Mike Welland
Jan 2004.
Arhus Denmark.

Is this to be my Souvenir?

Is this to be my Souvenir?

Jazz Photos
From The Timme Rosenkrantz
Collection 1918–1969

Frank Büchmann-Møller

Odense University Press 2000

Is this to be my Souvenier?

Publication of this book was made possible thanks to the cooperation
and generous support from The Carl Nielsen Academy of Music Odense
and The University Library of Southern Denmark.

It was furthermore supported by a grant from The Ben Webster Foundation.

Cover design and typographical layout by UniSats
Printed by Special-Trykkeriet Viborg
ISBN 87-7838-465-6

Language revision by:
Christen Kold Thomsen

Cover illustration:
Frankie Newton (1906-1954). For further details please see pages 133.

The Music Department
University Library of Southern Denmark
Islandsgade 2 • 5000 Odense C • Denmark
Phone: + 45 66 11 06 63 • Fax: +45 66 17 77 63

Odense University Press
Campusvej 55 • 5230 Odense M • Denmark
Phone: +45 66 15 79 99 • Fax: +45 66 15 81 26
E-mail: press@forlag.sdu.dk • Internet bookstore: www.oup.dk

Customers in the United States and Canada please contact:

International Specialized Book Services
5804 NE Hassalo St • Portland, OR 97213 • USA
Phone: + 1-800-944-6190 • E-mail: info@isbs.com

PREFACE

Timme Rosenkrantz was born on July 6th, 1911 in Hellerup, a suburb of Copenhagen. He inherited the title of baron from his father, the author Palle Rosenkrantz, and was educated as a journalist. Already as a teenager Timme Rosenkrantz became interested in jazz, and in 1934 he made the first of several trips to New York. In Denmark he founded one of the first European jazz journals, *Jazzrevy*, in 1935. Shortly after he began to write for the Swedish music magazines *Orkester Journalen* and *Estrad*, and he also contributed to English *Melody Maker* and American *Metronome*. When war broke out in 1939 he was in New York and decided to stay abroad. First he lived in the Sugar Hill district in Harlem, but later on he moved to an apartment on 46th Street. In Harlem he ran a music shop, The Melodee-Music Shop, for a couple of years, after which he had his own radio program on WNEW New York entitled "Rhythm Is Our Business".

His apartment on 46th Street was open day and night to friends and musicians. Many jam sessions were held there, and several were also immortalized on his home recording equipment. Later on some of these were brought out by his own record companies, "New York", "Baronet" and "Embassy Records". In the mid-40's he organized jazz concerts at New York's Time Hall, and in 1946 he was instrumental in bringing the first American jazz big band to Europe after the war. The band was an all-star group directed by Don Redman, and featured among others Don Byas, Tyree Glenn, Quentin Jackson, Peanuts Holland, the pianist Billy Taylor, and singer Inez Cavanaugh. He also organized Friday jam sessions at New York's Café Bohemia during the autumn of 1947, where he introduced the Danish drummer Uffe Baadh and the Swedish clarinetist Åke Hasselgård to an American audience.

For a number of years, in the late 40's, Rosenkrantz lived in Paris where he ran an American restaurant, Chez Inez, together with his long-time companion, Inez Cavanaugh.

During the 50's and 60's Rosenkrantz continued to write for newspapers and magazines, and all the time he continued to collect jazz photos, some of which were published in his *1939 Swing Photo Album* (republished 1964) and *Jazz Profiles* (1946). He also collected biographical data of jazz musicians and singers, as one of his intentions was to publish a jazz encyclopedia. But when Leonard Feather published his *Encyclopedia of Jazz* in 1955, Rosenkrantz abandoned plans for his own. During these years he also had various jazz shows on Swedish and Danish national radio. A humorous writer he published four books after 1933 (novels and collections of short stories). In 1964 his memoirs came out, aptly titled *Dus med Jazzen* (*Getting familiar with jazz*). These memoirs certainly ought to be translated into English as they offer a unique view of jazz and some of its famous musicians by a very funny, but also most devoted fan.

In the autumn of 1968 he opened his own jazz club in Copenhagen, Timme's Club, in Nørregade 41. The opening attraction was Mary Lou Williams, who later on was followed by Teddy Wilson, Ben Webster, Inez Cavanaugh and others.

While at work in New York for Danish national radio he suddenly died on August 11th, 1969. A memorial service was held on August 22nd at New York's St. Peter's Church, where pastor John Gensel, Duke Ellington, Dan Morgenstern, Stanley Dance, John Hammond, and the Danish Consul General in New York, J.O. Stephensen, paid tributes, and Tyree Glenn played "Mood Indigo" and "Satin Doll". A memorial concert was held in Copenhagen at the Odd-Fellow Palace on November 14th, with musical contributions by Teddy Wilson, Ben Webster, the Saints and Sinners, Kenny Drew, Inez Cavanaugh, Don Byas, Charlie Shavers, and many more.

The idea of publishing a book like this came to me one day as I was going through more than 2000 photographs of jazz musicians and orchestras which are one part of the Timme Rosenkrantz collection which also includes books, records, reel-to-reel tapes and memorabilia of a long life in jazz in Denmark and USA. I have been interested in jazz and its history since I was a teenager, and in my own collection of books about the subject I especially treasure photo books. In the Rosenkrantz collection, however, I found hundreds of interesting pictures completely new to me, several taken by himself during his visits to New York from the mid-30's to the mid-60's.

Many of the photographs were taken in studios for publicity purposes, and among these several are with personal dedications and regards to him. *These are reproduced in the text in italics.* Other photos were presented to him by such photographers as Charles Peterson, Jack Bradley, Charles B. Nadell, Jan Persson, Ole Brask and Erik Wraae. Many photos cannot be credited, however, as no information about photographer, date or occasion is available.

The photographs for this publication were selected to show famous musicians in new surroundings, to raise the reader's curiosity about lesser-known and, in some cases, unkown musicians, and also to throw new light upon facts about photos that have been published before. Hundreds of photographs in the collection still remain to be identified.

In several cases I have benefited from the expertise of Bente Arendrup, Arne Astrup, John Chilton, Erik Kjellberg, The Library of the Danish Film Museum, Jens Lindgren (Svenskt Visarkiv), Arnvid Meyer, Richard M. Sudhalter, Lars Westin, and Erik Wiedemann. I am grateful for their generous assistance and interest. Also heartfelt thanks to my employers Bertel Krarup, head of The Carl Nielsen Academy of Music, and to Aase Lindahl, head librarian of The University Library of Southern Denmark, to which the Timme Rosenkrantz collection belongs. Both of them took great interest in this project and helped provide me with the necessary financial support and time for research. I am also very grateful for the donation granted by the Ben Webster Foundation.

Frank Büchmann-Møller
Odense
October, 1999

FOREWORD

Wonderful characters have always been part of the world of jazz. One of them was Timme Rosenkrantz. As far as I know he was the only one actually born an aristocrat in contrast to a couple of other jazz greats who had to struggle to earn their titles; Count Basie and Duke Ellington come to mind.

Despite his interest in jazz Timme hailed from an entirely respectable family. That is why at an early age he enjoyed possibilities which were beyond the range of other youngsters. According to Timme himself, he first arrived in New York on a cold Monday in February, 1934 in order to take a good look at the attractive jazz life in that city. This was the beginning of a love affair which lasted for the rest of his life.

Timme was the sort of jazzfan you will not find today. His sole interest was to be where it all happened. And a lot of things happened during the 30's, 40's and 50's, the most important periods in jazz. As a natural consequence of this interest he began collecting photographs of his friends, at first to complement his journalistic writings, but later also for personal reasons.

His collection of jazz photos comprises more than 2000 items, collected between 1930 and 1969, the year he died. And what do we find? Well, just take a look in this book! Still, a few accompanying words may not come amiss.

The collection is of a typically personal kind which reflects the varied nature of Timme's interests and contains many rare photos.

The photos can be divided in two broad categories: Publicity photos of bands and soloists, some taken by press photographers like Jack Bradley, Otto F. Hess and Francis Wolff; and Timme's own snapshots.

Both from artistic and documentary points of view the most interesting items are to be found in the publicity material. Firstly, they give a picture of a period long gone and, secondly, they convey a style and an elegance which have rarely been seen ever since. Only the extremely elegant look of Duke Ellington, which along the way also infected the style of many of his musicians, comes close.

Many of these photos are of a technically enviable quality. There has been no question of finding quick or easy solutions. It has been done the hard way. The photographers have probably used big-size format cameras with glass plates of 4x5 inches or more. A fine example is the photo of Don Redman and His Orchestra in 1934. Every feature is clear and every musician can easily be identified. Other shining examples are photos taken by Bloom in Chicago of Fletcher Henderson's band sections, of which the trumpet section of Dick Vance, Joe Thomas and Roy Eldridge is especially marvellous. Danish photographers also mastered these techniques, as the photo of We Three (Leo Mathisen, Anker Skjoldborg and Otto Lington) dated 1927/28, exemplifies.

As for the classic photos, one notes that of Jo Jones with his trousers pulled up to his chin by a pair of solid suspenders. There are also interesting photos by Francis Wolff, one of the owners of Blue Note and one of the finest photographers of the period. But it has to be said that not everything worked out for him.

Timme's own snapshots are miscellaneous. Most of them portray musicians met on his way through the jazz life of New York. They are of historical and documentary interest, but of little artistic value. One of them is my absolute favorite, though, namely the picture taken on top of a hotel, showing Jack Teagarden after a particularly hard night. That one captures the art of the moment.

Finally a few words about the most surprising discovery in the collection, the old, ragged, yellow-toned photo of King Oliver. According to Frank Büchmann-Møller it is probably the earliest photo of King Oliver in a band. But most interestingly, it has never been published before and is probably the only existing copy in the world.

Much more could be said about many more photos, but go and explore for yourself – and dream.

Jan Persson
Photographer

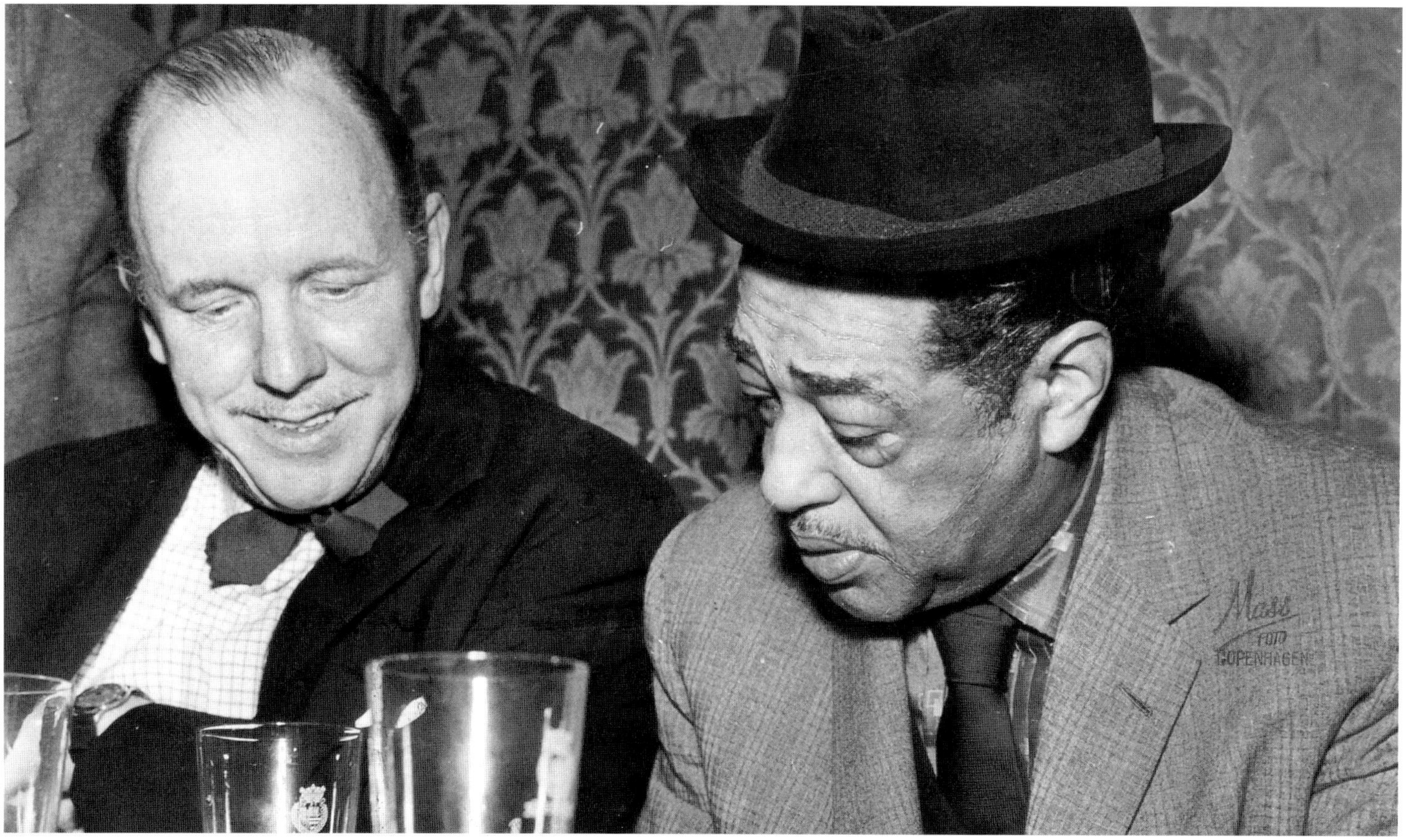

Timme Rosenkrantz and Duke Ellington in Copenhagen November 1958.

THANKS FOR THE MEMORY

When Timme returned from his many visits to the U.S. – (he actually never went any further than New York, Yonkers and Newport) – he always returned to his parents' home in Hellerup where I also lived with my mother and my kid brother.

There we stood, wide-eyed, as one trunk after another arrived full of records and photos. I especially remember once around 1936 when there was a particularly large stack of black and white glossy photos. I was very proud when he handed me a pair of scissors and asked me to cut off the white edges, so the pictures could be printed in his new jazz magazine *Jazzrevy*. Later many of them appeared in the first edition of his *Swing Photo Album*.

Many photos had dedications. Duke had of course scribbled: "*Love you madly*" and Fats Waller, wearing an elegant grey derby, had written in big letters: "*To Timmie Rosenkrantz, you louse! I received your card! You master mind of filth – from soup-nuts Thomas "Fats" Waller*".

1936 was also the year when Timme set his mind on making the Danish pianist, bandleader and composer, Leo Mathisen, famous in America. Leo had written a tune "Song of Souvenirs" which Timme was certain would make him a big success in the States. He had it printed as a supplement to *Jazzrevy*, but that hadn't done the trick. So now he tried his luck in New York and succeeded in getting W.C. Handy to publish it. Handy didn't think much of the title and asked the well-known lyricist, Maceo Pinkard, to write the lyrics. He changed the title to "Anytime", and Timme happily wrote home that now Leo was on his way to world fame!

It turned out he wasn't. So Timme's long time companion, Inez Cavanaugh, wrote new lyrics and they called it "Is this to be my Souvenir?" As no one else wanted to record it, Timme persuaded "RCA Victor" to let him do it. So on May 27th, 1938, at the Victor recording studios, he made his first recordings with "Timme Rosenkrantz and his Barrelhouse Barons". He had succeeded in getting together some of the finest swing musicians in town: Brick Fleagle, Tyree Glenn, Rudy Williams, Don Byas, Russell Procope, Rex Stewart, Billy Hicks, Billy Kyle, Jo Jones and Walter Page. The other tunes were Leo's "A Wee Bit of Swing" plus "When Day is Done" and "The Song is Ended".

Here Inez Cavanaugh made her debut as a singer and in *Melody Maker* Leonard Feather named it "The most thrilling recording ever made". He also confessed that it was he who had once given Timme the barrelhouse nickname in a news story about the Danish baron who digged jazz. It has stuck with Timme ever since – *honi soit qui mal y pense.*

And it was just like Timme to gracefully adopt it.

Warm thanks to Frank Büchmann-Møller, The Carl Nielsen Academy of Music and The University Library of Southern Denmark for reviving a truly swinging era.

Bente Arendrup
Timme's niece

HENRY "RED" ALLEN

Trumpet player and singer Henry "Red" Allen (1908-1967) was born into a musical family in New Orleans. His father, Henry Allen, Sr. (1877-1952) was for more than 40 years the leader of the Allen Brass Band and taught little Henry how to play the trumpet. "Red" Allen joined King Oliver in St. Louis in 1927 and went with his band to New York, but his career really took off in 1929 when he joined Luis Russell's band, after having made some sensational recordings which made him the rival of Louis Armstrong. After stints with Fletcher Henderson and Mills Blue Rhythm Band he returned in 1937 to Russell, whose band at that time was backing Louis Armstrong. In 1940 Allen left to take part in the mainstream jazz movement leading his own groups. From originally being an Armstrong imitator like most of the trumpet players of his generation, Allen from the 40's developed a highly personal style of playing and singing, exploring the possibilities of the trumpet to the utmost, and as a blues interpreter he reached new heights.

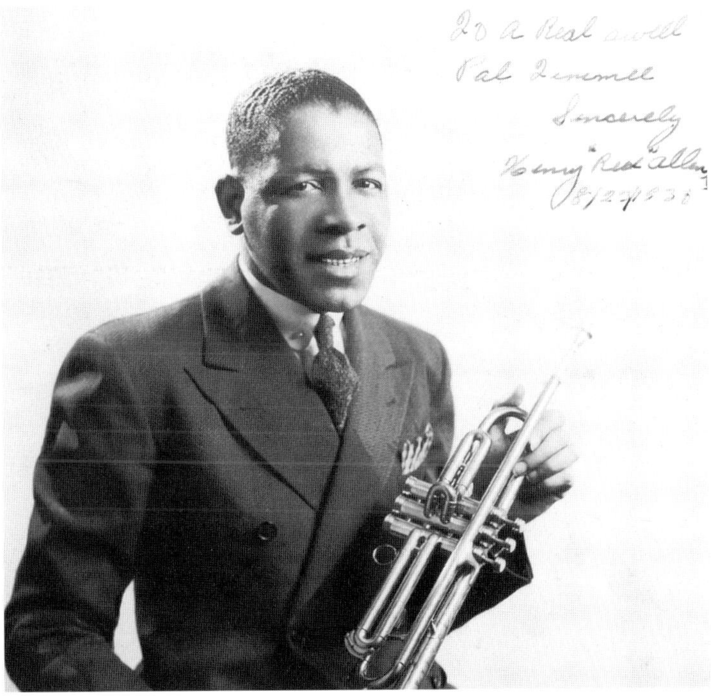

Promotion photo of Henry "Red" Allen. *To a Real swell Pal Timmie. Sincerely Henry "Red" Allen, Jr. 8/23/1935.*

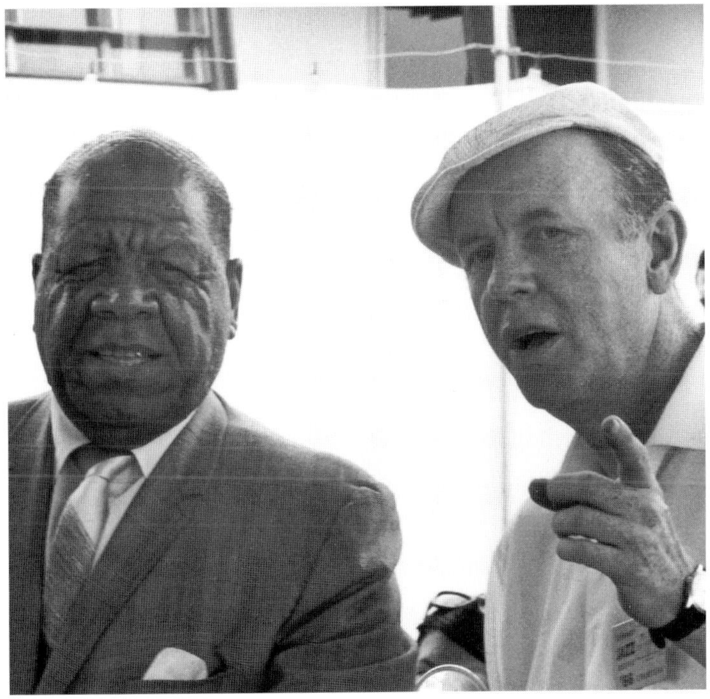

Henry "Red" Allen and Timme Rosenkrantz at the Newport Jazz Festival 1966.

Bert Ambrose

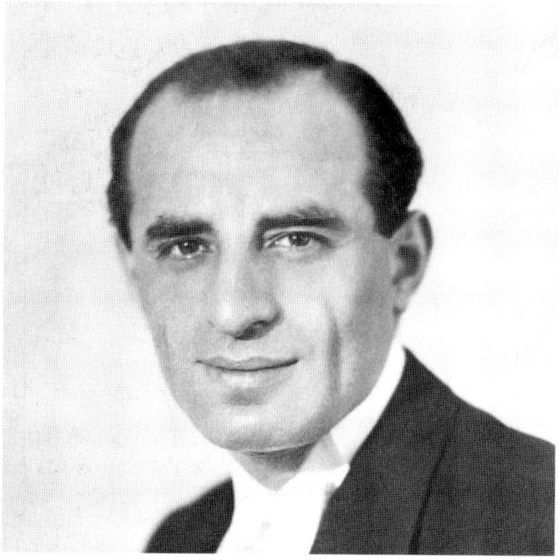

English band leader Bertram "Bert" Ambrose (1896-1971) emigrated at fifteen with his aunt to New York. From 1917 he fronted his own bands and played in hotels, but in 1920 he returned to London. He left again the following year for another stint in the Big Apple playing at the Clover Gardens, but moved back to London in 1922 to lead a band at the Embassy Club. In 1927 he formed a big band with which he played various venues in London until 1938, after which he had smaller groups. Due to ill health he only sporadically led his own bands during the 50's, and after a widespread tour of Britain in 1956 he disbanded for good. Ambrose regularly included American musicians in his bands, always used skilled arrangers, and rehearsed the band to play with extraordinary discipline. All this made it the most highly rated band in England of its time.

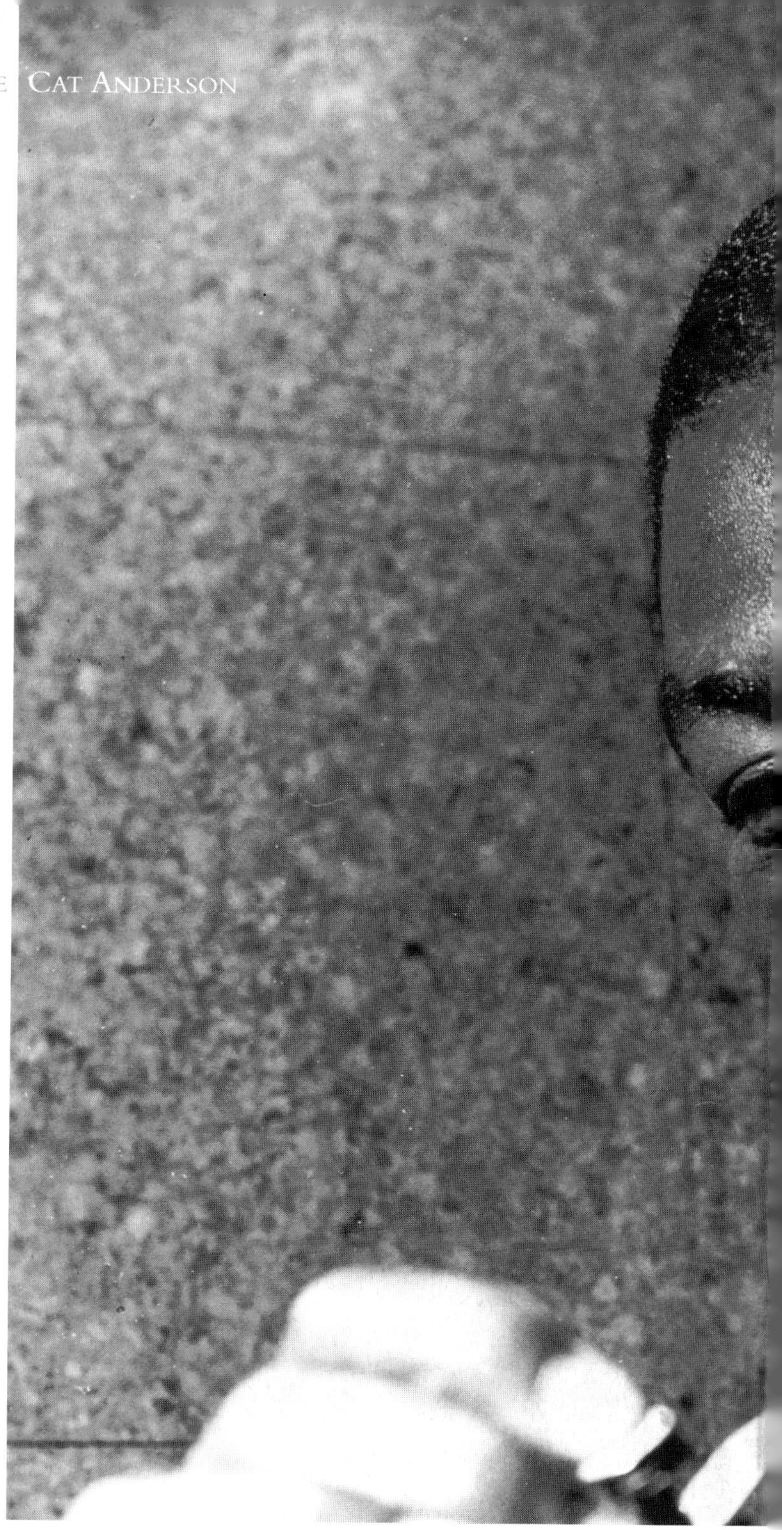

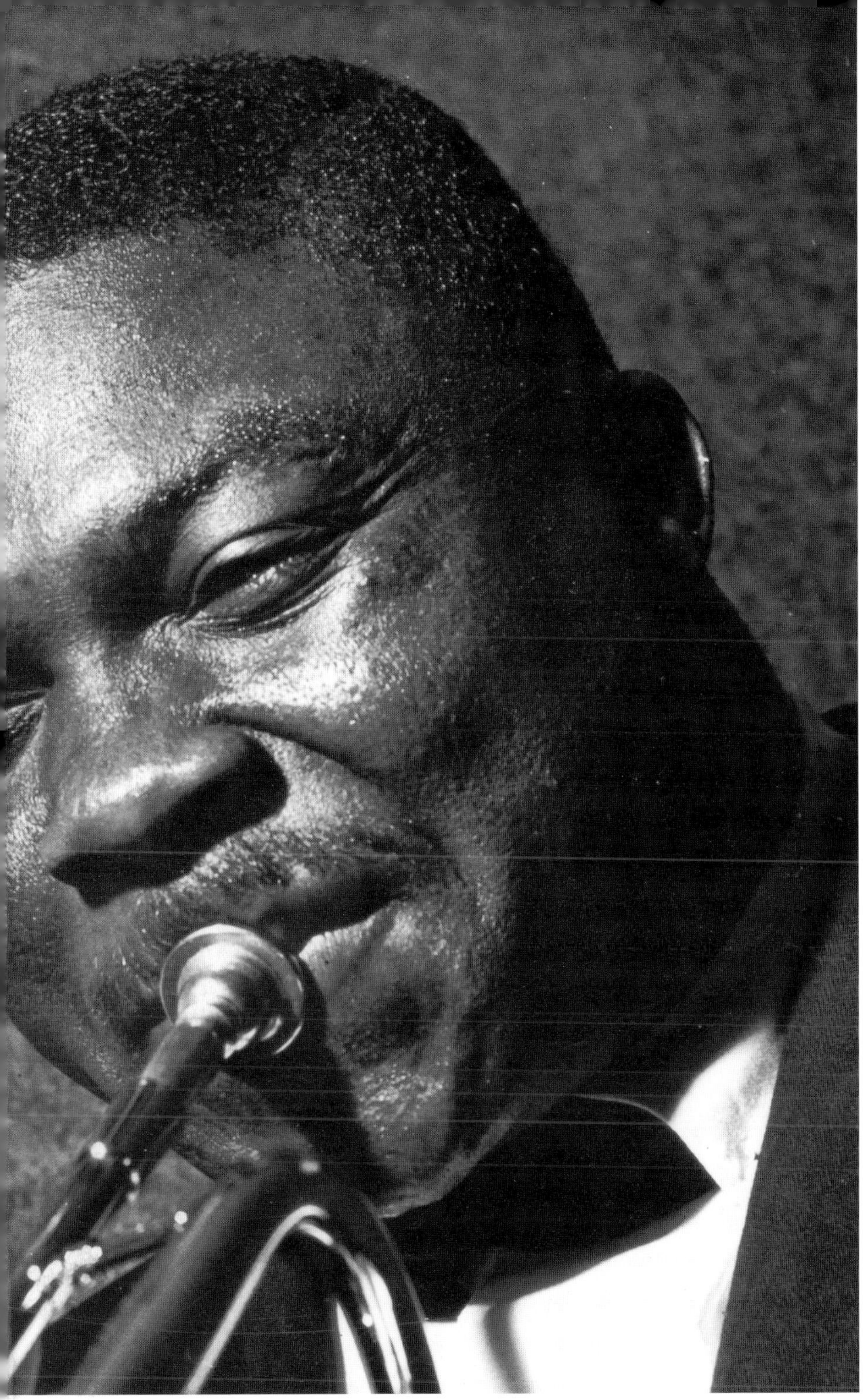

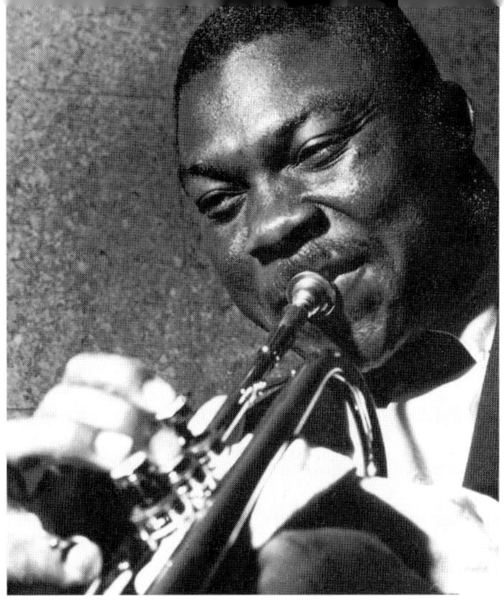

Cat Anderson

High-note specialist William Alonzo "Cat" Anderson (1916-1981) learned music while growing up in the Jenkins' Orphanage in Charleston, S.C., and played trumpet in its famous student bands. After leading his own band for a couple of years he joined the big bands of Claude Hopkins, Lionel Hampton, and others before Duke Ellington hired him as a high-note specialist in 1944. Apart from 1947-49 and 1959-61, when he either led his own small groups or played with others, he remained with Ellington until 1971 after which he settled in Los Angeles to freelance. Although best known for his five-octaves range on the trumpet, Anderson was highly accomplished in all other features of the instrument, and he was very well suited to the Ellington band and contributed to its colorful palette by using half-valve technique á la Rex Stewart and plunger technique á la Bubber Miley.

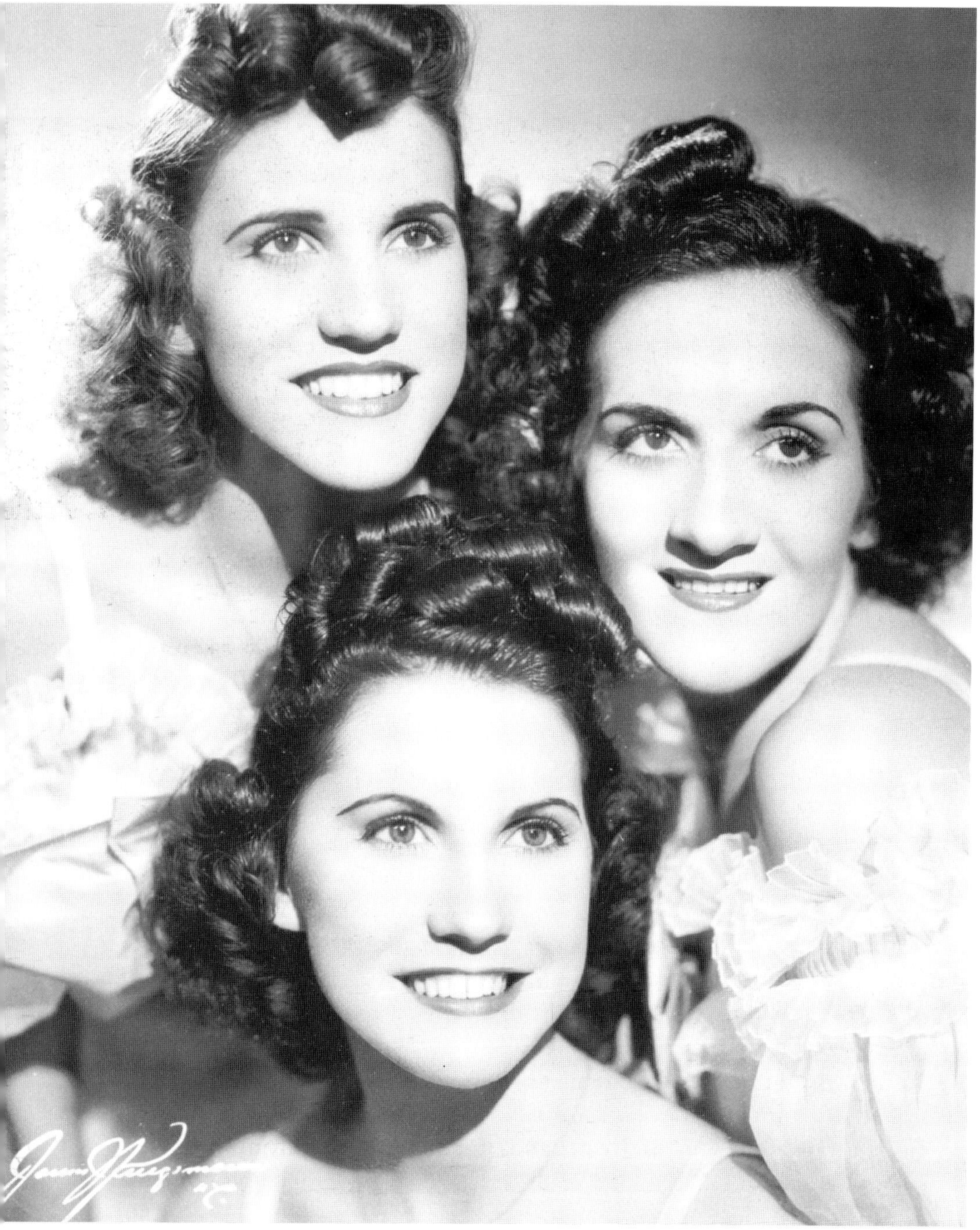

THE ANDREWS SISTERS

The vocal trio The Andrews Sisters came from the little town Mound near Minneapolis, Minnesota and consisted of LaVerne (1911-1967), Maxene (1916-1995) and Patti Andrews (1918-), and had the Boswell Sisters as their models. They toured together in vaudeville during the early 30's but got their breakthrough in 1938 with "Bei mir bist du schön", after which success followed success. Bandleader Victor Schoen wrote their arrangements and led the backing bands which often consisted of the best musicians available, taken from, for example, Jimmy Dorsey's, Woody Herman's, Eddie Heywood's, and Glenn Miller's orchestras. The music was a popular mixture of novelty, commercial boogie woogie, calypso, jazz and ballads which the sisters delivered with a delightful swing and in easily identifiable close harmony. The trio kept together until 1953 when Patti left to go solo, but the sisters still worked together occasionally until LaVerne's death. Maxene and Patti were reunited in 1974 for the Broadway show "Over There", which ran for more than a year, but afterwards they never worked together again. From the left Patty, Maxene, LaVerne.

IVIE ANDERSON

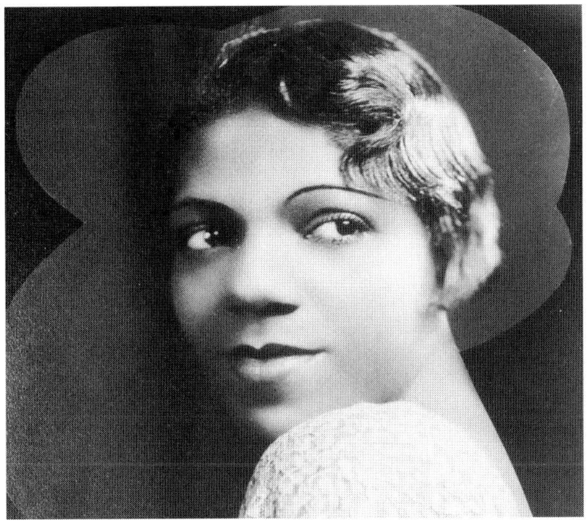

Los Angeles born singer Ivie Anderson (1905-1949) toured throughout the 20's in clubs and stage revues. After a period with Earl Hines in 1930 she came to Duke Ellington where she remained 1931-42. Her style blended perfectly with the band and she was a consistently superior singer. She was also the most versatile of Ellington's different vocalists. She could scat like Louis Armstrong, her voice could be warm, low-pitched and beautifully rounded, and she could perform a blues with an intuitive feeling like a Billie Holiday. Due to chronic asthma she left Ellington and returned to Los Angeles, and performed only locally during her final years.

FOLKE ANDERSON

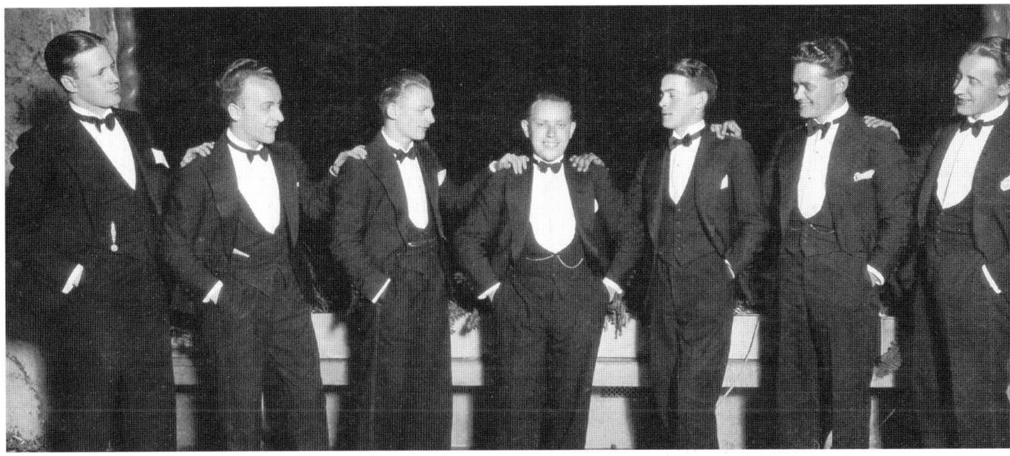

The photo shows a reunion of the Paramount Orchestra in 1931 with, from the left, Nisse "Bagarn" Lind (p), Acke Sundin (bj), Gösta "Smyget" Redlig (tp), Folke "Göken" Anderson (vl), Anders "Tran Anders" Soldén (dr), Olle Henricson (cl), and Sune Lundwall (sax, b). *Till min gode vän Timme till minne av Folke Anderson. Stockholm den 24/10-31.*

The Swedish violinist and bandleader Folke "Göken" Anderson (1902-1976) had a great influence on the development of jazz in Sweden. As early as in the early 20's he was playing jazz in Stockholm, and he visited USA for the first time in 1925. The following year he played on board the American liner "Gripsholm", which enabled him and the other band members to hear jazz greats like Joe Venuti, Bix Beiderbecke, Fletcher Henderson, Paul Whiteman, Frankie Trumbauer and others in person, when ashore in New York. After the "Gripsholm" engagement Anderson took over as leader, and he made some ground-breaking recordings in 1928-29 in Stockholm and London with a band known as the "Paramount Orchestra". He led his own bands until 1936, but from 1931 he withdrew from playing jazz and concentrated on dance and concert music.

LOUIS ARMSTRONG

The most influential jazz musician of all, and also the one who almost single-handedly put jazz on the world map as a form of popular music, was New Orleans-born Louis Armstrong (1901-1971). He learned the trumpet while at the Colored Waifs' home in his early teens, and after some years of playing in his home town his big break arrived when he joined King Oliver in Chicago in 1922. After leaving Oliver two years later he stayed on for a while in the Windy City before accepting an offer from Fletcher Henderson to join his orchestra in New York. For a year Armstrong was in the Big Apple working in Henderson's band and also recording prolifically with others. He returned to Chicago in late 1925, and by early 1926 worked with both Carroll Dickerson and Erskine Tate. In 1929 Armstrong once more moved to New York, but in 1930 he left to play in Les Hite's band in California. In the Spring of 1931 Armstrong returned to Chicago forming his own big band, with which he toured extensively the following years. In 1947 he returned to a small band unit – the All Stars – which he led until his death. During the years the personnel underwent many changes, but at its best – the REAL All Star band – numbered both Jack Teagarden and Earl Hines.

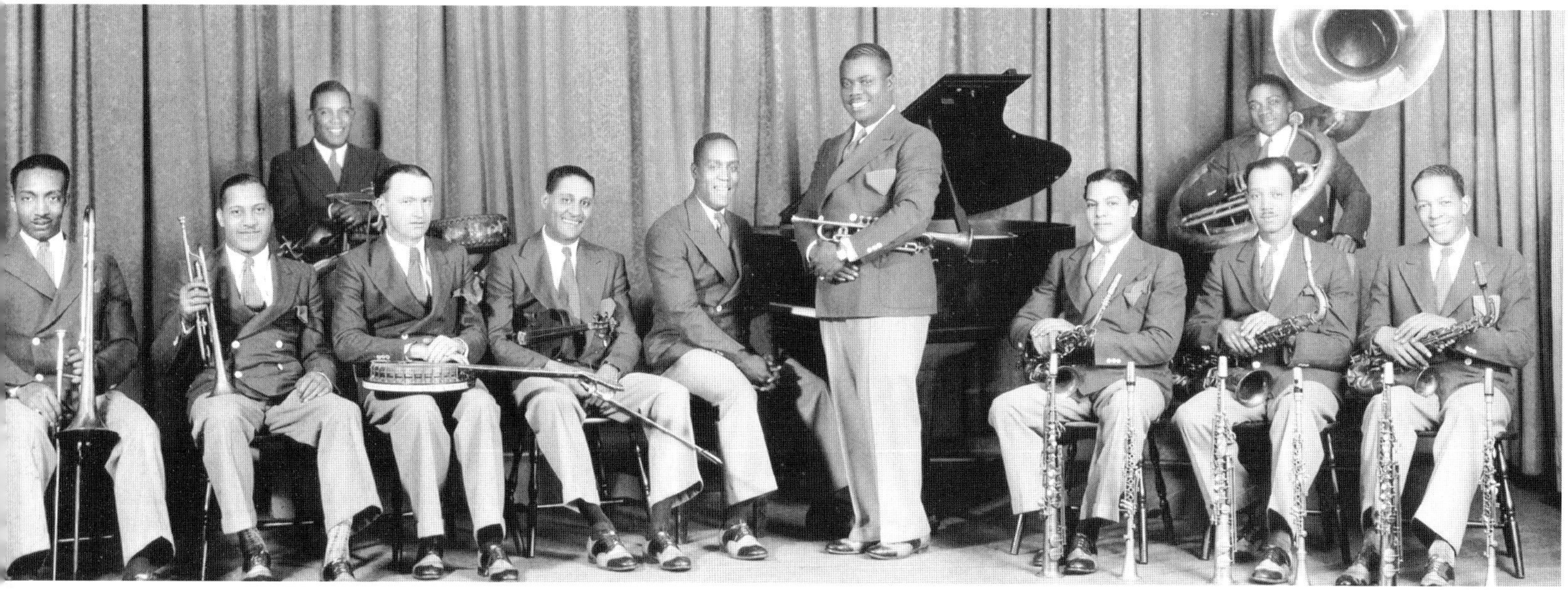

Armstrong with Carroll Dickerson's Orchestra in 1927. From the left Fred Robinson (tb), Willie Hightower (tp), Zutty Singleton (dr), Mancy Cara (bj), Carroll Dickerson (vl), Gene Anderson (p), Armstrong, Darnell Howard (as), Jimmy Strong (ts), Pete Briggs (tu), and Crawford Wethington (as).

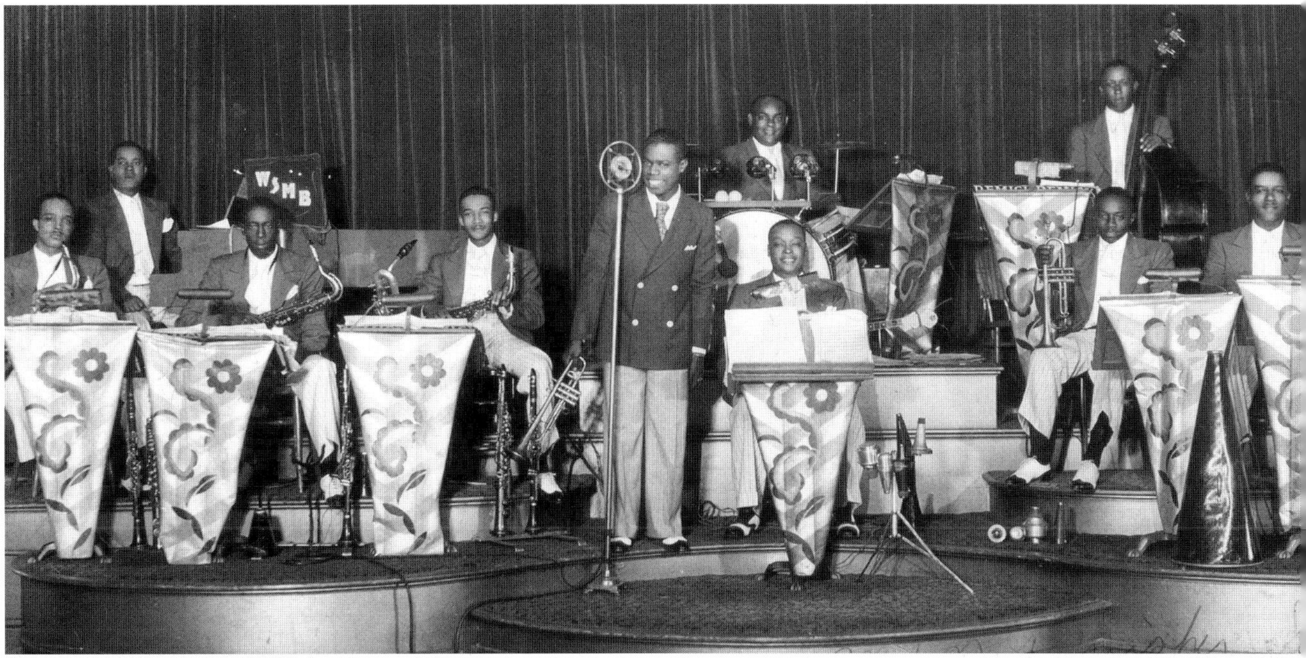

Louis Armstrong's band at the Suburban Garden in New Orleans 1931, showing from left Lester Boone (as), Charlie Alexander (p), Al Washington (ts), George James (as), Armstrong, Tubby Hall (dr), Mike McKendrick (g), John Lindsay (b), Zilner Randolph (tp), and Preston Jackson (tb). *My Best Wishes To The Harlem Music Shop From Louis Armstrong.*

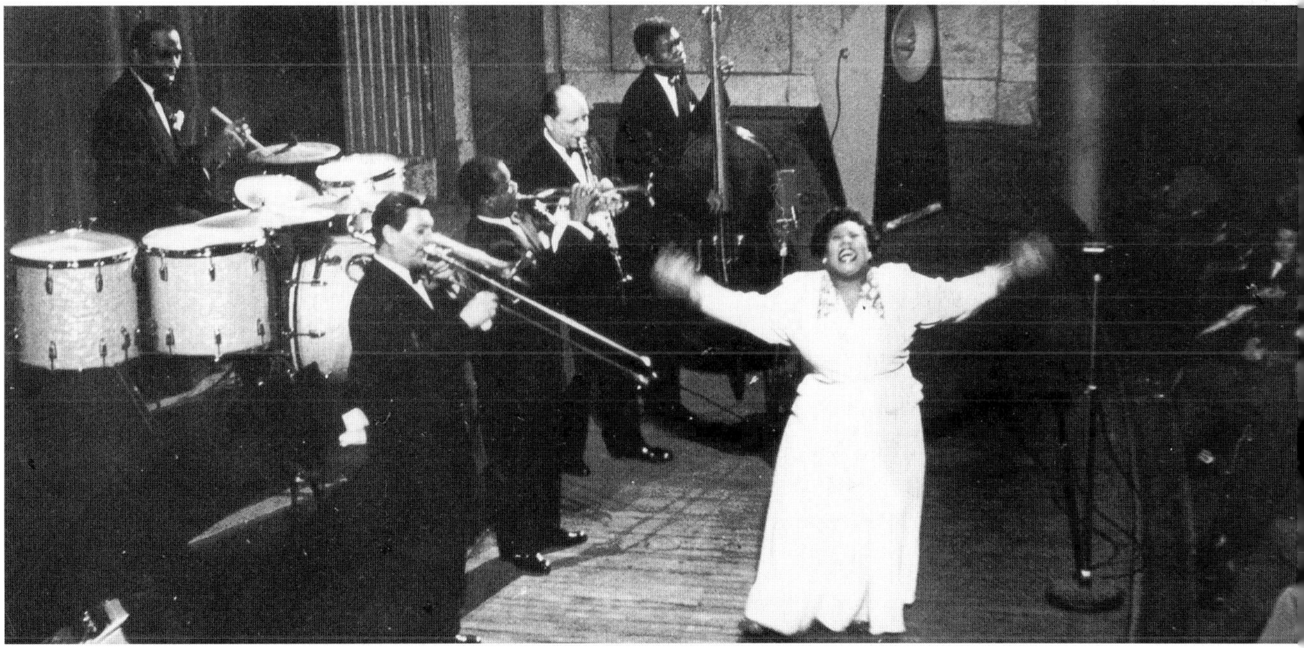

Louis Armstrong and His All-Stars around 1950 during a concert in Sweden with from left Cozy Cole, Teagarden, Armstrong, Barney Bigard, Arvell Shaw and Velma Middleton.

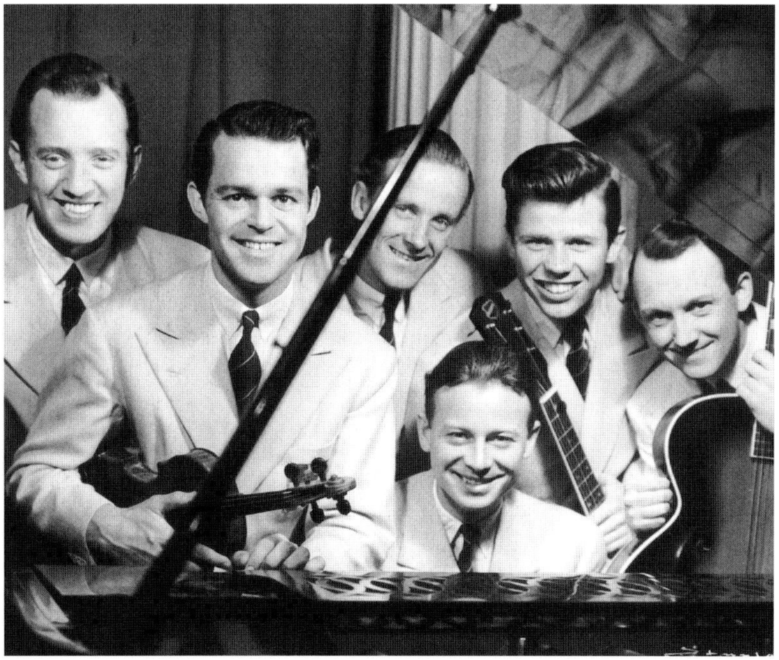

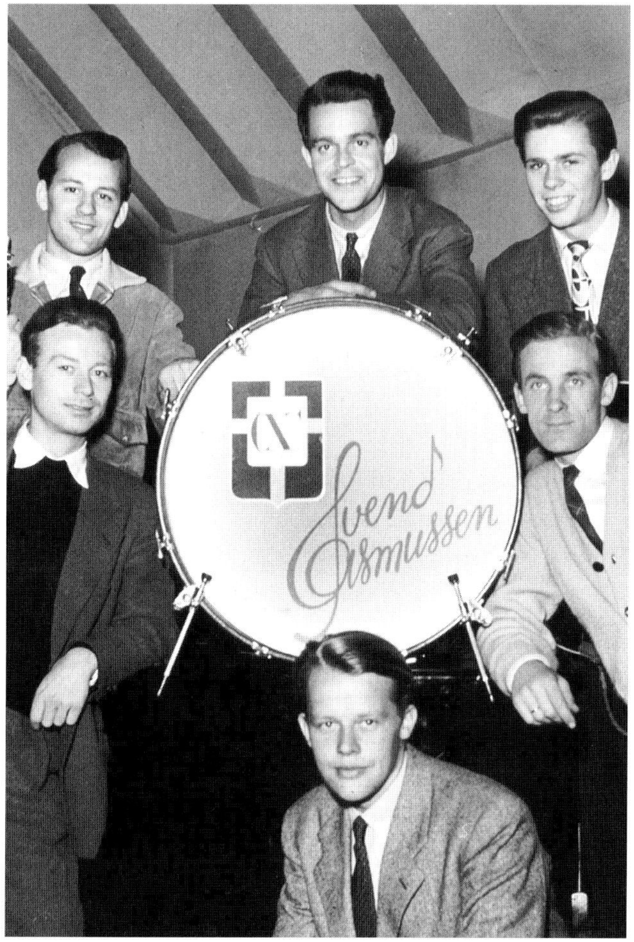

SVEND ASMUSSEN

The Danish violin player and entertainer Svend Asmussen (1916-) started out as early as 1933 in a Joe Venuti-inspired quartet. He was born in Copenhagen, and played mostly for shows and cabarets throughout the 30's. In the early 40's he led his own jazz trio, but in 1945 he assembled a sextet which created an elegant show routine. In the autumn of 1945 the sextet went to Sweden for a year-long stay. Asmussen disbanded his group around 1955. In the following years he performed on and off with singer Alice Babs in pop-oriented groups, but also played with Stuff Smith, John Lewis, and Duke Ellington. Throughout the 70's, 80's, and 90's he continued to record and appear at international festivals and is still active with his own quartet.

(Top) Svend Asmussen Sextet at the Swedish Radio in Stockholm 1945, showing clockwise left to right Max Leth (p), Svend Hauberg (cl), Asmussen, Jørgen Ingmann (g), Erik Frederiksen (dr), and Børge Ring (b) sitting.

(Left) Asmussen with his 1954 sextet which from left include Poul Gregersen (b), Asmussen, Erik Frederiksen (dr), Max Leth (p), Jørgen Ingmann (g), and Ulrik Neumann (g).

UFFE BAADH

The Danish drummer Uffe Baadh (1923-1980) began his career in the early 40's playing with Niels Foss and Kai Ewans in Copenhagen. In December 1943 he had to flee to Sweden as Gestapo wanted him because of his connection with the resistance movement. In Stockholm he played with Rolf Ericson, Thore Ehrling, Charles Norman and Carl-Henrik Norin and made his first recordings, but when peace came in May 1945 he returned to Copenhagen. In 1947 he emigrated to the USA, and almost immediately got jobs with Jack Teagarden and Teddy Wilson in New York, and also took part in the weekly jam sessions at the Café Bohemia arranged by Timme Rosenkrantz during August and September. Baadh soon moved to Los Angeles where he began playing with other Scandinavian jazz musicians in town such as Åke Hasselgård, and at the same time he changed his name to Frank Bode. He also took part in some of Gene Norman's concerts with Wardell Gray and Dodo Marmarosa, and having achieved a reputation as a good swing drummer he soon got jobs with Benny Goodman, Claude Thornhill, Ray Anthony and Harry James. In 1964 he visited Denmark and played with Otto Francker but returned after a while to California. Due to bad health he was inactive during his last years.

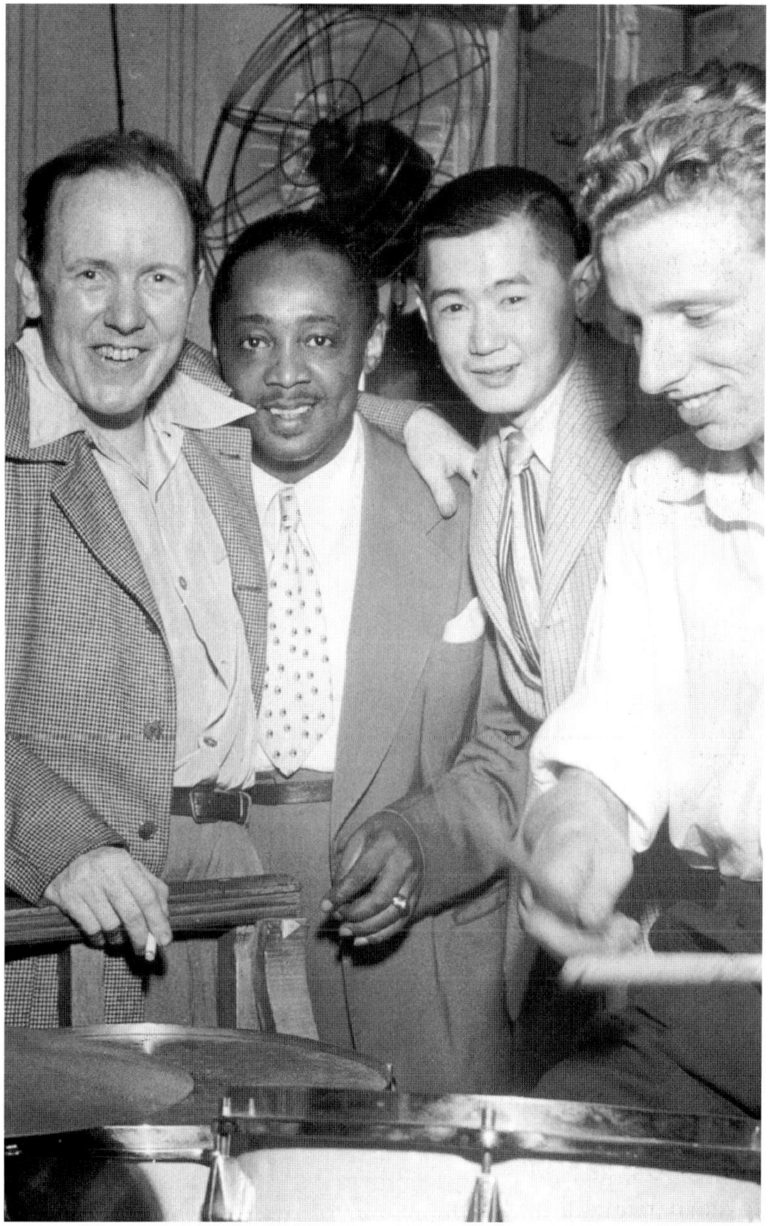

Baadh at one of the jam sessions at the Café Bohemia in New York 1947 with Rosenkrantz, trumpet player Joe Thomas and record producer for the Keynote Company, Harry Lim.

BUSTER BAILEY

Clarinetist William C. "Buster" Bailey (1902-1967) was a master technician. Born in New York he first played in a band led by W.C. Handy but in 1919 he settled in Chicago to work with Erskine Tate and King Oliver. In 1924 he returned to New York and began a long collaboration with Fletcher Henderson. From 1934-35 he was with Mills Blue Rhythm Band, after which he became a member of John Kirby's Sextet. From 1947 he played with Henry "Red" Allen, Wilbur De Paris, Big Chief Russell Moore, Wild Bill Davison, and the Saints and Sinners, and spent his final years as a member of Louis Armstrong's All Stars. When playing in big bands he had to double on saxophone, as was the custom at that time, but he was best known for his work on clarinet. He always played with conviction no matter how fast the tempo, but he was never a swinger, and he lacked passion in his playing.

MILDRED BAILEY

From an early age singer and pianist Mildred Bailey (1907-1951) received musical training. Partly of American-Indian origins she grew up in the state of Washington, but her career began in California where she already in the early 20's was singing and playing piano in silent movie theatres, performing in revues and on the radio as well as in nightclubs in Hollywood. In 1929 she joined Paul Whiteman's big band where she met her future husband, xylophonist Red Norvo. She remained with Whiteman until 1933, after which she for a while concentrated on radio shows. 1936-39 she co-led a band with Red Norvo – they were referred to as "Mr. and Mrs. Swing" – but later on she worked mainly as a solo act besides having her own radio show on CBS. Her health was never strong, but she continued to perform even when she suffered from recurrent illnesses in the 40's. She was inspired by Bessie Smith, Ethel Waters and other early blues singers and was the first white female singer accepted in jazz. She sang with a fragile, sweet-toned, high-pitched voice, and mastered the many aspects of jazz phrasing, had good improvisatory skills and swung with ease. She died all too early at 44 of heart-related problems, at the same age as Billie Holiday.

PEARL BAILEY

Singer Mae "Pearl" Bailey (1918-1990) was born in Philadelphia and started out as a dancer, but later sang in vaudeville and came to New York in the early 40's with Noble Sissle's orchestra after which she was hired first by Cootie Williams and later by Count Basie. She then began a solo career at the Village Vanguard, followed by an engagement at the Blue Angel which led to her association with Cab Calloway. From 1946 she began to appear in Broadway musicals as well as in films, such as "Carmen Jones" (1954), "St. Louis Blues" (1958) and "Porgy and Bess" (1959). In 1952 she married drummer Louie Bellson who later became her musical director. For her performance in the Broadway show, "Hello, Dolly!" (1968), she received a Special Tony Award and was posthumously inducted into the New York Theater Hall Of Fame in 1991.

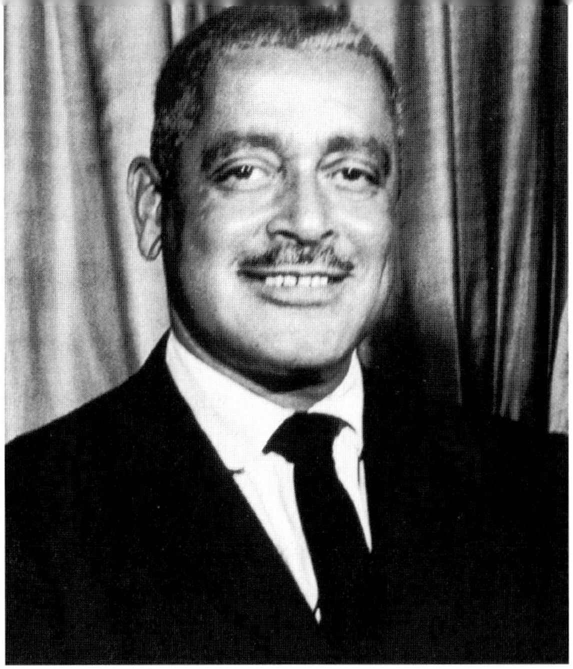

Buster Bailey

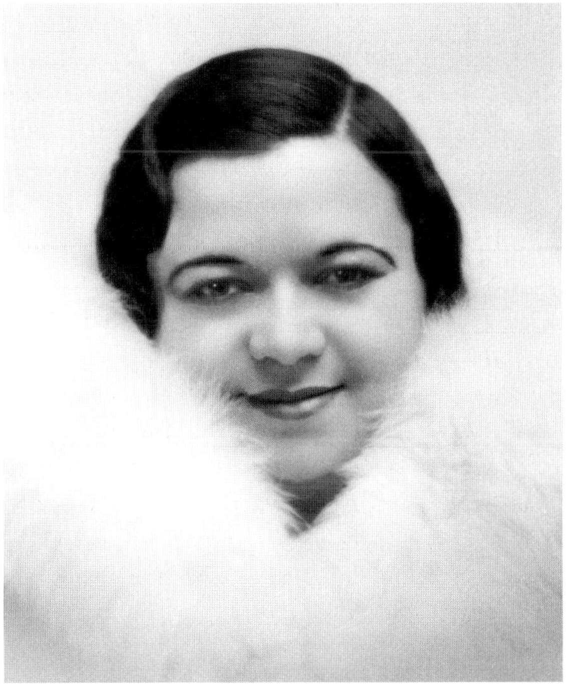

Mildred Bailey

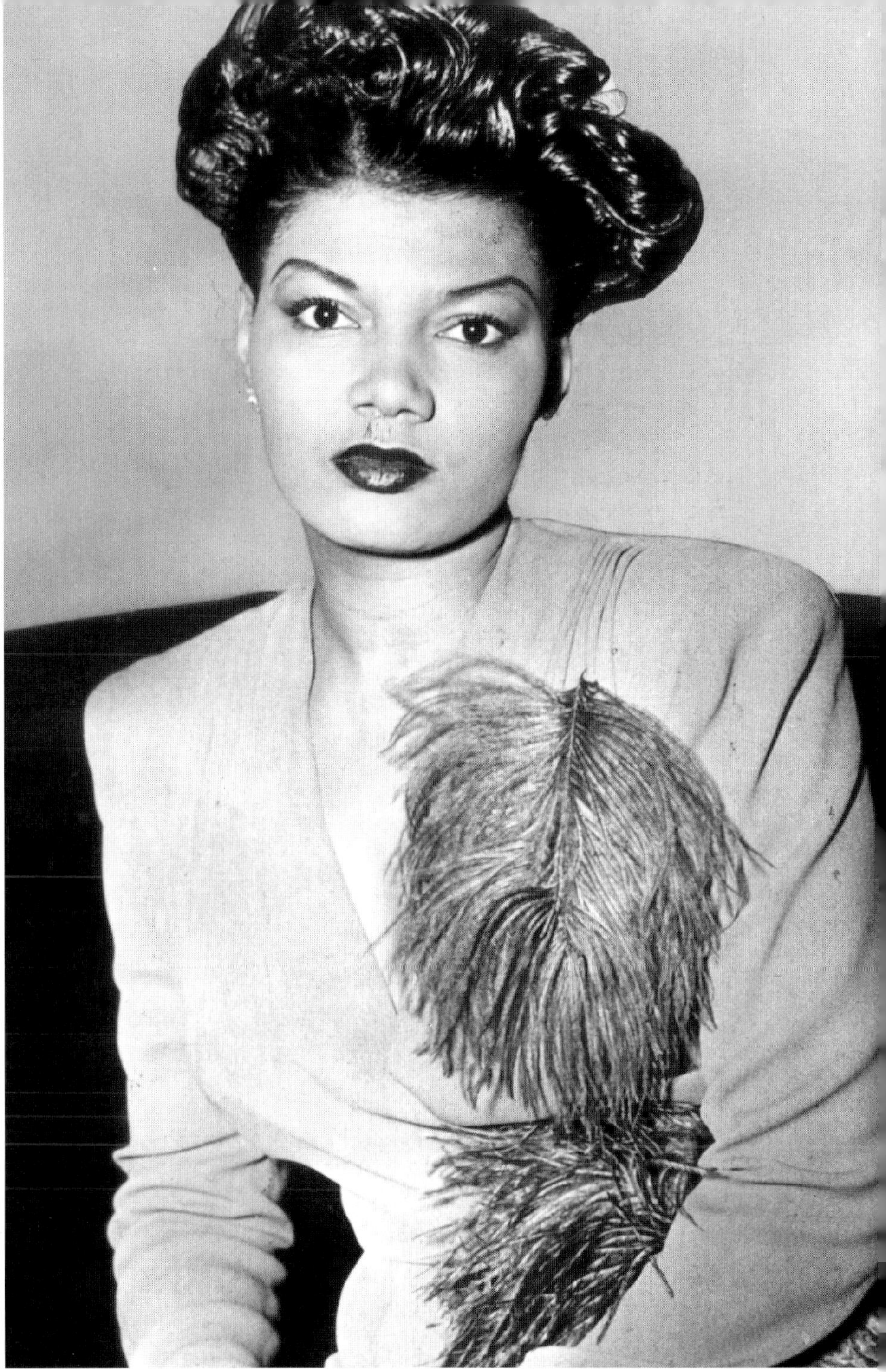

Publicity photo of Pearl Bailey from the mid 40's.

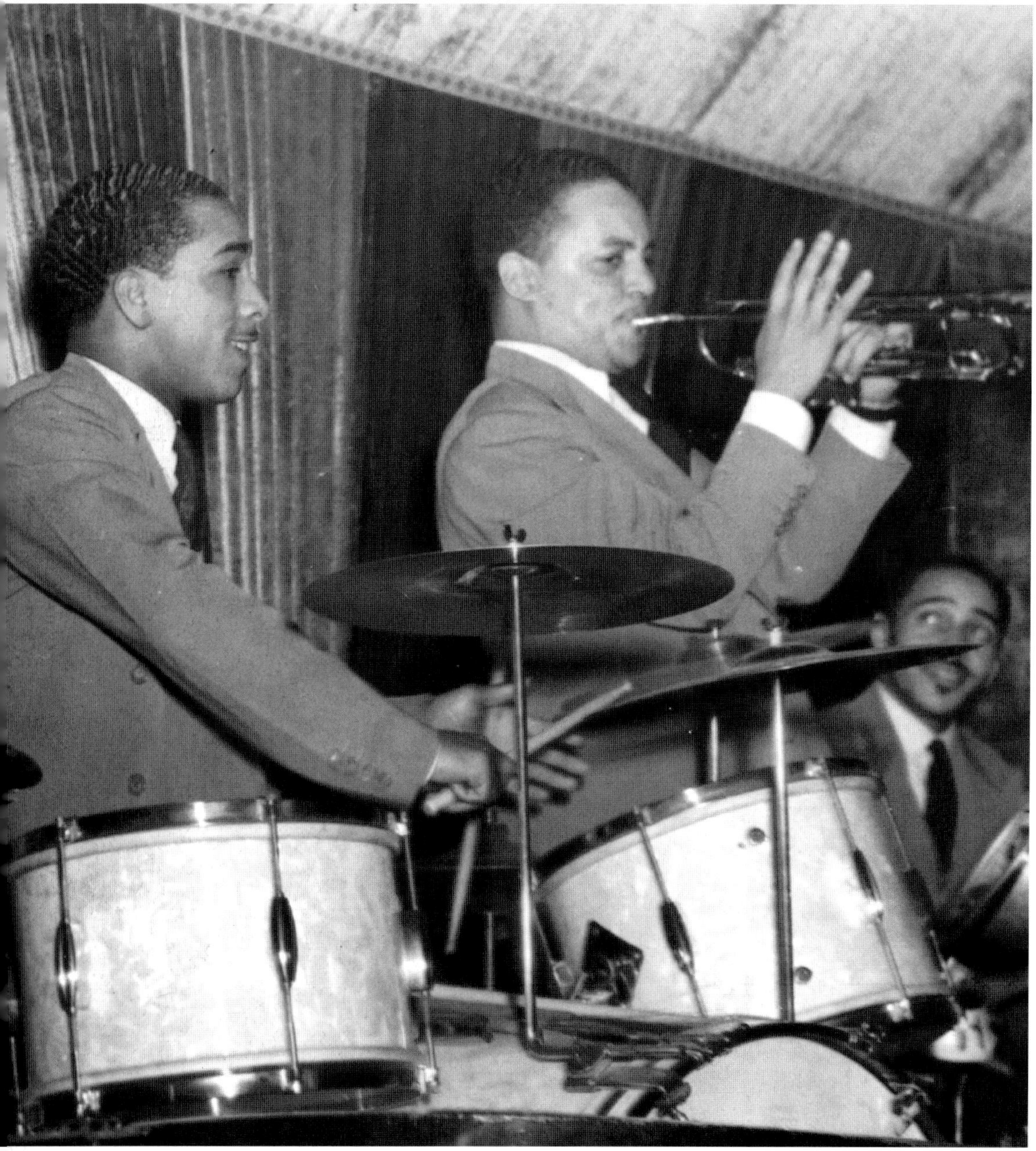

In this 1939/1940 photo Shorty Baker is soloing in Teddy Wilson's Big Band, his sound admired by drummer J.C. Heard and trumpeter Karl George.

SHORTY BAKER

One of the most beautiful trumpet sounds in jazz was played by Harold "Shorty" Baker (1914-1966). He was highly regarded by other musicians as an accomplished lead player with careful dynamics and phrasing and as a fine, lyrical soloist. Born in St. Louis his first professional job was with his brother's band, after which he worked with Fate Marable, Eddie Johnson and Erskine Tate. In the late 30's he played in the bands of Don Redman, Duke Ellington and Teddy Wilson, and 1940-42 he was with Andy Kirk and Mary Lou Williams, whom he married in 1942. He returned to the Ellington unit at various intervals between 1942 and 1962, but otherwise he freelanced or led small bands at the Metropole in New York.

DAVE BARBOUR

Like most guitarists of his generation Long Island-born David Michael "Dave" Barbour (1912-1965) started out on the banjo but switched instrument in the early 30's. He played with Wingy Manone in 1934 and with Red Norvo 1935-36, after which he was a much sought-after studio musician, recording with top names like Louis Armstrong, Mildred Bailey, Teddy Wilson and Bunny Berigan. In 1939 he played in the big band of Artie Shaw, and 1942-43 he was with Benny Goodman where he met his future wife Peggy Lee. In the mid-40's he led a little band with her, and during that time they wrote several hit songs together, including "Manana" and "It's a Good Day". During the 40's Barbour was still very active in the studios, and in the early 50's he had a short career in Hollywod as an actor. In 1952 he retired as a professional musician due to illness after which he played the guitar only sporadically again. Most of his work was as a section man, but he was also capable of playing fluent solos in the style of Charlie Christian.

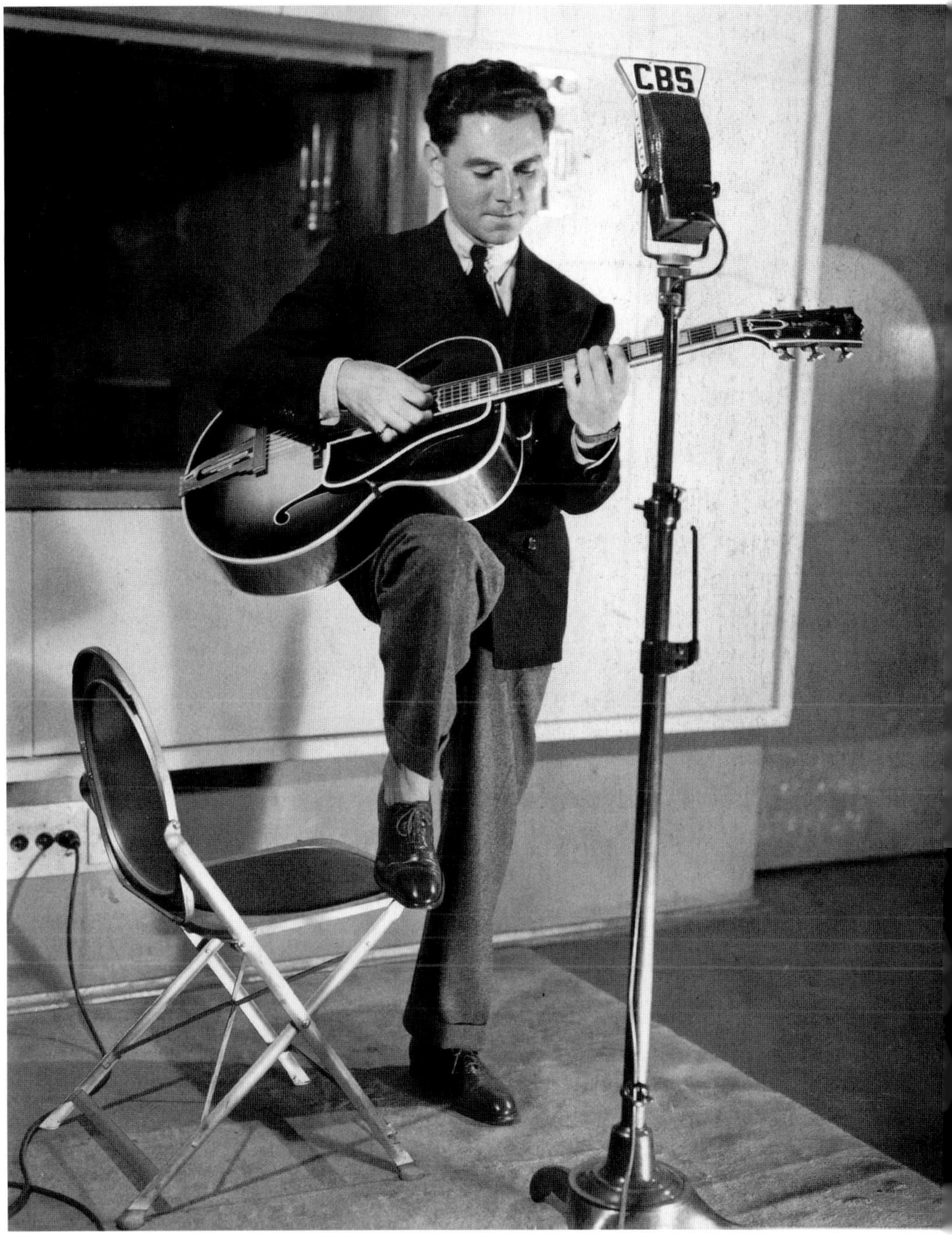

PUDDINGHEAD BATTLE

Trumpeter, arranger and composer Edgar William "Puddinghead" Battle (1907-1977) began playing the trumpet from the age of eight. While at college he formed the Dixie Serenaders and later led the Dixie Ramblers in his hometown Atlanta. During the 30's he played with Andy Kirk, Blanche Calloway, Sam Wooding, Benny Carter, Alex Hill and Willie Bryant. He led his own band during 1937 but disbanded to devote himself to composing and arranging. Among the bandleaders who profited from his music were Count Basie, Cab Calloway, Earl Hines, Louis Prima, Jack Teagarden, Fats Waller, and Paul Whiteman. He returned as a leader of big bands again in the 40's and 60's.

CHARLIE BARNET

Saxophonist and bandleader Charles Daly "Charlie" Barnet (1913-1991) was born in New York into a very wealthy family. He gave up studies at Yale University to play jazz, and afterwards led his own bands from 1933. He was a great admirer of Duke Ellington and many of the early band arrangements were imitations of Ellington's. Economically independent as he was, Barnet hired the best musicians available, black or white, and he was one of the first white bandleaders to employ black musicians, a fact which probably prevented his band from getting into one of the big commercial radio shows. He was a happy-go-lucky fellow who was very much liked by his band members. With the decline of the big bands after the war he disbanded his orchestra, settled in Palm Springs with his 11th (!) wife, moved into management, bought a chain of hotels, and played with his own small groups. On a few occasions he fronted a big band once more.

EDDIE BAREFIELD

Clarinetist, saxophonist and arranger Edward Emmanuel "Eddie" Barefield (1909-1991) was born in Scandia, Iowa and spent several of his teen years in both territory bands and name bands, including those of Bernie Young, Bennie Moten, Zack Whyte, and McKinney's Cotton Pickers. 1933-36 he was with Cab Calloway, after which he settled on the West Coast. In 1938 he returned to New York as a member of Fletcher Henderson's orchestra, and in the 40's he was a staff musician for ABC and for WOR radio besides playing with Benny Carter, Ella Fitzgerald and Duke Ellington. His all-round competence as both musician and arranger made him a first call by studios and ensured that 1948-70 he worked as musical director in Broadway shows. During those years he also worked as musical director for Cab Calloway and found time to play jazz and making film music. 1971-82 was spent in the house band of the Ringling Brothers and Barnum and Bailey Circus after which he freelanced and played with Dick Vance, The Harlem Blues and Jazz Band, Stan Rubin and Illinois Jacquet. After World War II Barefield abandoned the clarinet and concentrated on playing tenor saxophone influenced by the style of Lester Young. *The Greatest of all things To My boy Timme from Eddie Barefield.*

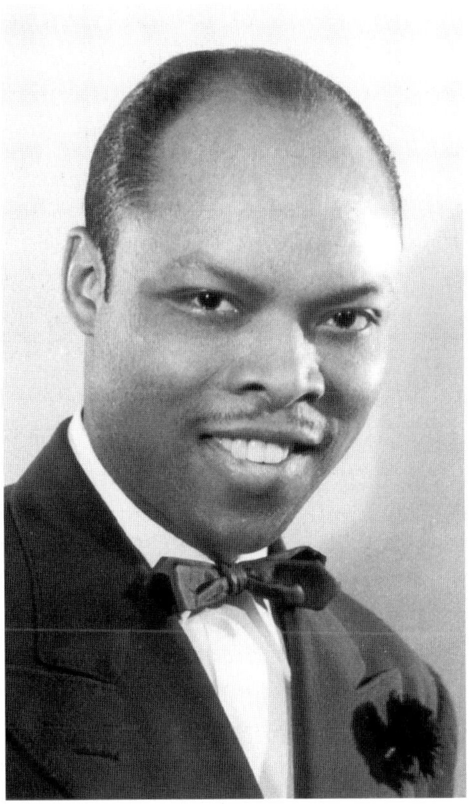

Eddie Barefield.

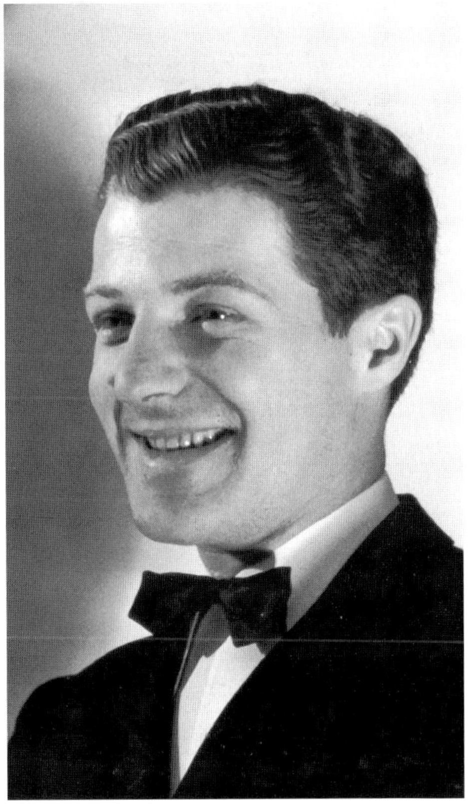

Charlie Barnet.

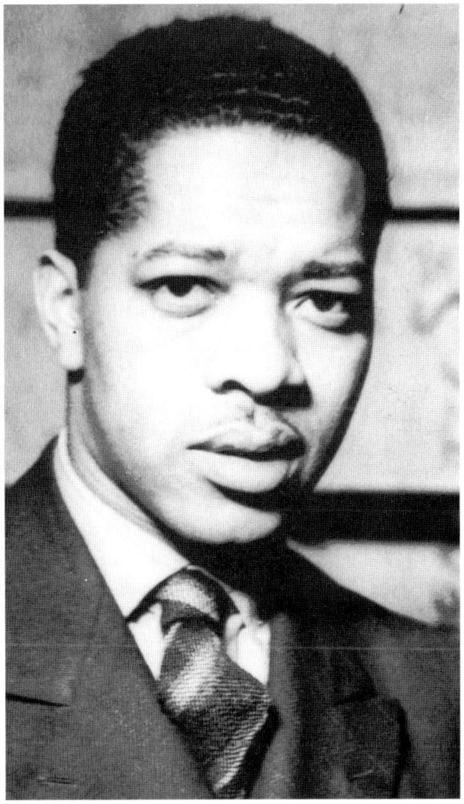

Puddinghead Battle.

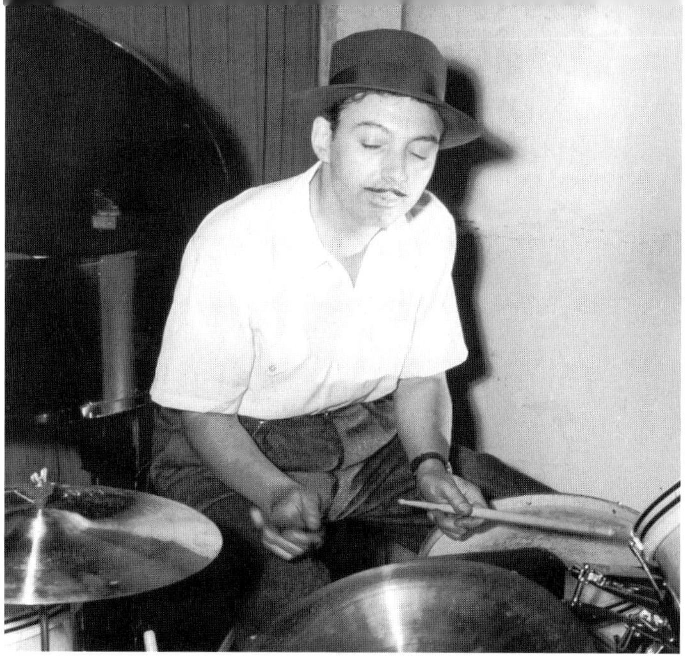

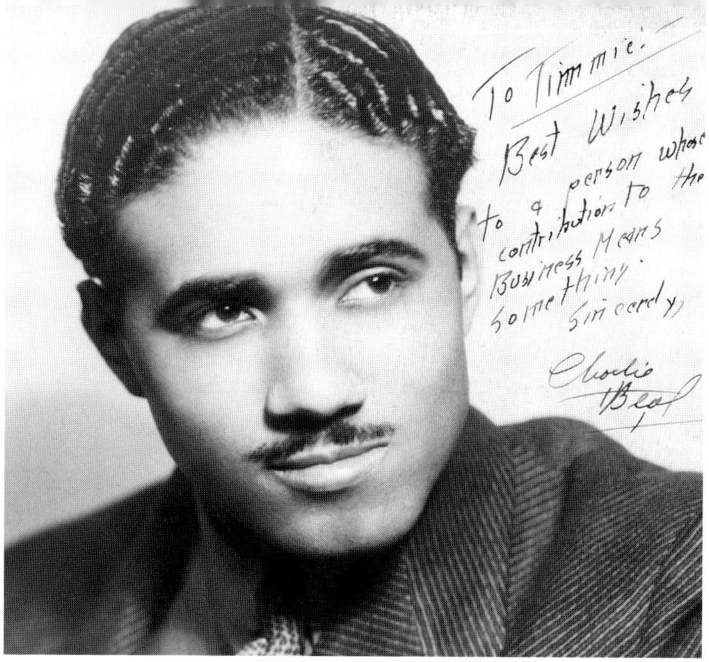

Ray Bauduc

New Orleans born drummer Raymond "Ray" Bauduc (1909-1988) came out of a musical family. Already before leaving school he played professionally in silent movie theatres, and after playing with local bands he played with Joe Venuti, Eddie Lang, and Fred Rich from the mid-20's. From 1928 he worked with Ben Pollack, and in 1935 he joined the Bob Crosby Orchestra. After military service he co-led a band with Gil Rodin, worked with Jimmy Dorsey and Jack Teagarden after which he led a group with Nappy Lamare. In the 60's he freelanced on the West Coast, but his last years were spent in Bellaire, Texas. The New Orleans two-beat drumming remained deep in Bauduc all his life, and he even used it when playing in swing big bands. He played cymbals superbly and was an intelligent soloist.

Charlie Beal

Pianist Charlie Beal (1908-1991) was born in Los Angeles where he played with Speed Webb and Les Hite. In 1932 he moved to Chicago to work as a soloist at the Grand Terrace, but he also played with Jimmie Noone, Erskine Tate, Louis Armstrong, Carroll Dickerson and Noble Sissle. He settled in New York in 1934 where he played a succession of long residences at 52nd Street clubs like the Onyx and the Famous Door, before joining Eddie South in 1936. After World War II he moved to his hometown where he appeared with Armstrong and Billie Holiday in the movie "New Orleans" (1947), and from 1948 to 1956 he toured European cities like Milan, London and Paris before returning to New York. Beale was a solid player who as a solo pianist had a penchant for the popular end of the jazz repertoire. *To Timmie! – Best Wishes to a person whose contribution to the Business Means Something. Sincerely, Charlie Beal.*

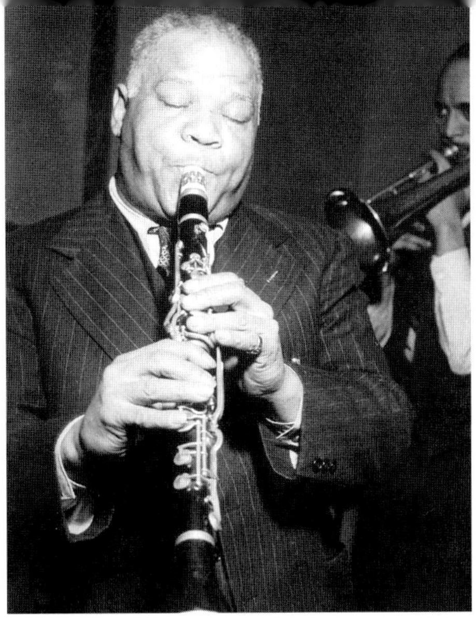

Bechet at a recording session in December 1944 for Blue Note with trombone player Vic Dickenson as one of his Blue Note Jazzmen.

Sidney Bechet

Clarinetist and soprano saxophonist Sidney Joseph Bechet (1897-1959) was one of the real jazz greats; a powerful and passionate player, a stylist, and a wonderful, majestic improviser. He was born in New Orleans into a musical family where also his four brothers played instruments, and was mainly self-taught. Already in 1913 he played in various bands, but in 1916 he left his home-town to play in touring shows and carnivals throughout the South and Midwest. He came to Chicago in 1917, where he played with Freddie Keppard and King Oliver among others, and in 1919 he joined Will Marion Cook's concert band with which he travelled to Europe. Here he left to work in England and France, and throughout the 20's he constantly travelled between Europe and the USA. In early 1933 Bechet temporarily left music, but the following year he joined Noble Sissle's band and toured with him until 1938 when he formed his own group. In 1949 he went to Europe again and his reception there was so enthusiastic that he settled permanently in France in 1951. He died of lung cancer in his home in Garches Haut-de-Seine, outside Paris.

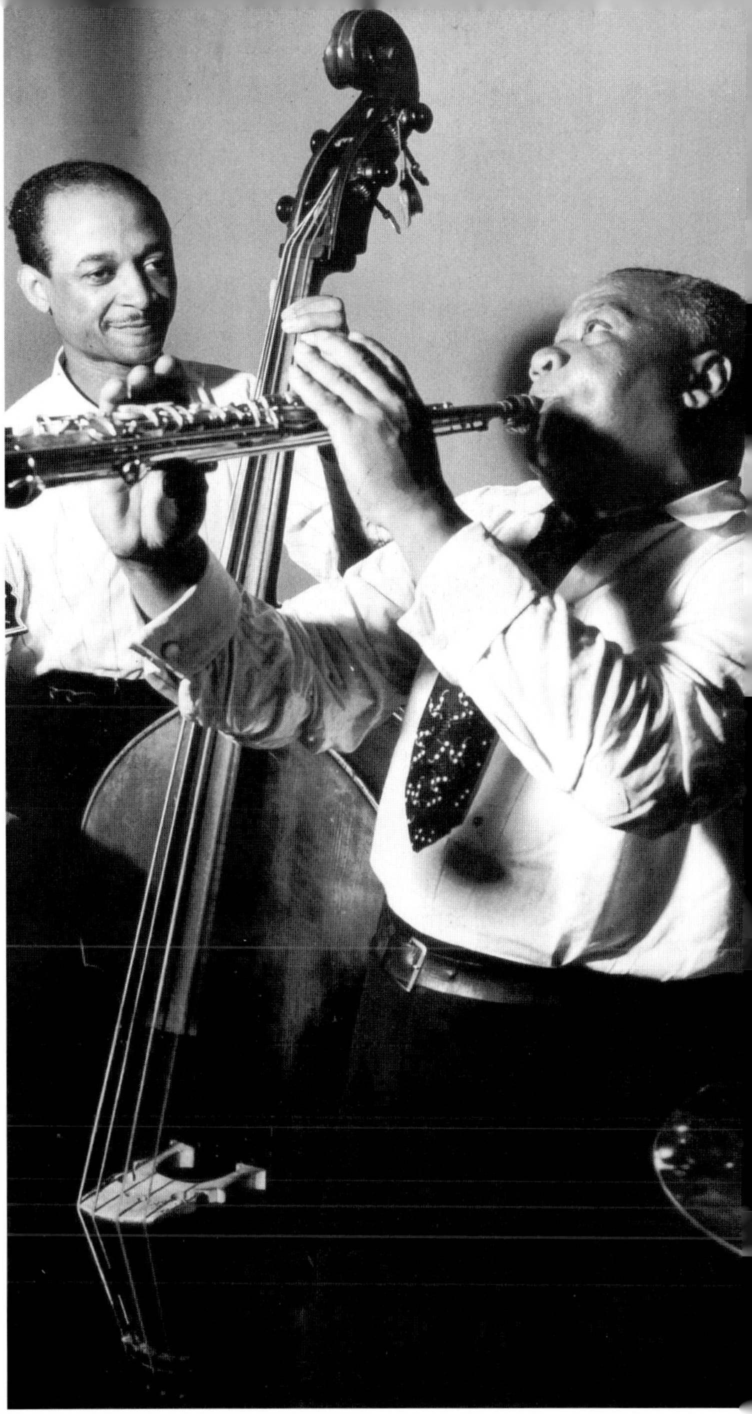

Bechet wailing on his soprano saxophone during a recording session for Blue Note June 8, 1939. The bass player is Johnny Williams.

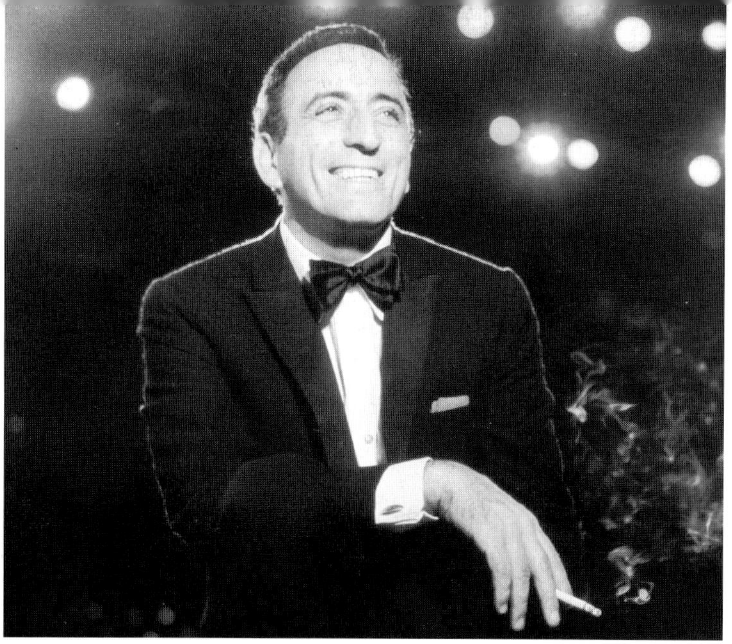

Tony Bennett

New York born singer Anthony Dominick Benedetto, "Tony Bennett" (1926-), is the son of an Italian father and an American mother. He studied music and painting and became a talented artist who exhibited in New York, Paris and London. During service in the US Army he began singing, and after his discharge he worked under the name of Joe Bari, until Bob Hope discovered him, brought him to his own show and changed his name a second time to Tony Bennett. Later on he worked with big bands such as Count Basie, Duke Ellington and Woody Herman, and in the 70's he recorded with Bill Evans, Ray Charles, Ruby Braff a.o. Bennett, whose singing is inspired by Mildred Bailey, Billie Holiday and Louis Armstrong, has won several Grammys, and he seems to get better with the years as his voice has deepened to a beautiful baritone. This photo, taken in the early 60's, was given to Rosenkrantz by Stuff Smith. *To Stuff, Do one for me! (Best Wishes) Tony Bennett.*

George Benson

Guitarist and singer George Benson (1943-) was born and raised in Pittsburgh where he already at the age of eight sang in nightclubs. In 1960 he formed his own rock-and-roll band, and 1962-65 he played jazz with Brother Jack McDuff after which he formed his own quartet with organist Lonnie Liston Smith. Due to his speed and agility on the guitar he was much used as a sideman in the studios and recorded with Billy Cobham, Miles Davis, Ron Carter, Freddie Hubbard and Lee Morgan. From the early 70's he became more commercial and reached a large audience with recordings on which he concentrated on singing, but he has continued to play jazz occasionally. As a guitarist he is influenced by Wes Montgomery and Tal Farlow, and one of his distinctive traits is his scat singing in unison with his guitar lines.

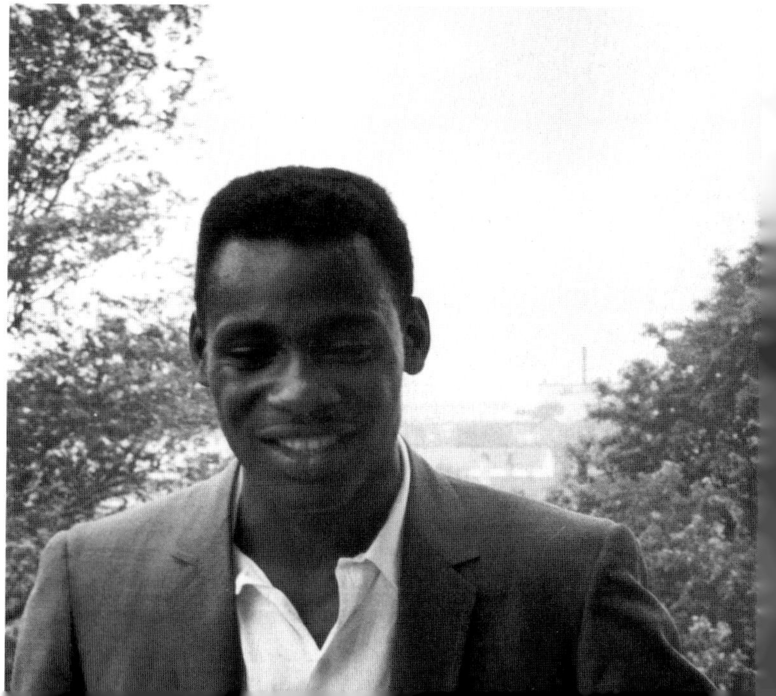

EDDIE BERT

A very flexible musician, trombonist Eddie Bert (1922-) is just as strong in a big band setting as in small groups. Born in Yonkers, N.Y. he joined Sam Donahue in 1940 after which he worked with Red Norvo, Charlie Barnet and Woody Herman. After Army service he played other big band jobs up to the mid-50's with Benny Goodman, Stan Kenton and Ray McKinley a.o. For the rest of the decade, he played mostly in small groups including those of his own bands and with Charlie Mingus. Most of the 60's was spent in theatre bands, but he also played jazz as often as possible. Later on he played in Dick Cavett's TV shows, but he also played and toured with the Thad Jones-Mel Lewis Orchestra and Lionel Hampton's All Star Orchestra.

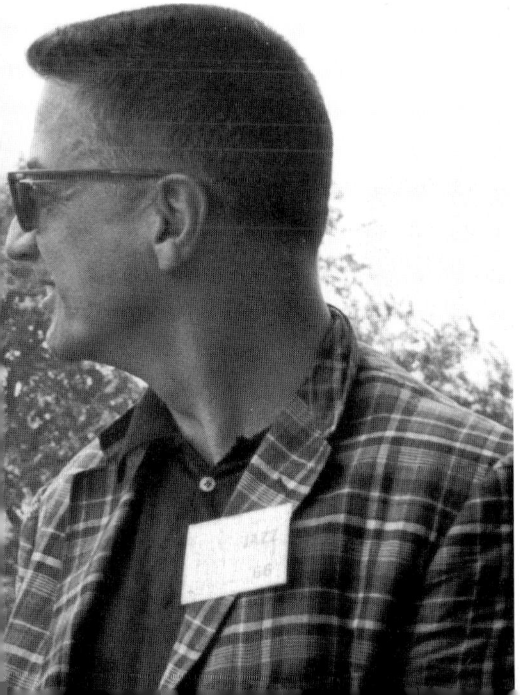

George Benson and critic John Hammond (1910-1987) at the 1966 Newport Jazz Festival.

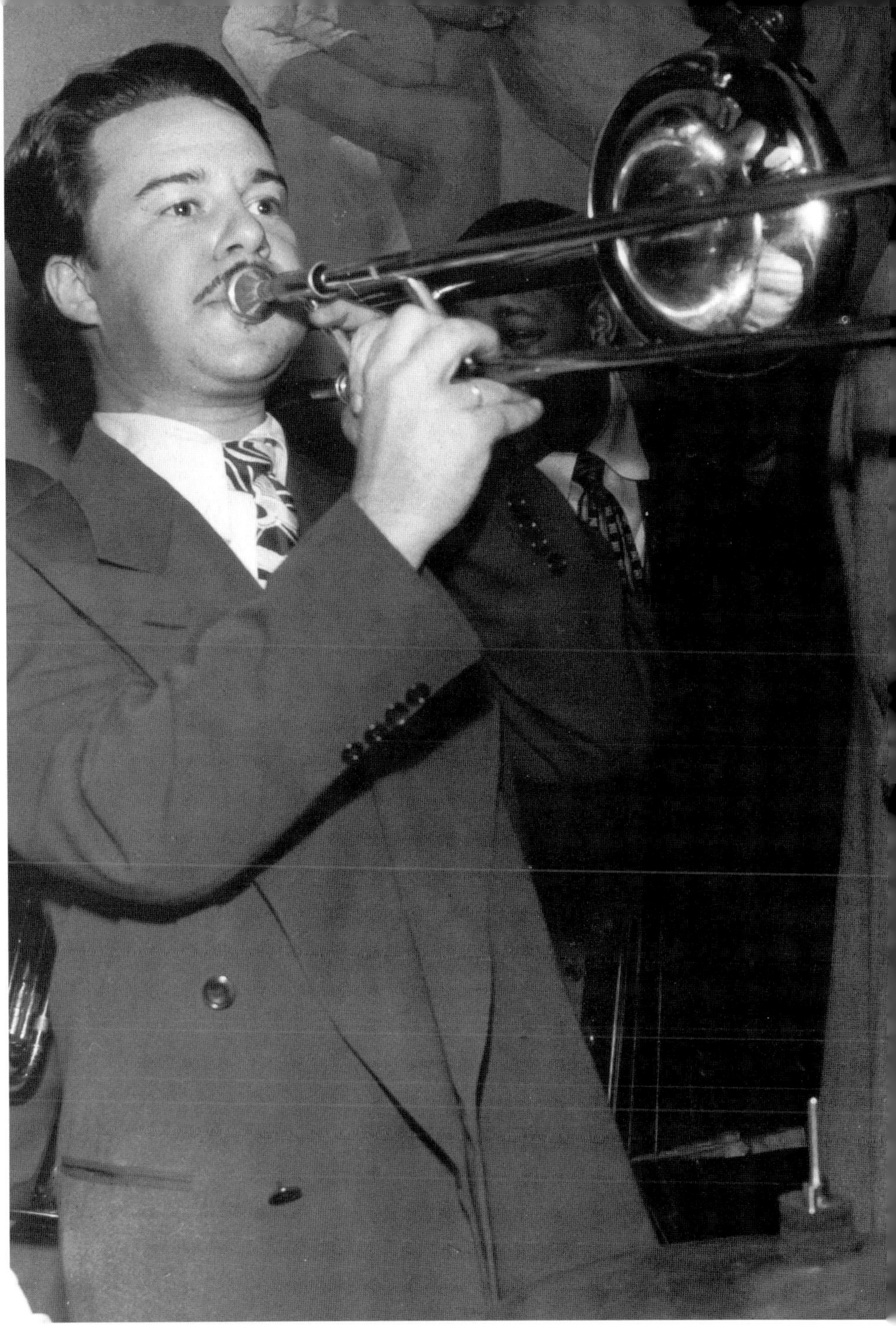

Eddie Bert at a Café Bohemia jam session on September 5, 1947 with bass player Al Hall.

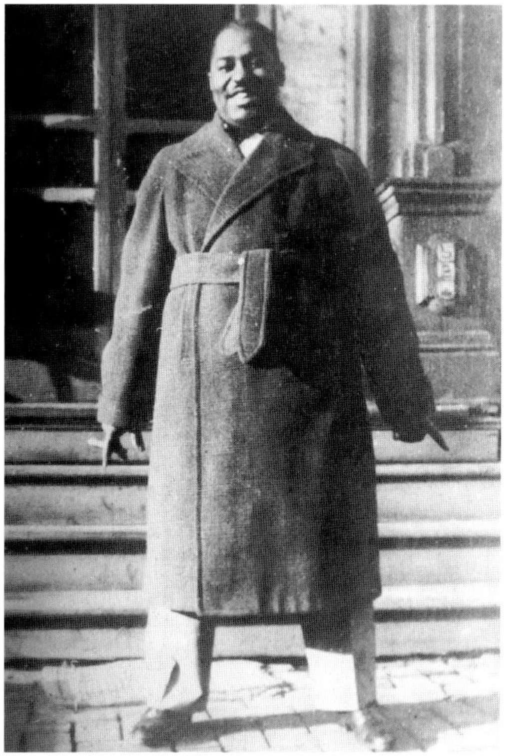

Chu Berry with a new, warm coat, ready to tour during the winter season.

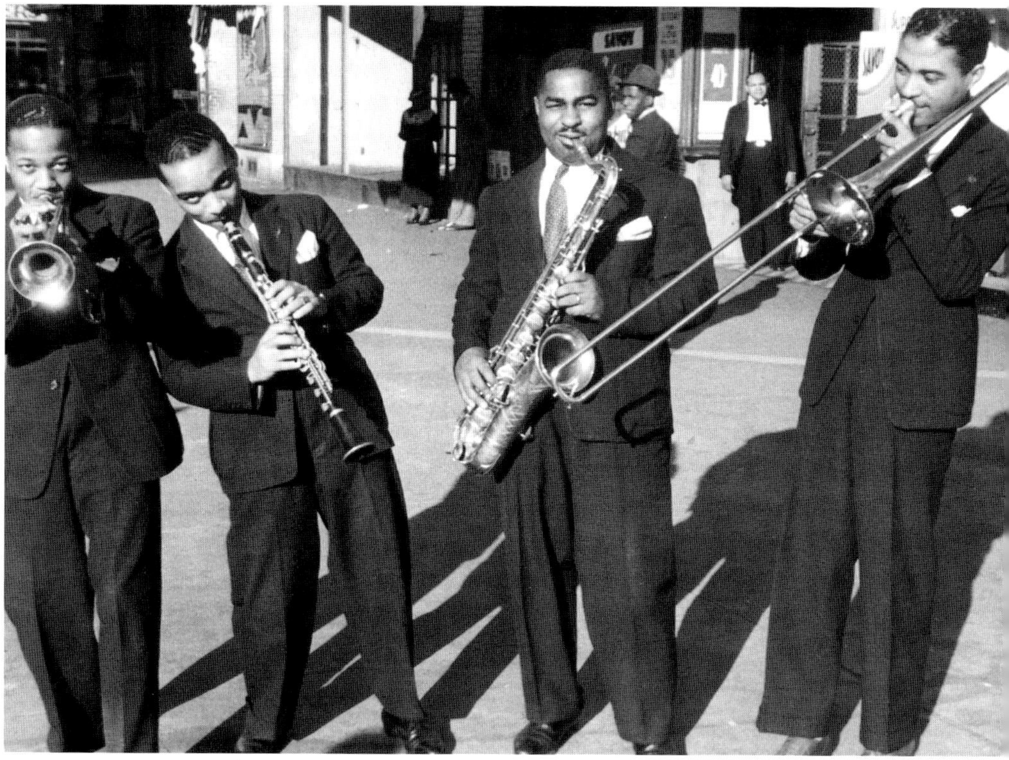

This photo is taken by Rosenkrantz in 1935 outside the Savoy Ballroom in Harlem during Berry's engagement with Teddy Hill. Berry is seen with Hill mates Roy Eldridge (tp), Russell Procope (cl) and Dicky Wells (tb).

CHU BERRY

Tenor saxophonist Leon "Chu" Berry (1910-1941) was born in Wheeling, West Virginia and raised in a musical family. In 1929 he moved to Chicago to join Sammy Stewart's big band, and the following year he settled in New York, where he played with Cecil Scott and Kaiser Marshall before Benny Carter hired him in 1932. He left Carter the following year for a stint with Charlie Johnson after which he worked with Teddy Hill and Fletcher Henderson before joining Cab Calloway in 1937. While on tour with Calloway he received severe head injuries in a car accident and died a few days later. Berry was strongly influenced by Coleman Hawkins. He was a superb soloist with an emotional sound, and his imaginative ideas were delivered with a strong swing and drive. Unfortunately he died without leaving a lasting impact on the development of jazz, and therefore is still very underrated.

Beryl Booker

Like Erroll Garner pianist Beryl Booker (1922-1978) was self-taught and never learned to read music. She was born in Philadelphia and played in local clubs until she in 1946 became a member of Slam Stewart's trio, an association which lasted on and off until the late 50's. In between she accompanied Dinah Washington (1952-54), toured with Billie Holiday (1954), and also led her own trios. She was active right up to the year she died.

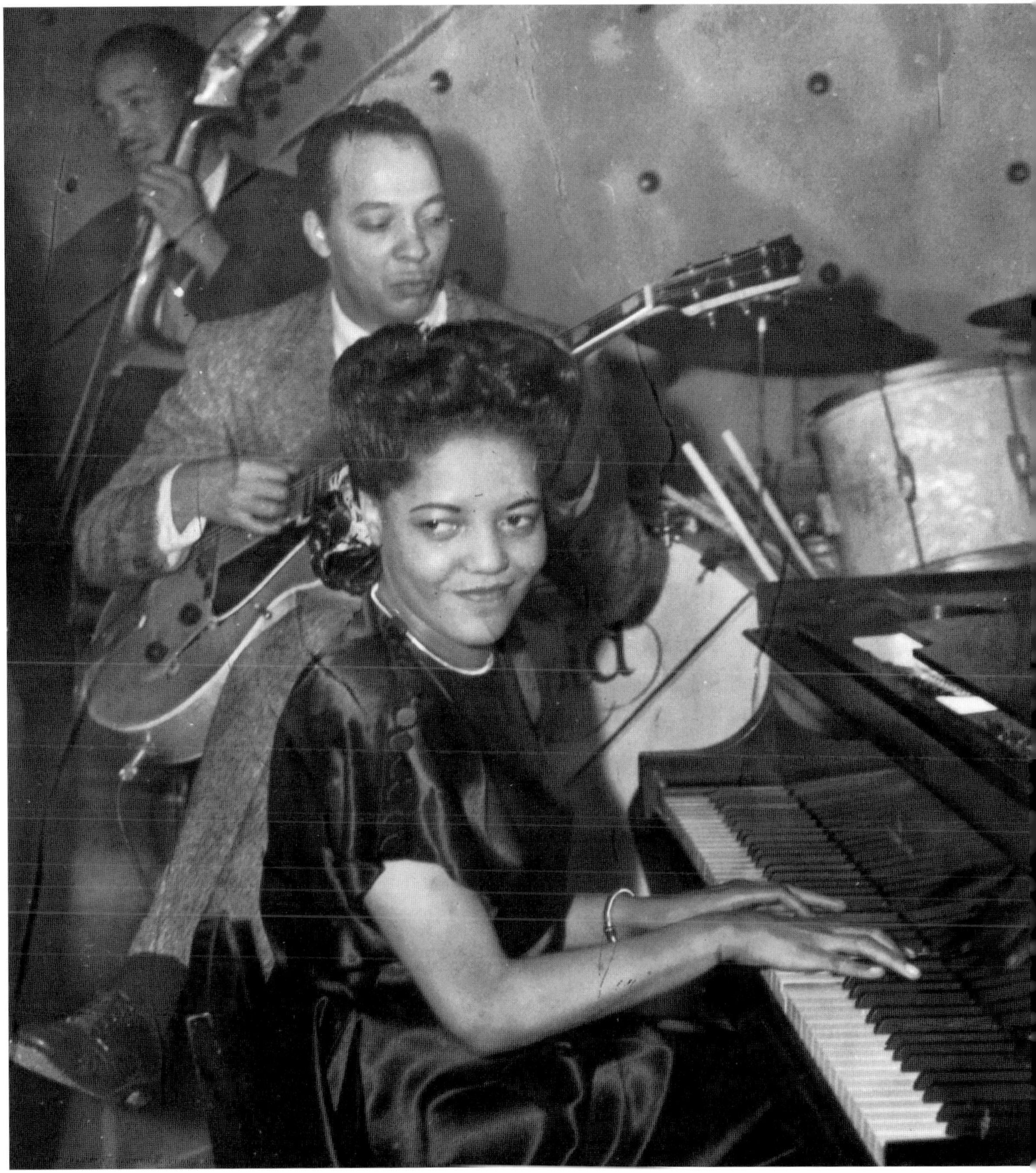

Bery Booker at the Three Deuces in 1946 when she was part of Slam Stewart's Trio. The guitar player is John Collins.

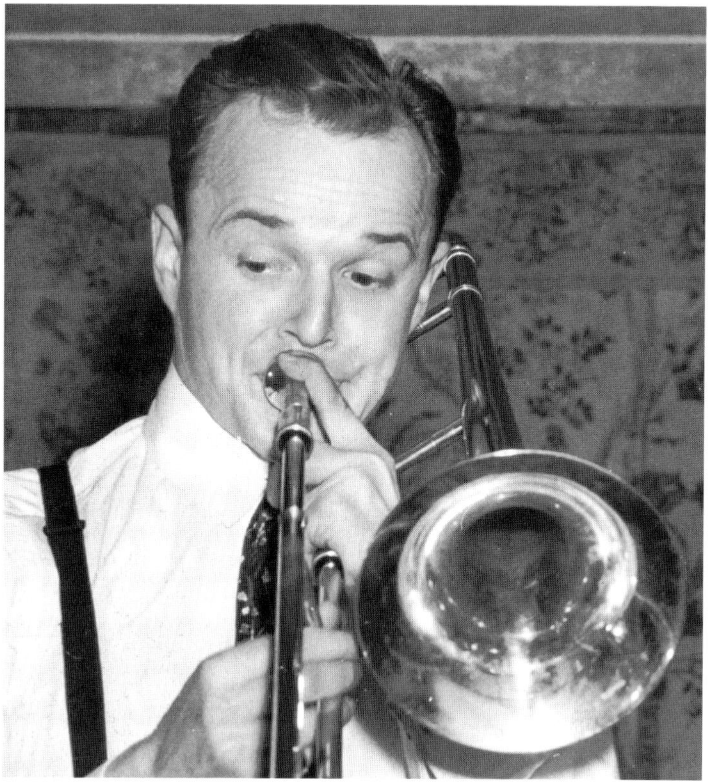

Will Bradley during the 40's.

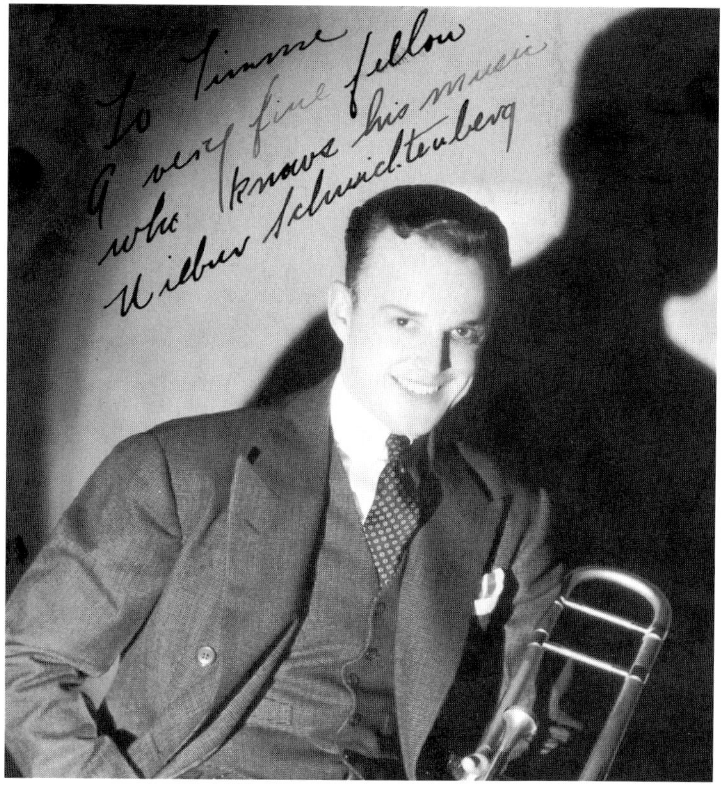

Publicity photo of Will Bradley from the mid-30's. *To Timme. A very fine fellow who knows his music. Wilbur Schwichtenberg.*

WILL BRADLEY

Trombonist and bandleader Wilbur Schwichtenberg, "Will Bradley" (1912-), came to New York from New Jersey in 1928 to play with Milt Shaw. He was then with Red Nichols and Ray Noble until 1936 and was much in demand in the studios of CBS and other companies. In 1939 he formed a big band with drummer Ray McKinley which specialized in boogie-woogie. The band was an instant success but broke up in 1942. Hereafter he returned to the studios and played the Tonight Show, but he also studied composition and worked freelance. Apart from jazz he is much interested in classical music and has composed several extended works for symphony orchestras and chamber ensembles. As a trombonist he modelled his playing after Tommy Dorsey and is widely respected among other musicians for his skills. He is equally at home in all tempos but enjoys playing ballads in a polished and graceful style.

TINY BRADSHAW

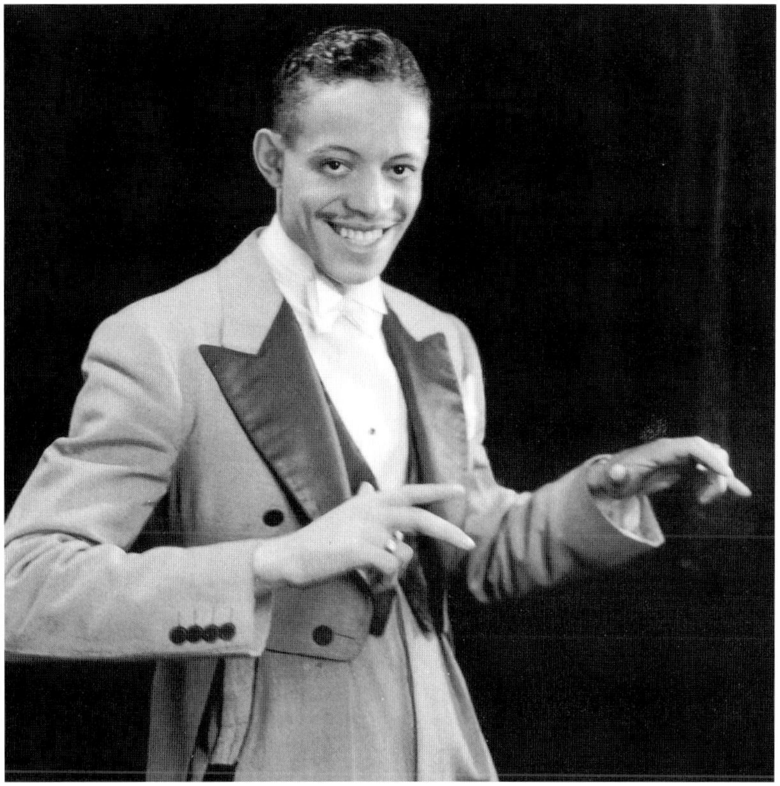

Bandleader, drummer and singer Tiny Bradshaw (1905-58) came to New York in 1932 where he worked with Marion Hardy's Alabamians, the Savoy Bearcats, Mills Blue Rhytm Band and Luis Russell's orchestra. In 1934 he organized his own big band with which he toured extensively, playing long engagements at hotels and dance halls. During this time he modelled his singing after Cab Calloway, but he never quite made the big time despite hiring first-rate musicians and arrangers for his band, amongst them trumpeters Shad Collins and Charlie Shavers, saxophonists Russell Procope, Happy Caldwell, Charlie Fowlkes, Sonny Stitt, Gigi Gryce, and pianist Billy Kyle. In the late 40's he adapted the band to fit the rhythm-and-blues style, but two strokes forced him to disband in the mid-50's.

AARON BRIDGERS

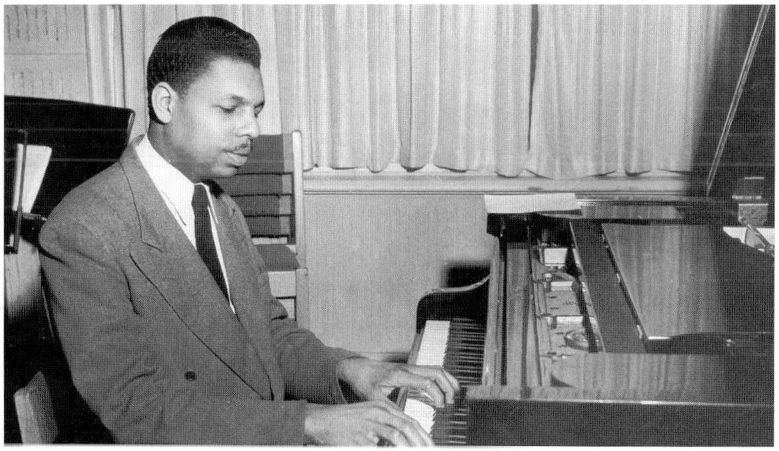

Pianist Aaron Bridgers was a friend of Timme Rosenkrantz and came to Europe in 1951 as accompanist for singer Inez Cavanaugh, Rosenkrantz's girlfriend for many years. Bridgers remained in Europe, settled in Paris and recorded under his own name in 1955-56.

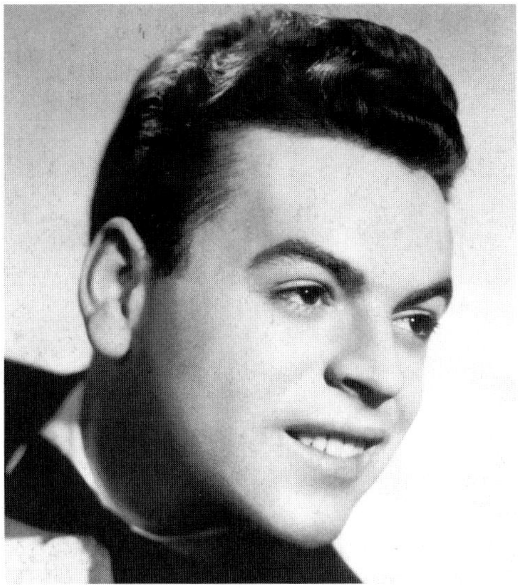

Publicity photo of Les Brown taken around 1938 at the time he formed his first band.

Les Brown

Bandleader, composer and arranger, Lester Raymond "Les" Brown (1912-), was born in Reinerton, PA. In 1932 he entered Duke University in Durham, NC where he joined the university's dance band and soon became its leader. In 1937 he moved to New York and began writing arrangements for Jimmy Dorsey and Isham Jones, and the following year he formed his own band. Most of the repertoire consisted of easy, swinging dance music, but he nevertheless had good jazz soloists and vocalists in the band such as Abe Most and Doris Day. In 1947 he began a long association with Bob Hope, and since then Les Brown and His Band of Renown have remained popular on television programs like "The Steve Allen Show" and "The Dean Martin Show".

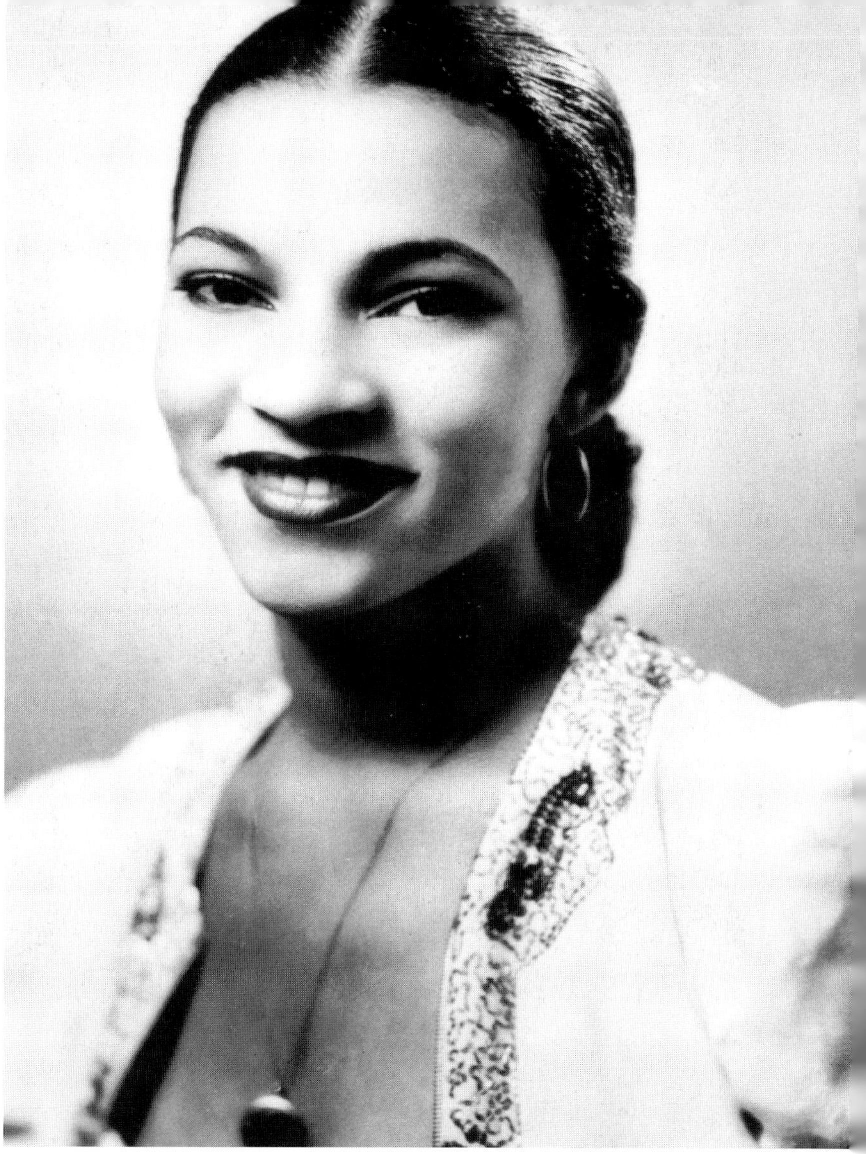

Dolores Brown

This publicity photo of singer Dolores Brown is from 1943-44, at the time she was featured with Don Redman's big band. Before this job she performed with Erskine Hawkins's big band with which she recorded in 1939-40.

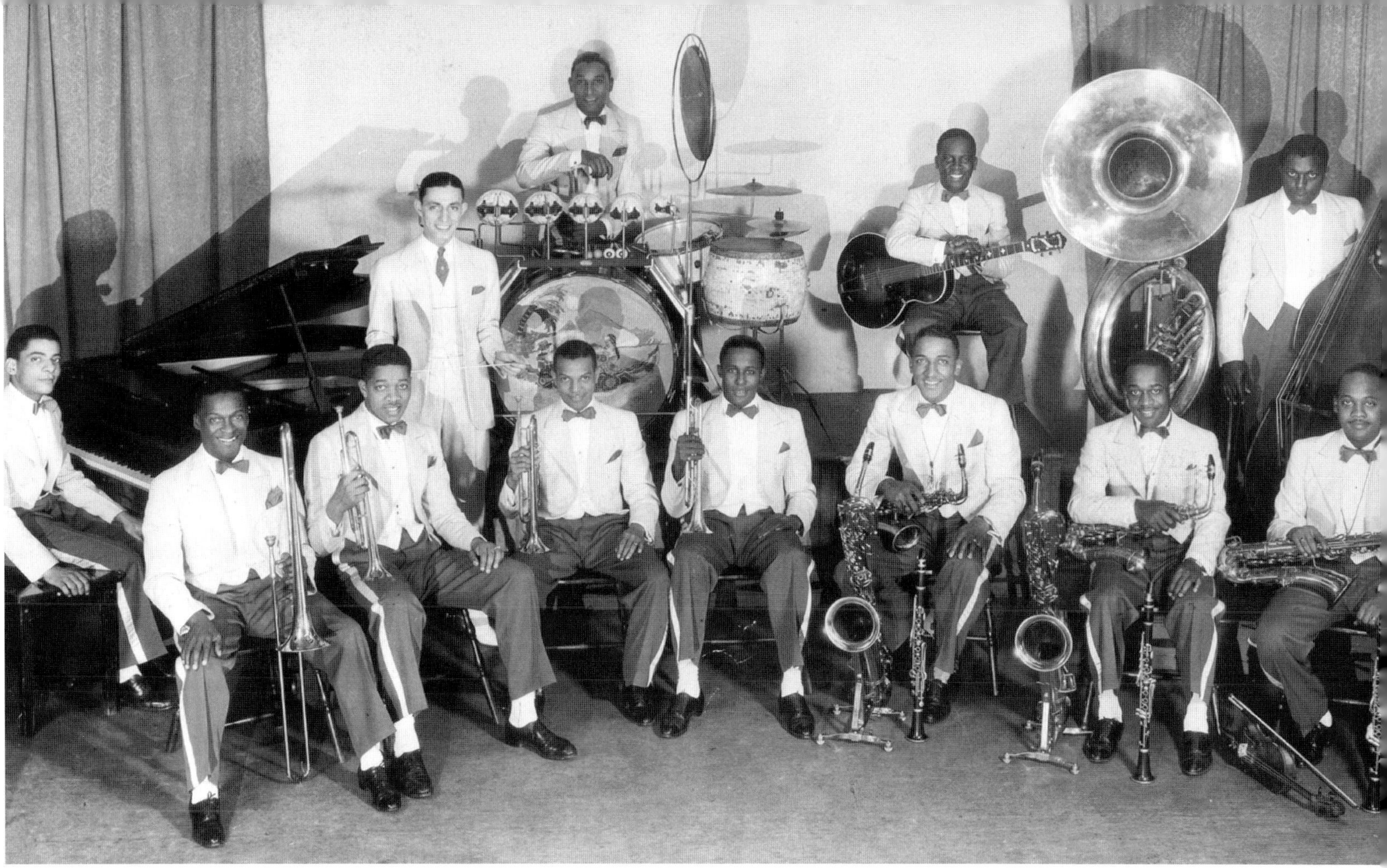

Willie Bryant's first band with an excellent rhythm section consisting of Teddy Wilson (p), Cozy Cole (dr), Arnold Adams (g), and Louis Thompson (b). In the front row from left: John Haughtone (tb), trumpeters Edgar "Puddinghead" Battle, Robert Cheek and Dick Clark, and saxophonists Glyn Pacque, Stanley Payne, and Johnny Russell. Bryant is between the piano and the drums.
To My Pal Baron Timme Rosenkrantz From Willie Bryant And Band New York.

Willie Bryant

New Orleans born dancer and singer, Willie Bryant (1908-64), toured extensively in vaudeville before organizing his own big bands 1934-38 and again 1945-48. Later on he was master of ceremonics at the Apollo Theater in New York and also worked as a disc jockey, an actor, a radio announcer, and organizer of various tv series for CBS. His first band came close to attaining top rank status but musically never quite made it.

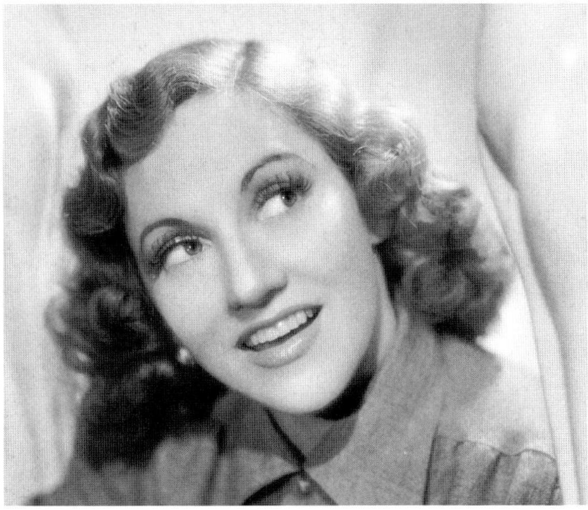

CONNEE BOSWELL

Singer Connee Boswell (1907-1976), and her sisters Martha (1908-1958) and Helvetia (1909-1988), were born into a middleclass family in New Orleans. While still teenagers they formed a vocal trio The Boswell Sisters, performed on radio, and recorded from 1931 with jazz greats like Bunny Berigan, Joe Venuti, Jimmy and Tommy Dorsey, and Benny Goodman. In the mid-30's all three sisters married, and in 1935 the group broke up. Although being in a wheelchair since contracting polio at the age of four, Connee continued with her career and worked extensively into the 60's in radio, films and television. Besides singing she was remarkably multi-instrumental, playing saxophone, piano, trombone and cello.

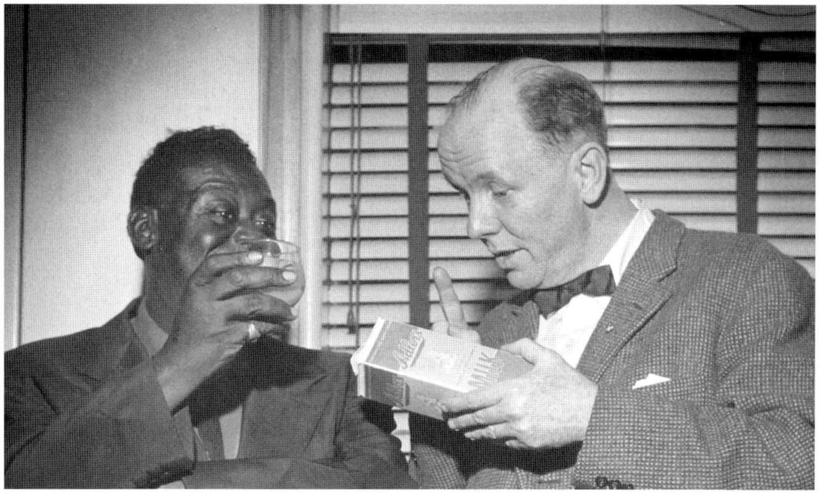

Pete Brown at a private recording session in Rosenkrantz's New York apartment. It appears that Rosenkrantz is trying to convince Brown of the virtue of drinking milk.

PETE BROWN

Alto saxophonist James Ostend "Pete" Brown (1906-1963) came to New York in 1927 after having worked in several bands in his home town, Baltimore, and in Atlantic City. In the Big Apple he freelanced until he became a member of John Kirby's Sextet in 1937. He left the following year to form his own band which played several 52nd Street clubs, such as the Onyx and Kelly's Stable, sometimes with Frankie Newton as co-leader. He continued to play into the 60's, even as his health deteriorated due to diabetes and weight problems. He was also busy as a teacher, Cecil Payne and Flip Phillips being among his pupils. Brown was a highly original musician with a distinctive style dominated by intense, rhythmic phrasing and a hard swing which was well suited to the popular jump bands of the 30's. His playing inspired many saxophone players in later rhythm-and-blues bands.

BUTTERBEANS AND SUSIE

This team was one of the most popular and durable in black vaudeville appearing together for almost half a century. Butterbeans was born in Georgia and baptised Jody Edwards (1895-1967), while Susie (1896-1963) was born Susie Hawthorn in Pensacola, Florida. They had begun to perform together before they married in 1916. They headlined in their revues from the 20's and supported numerous stars from Trixie Smith (1920) to James Brown (1959). On their recordings, comic sketches in song and speech, they were sometimes backed by top jazz musicians. This publicity shot gives a fair picture of their show characters. Susie always performed as the dominant wife, while Butterbeans was the henpecked, put-upon husband.

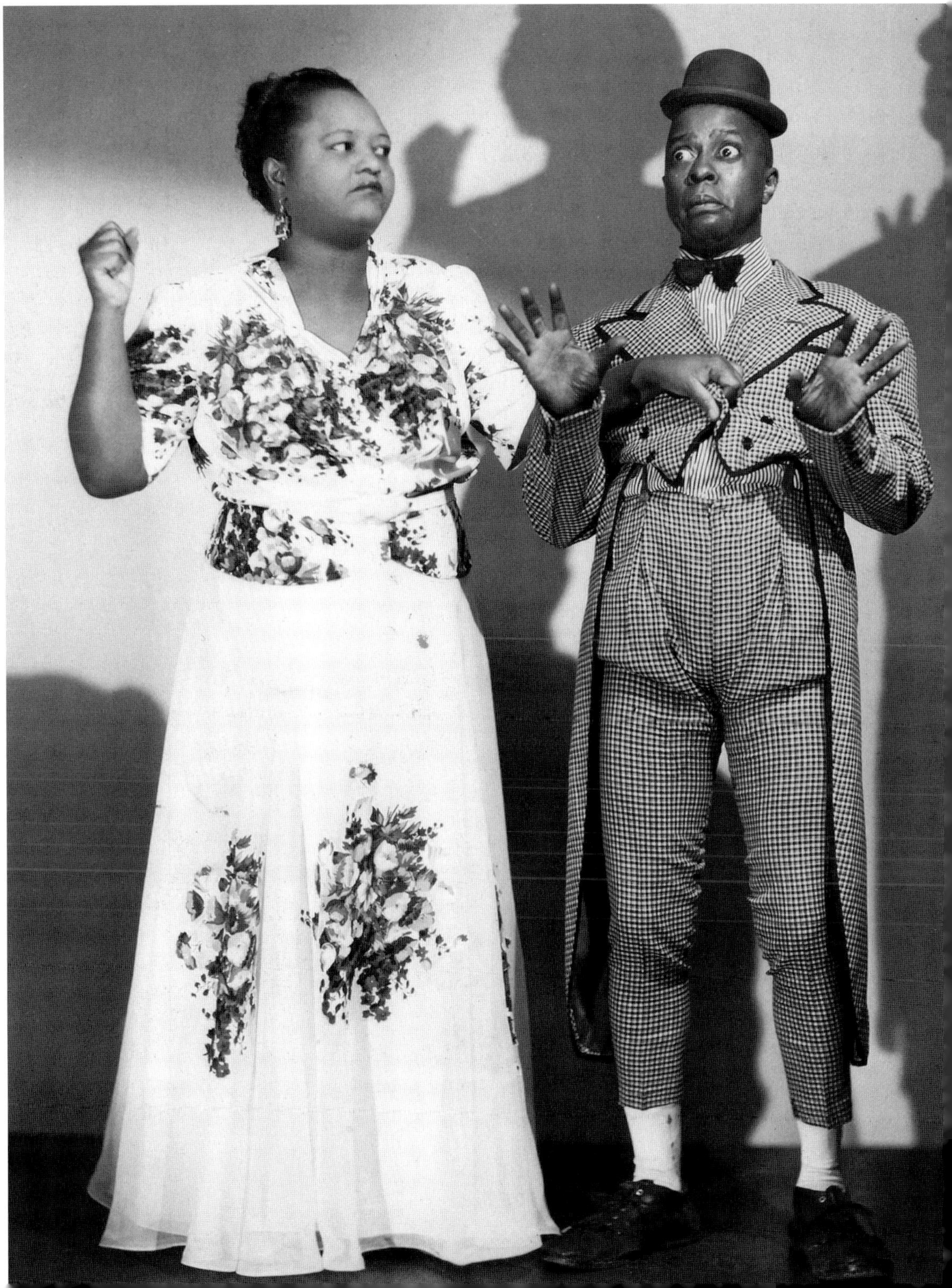

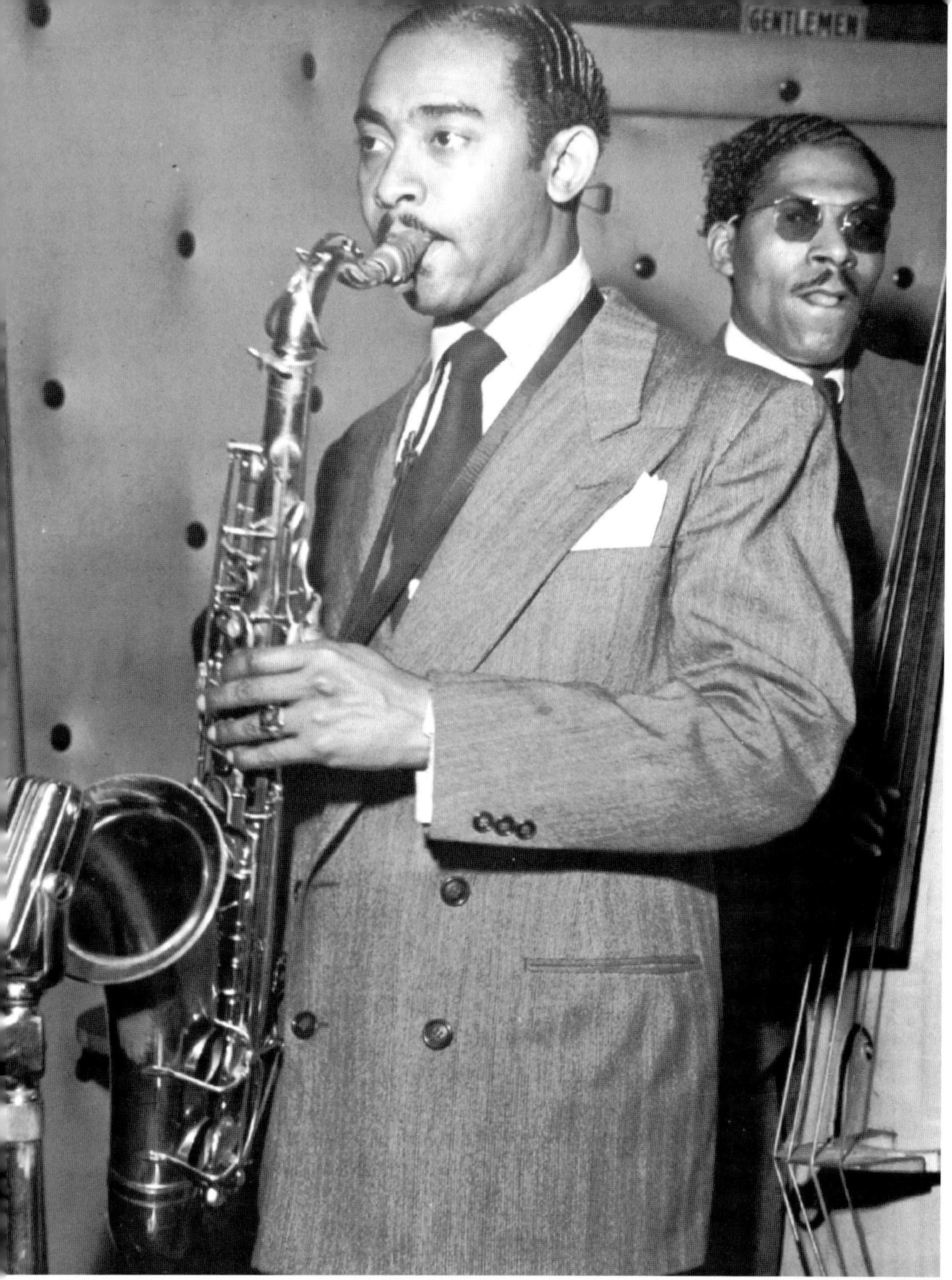

Don Byas at the Three Deuces, New York, in 1945 with bass player Slam Stewart.

DON BYAS

Tenor saxophonist Carlos Wesley "Don" Byas (1912-1962) was born in Muskogee, Oklahoma and gained his first professional experiences in the territory bands of Bennie Moten, Terrence Holder and Walter Page's Blue Devils. He formed his own band in 1931, but in 1933 he left Oklahoma and settled in Los Angeles to play with Lionel Hampton, Eddie Barefield and Buck Clayton. He came to New York in 1937 with Eddie Mallory's band, and in 1939 he joined Andy Kirk. In 1941-43 he became famous nation-wide as featured soloist with Count Basie's orchestra, after which he worked in many small bands in the clubs of 52nd Street. In 1946 he came to Europe with Don Redman's Big Band and remained there until his death, living in France, the Netherlands and Denmark. Byas was a transitional musician who linked swing with bop. His playing in the mid-40's was marked by long, fluid lines of exceptional creativity and beauty, and around this time he even overshadowed his idol Coleman Hawkins. His first recordings were made for Timme Rosenkrantz in 1938, and during 1944 he made several private recordings at Rosenkrantz's home, too.

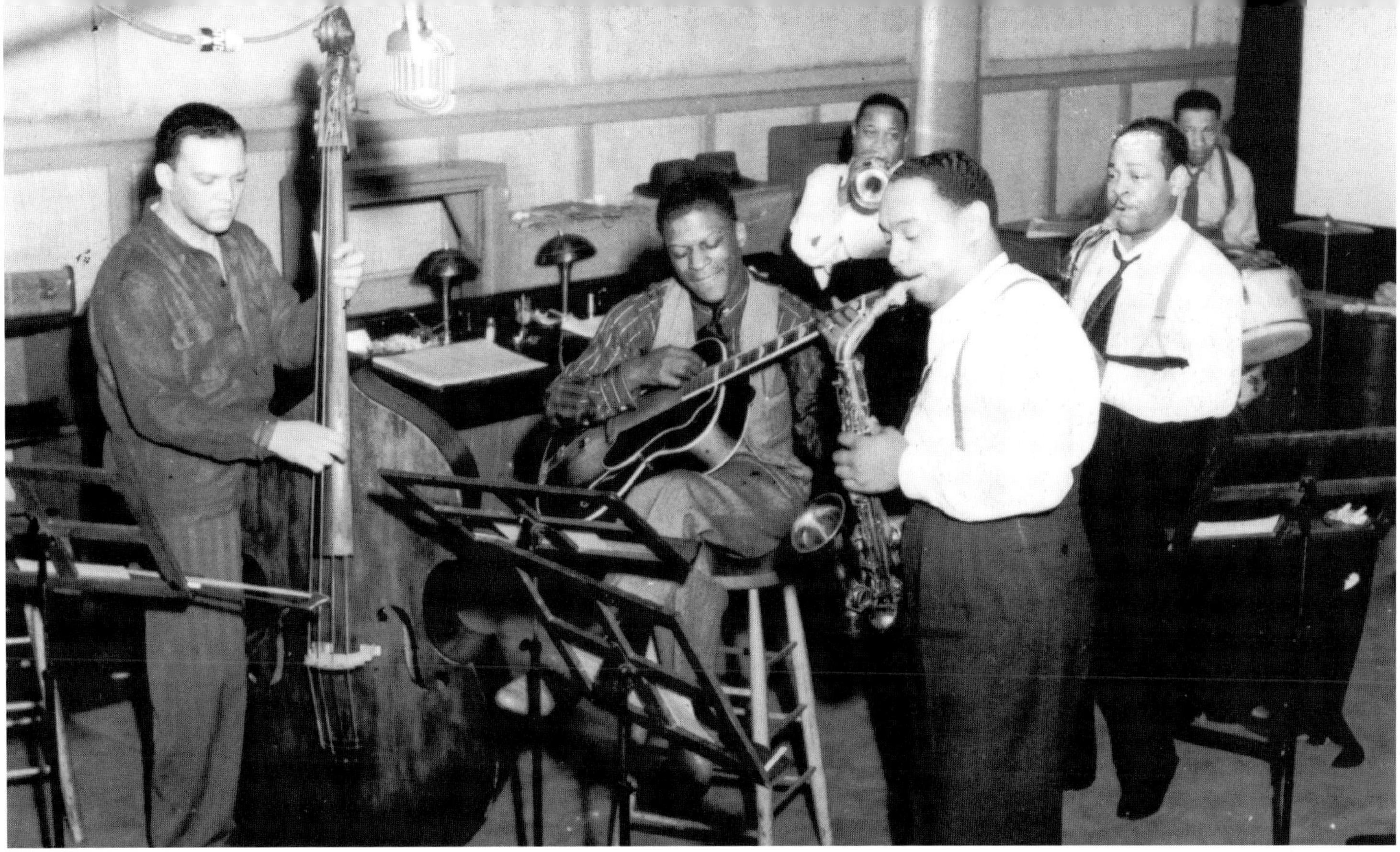

Benny Carter

One of the really great musicians in jazz is Bennett Lester "Benny" Carter (1907-). He is a true multi-instrumentalist, playing trumpet, alto saxophone, clarinet, trombone and piano, besides being one of the finest composers and arrangers. He was born in New York and started out on trumpet but took up the saxophone later on. As a member of Fletcher Henderson's orchestra 1930-31 he attracted widespread attention for his arrangements, and the following year he followed Don Redman as musical director of McKinney's Cotton Pickers. In 1935 he moved to Europe, but back in New York in 1938 he formed a big band which played the Savoy Ballroom most of the following two years. In 1943 he went to the West Coast where he quickly became involved in writing film music. Over the next five decades he wrote scores for films and television series but also found time to play clubs, record and tour several times, and he is still performing on saxophone at his immaculately high level. The photo shows him recording for Commodore on May 25, 1940 with the Chocolate Dandies. From left John Kirby, Bernard Addison, Roy Eldridge, Benny Carter, Coleman Hawkins, and Sidney Catlett.

THE CALIFORNIA RAMBLERS

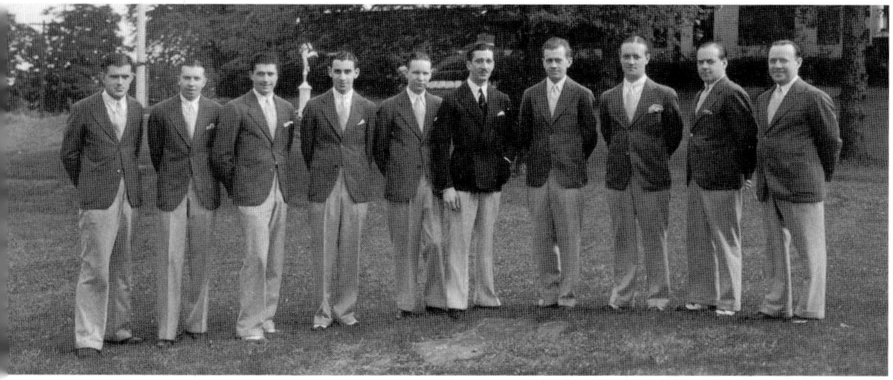

The name of this constantly changing group was used for hundreds of recordings for a plethora of companies between 1921 and 1937. Singer – and manager for Fats Waller – Ed Kirkeby assembled between nine and fourteen of some of the best white musicians for these dates, and their records show that they were among the pioneers of big band jazz, playing forward-thinking, tight arrangements with an infectious swing, great collective skill and fluent, melodic improvisations. Sometimes they recorded under the name of the Golden Gate Orchestra, and smaller units used names like the Goofus Five, the Varsity Eight, the Vagabonds, or the Five Birmingham Babies. Besides recording the group appeared for several years at the Pelham Bay Park near New York which Kirkeby renamed the California Ramblers' Inn. On this photo, taken in December 1930, the group is standing in front of the Hunters Island Inn, showing from left Carl Smith (b), Johnny Rude (as), Herbert Weil (dr), Arthur Rollini (ts), Noel Kilgen (g), Adrian Rollini (bass sax), Lew Cobey (p), Chelsea Quealey (tp), Bobby Davis (as), Jack Wechsler (vl).

CAB CALLOWAY

Singer and dancer Cab Calloway (1908-1994) was born in Rochester, NY, but moved to Chicago to attend law school. Inspired by his sister Blanche who performed as a singer, he dropped out and began working as a singer and a dancer at theatres. From 1929 he worked regularly with the Missourians, and after a while the name changed to Cab Calloway and His Orchestra. A long, successful stay at the Cotton Club helped make the band known nationwide, and with replacements by better musicians Calloway had a first-class big band around 1940 which included such stars as Chu Berry, Milt Hinton, Cozy Cole, Danny Barker, Dizzy Gillespie, Jonah Jones, Russell Smith, and Quentin Jackson. At this time Calloway had become the highest-paid and most successful black entertainer and bandleader, and he appeared in several films such as "The Singing Kid" (1936), and "Stormy Weather" (1943). He disbanded his big band in 1948 to perform in musical theatre, but once in a while he assembled a band for special occasions. He continued to perform and tour up through the 80's, and also did tv-shows and films, such as "The Blues Brothers" (1980), and "His Royal Highness Of Hi-De-Ho; The Legendary Cab Calloway" (1987).

Cab Calloway and His Orchestra 1931, probably taken before opening at New York's famous Cotton Club. From left Earres Prince (p), Walter "Foots" Thomas (as), Calloway (standing), Andrew Brown (ts), Morris White (bj), William Thornton Blue (sax), Leroy Maxey (dr), R.Q. Dickerson (tp), Reuben Reeves (tp), Jimmy Smith (tu, b) and DePriest Wheeler (tb).

This photo, in typical publicity fashion, is from the mid-30's and could be taken from one of Calloway's film appearances. In the back row are Bennie Payne (p), DePriest Wheeler, Harry White (tb), Leroy Maxey (dr), Morris White (g), and Al Morgan (b). In the front from left: Lammar Wright, Edwin Swayzee, and Doc Cheatham (tp), Calloway, Eddie Barefield (as), Andrew Brown (cl), Arville Harris (as), and Walter "Foots" Thomas (ts).

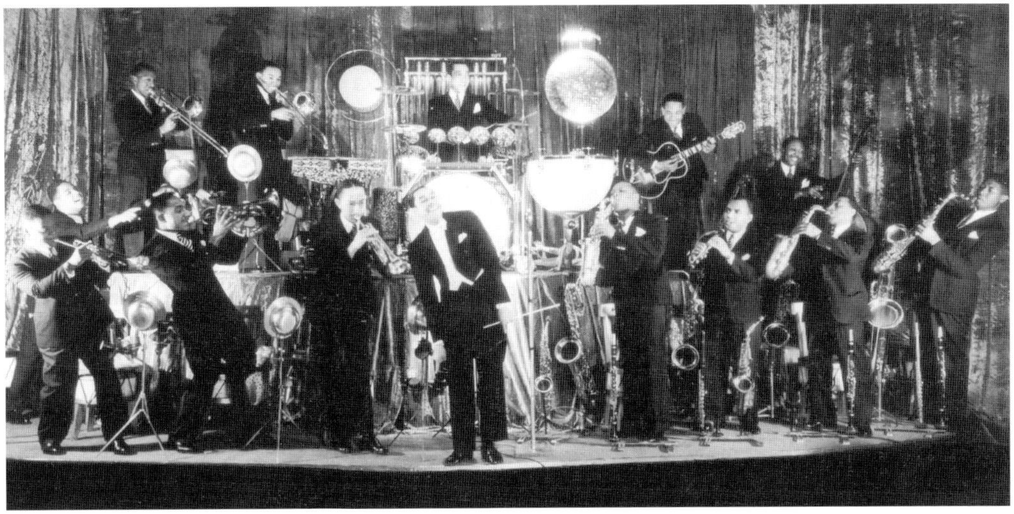

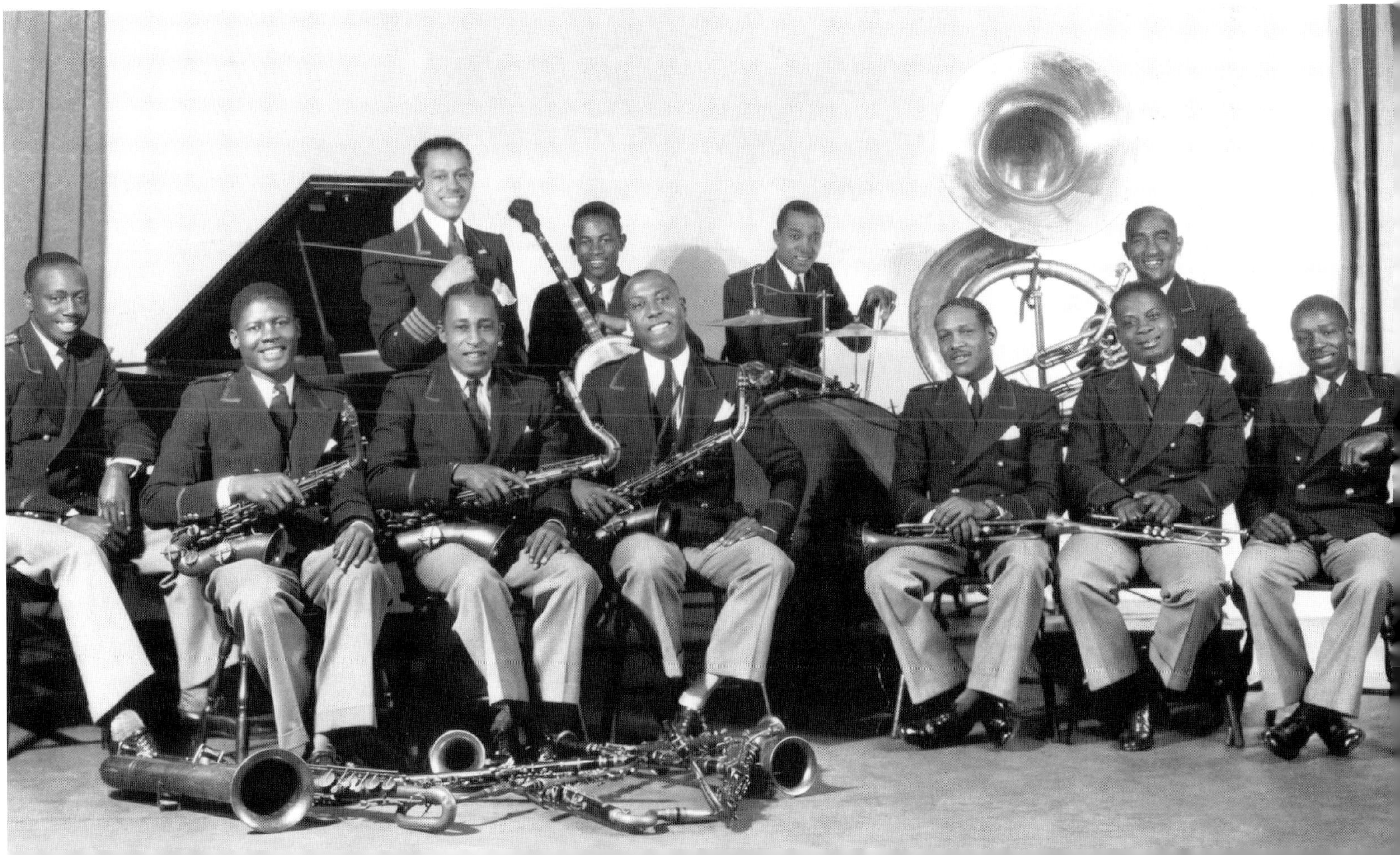

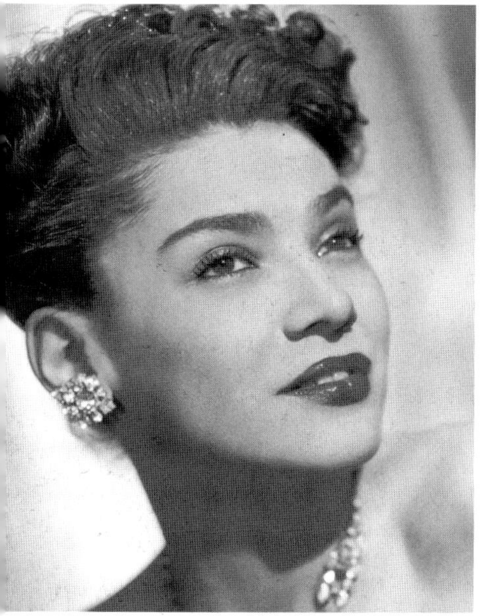

UNA MAE CARLISLE

Pianist, composer and singer Una Mae Carlisle (1915-1956) came from Xenia, Ohio. Her father was white, while her mother was a Cherokee Indian, and already as a teenager she worked as a radio musician in Cincinnati in 1932, where Fats Waller heard her. She joined his band and played in his show for a while but continued afterwards as a solo act. In 1937 she went to Europe and appeared and recorded in England, Germany and France but returned to USA shortly before the outbreak of World War II. Back in New York she worked at the Village Vanguard, Kelly's Stable, the Plantation Club, Hotel Dixie and elsewhere, but she also toured and had her own radio and TV series from the late 40's. Unfortunately she suffered from mastoid trouble which in the end forced her to retire in 1954. Her piano playing was based on Fats Waller's style, and her voice was warm, sensual and expressive, as can be heard on her recordings which featured such musicians as Lester Young, Benny Carter, Charlie Shavers, Don Redman, Russell Procope, Ray Nance and John Kirby.

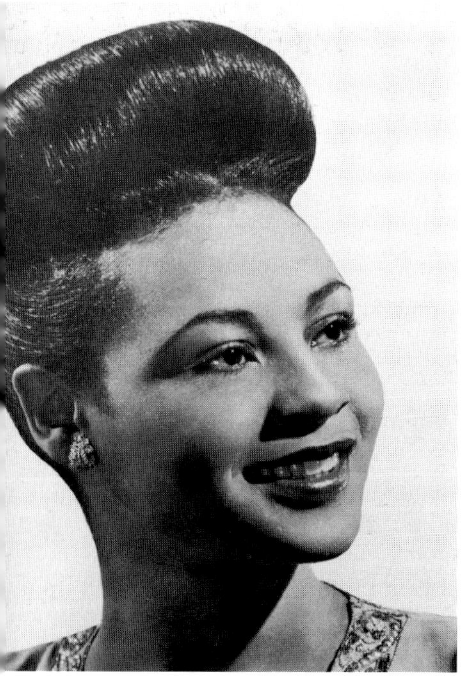

THELMA CARPENTER

New York born singer Thelma Carpenter (1920-1997) began singing while still in the cradle. She made her radio debut at the age of five, and at the age of eleven had her own show on WNYC. In 1938 she won an amateur contest at the Apollo Theater, after which she got a job at the Onyx Club on 52nd Street as a sub for Maxine Sullivan. Here John Hammond discovered her and recommended her to Teddy Wilson. He hired her for his new big band which was soon to open at the Famous Door. Carpenter was with Wilson 1939-40, after which she became the vocalist in Coleman Hawkins' orchestra. 1943-44 she was with Count Basie, after which she returned to 52nd Street clubs like Kelly's Stable and La Commedia in the early 50's. As she was much more a supper club type of singer than an interpreter of jazz songs, she soon changed from the intimate clubs of Swing Street to the theatres on Broadway. In 1968 she became Pearl Bailey's understudy in "Hello, Dolly!". She performed the title role more than a hundred times, which meant a comeback for her and a lot of activity on TV and radio, in films and theatre right up to a few months before her death.

The Al Casey Trio in 1945 with Al Matthews and Sammy Clanton.

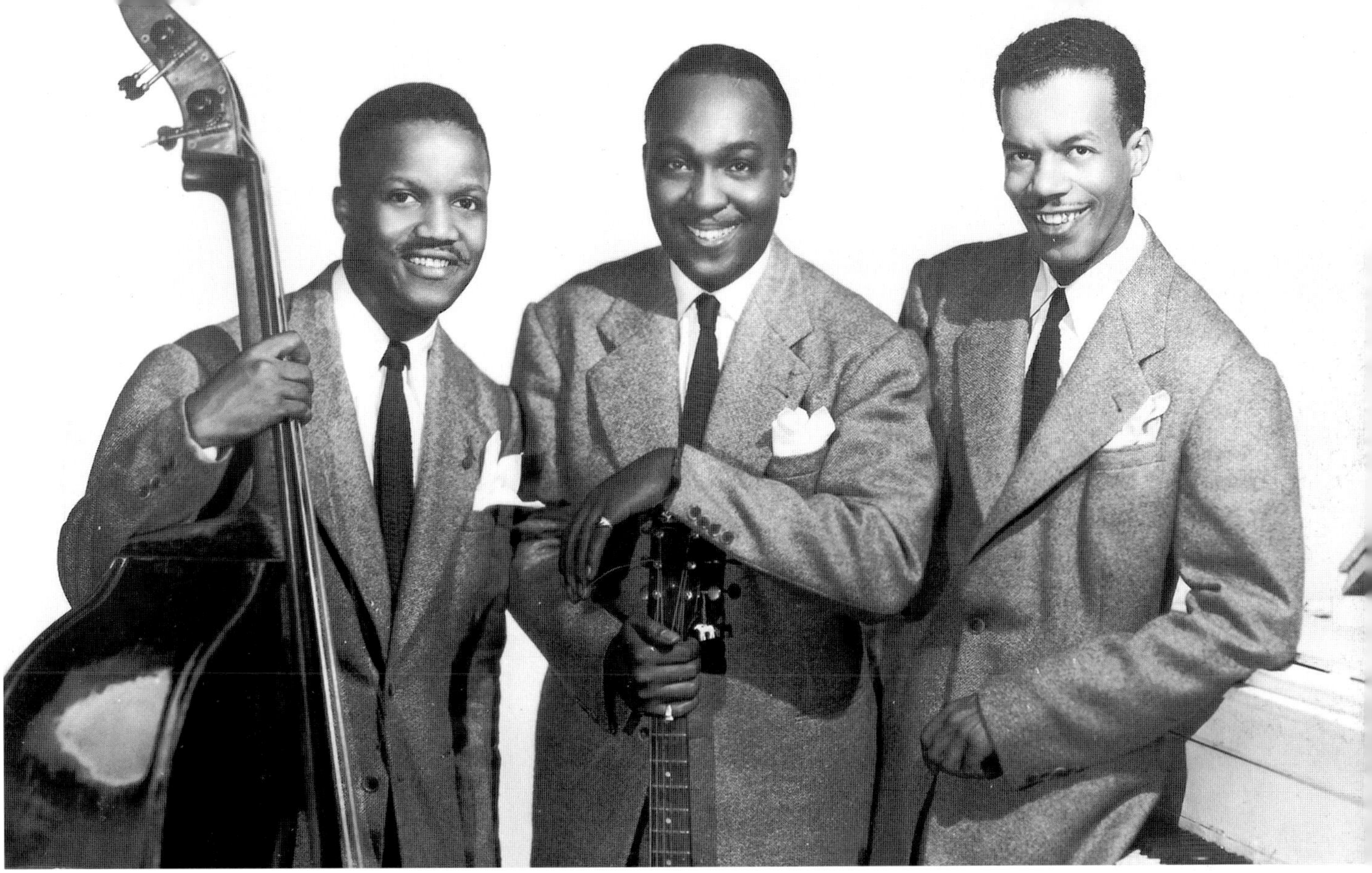

AL CASEY

Guitarist Albert Aloysius "Al" Casey (1915-) was born in Louisville, Kentucky, but moved to New York with his family in 1930. He worked with Fats Waller from 1933 until Waller died in 1943 except for a year with Teddy Wilson's big band 1939-40. After Waller's death Casey joined Clarence Profit's trio at George's Tavern in Greenwich Village for a while in 1944, before he started his own trio which played 52nd Street clubs like the Onyx and the Down Beat for a long time, besides working at Randini's in Los Angeles and Garrick's in Chicago. The trio with Al Matthews on bass and Sammy Clanton on piano proved very successful, and because of Clanton's ability to sing and play like Nat Cole they were called "The Nat Cole group of the East Coast". In the 50's jazz jobs were more scarce so Casey entered the r&b field, playing with King Curtis, followed by a long stint with Curley Hammer's Sextet in New York. In the early 70's Casey only played week-ends, but by 1980 he was back in full swing, touring extensively with the Harlem Blues and Jazz Band.

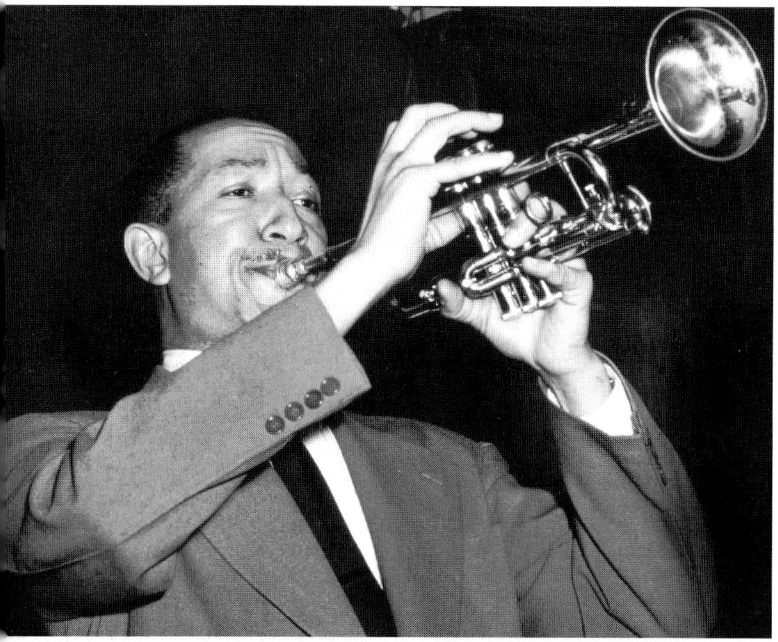

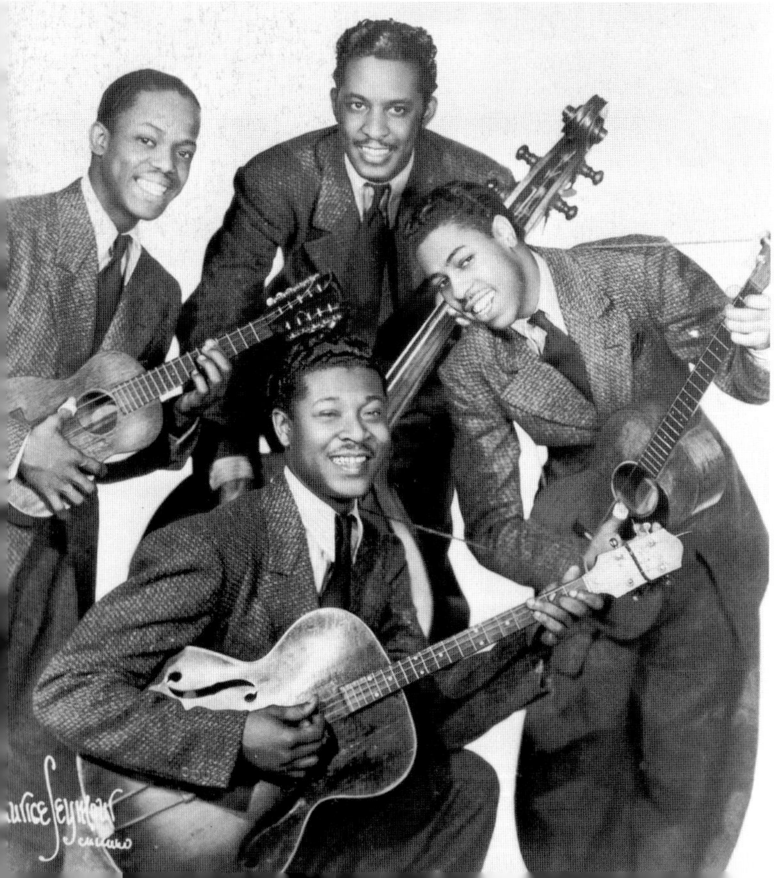

DOC CHEATHAM

Trumpet player and singer Adolphus Anthony "Doc" Cheatham (1905-1997) grew up in Nashville, Tennessee. He started out on both saxophone and trumpet, playing in burlesque shows and vaudeville in the early 20's accompanying some of the best blues singers at the time. By 1926 he was in Chicago, but after hearing Louis Armstrong in person he concentrated solely on the trumpet, developing an admirable technique, a delicate style and a lovely tone, even in the high register. Much of the late 20's and the 30's was spent in the big bands of Sam Wooding, Chick Webb, Cab Calloway, Teddy Wilson and Benny Carter, where he mostly did section work, but from the early 40's he gained a reputation as a fine soloist while with Eddie Heywood's Sextet. From the late 40's he played in a variety of Latin American bands before joining small groups led by Wilbur De Paris, Sammy Price and Herbie Mann. During the 60's he led his own band for several years but also played with Benny Goodman. During the last 20 years of his life he was busy touring and recording worldwide besides fronting his own quartet on Sunday residencies at New York's Sweet Basil.

THE CATS AND THE FIDDLE

Regarded as one the finest vocal/string bands, this quartet from Chicago was formed in 1937 inspired by the Mills Brothers. They first appeared on local radio and in local clubs, particularly the Pioneer Lounge, which was their home base for 15 years. During the years there were some changes in personnel, but this photo from around 1940 shows the original group with Austin Powell (guitar) in front, flanked by Jimmy Henderson and Ernie Price (tipple) and Chuck Barksdale at the bass.

COZY COLE

William Randolph "Cozy" Cole (1909-1981) was a brilliant technician who was effective in pushing soloists to do their best, and he belongs, with Sidney Catlett and Zutty Singleton, among the greatest classic drummers. Cole was born in East Orange, New Jersey and took up drumming as a child. By the end of the 20's he had played with Wilbur Sweatman in several New York clubs and theatres besides leading his own groups. During the early 30's he played with Blanche Calloway, Benny Carter and Willie Bryant, and in 1936 he joined Stuff Smith's group at the Onyx Club. 1938-42 he was with Cab Calloway after which he led his own groups. 1949-53 he was a member of Louis Armstrong's All-Stars but left to manage a drum school in New York with Gene Krupa. In 1957 he toured Europe as part of an all-star unit with Jack Teagarden and Earl Hines, and throughout the 60's and 70's he freelanced, touring internationally and appearing at numerous festivals.

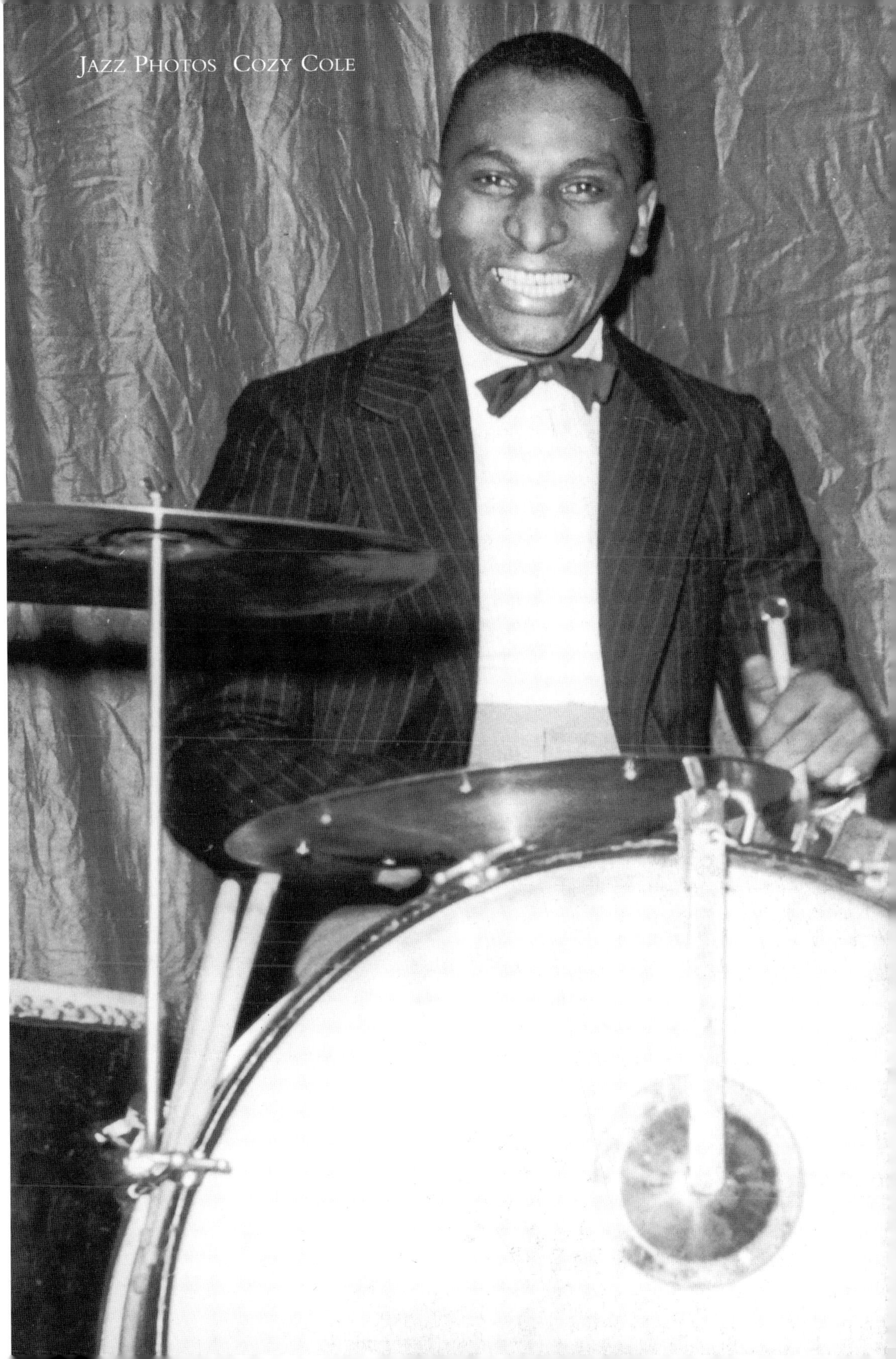

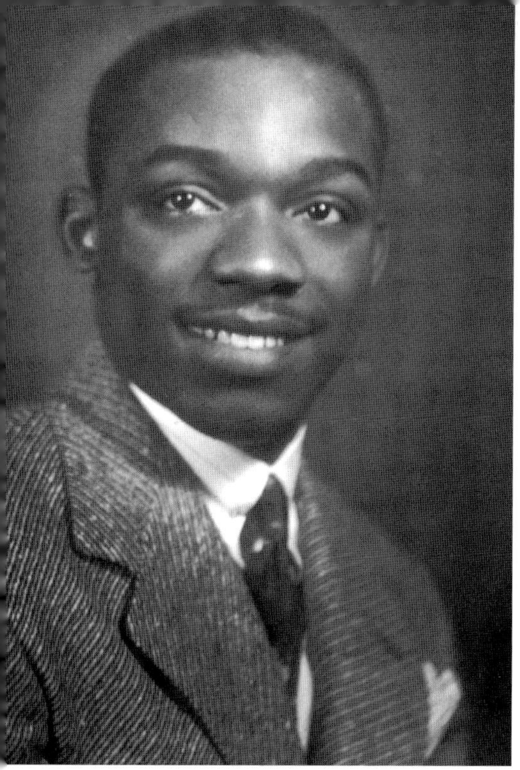

Kenny Clarke

Drummer Kenneth Spearman "Kenny" Clarke (1914-1985) was among the most influential and innovative jazz musicians. He was born in Pittsburgh, Pennsylvania and while still in his teens played in several bands. Later on he joined Roy Eldridge, after which he played in the Jeter-Pillars Orchestra and in bands led by Edgar Hayes, Claude Hopkins and Teddy Hill. In 1941 he led the house band at Minton's Playhouse in New York where he constantly encouraged young, advanced players like Charlie Christian, Dizzy Gillespie, Charlie Parker, Bud Powell and others to sit in. In the late 40's he worked in Dizzy Gillespie's big band, after which he was with Milt Jackson's quartet. In 1956 he settled in France, accompanying numerous visiting American musicians, such as Stan Getz, Lester Young, and Miles Davis at Parisian clubs. Clarke was the father of modern jazz drumming, responsible for shifting the steady pulse from the bass drum to the ride cymbal, using the bass and snare drums for counterrhythms and punctuations.

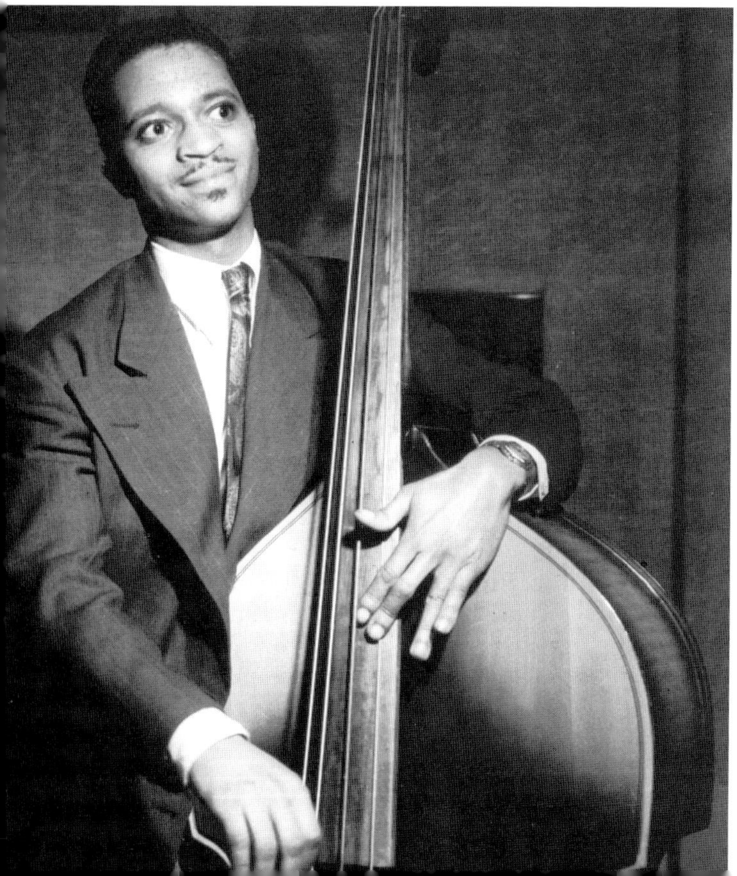

Israel Crosby

Double bass player Israel Crosby (1919-1962) ought to be better known for his contributions on his instrument. Born in Chicago he took up the trumpet at five, switched later to trombone and tuba, but changed finally in 1934 to the string bass, and played with Johnny Long and later with Albert Ammons at the Club de Lisa in his home town. He then played with big bands led by Fletcher Henderson, Horace Henderson and Teddy Wilson, after which he began a long association with CBS as a studio musician in 1944. He was a member of Ahmad Jamal's trio on and off between 1951 and 1962, after which he joined George Shearing. He died unexpectedly from a blood clot in the heart. Crosby was one of the earliest virtuoso string bass players, almost on a par with Jimmy Blanton. He made interesting and exciting rhythmic patterns and walking bass lines as an accompanist and produced lovely melodic solos.

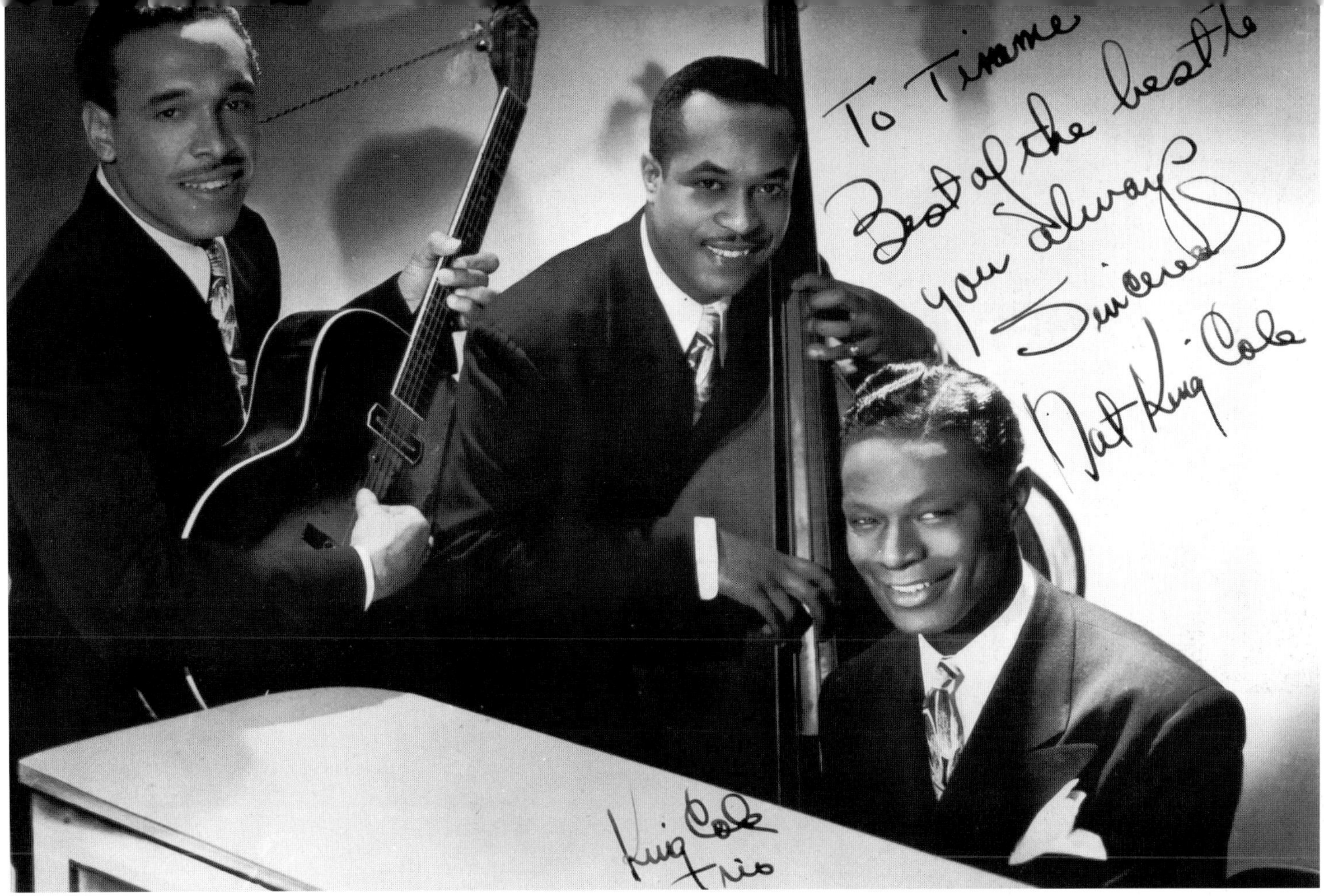

The Nat King Cole Trio around 1944 with Oscar Moore and Johnny Miller. *To Timme. Best of the best to you always. Sincerely Nat King Cole.*

Nat King Cole

Born in Montgomery, Alabama, pianist, singer and band leader, Nathaniel Adams "Nat King" Cole (1917-1965), came to Los Angeles with a revue in 1936 and remained there when it dissolved. Cole then played as a solo pianist for a couple of years, but in 1939 he formed a trio with guitarist Oscar Moore and bassist Wesley Prince. In 1942 Red Callender replaced Prince, but as he only stayed for a short while Johnny Miller became the bass player. As the trio's success grew bigger Cole became more and more commercial and from 1947 he began performing and recording with a big band. Although Cole was an excellent piano player, and the model of many modern pianists such as Oscar Peterson, he gave up piano playing for a career as singer.

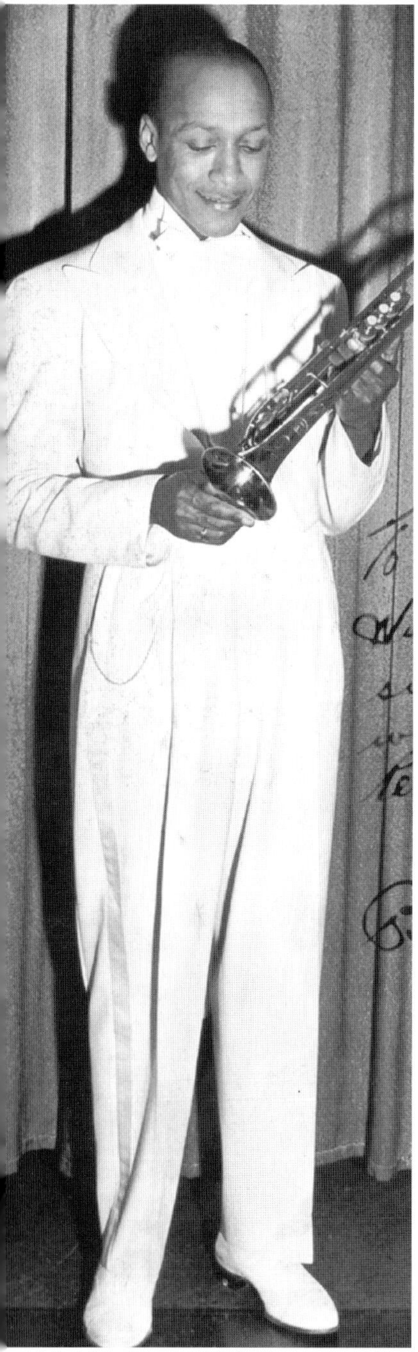

BILL COLEMAN

Trumpet player William Johnson "Bill" Coleman (1904-1981) took up various reed instruments at first, but like Doc Cheatham he permanently switched to the trumpet after hearing Louis Armstrong. Coleman was born in a little town, Centreville, Kentucky, and played in many local bands before coming to New York in 1927. The following years he played with Luis Russell, Charlie Johnson, Lucky Millinder, Benny Carter and Fats Waller, but in 1935 he came to France with dancer and bandleader Freddy "Snake Hips" Taylor. From Paris he travelled to Bombay, India as a member of Leon Abbey's Orchestra, after which he returned to Paris to play with Willie Lewis. 1938-40 he co-led a band with pianist Herman Chittison which worked in Cairo, Egypt. Back in the USA he played with various band-leaders such as Teddy Wilson, Ellis Larkins and Mary Lou Williams, but in the late 40's he once more went to Europe where he finally settled in France. Occasionally he toured other European countries but only returned to his home country on few occasions. *To Inez & Timmie. Wishing you all the success in the world with your record shop. Sincerely Bill Coleman 7/8/41.*

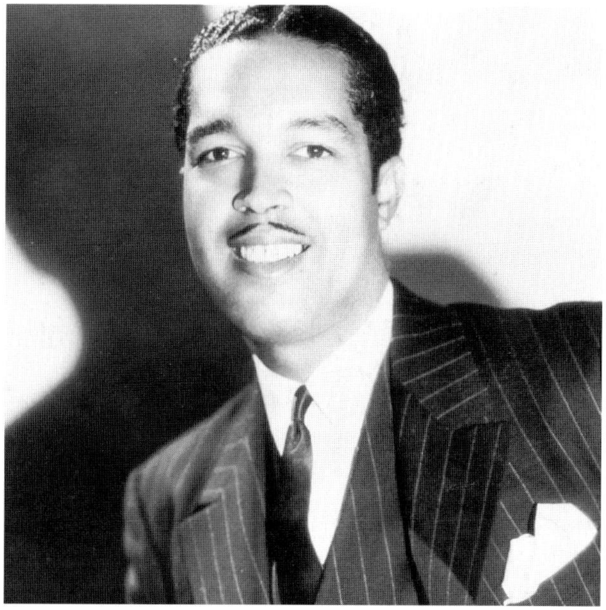

Publicity photo of Al Cooper.

Al Cooper's Savoy Sultans with from left Grachan Moncur (b), Alex "Razz" Mitchell (dr), Rudy Williams (as), Pat Jenkins (tp), Ed McNeil (ts), Cyril Haynes (p), Sam Massenberg (tp), Al Cooper (as).

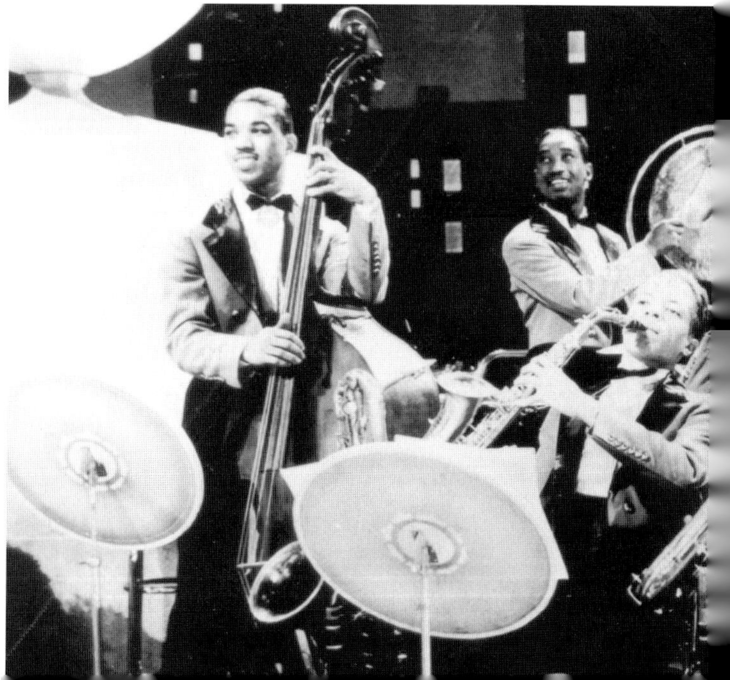

AL COOPER

Alto saxophonist, clarinetist and bandleader Lofton Alfonso "Al" Cooper (1911-1981) played around the New York area early in his career. In 1937 he formed a group, the Savoy Sultans, which became the house band at New York's Savoy Ballroom from September 1937 until they disbanded in 1946. The group consisted of two trumpets, three reeds and a rhythm section which from time to time included a guitarist. Although the Savoy Sultans never had any outstanding soloists, its full sound, a tight ensemble playing based on heavy use of effective riffs, and a hard-driving swing became very popular among dancers. It was feared by other bands, because the Sultans were almost unbeatable in band battles. After the break-up of the band Cooper's career dwindled away and he died in New York almost forgotten.

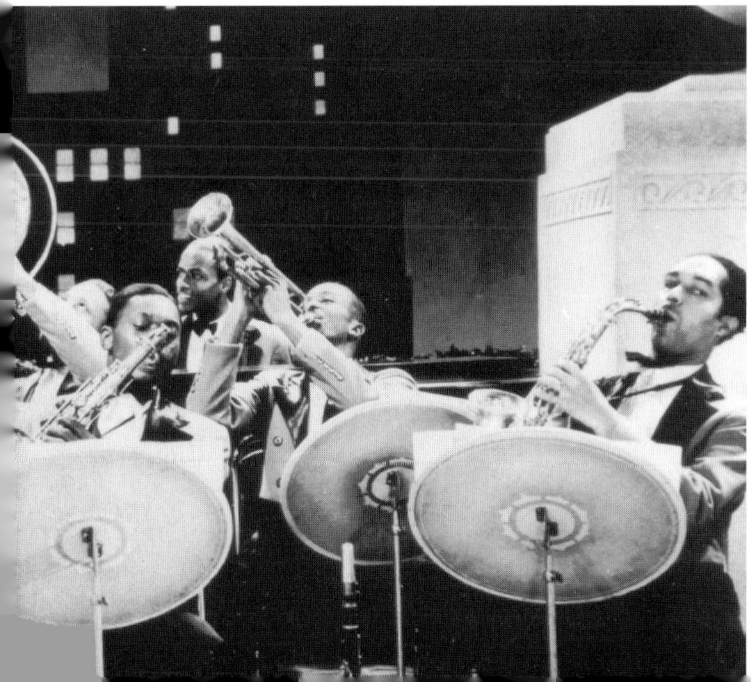

EDDIE CONDON

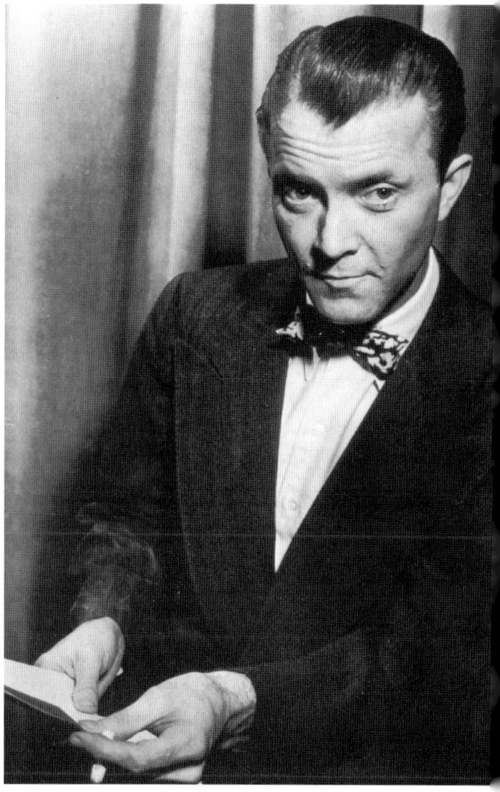

Eddie Condon in his own club around the time of its opening in December 1945.

Banjoist and guitarist Albert Edwin "Eddie" Condon (1905-1973) was born in Goodland, Indiana. After working in several local bands he moved to Chicago in the early 20's where he began playing with members of the Austin High School Gang, including Frank Teschemacher, Bud Freeman and Dave Tough. By 1928 he was in New York and with Red McKenzie he was instrumental in setting up some of the first interracial recording dates, mixing black musicians such as Louis Armstrong and Happy Caldwell with white musicians like Jack Teagarden and Joe Sullivan. From 1937-44 he was a regular at Nick's Tavern in New York, but in December 1945 he opened his own club Eddie Condon's on West 3rd Street in Greenwich Village. With Ernie Anderson he organized a series of jazz concerts at Carnegie Hall and at Town Hall (1942-46), and from 1942 he presented "Eddie Condon's Floor Show", one of the first jazz programs on TV. By the late 40's he was also busy recording and touring internationally. It is hard to overestimate his contributions to jazz, both as a fine rhythm guitarist and as entrepreneur.

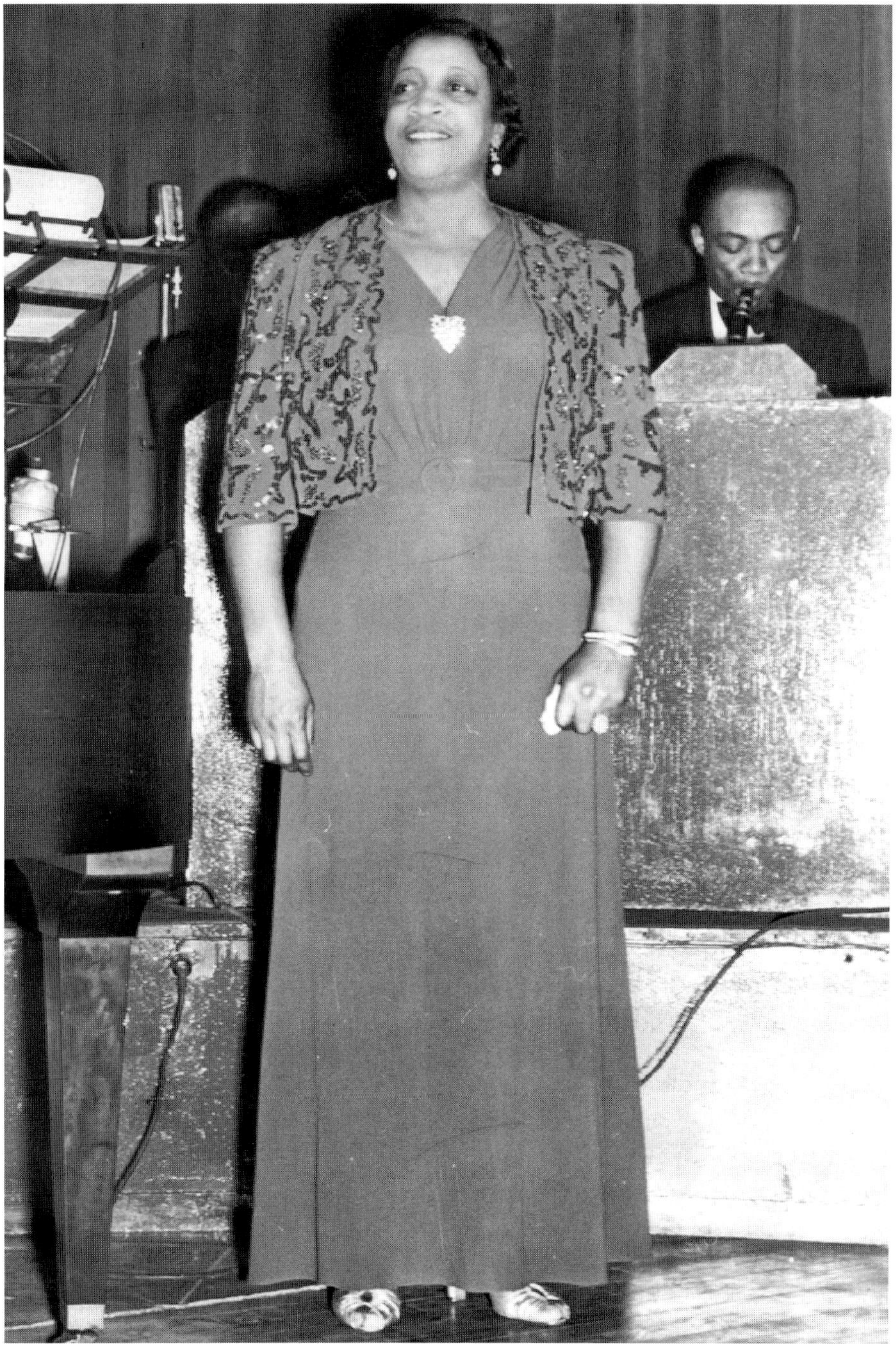

IDA COX

One of the greatest blues singers, Ida Cox (1896-1967), was born in Toccoa, Georgia. During childhood she sang in a local Methodist choir. She ran away from home at the age of 14 to join White and Clark's Minstrel Show with which she toured the TOBA (Theater Owners' Booking Association) circuit extensively. Later on she became a soloist; for some years accompanied by Lovie Austin, and later on by her husband Jesse "Tiny" Crump. During the 30's she toured successfully with her own tent show, and in 1939 she played New York's Café Society. From 1941 she again toured with her own shows until she suffered a stroke in 1945 in Buffalo, N.Y. She retired to Knoxville, but made a comeback recording in 1961 with an all star group including Coleman Hawkins. Unlike other blues singers who included vaudeville songs and other popular songs into their repertoire, Cox almost entirely relied on the traditional blues form, often composed by herself, and performed in her characteristical, nasal, slightly monotone, but nevertheless passionate way.

Ida Cox at the Café Society in 1939 with Edmond Hall playing the clarinet.

TOMMY DORSEY

After Tommy Dorsey and his brother Jimmy went their separate ways in the 20's, Tommy worked with Jean Goldkette and Paul Whiteman after which he became busy in studio and pit orchestras in New York. After the experience with the Dorsey Brothers Orchestra he took over the big band of Joe Haymes, and with good arrangers he turned the band into one of the most successful dance bands of the swing era. He also ensured that good soloists were hired, like Bunny Berigan, Buddy Rich, Yank Lawson, Bud Freeman, Charlie Shavers and Buddy DeFranco. As good vocalists were crucial, he employed some of the finest of the time, such as Jack Leonard, Edythe Wright, Jo Stafford and Frank Sinatra. The band was so popular that it survived for some time after the heydays of the big bands were over, but the early 50's were hard times, and he had to reunite with his brother in 1953.

The Tommy Dorsey Orchestra 1936. From left in the back row: Max Kaminsky, Sam Skolnik, and Joe Bauer (tp), Dave Tough (dr), Carmen Mastren (g), Gene Traxler (b), and Dick Jones (p). Sitting in front are from left Les Jenkins and Walter Mercurio (tb), Jack Leonard, Axel Stordahl, and Edythe Wright (vocalists), Joe Dixon, Clyde Rounds, Bud Freeman, and Bob Bunch (reeds). The proud band leader is standing between Wright and Stordahl.

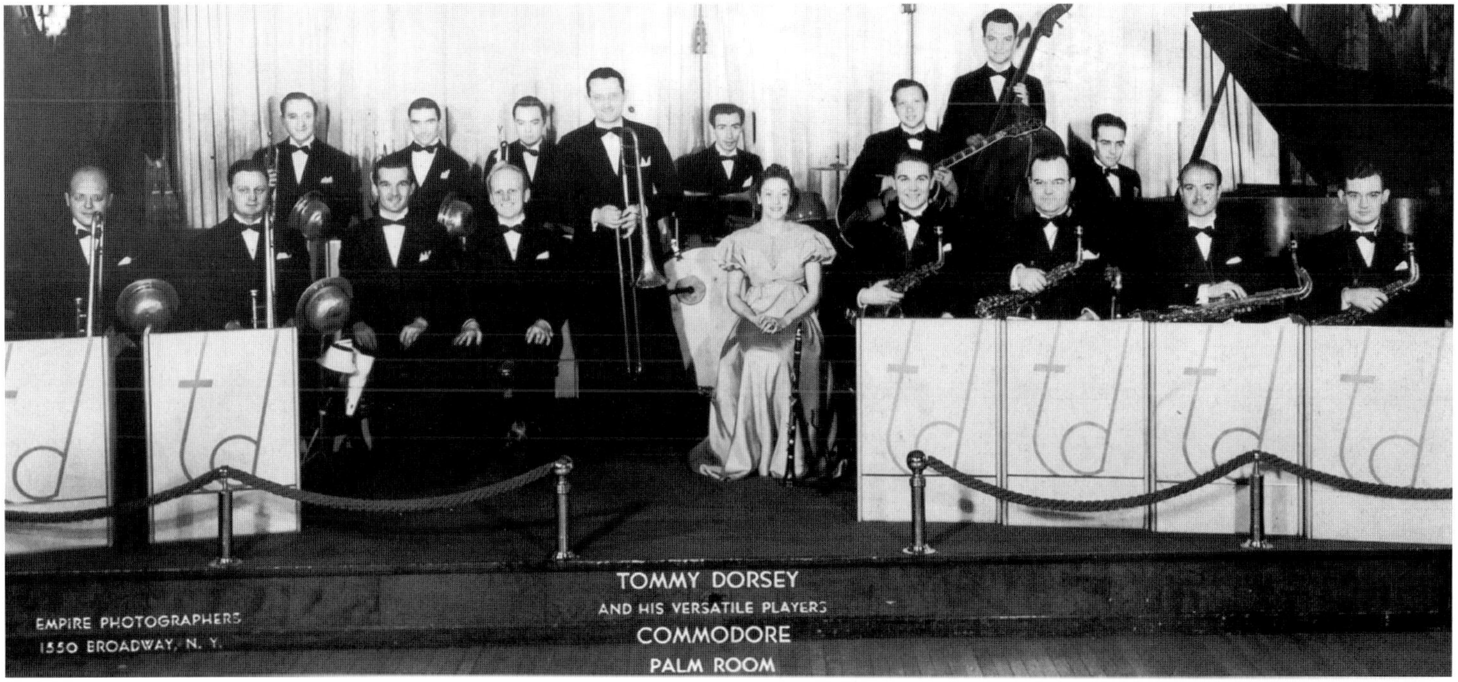

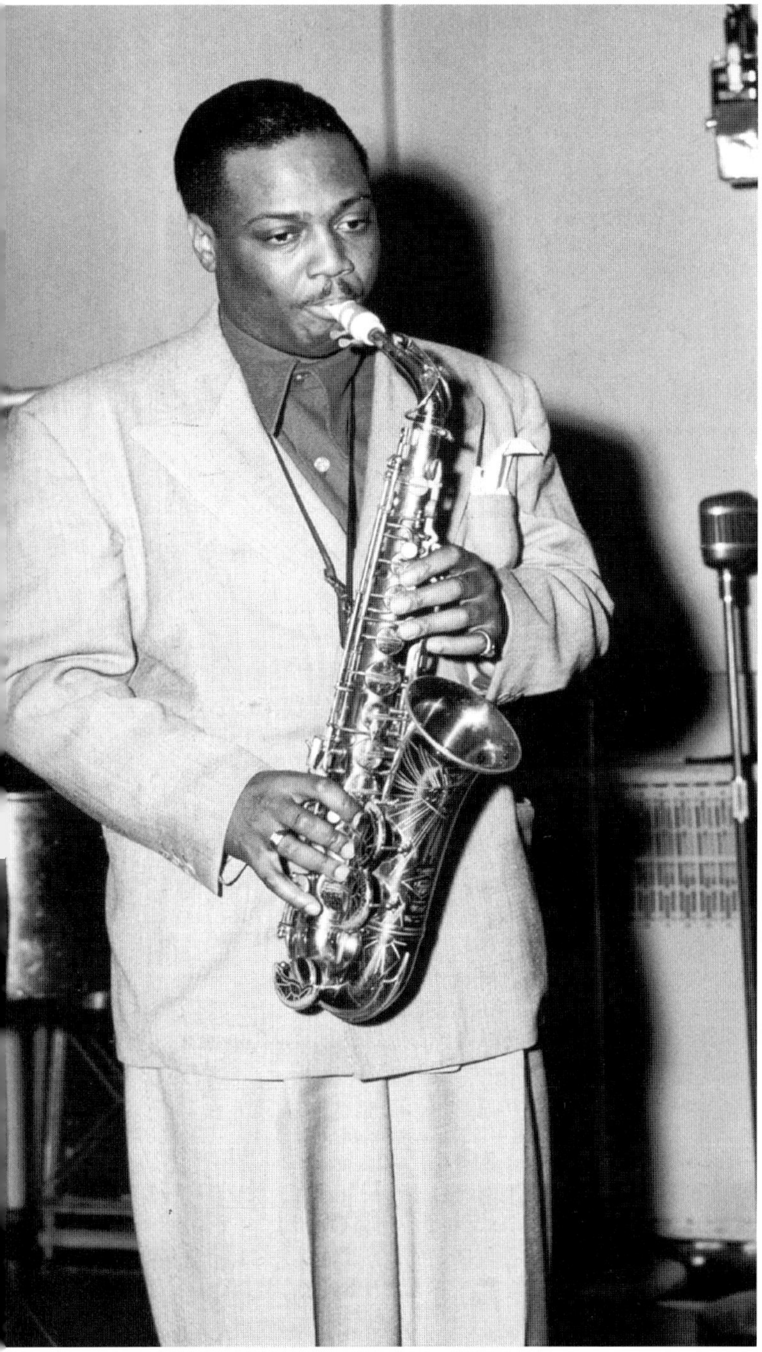

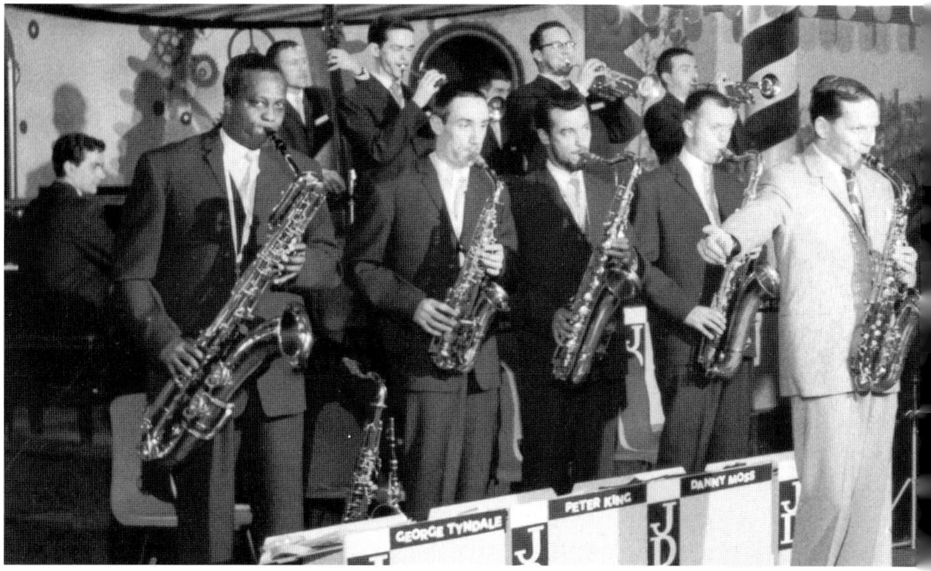

LEM DAVIS

Alto saxophonist Lemuel Arthur "Lem" Davis (1914-1970) was born in Tampa, Florida and played in local bands before he came to New York in 1941, where he made quite an impression. He became a member of Coleman Hawkins's Septet in 1943, and the following year he joined Eddie Heywood's successful group. During the 50's and 60's he worked in New York with Buck Clayton and pianist Teacho Wiltshire besides fronting his own bands. As a swing musician Davis, like Pete Brown, Roy Eldridge, Vic Dickenson and many more of his generation, had difficulties finding his own identity when bebop entered the scene, and judging by some of his later recordings, it seems that he never quite overcame this crisis.

Lem Davis recording for Savoy on May 10, 1946.

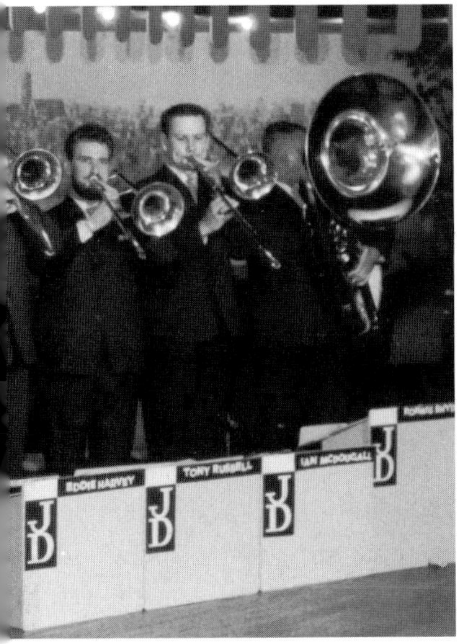

John Dankworth fronting a 1960 version of his big band. In the front row from left: George Tyndale, Peter King, Danny Moss, Art Ellefson (reeds), Eddie Harvey, Tony Russell and Ian McDougall (tb), and Ronnie Snyder (tu). In the back row: Dudley Moore (p), Spike Heatley (b), Dickie Hawdon (tp), Kenny Clare (dr), and Kenny Wheeler and Gus Galbraith (tp).

JOHN DANKWORTH

English alto saxophonist, bandleader, composer and arranger John Philip William Dankworth (1927-) was born in London and started out on the clarinet playing traditional jazz in the mid-40's. After hearing Charlie Parker in New York he switched to alto saxophone and soon became a leading figure in British jazz. In 1953 he formed his first big band, which ran until 1964 featuring his wife by 1958, singer Cleo Laine. From 1971 he acted as musical director for his wife, and from the early 80's he led a touring quintet and occasionally formed big bands. Dankworth's compositional skills are plentyful as he has written scores for big bands and for small jazz orchestras, besides written film music and classical music, including suites and an opera-ballet as well as third-stream music.

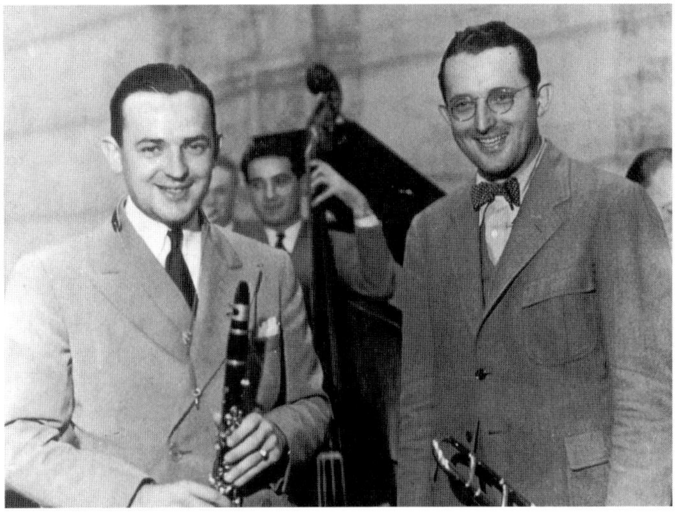

DORSEY BROTHERS ORCHESTRA

The two brothers, clarinetist and alto saxophonist James "Jimmy" Dorsey (1904-1957) and trombonist Thomas "Tommy" Dorsey (1905-1956), grew up in Shenandoah, Pennsylvania where in the early 20's they led Dorsey's Novelty Six and Dorsey's Wild Canaries. They then made separate careers until May 1934 when they formed the Dorsey Brothers Orchestra, a successful band which unfortunately was short-lived due to feuding between the brothers. Tommy went off the bandstand in June 1935 after a violent argument after which Jimmy took over the band. In 1953 Tommy brought Jimmy into his own band, and together they ran another version of the Dorsey Brothers Orchestra which lasted until Tommy's death. This photo is from the 1934 version, showing bassist Delmar Kaplan between the two leaders, while everything still was new and all smiles.

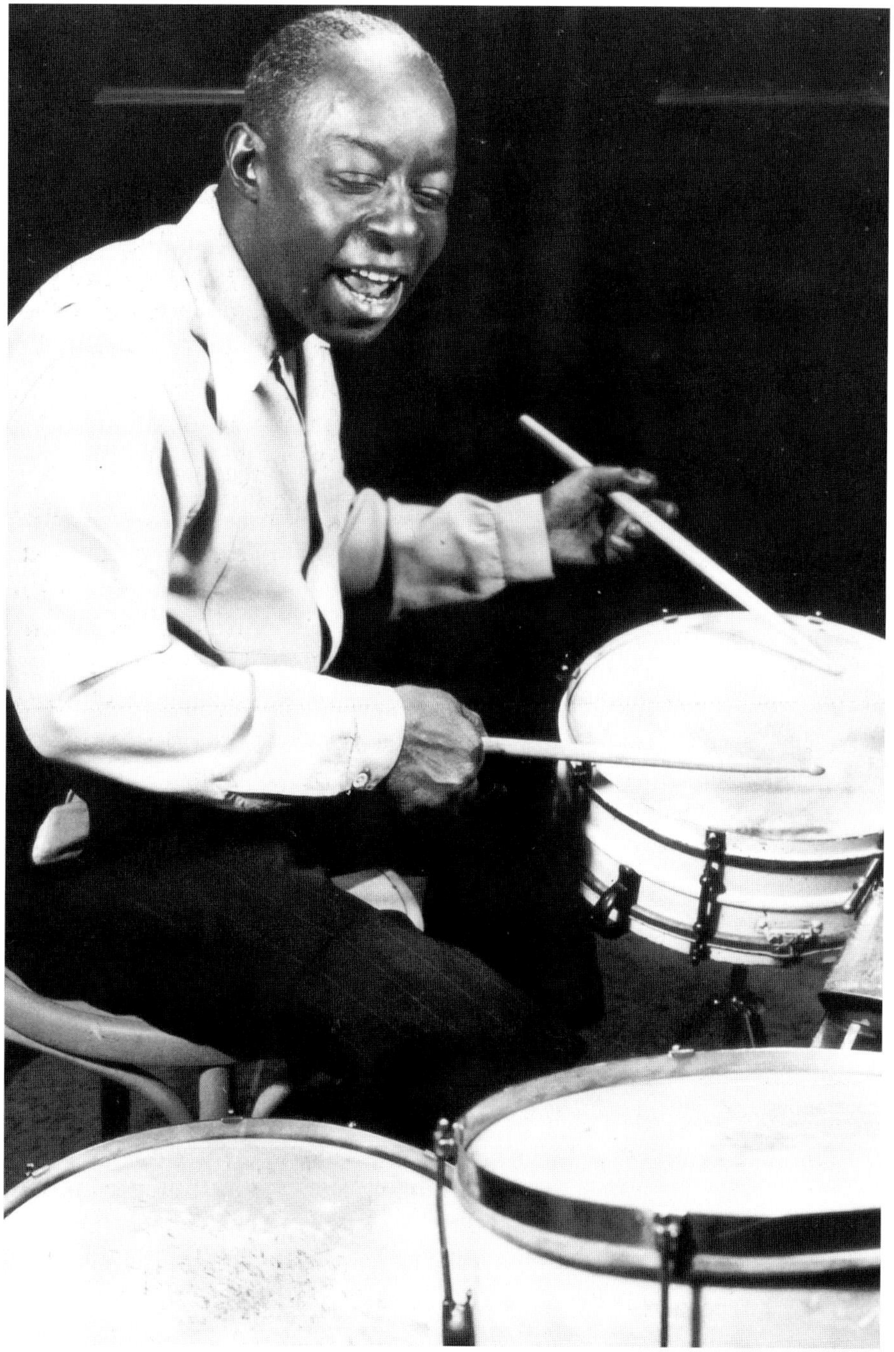

BABY DODDS

Drummer Warren "Baby" Dodds (1898-1959) was the kid brother of clarinetist Johnny Dodds. He was born in New Orleans and a natural on the drums, using every one of them in a varied way through a performance, almost as a solo in itself, but without disturbing the coherence of the tune. Getting his first drums at 16 he soon played with the best musicians in town, including the bands of Willie High-tower, Bunk Johnson, Papa Celestin and Fate Marable. He then joined King Oliver in 1922 in California and moved with him to Chicago where he spent the following two decades playing with his brother or freelancing. In 1945 he went to New York to play with Bunk Johnson after which followed stints with other revivalists like Jimmie Noone and Sidney Bechet. Contrary to his brother, who lived a straight and exemplary life, Baby Dodds loved to drink and have a ball and this led to a series of strokes which by 1949 forced him to slow down until he totally stopped playing in 1957. Dodds was the epitome of the New Orleans style of drumming, and his technique and equipment became the standard of this style. As can be seen on this photo from the mid-40's, he never purchased modern outfits like a high-hat.

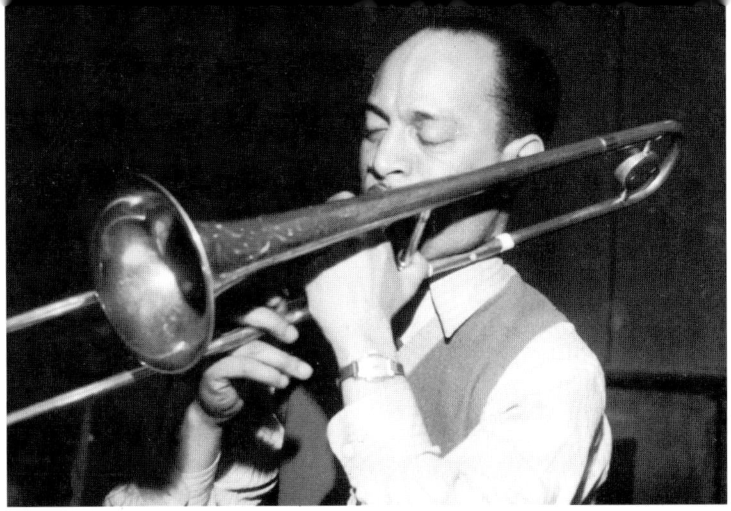

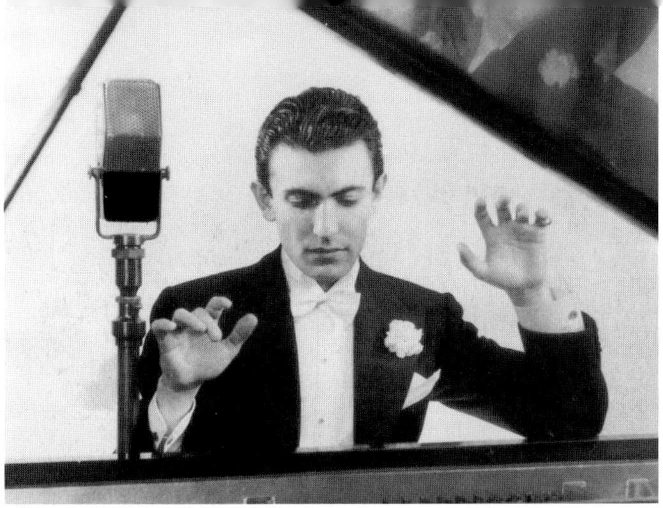

Vic Dickenson

Besides being a very fine section man, trombonist Victor "Vic" Dickenson (1906-1984) had a great sense of musical humour, which he used in a very personal, relaxed way in solos. He was born in Xenia, Ohio and received only little formal musical training. He played his way through the early 30's in territory bands like those of Speed Webb and Zack Whyte before joining the big bands of Blanche Calloway, Bennie Moten, Claude Hopkins, Benny Carter and Count Basie. During the 40's he played with Frankie Newton and Eddie Heywood with whom he came to the West Coast where he freelanced 1947-48. The following decade was spent in and around Boston leading his own bands, after which he moved to New York to play with Henry "Red" Allen at the Metropole. In the 60's he co-led the Saints and Sinners with Red Richards, worked as a regular at Eddie Condon's and toured with various groups. From 1968-70 he co-led a fine quintet with Bobby Hackett, after which he had spells with the World's Greatest Jazzband.

Vic Dickenson during a recording session for Blue Note, probably with Sidney Bechet, on December 20, 1944.

Eddy Duchin

Pianist and bandleader Eddy Duchin (1910-1951) was born in Cambridge, Massachusetts. He came to New York in 1928 and joined Leo Reisman's orchestra at the Central Park Casino, then the most popular spot for dancing. Three years later he took over Reisman's band and soon became one of the most popular dance band leaders in the country. Besides playing seven nights a week the band was also broadcast coast to coast every Saturday afternoon during its tea dances, which helped to ensure Duchin's incredible national popularity. It did not last long before Duchin did several radio series and also appeared in a couple of films. Besides Central Park Casino the band played other class dancing spots such as the Persian Room at the Plaza Hotel in New York and the Cocoanut Grove at the Ambassador in Los Angeles. During the early 40's he made a successful South American tour, after which he did military service. In the late 40's he formed another band, but illness began to affect him, and he died in 1951 from leukemia. Duchin's piano style was flashy and sophisticated, and his band played mostly supper-club type arrangements.

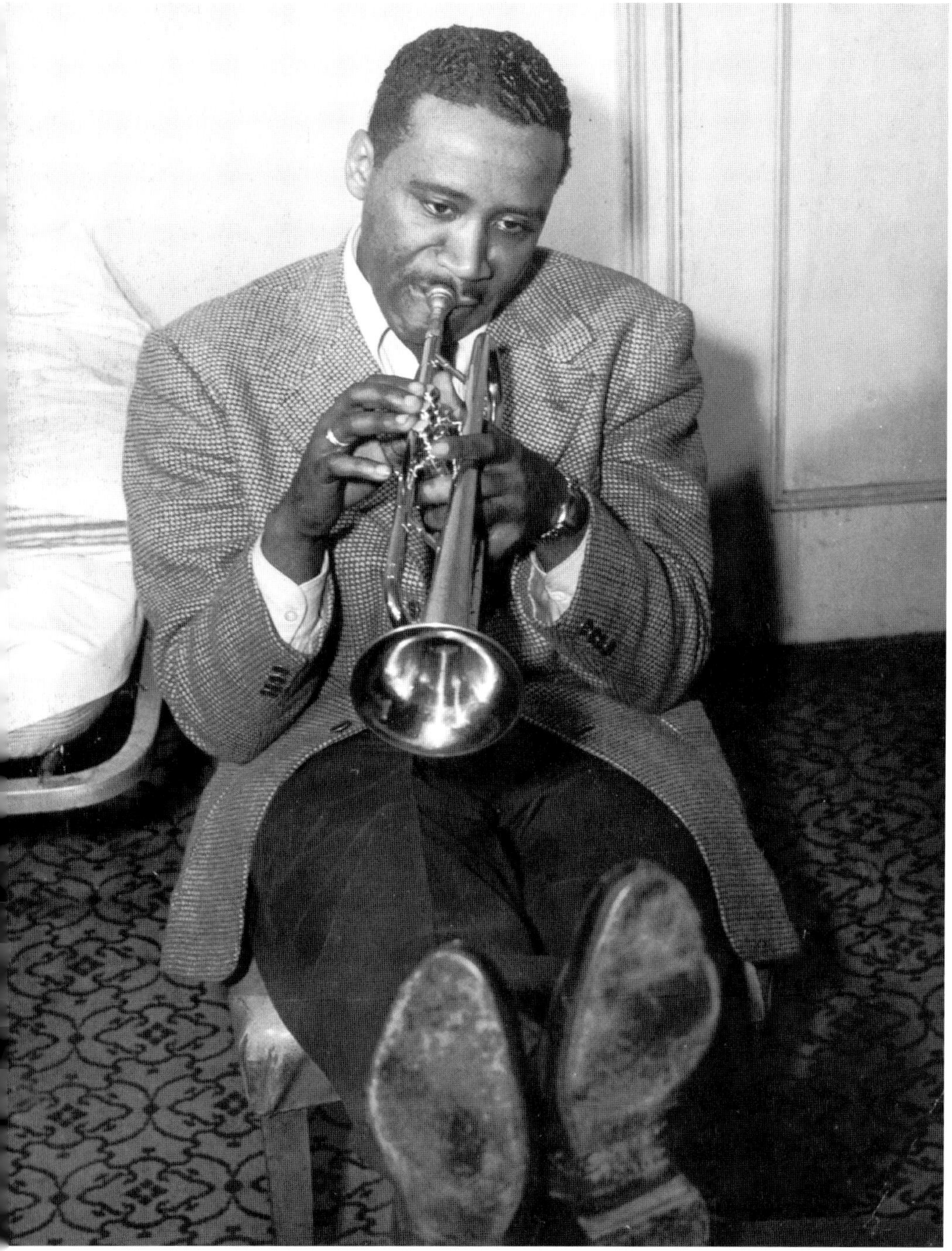

HARRY "SWEETS" EDISON

Born in Columbus, Ohio, trumpeter Harry Edison (1915-1999) was of half American-Indian origin. He began playing trumpet inspired by hearing Louis Armstrong on records and worked in some of the best territory bands, such as the Jeter-Pillars Orchestra, in the early 30's. He joined Count Basie in early 1938 and remained with him until 1950, when Basie reduced his big band to a small unit. While with Basie Lester Young nicknamed him, a reference to both his style of playing and his nice personality. After the years with Basie Edison's career became more varied. He toured with Jazz at the Philharmonic and Josephine Baker, and began in 1952 a long association with Frank Sinatra. He settled in Los Angeles, leading his own bands from time to time, and toured extensively with Eddie "Lock-jaw" Davis between studio jobs as well as appearing as a guest soloist with Basie on several occasions. Edison's style is easily recognizable. He played in a sparse manner, mostly in the middle register, with a perfect sense of time and much humour.

Edison in his hotel room around 1950.

ZIGGY ELMAN

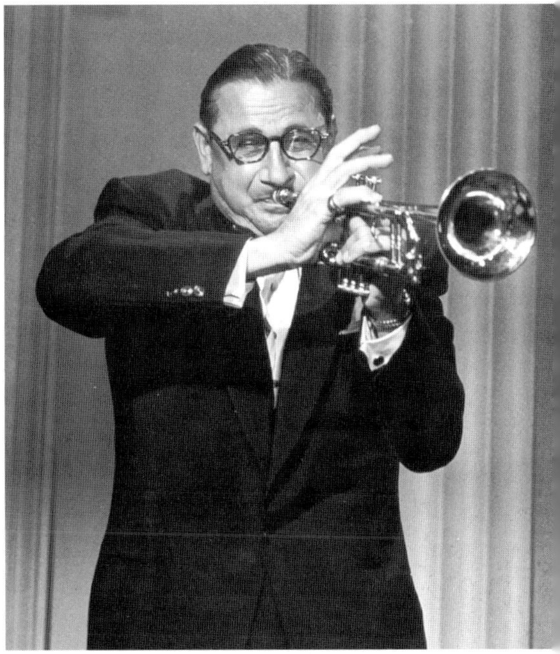

Trumpeter and multiinstrumentalist Harry Finkelman "Ziggy Elman" (1914-1968) was born in Philadelphia, and early in his career he played both reed and brass instruments. While playing in Atlantic City's Steel Pier ballroom with Alex Bartha in 1936 Benny Goodman noticed his versatility and recruited him. He was with Goodman until 1940 and after a short spell with Joe Venuti played regularly with Tommy Dorsey the following eight years. After an unsuccessful try to lead his own big band he moved to Los Angeles in 1948 and began working in film, radio and TV. In 1956 he had to semiretire due to a nervous breakdown and alcohol problems. Besides playing various reed instruments and trombone Elman is best known for his trumpet playing, possessing the rare capability of being both a fine lead trumpeter and a creative soloist.

HERSCHEL EVANS

Clarinetist and tenor saxophonist Herschel Evans (1909-1939) was, like Chu Berry, one of the leading swing saxophonists of his time who died tragically all too soon. He came from Denton, Texas, and played professionally from 1926 on in southwestern territory bands led by Alphonso Trent, Troy Floyd and Bennie Moten. After stints with Dave Peyton in Chicago he moved to Los Angeles to play with Charlie Echols, Lionel Hampton and Buck Clayton. In 1936 Clayton brought Evans with him to join Count Basie in Kansas City where Evans formed the famous tenor sax team with Lester Young. In late 1938 Evans became ill with dropsy which unfortunately went untreated. He collapsed on stage during a performance at the Crystal Ballroom in Hartford, Connecticut and died two weeks later at the Wadsworth Hospital in New York. Evans developed a personal style with a rich, dark and powerful tone, and his solos were delivered with energy and authority in relatively short phrases.

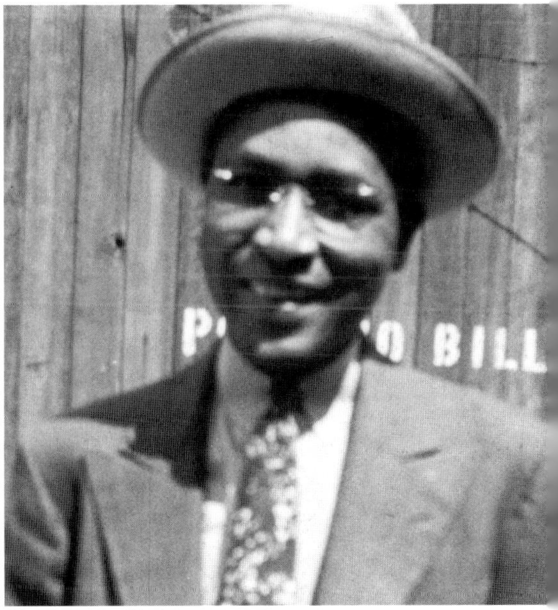

Herschel Evans photographed by Rosenkrantz in New York 1938 during the Basie band's long summer residency at the Famous Door.

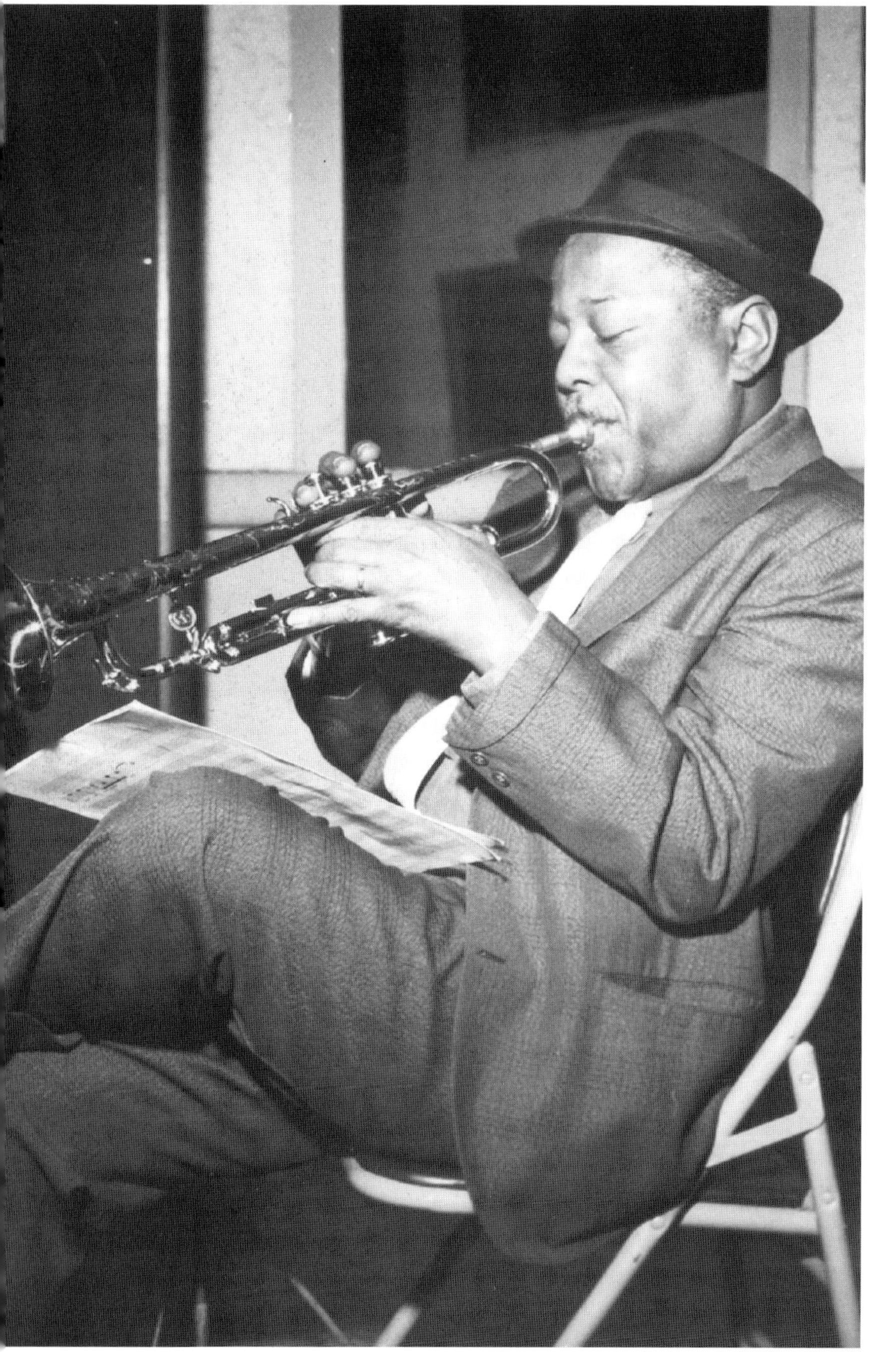

ROY ELDRIDGE

A major force in jazz and an outstanding soloist and stylist, David Roy Eldridge (1911-1989) was, unlike most trumpet players of his generation, not inspired by Louis Armstrong. Instead he modeled his style after the tenor saxophonist Coleman Hawkins, which meant that he developed an incredible three-octave range and an unprecedented dexterity, particularly in the high register. His solos were furthermore marked by an emotional intensity which made a great impact on many young bop players, among them Dizzy Gillespie and Howard McGhee. Eldridge began his career in carnival bands and midwestern territory bands. He joined Teddy Hill in New York 1935, where he and Chu Berry became close friends. Both were competetive players who loved to go out and jam and cut everybody else. After a spell with Fletcher Henderson he led his own bands until 1941 when he was hired by Gene Krupa, thus being one of the first black musicians to be a permanent member of the brass section of an otherwise white big band. In 1944 he joined Artie Shaw's big band, and the following year he formed his own band, but soon returned to smaller groups. From 1951 he took part in the mainstream movement playing with Johnny Hodges, Benny Carter and Coleman Hawkins, and during the 70's he fronted his own traditional band at Jimmy Ryan's in New York. After a stroke in 1980 he was forced to slow down, so he gave up the trumpet and from then on performed occasionally as a singer, drummer and pianist.

Eldridge in a New York recording studio sometime in the 40's.

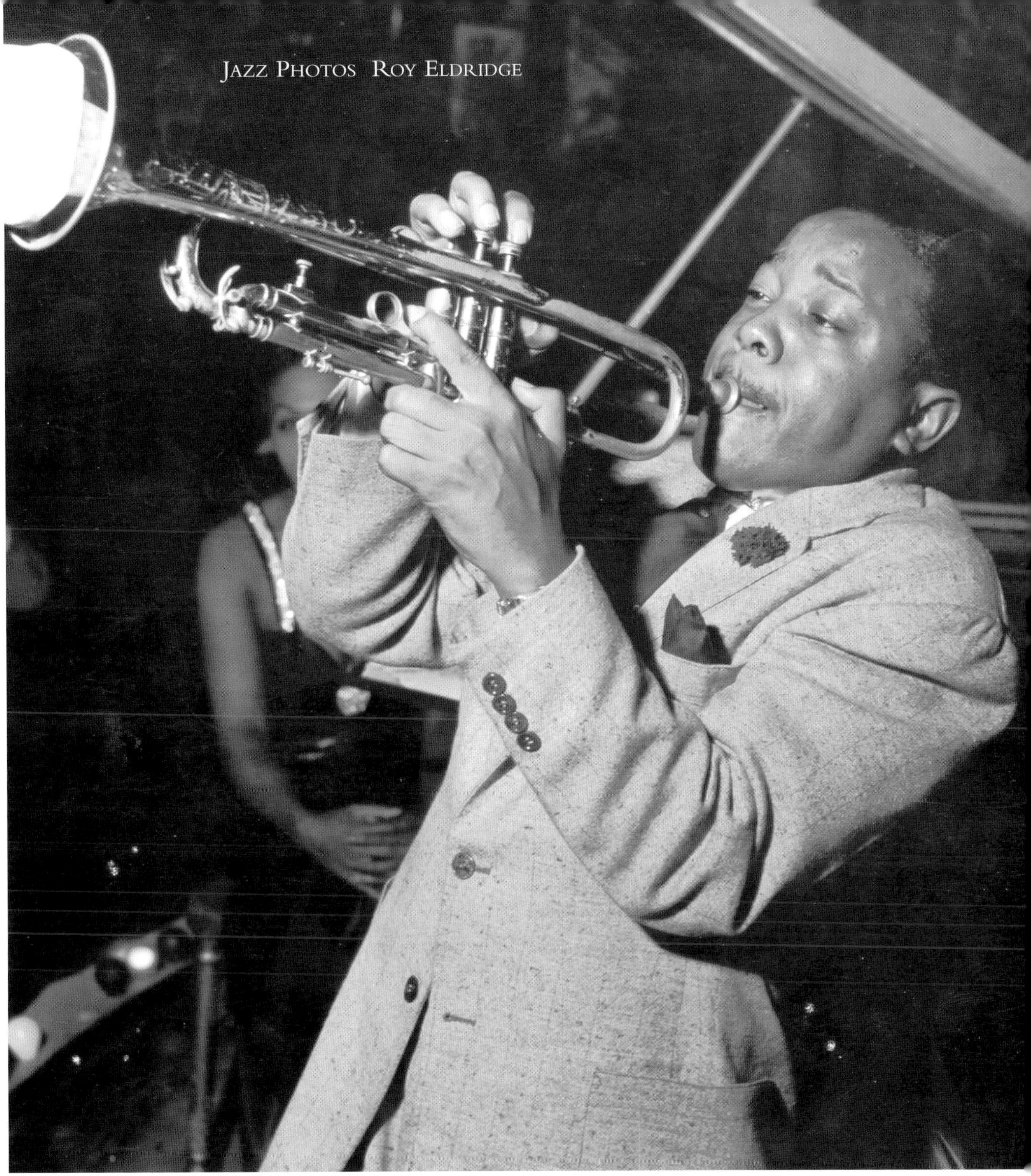

Eldridge fronting his band at the Arcadia Ballroom in New York, July 1939. Singer Laurel Watson is halfway hidden.

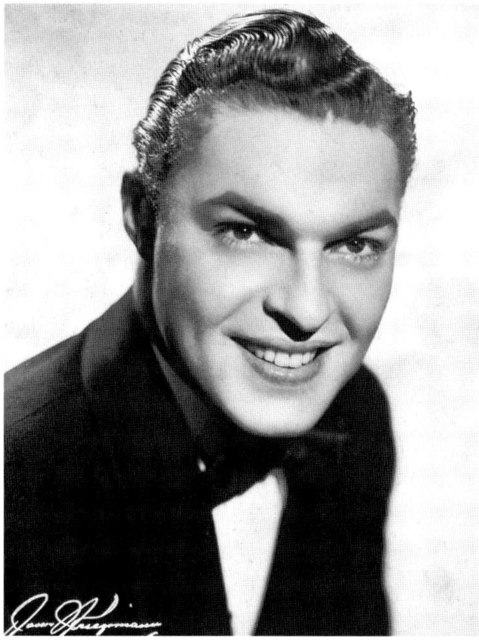

BOB EBERLY

Singer Robert Eberle "Bob Eberly" (1916-1981) was born in Mechanicville, New York. Early in his career he changed his surname to avoid confusion with his younger brother Ray, who was also a singer. Eberly worked around New York for some time before he joined the Dorsey Brothers' Orchestra in 1935. After the brothers split he remained with Jimmy Dorsey until 1943 when he had to do military service. After the war he returned to a solo career and appeared in the film "The Fabulous Dorseys" (1947). From the 50's he was featured regularly on TV, and his last engagement was in 1980 in Disney World, just before he had one of his lungs removed because of cancer. Eberly was one of the most popular band vocalists of the 40's and he enjoyed an especially productive partnership with vocalist Helen O'Connell, who joined the Dorsey band in 1939, and with whom he had several hits.

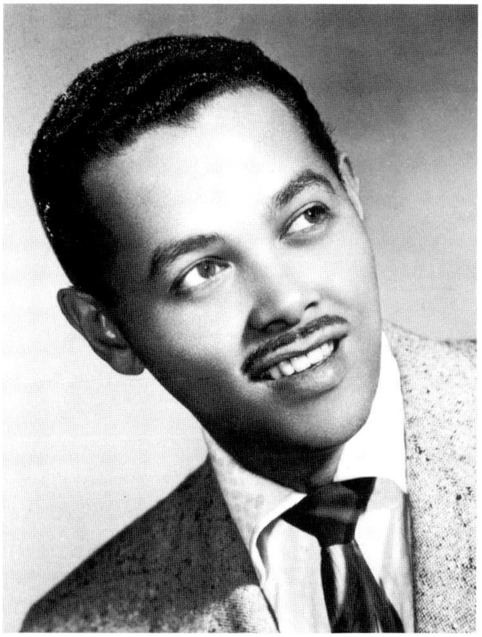

BILLY ECKSTINE

Singer, bandleader, trumpeter and trombonist William Clarence Eckstein "Billy Eckstine" (1914-) was born in Pittsburg, Pennsylvania and started his professional singing career in the early 30's working in Washington, Pittsburgh, Buffalo and Detroit before he came to Chicago in late 1937. He joined Earl Hines's big band in 1939 where he learned to play trumpet and remained with Hines until 1943 when he left to form his own big band. Though his band contained many young bebop players through the years, such as Dizzy Gillespie, Charlie Parker, Dexter Gordon, Gene Ammons, Miles Davis, Sonny Stitt and Art Blakey, it was economically unsuccessful and he was forced to disband in 1947. After a short spell with a septet he returned to a solo career, accompanied by pianist Bobby Tucker, drummer Charlie Persip and others, touring nightclubs in the USA as well as abroad. Famous for his beautiful, vibrant baritone Eckstine is best known as a romantic interpreter of ballads.

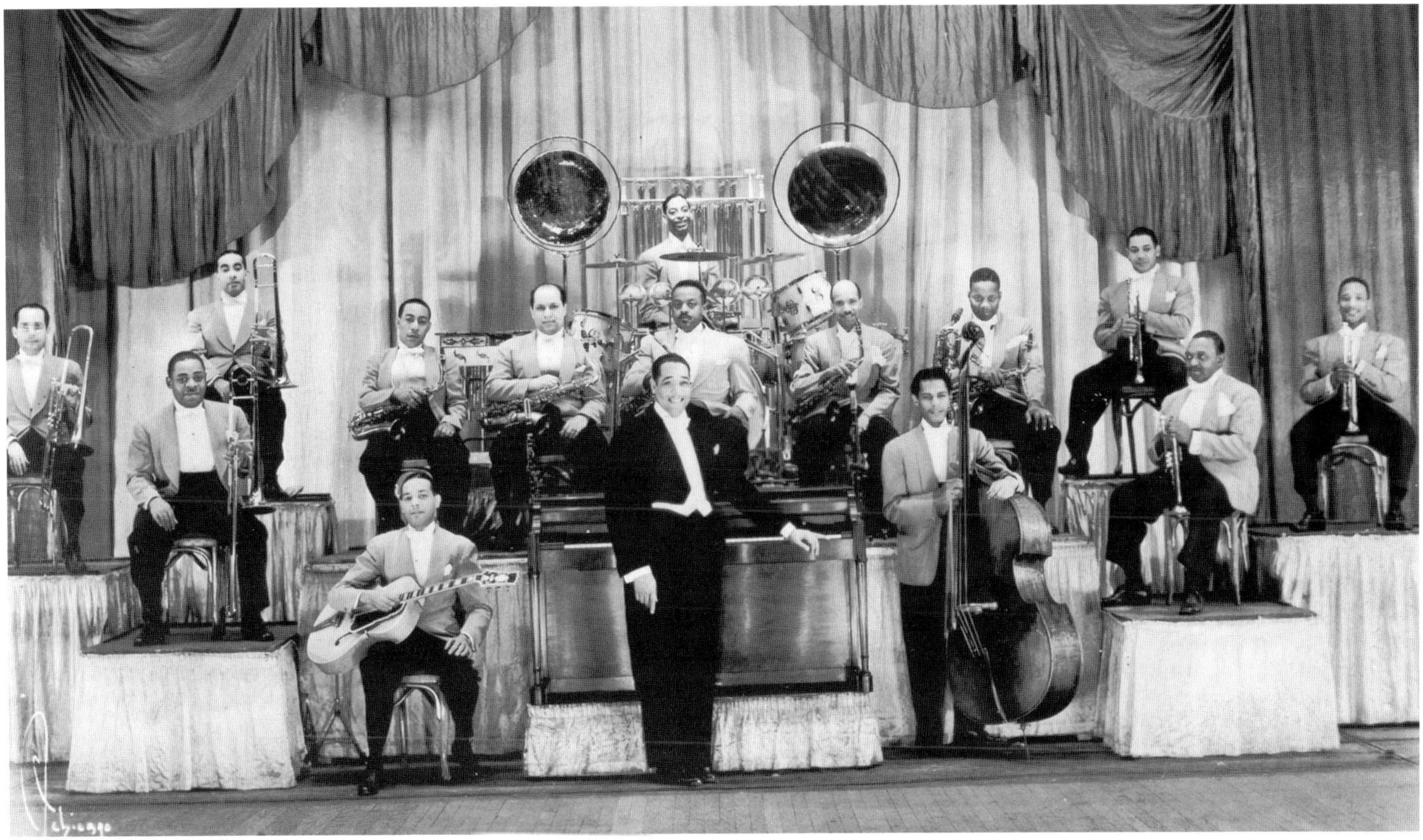

One of Duke Ellington's finest bands. From left: Juan Tizol, "Tricky Sam" Nanton, and Lawrence Brown (tb), Fred Guy (g), Johnny Hodges, Barney Bigard, Ben Webster, Otto Hardwick, and Harry Carney (reeds), Sonny Greer (dr), Junior Raglin (b), and Wallace Jones, Rex Stewart, and Ray Nance (tp). Ellington is in the middle. The photo was taken around 1942.

DUKE ELLINGTON

Composer, arranger, pianist and bandleader Edward Kennedy "Duke" Ellington (1899-1974) formed his first band in Washington D.C. in 1919, but three years later he became a member of Wilbur Sweatman's orchestra in New York. In 1923 he worked at Baron's in New York with Elmer Snowden's band, and when Snowden left that year Ellington took over. For the rest of his life Ellington toured extensively with his own band, nationally as well as worldwide.

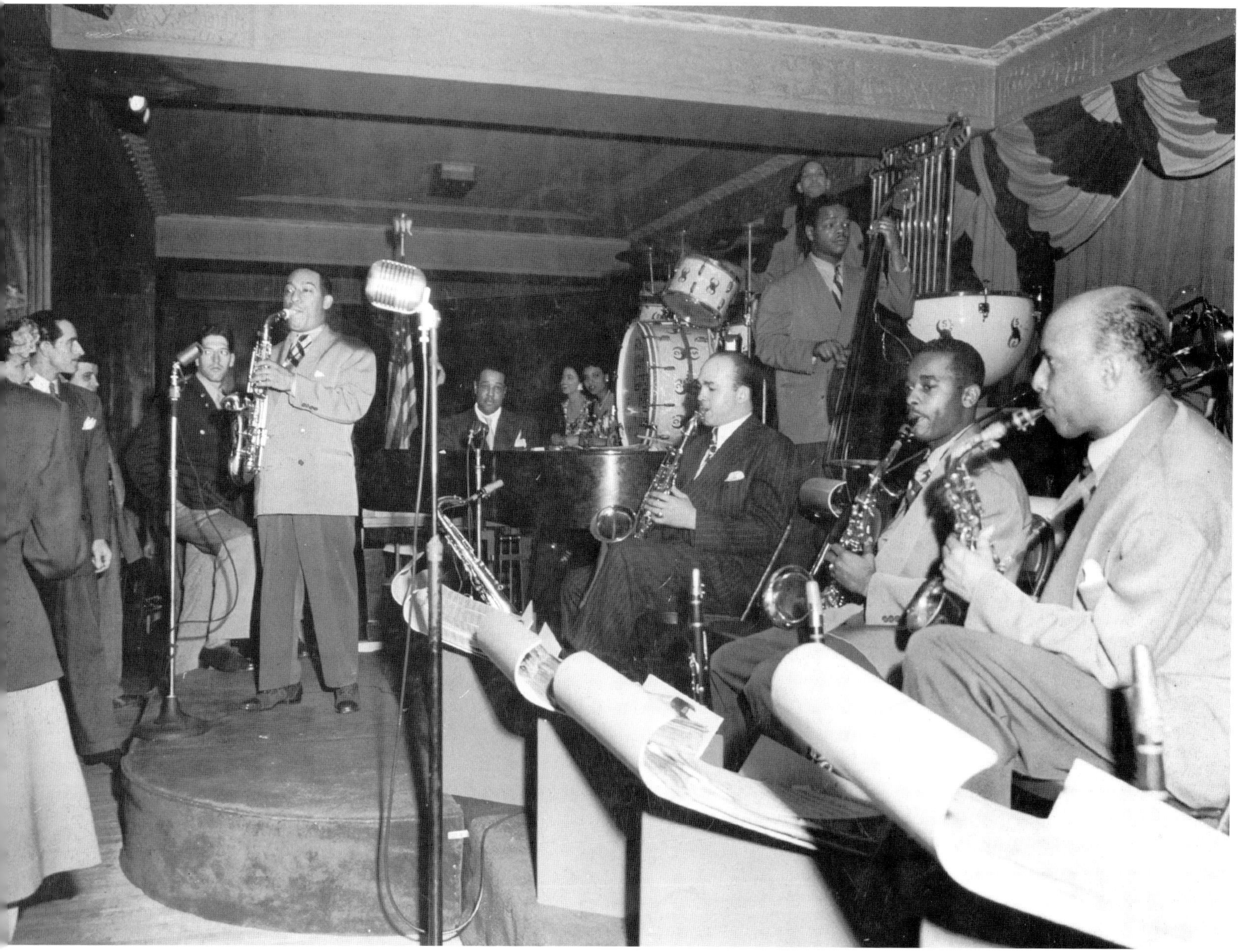

A rare photo from a 1945 club date. Soloist is Johnny Hodges, and among the other band members are Duke Ellington (p), Al Sears (ts), Junior Raglin (b), Sonny Greer (dr), Jimmy Hamilton (ts) and Otto Hardwick (as). Behind Ellington vocalists Kay Davis and Joya Sherrill are listening.

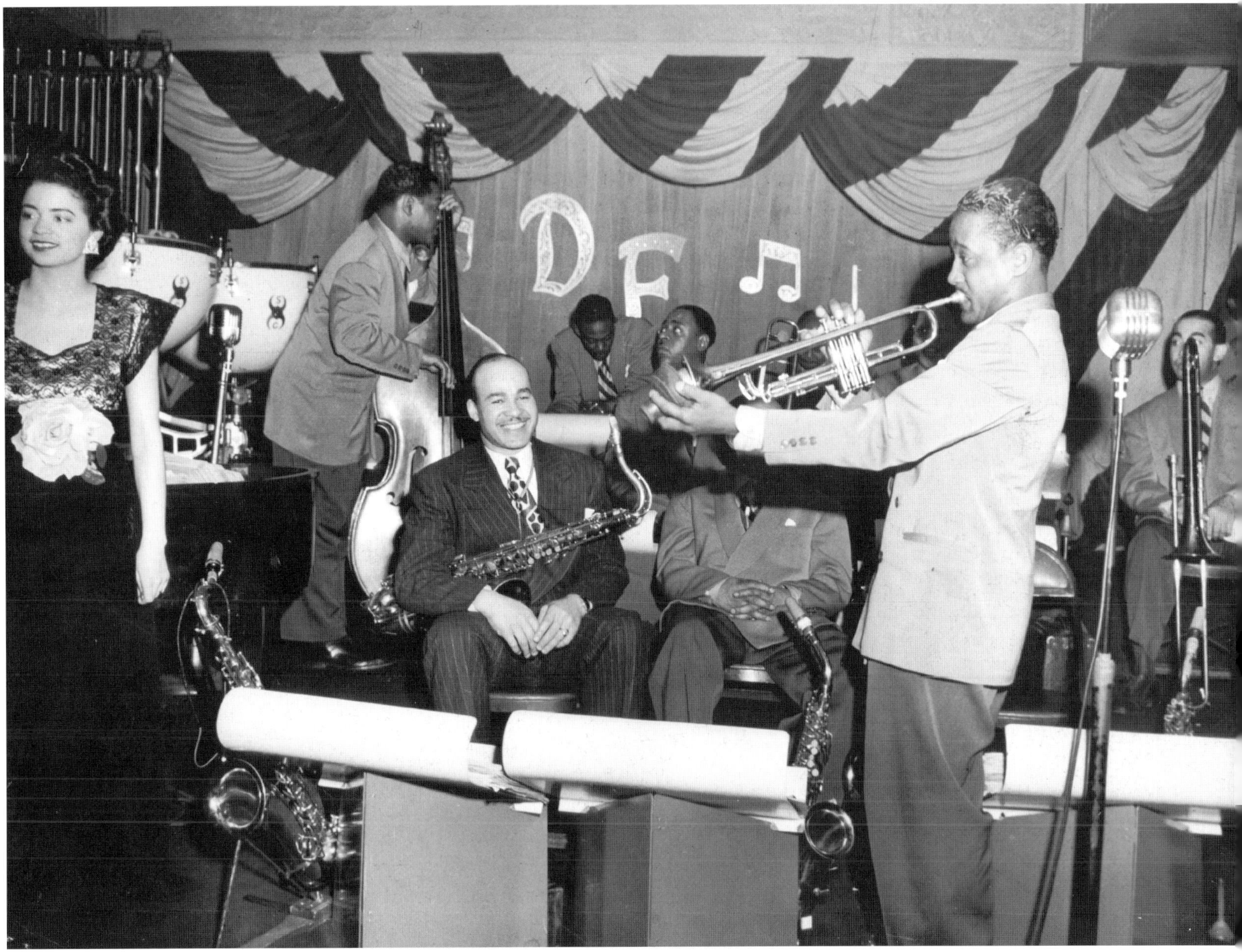

Another photo from the same club date as the previous one. Ray Nance is soloing on trumpet, and Kay Davis and Al Sears seem to enjoy it, while Junior Raglin and "Tricky Sam" Nanton are looking at each other. Trombonist Lawrence Brown is on the extreme right.

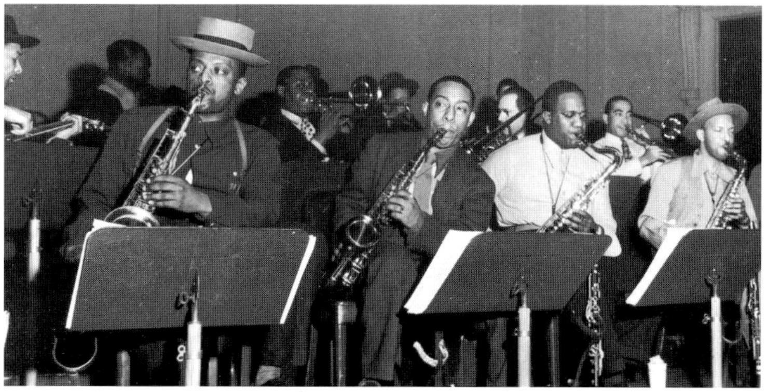

The Duke Ellington band during a rehearsal at Carnegie Hall, New York, January 1943. From left Fred Guy (g), Rex Stewart (tp), Ben Webster (ts), "Tricky Sam" Nanton (tb), Johnny Hodges (as), Juan Tizol (tb), Chauncey Haughton (ts), Lawrence Brown (tb) and Otto Hardwick (as) can be seen.

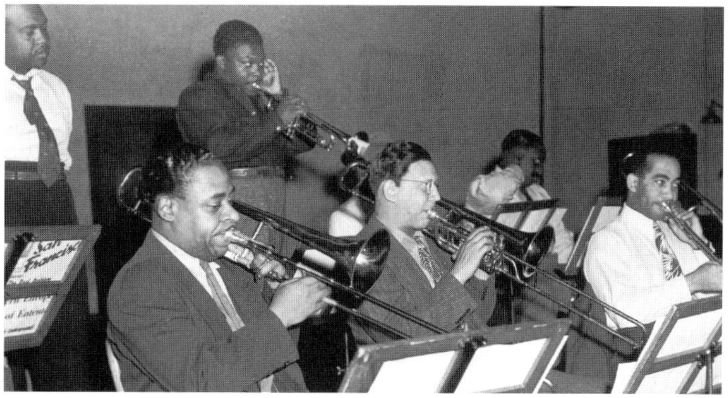

Duke Ellington's brass section during a rehearsal in 1944. Left to right: "Tricky Sam" Nanton, Juan Tizol, and Lawrence Brown (tb), and Shelton Hemphill, Cat Anderson, Ray Nance (hidden behind Tizol), and Rex Stewart (tp).

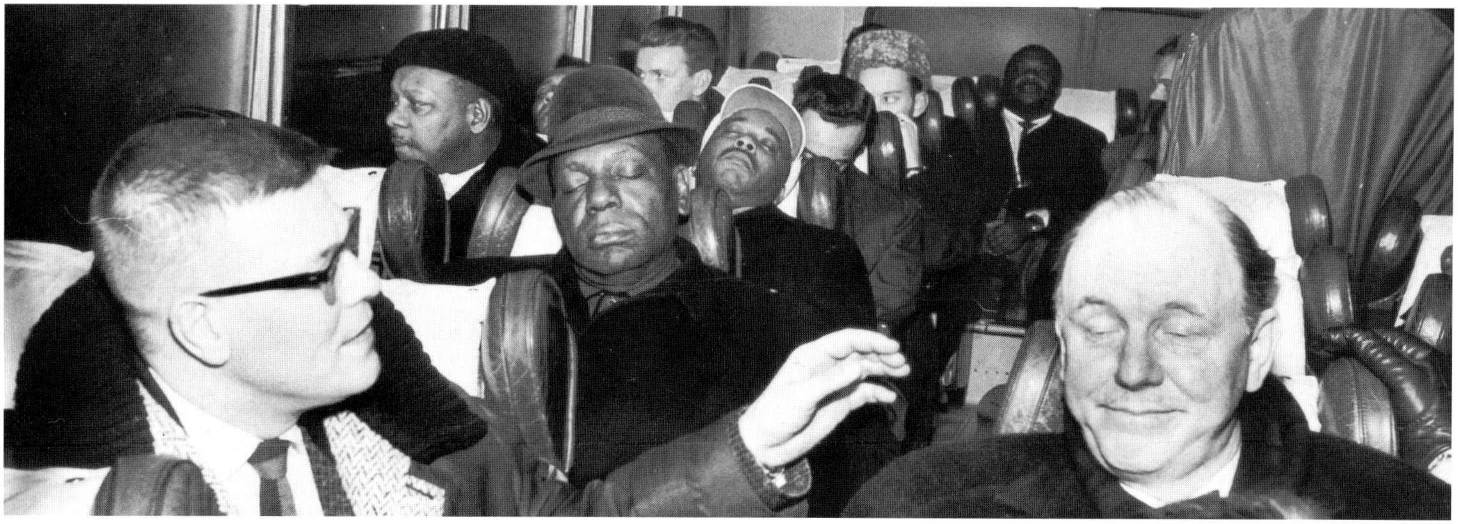

This photo from 1963 shows the Ellington band in a bus on its way to Lund, Sweden, after a concert in Copenhagen. It is obvious how tired you get from touring as the only musician awake is Harry Carney who is looking out into the night. Next to him Jimmy Hamilton is sleeping. Just in front of him Cootie Williams sits. Sleeping in the seats behind Carney and Hamilton are Johnny Hodges and Paul Gonsalves, while Timme Rosenkrantz, who remained one of Ellington's closest friends for more than 30 years, is dosing with a Mona Lisa-like smile on his face on the far right.

IRVING FAZOLA

Reedman Irving Henry Prestopnik "Fazola" (1912-1947) was a New Orleansian. He received classical training from the age of 13, and this was the reason that Louis Prima nicknamed him after the solfeggio notes "fa so la". In the Crescent City he played with Louis Prima, Sharkey Bonano and others, after which he joined Ben Pollack in 1935 with whom he went to New York. In the following years he was in and out of several big bands, with frequent visits to New Orleans in between. His hot and violent temper was often against him, Bob Crosby, for instance, had to fire him in 1940 after a spectacular fight with trombonist Ray Conniff. Three years later he returned to New Orleans where he settled for the rest of his life. Fazola was one of the finest of the clarinetists coming out of the swing era, a master technician and a fine improviser with a pure and smooth sound. His big appetite for the basic things in life, including food and drinks, brought on cirrhosis of the liver and high blood pressure which ended his life much too soon.

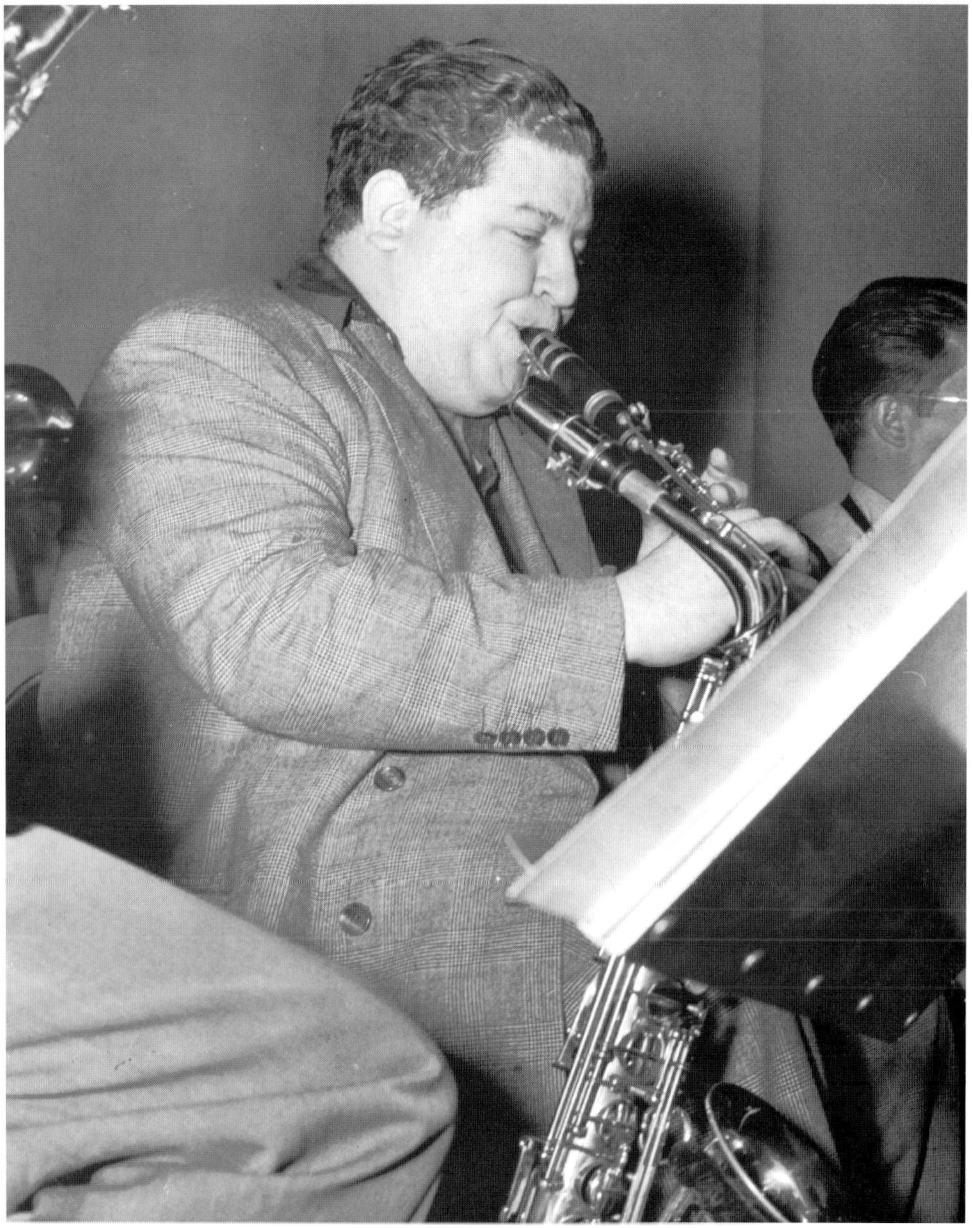

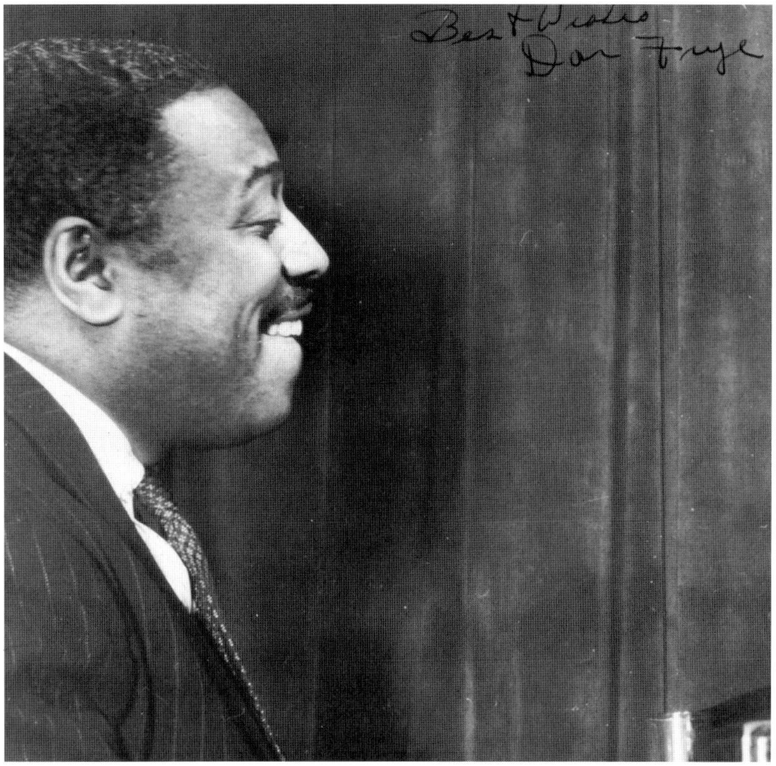

DON FRYE

Pianist Donald O. "Don" Frye (1903-1981) was born in Springfield, Ohio, but came to New York with Lloyd and Cecil Scott in 1924. He remained with the Scotts until the early 30's when he joined Freddy Moore's Trio. In 1937 he became the original pianist in John Kirby's Sextet and worked later on with Lucky Millinder, Frankie Newton and Zutty Singleton. From 1943 he performed as a soloist, playing long engagements at the Village Vanguard in New York, followed by more than a ten years' residency as the house pianist at Jimmy Ryan's. His style was influenced by both Fats Waller and Art Tatum. *Best Wishes Don Frye.*

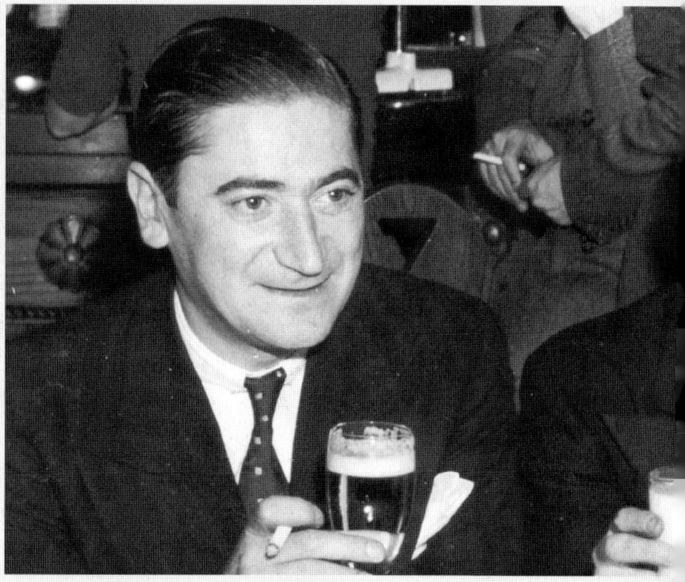

BUD FREEMAN

Tenor saxophonist Lawrence "Bud" Freeman (1906-1991) was a native of Chicago and in the early 20's a member of the Austin High School Gang. In 1927 he arrived in New York with Ben Pollack's band, and the following years he played and recorded frequently with a long list of leaders such as Joe Venuti and Joe Haymes. In 1936 he joined Tommy Dorsey's great band. In 1938 he was with Benny Goodman but didn't stay for the entire year and instead formed his own Cumma Sum Laude Orchestra. During the 50's and 60's he led other groups and became one of the

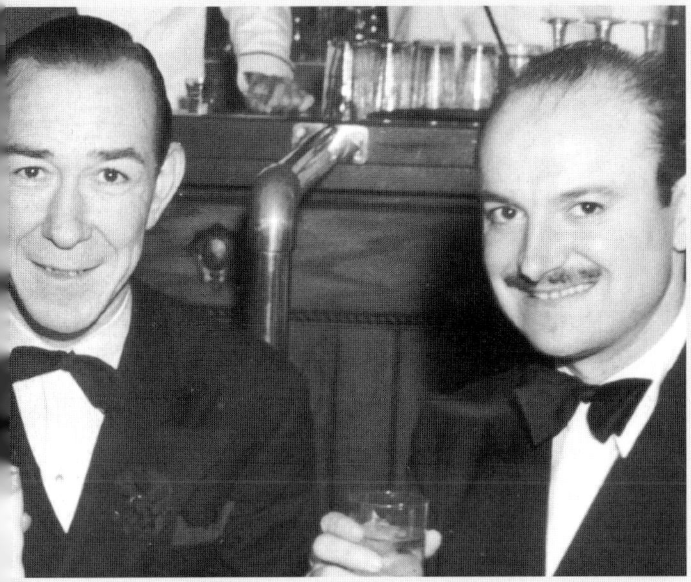

Bud Freeman at Nick's Tavern, New York in the mid-40's. Club owner Nick Rongetti is at the left with a glass of beer, trumpeter Muggsy Spanier – a regular at Nick's during that time – is sitting in the middle with a glass of milk, while Freeman looks forward to enjoy a whisky on the rocks.

founders of the World's Greatest Jazzband in 1968. In the 70's he lived for a while in London after which he settled in Chicago. He continued to play until illnes forced him to retire a few years before his death. Freeman was the first white saxophone player to create a recognizably alternative jazz style on the tenor saxophone to that of Coleman Hawkins.

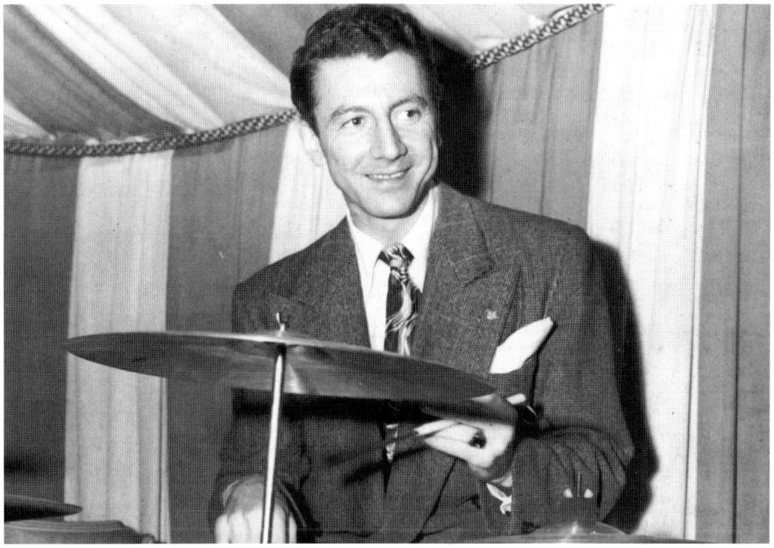

Morey Feld at Eddie Condon's in New York around 1950.

MOREY FELD

Morey Feld (1915-1971) was one of the best of the dixieland drummers. He came from Cleveland, Ohio, and studied drums from the age of 18. After a couple of years with Ben Pollack, Joe Haymes and Bud Freeman he joined Benny Goodman in 1943. From 1946 to 1955 he worked with many well-known dixieland and swing musicians such as Teddy Wilson, Eddie Condon, Billy Butterfield and Peanuts Hucko, after which he became a staff musician at ABC. In the 60's he returned to Benny Goodman and Eddie Condon, opened a drum school in 1966, and also led his own bands. After a number of overseas tours he moved to Colorado to join Peanuts Hucko once more, and in 1968 he was the first choice as a drummer with the World's Greatest Jazzband. He died tragically in a fire that destroyed his home in Bow Mar, near Denver.

ELLA FITZGERALD

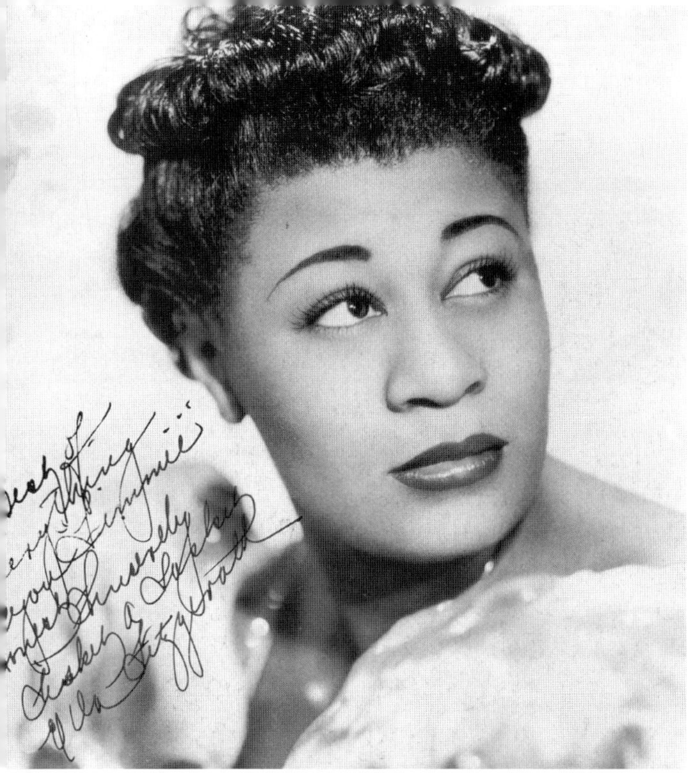

Ella Fitzgerald during her years with Chick Webb. *Best of everything to you Timmie. Honestly sincerely A Tisket a Tasket Ella Fitzgerald.*

Known as "America's First Lady of Songs" and for her distinguished interpretations, Ella Jane Fitzgerald (1917-1996) was one of the most popular jazz musicians, rivalled only by Louis Armstrong. She was born in Newport News, Virginia but raised in Yonkers, New York. At first she preferred dancing to singing, but having won a couple of talent shows at both the Harlem Opera House and at the Apollo Theatre she was recommended to Chick Webb, who hired her early 1935. After Webb's death in 1939 she led the band until 1942 when she began her solo career. From the late 40's impresario and record producer Norman Granz took control of her career and was instrumental in establishing her as one of the leading jazz singers. From the mid-80's her health deteriorated due to diabetes, and she was confined to a wheelchair in her final years. She performed with a never failing elegant swing, and her voice had a large range and retained a youthful, light timbre to the end. As a stylist she has influenced countless popular singers.

HELEN FORREST

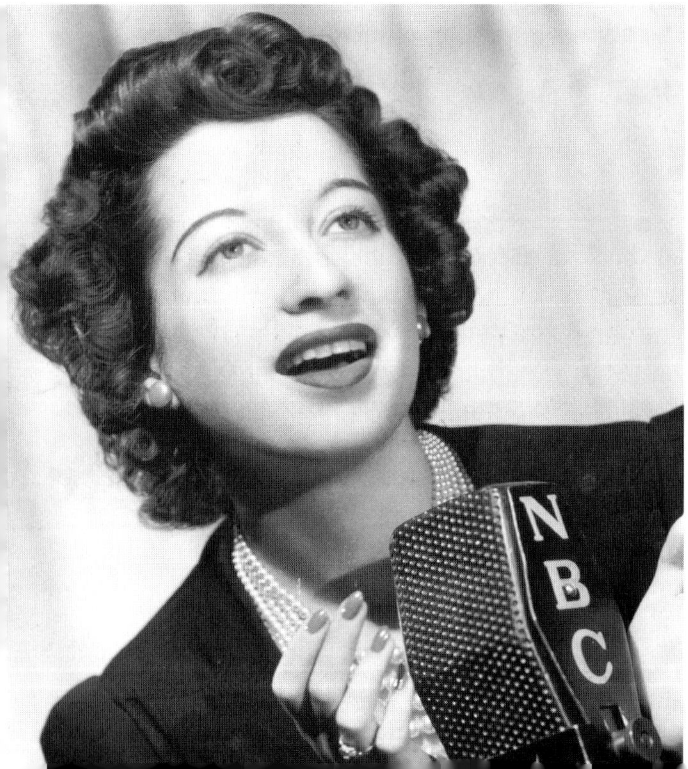

Born in Atlantic City, New Jersey, Helen Forrest (1918-1999) began her career singing on radio using various pseudonyms. She joined Artie Shaw in 1938, and from then on her career took off. From 1939 to 1941 she was with Benny Goodman, and 1941-43 Harry James featured her, after which she went on as a solo act. From 1944 she teamed with singer Dick Haymes on a popular radio show which lasted for years. In the late 50's she was less active, but in the 60's she went with the Tommy Dorsey Band fronted by Sam Donahue. She also appeared frequently on TV, and toured and performed in clubs up through the 70's, recording with Buddy DeFranco and others. A strong and warm voice, she is considered one of the greatest of the big band singers.

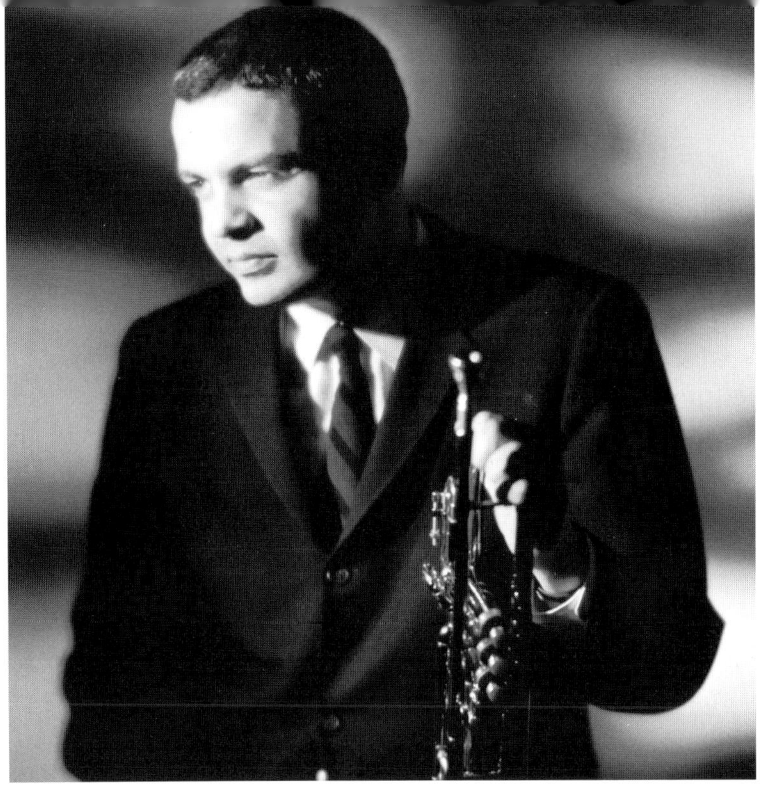

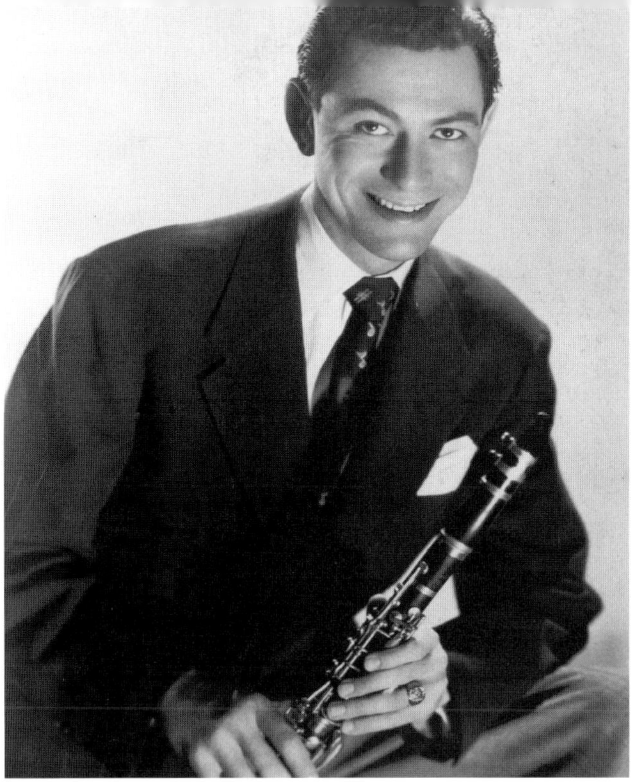

Maynard Ferguson

Maynard Ferguson (1928-) was born in Montreal, Canada, and plays both brass instruments and saxophones, but it is as a high-note specialist on the trumpet that he became internationally known. He moved to USA in 1948 and played with Boyd Raeburn and Charlie Barnet, after which he joined Stan Kenton, who featured him as an outstanding soloist from 1950-53. The following years he freelanced around Los Angeles, and from 1957 he has led bands of various sizes, always touring extensively. In the 70's he reached new audiences by playing jazz-rock and pop hits. Ferguson has an astonishing technique and an exceptional command of the stratospheric register of the trumpet. His bands have focused more on playing with high energy and at excessive volumes than with refinement and subtlety.

Herbie Fields

Clarinetist and saxophonist Herbert "Herbie" Fields (1919-1958) came from Elizabeth, New Jersey. After studies at Julliard 1936-38 he played with Leonard Ware, Woody Herman and Raymond Scott before his career temporarily was interrupted by military service 1942-43. After leading his own band he joined Lionel Hampton for a while – but from 1946 he again fronted his own bands. He moved to Florida in the 50's, where he began playing commercial music, but unhappy with his career and his life he committed suicide by taking an overdose of sleeping pills. Fields was an inconsistent player, but at his best he could create very imaginative solos, especially on the clarinet.

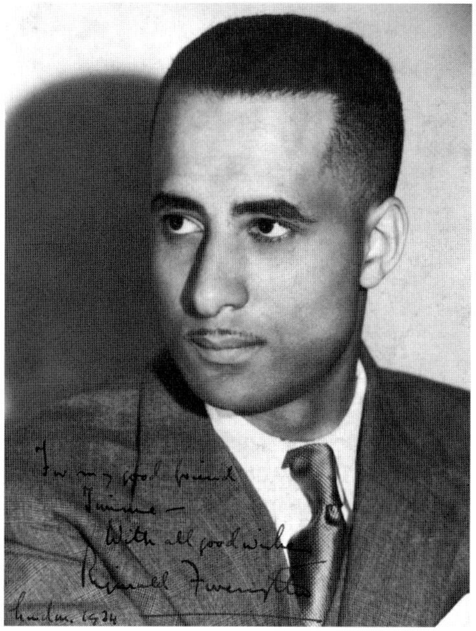

Foresythe in London 1934. *For my good friend Timme – With all good wishes Reginald Foresythe. London, 1934.*

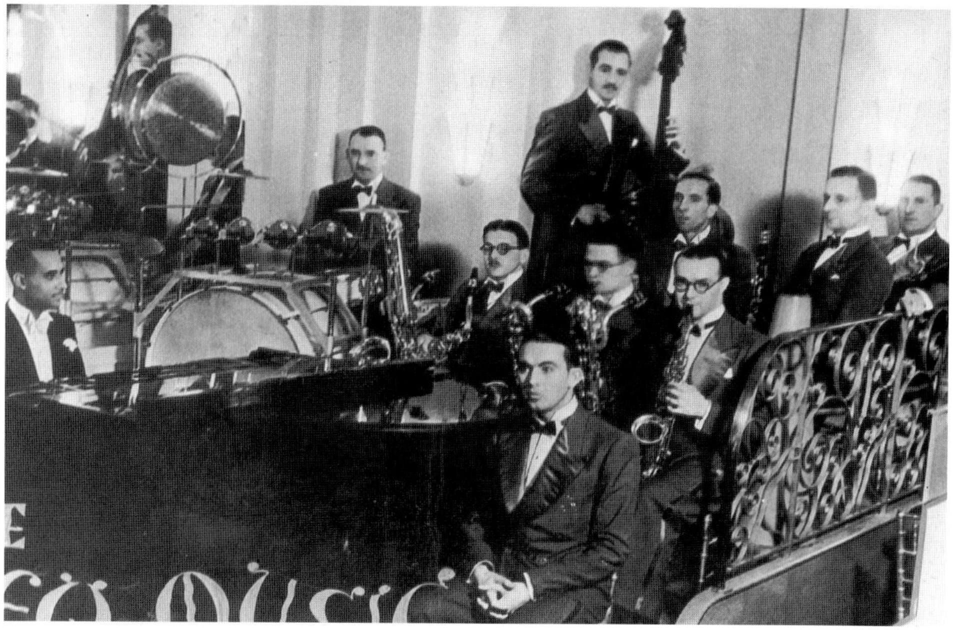

Publicity photo of Foresythe leading his "New Music" orchestra in London.

REGINALD FORESYTHE

English pianist, composer and arranger Reginald Charles Foresythe (1907-1958) wrote music ahead of its time. He was born in London as son of a Yoruba (Nigerian) barrister and an English mother and played his first gigs already by 1923. During the following years he worked in Paris, Australia and Honolulu before he arrived in California in 1929 and began writing film music for MGM and United Artists. Later on he went to Chicago and New York, wrote for Earl Hines, Duke Ellington, Wild Bill Davison and Paul Whiteman before returning to London 1933. Here he formed his revolutionary "New Music" band, in which two clarinets and a bassoon replaced the brass section. He joined the RAF during World War II after which he had his own band for a while, but in the 50's he worked mostly as a solo pianist in small clubs in London's Soho and Kensington, until he died from a fall down stairs. Foresythe's music was modernistic, using unusual instrumentation, voicing and harmony. Up-tempo numbers had a light swing, while the slow ones were moody. In 1934 Rosenkrantz visited London where he met Foresythe and received the two above photos.

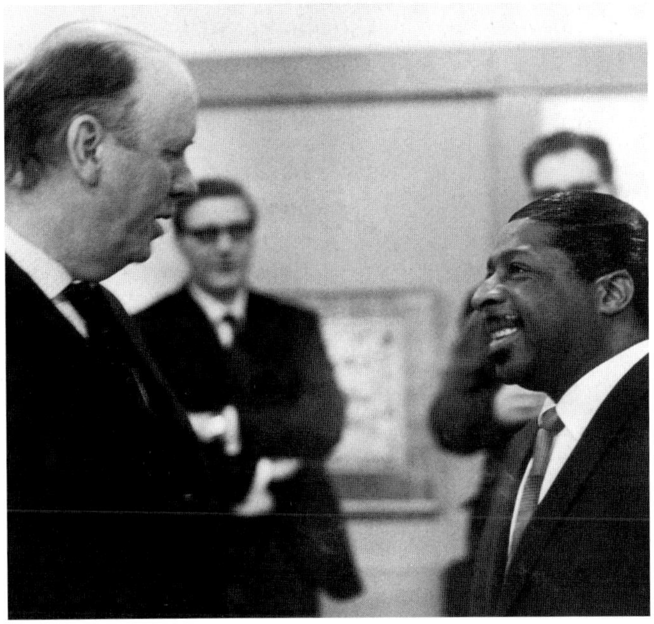

Rosenkrantz and Garner in Copenhagen, April 1966.

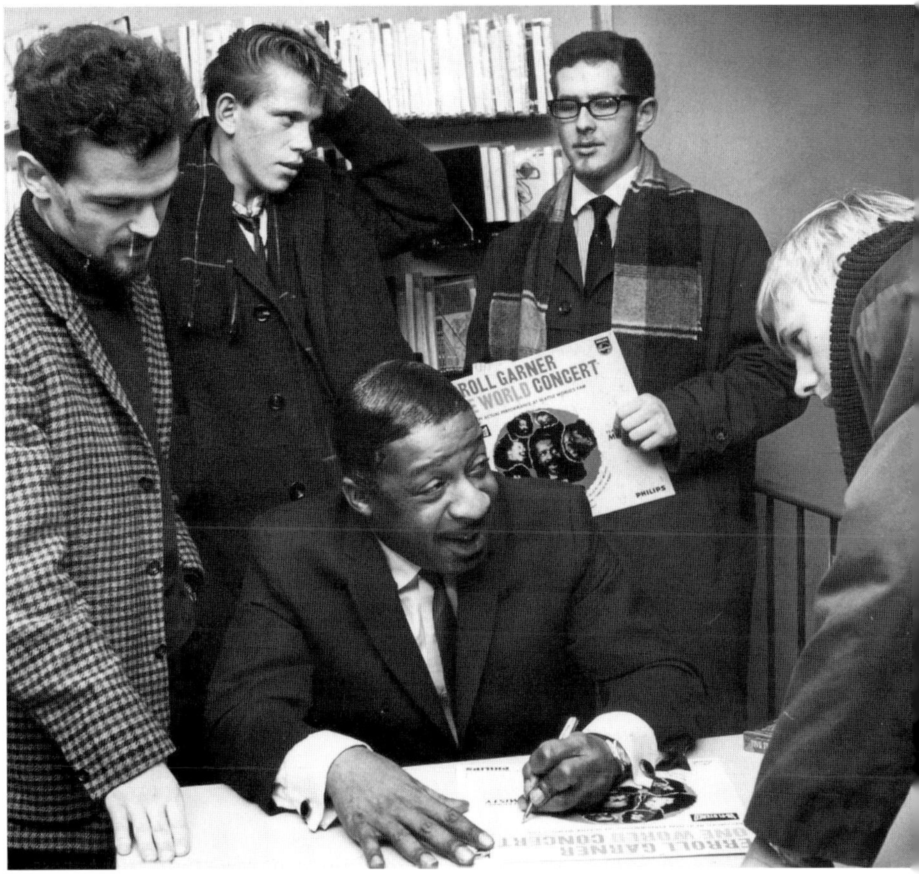

Garner in Copenhagen November 1964, signing his newest album "One World Concert".

ERROLL GARNER

Rosenkrantz and Erroll Louis Garner (1921-1977) shared a special relationship. Garner came to New York in 1944 from his hometown Pittsburgh where he had played professionally for a number of years. In the Big Apple he got a job as intermission pianist in a little 52nd Street club called Tondeleyo. Rosenkrantz heard him there, became his friend, recorded him at his home, and featured him at a concert at Times Hall. The rest is history. Garner became an instant success, and for the rest of his life he recorded and toured extensively, sometimes as a solo act, but mostly with his own trio. Besides possessing a virtuoso technique combined with an ability to create infectious swing, one of his trade-marks was long, fanciful introductions, almost small compositions by themselves.

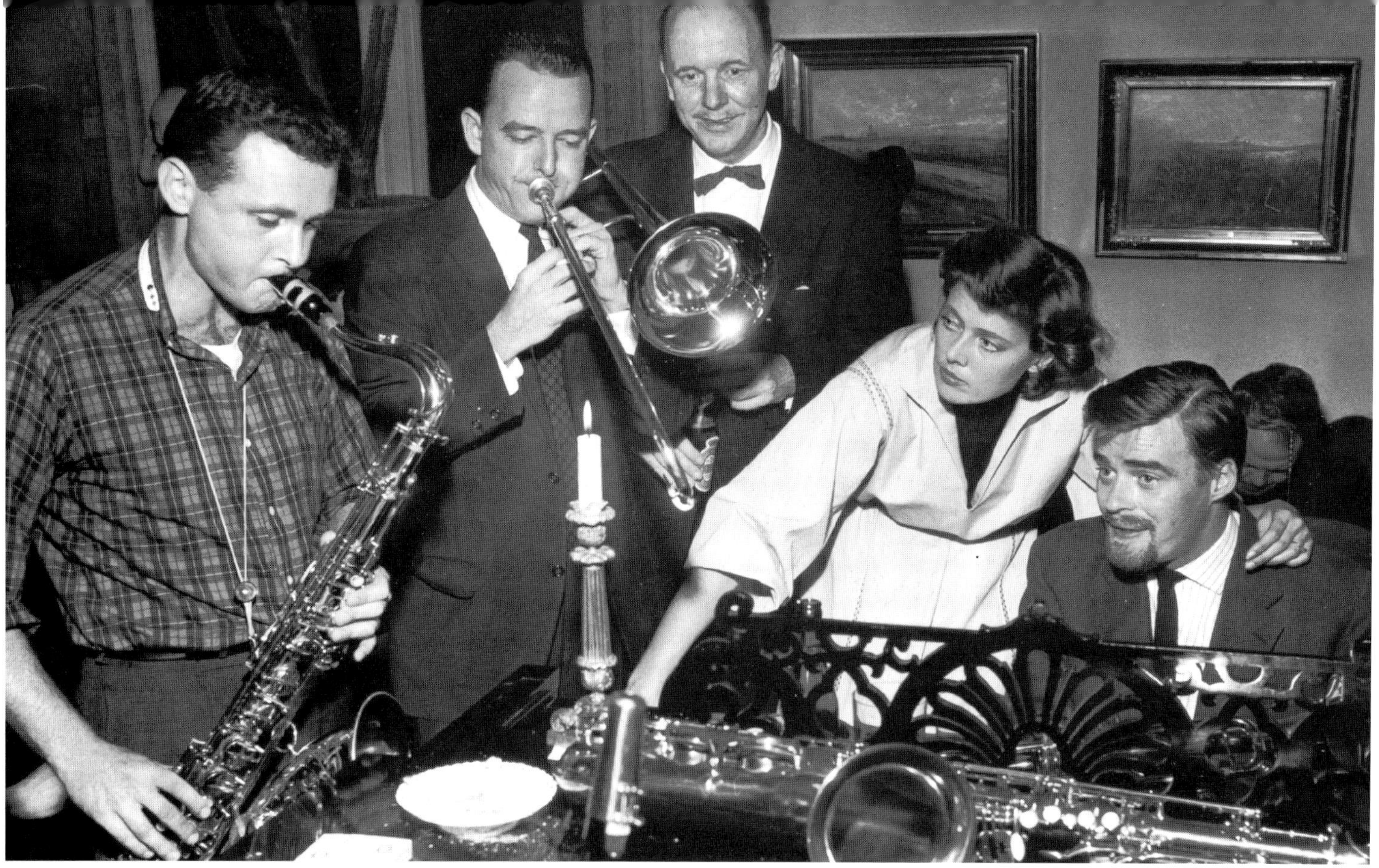

Stan Getz in September 1958 jamming at the home of Torben and Lone Ulrich in Hellerup, near Copenhagen, with Kai Winding trombone, and Jørgen Lausen piano. Rosenkrantz is looking on, and Lone Ulrich has her arm around Lausen.

Stan Getz

Tenor saxophonist Stanley "Stan" Getz (1927-1991) was one of the most renowned of jazz musicians. He was a native of Philadelphia and began his professional career already at the age of 15 playing with Jack Teagarden. He then spent the rest of the 40's playing in the big bands of Stan Kenton, Benny Goodman and Woody Herman. The 50's were tough years, due mostly to his drug problems, and the years 1958-61 were spent in Europe, where he settled in Copenhagen. Back in the USA he formed his own quartet and recorded bossa nova albums which made him extremely popular. The rest of his life he toured extensively. Besides being an exceptionally creative soloist, he was a talent scout who helped launch the careers of Chick Corea, Joanne Brackeen, Tony Williams, Billy Hart, Miroslav Vitous, Victor Lewis, Kenny Barron and others. He made his final tour a couple of months before he died of cancer.

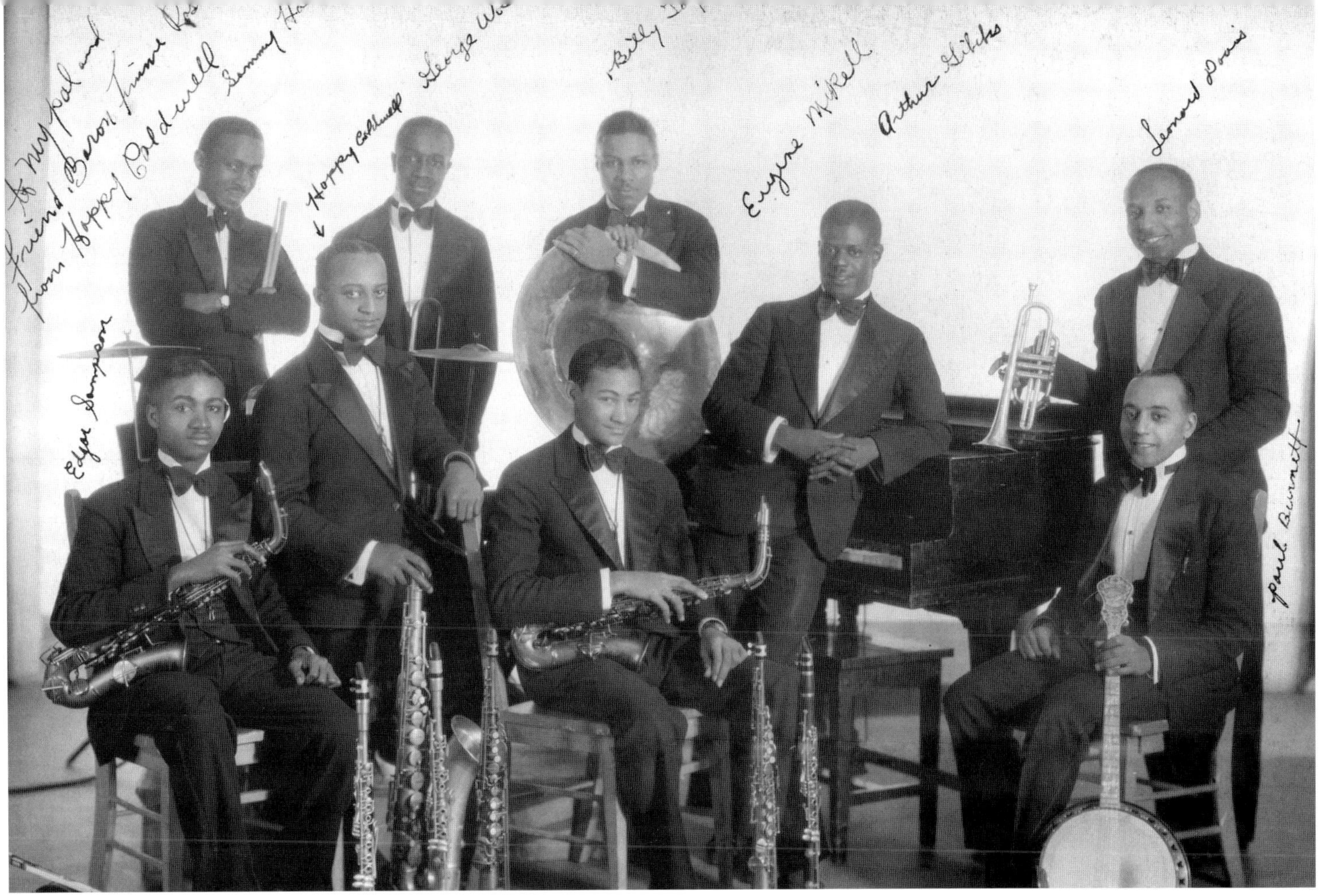

Arthur Gibbs with a highly interesting orchestra, which unfortunately never recorded. This short-lived group existed for a year only, from summer 1927 to summer 1928, and worked at both the Savoy and the Arcadia Ball Room in New York. Standing from the left are Sammy Hodges (dr), George Washington (tb), Billy Taylor (tu), Arthur Gibbs, and Leonard Davis (tp). Seated are Edgar Sampson (as and vln), Happy Caldwell (ts), Eugene Mikell (as), and Paul Burnett (bj). *To my pal and friend, Baron Timme Rosenkrantz from Happy Caldwell.*

Arthur Gibbs

Pianist Arthur Gibbs (1896-1956) organized and directed bands which in the twenties accompanied many prominent theatrical artists, among them Florence Mills, Tallulah Bankhead and Bill "Bojangles" Robinson. During 1929-30 he toured Europe with a small group working in London, Paris, Budapest, Barcelona, and Vienna. He then returned to New York and worked mostly in theatres for the rest of his life.

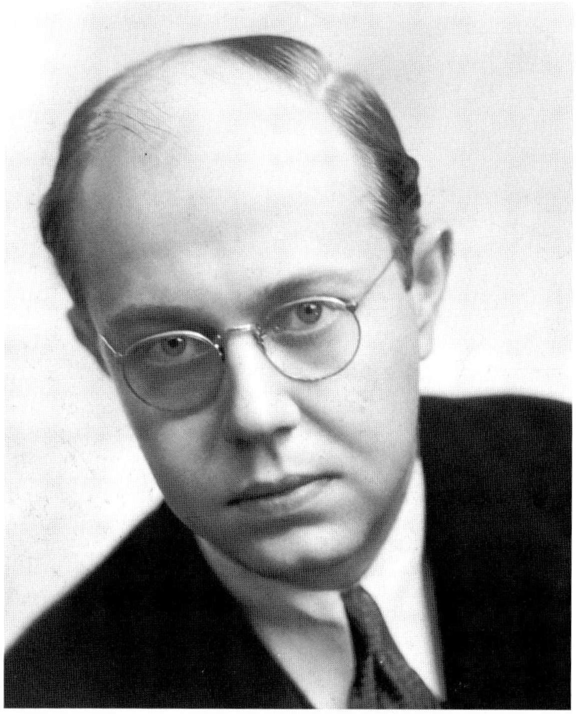

GENE GIFFORD

Although Harold Eugene "Gene" Gifford (1908-1970) started his musical career on banjo and guitar, he is best known for his ability as an arranger. He was born in Americus, Georgia, but moved early to Memphis. Here he formed and toured with his own bands from the mid-20's, and in 1929 he joined Jean Goldkette's Orange Blossoms. Shortly afterwards Goldkette broke up his bands, and the Orange Blossoms continued as the Casa Loma Orchestra. Gifford became its chief arranger and set the style of the band. In 1939 he left to freelance, but during the 50's he worked as a radio engineer and consultant after which he settled in Memphis as a music teacher. Gifford's scores were expertly drafted and technically complex, often with the use of call-and-reponse exchanges between the brass and the reeds sections, and in slow, moody pieces he made intelligent, colourful use of various woodwind instruments. His use of riff-based ensemble sound influenced many arrangers of black swing bands.

TYREE GLENN

Trombonist and vibraphonist Evans Tyree Glenn (1912-1974) was a Texan from Corsicana and played in local bands during his teens. He then worked in Washington and Virginia before he moved to Los Angeles where he played with Eddie Barefield. In 1939 he first joined Benny Carter and then Cab Calloway with whom he stayed until 1946 when he toured with Don Redman in Europe. Between 1947-51 he was with Ellington after which he mostly played studio jobs for CBS the following decade. In 1965 he joined Louis Armstrong but freelanced again from 1968. With Ellington he specialized in playing with the plunger mute like "Tricky" Sam Nanton before him, and on the vibraphone he played in the swing style inspired by Red Norvo and Lionel Hampton.

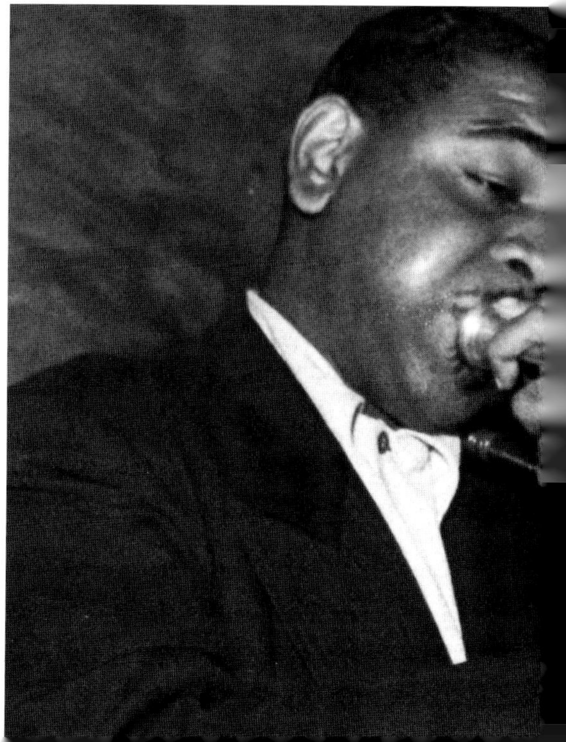

A.G. GODLEY

A.G. Godley (1905-1973) was a drummer and a showman of extraordinary talent who certainly ought to be better known. Very little has been written about him, but Jo Jones always referred to him as one of the biggest of all big band drummers. In the early 30's he worked in territory bands around Kansas City, such as Walter Page's Blue Devils and Fate Marable, after which he joined Alphonso Trent who billed him as "the originator of the drum solo". Then he was with the Jeter-Pillars Orchestra in St. Louis for some years, playing the Club Plantation. Teamed with bassist Abe Bolar, as witnessed on records made around 1940 with Pete Johnson and Hot Lips Page, he created one of the best rhythm sections in Kansas City. In the early 40's he was in New York, and 1945-46 he toured the Pacific for the USO with Leo "Snub" Mosley after which he moved to Seattle, Washington, where he died almost forgotten. *To Inez + Timme of the good old "Melody" A.G. Godley. 7/22/41.*

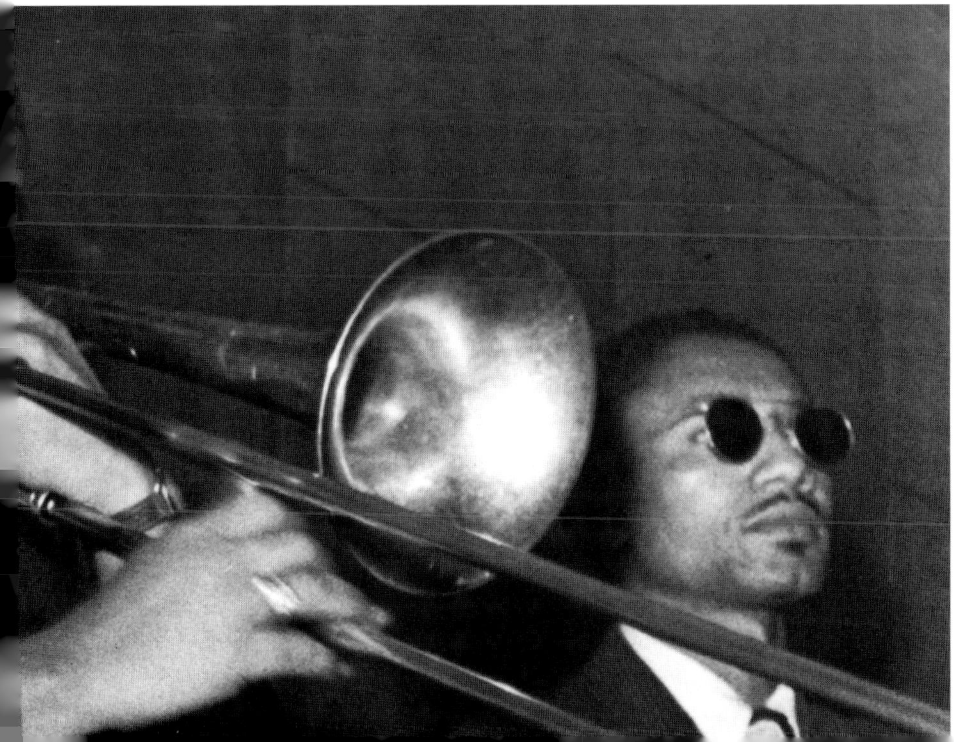

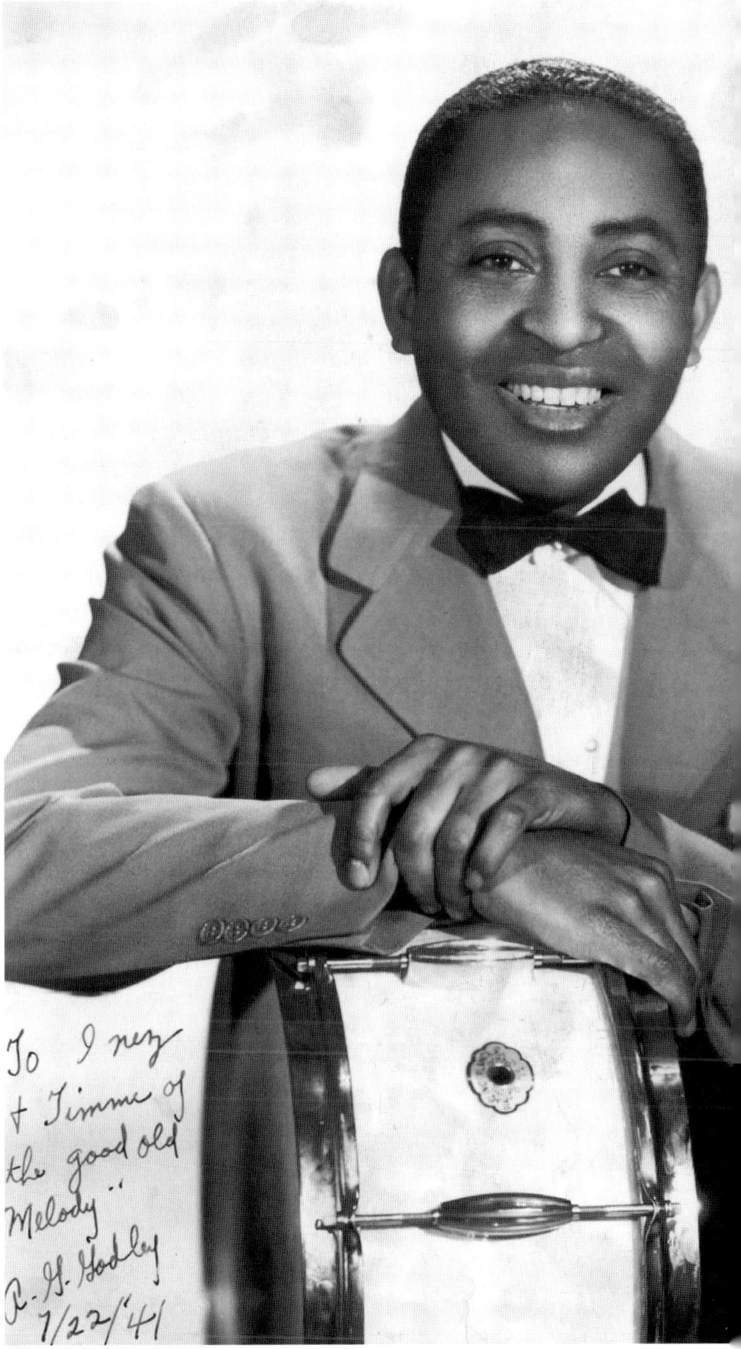

SONNY GREER

Drummer William Alexander "Sonny" Greer (c.1895-1982) began playing in local bands in and around his native town Long Branch, New Jersey. In 1920 he joined Duke Ellington's orchestra with which he played until 1951. From then on he freelanced with other small groups led by Johnny Hodges, Tyree Glenn, Eddie Barefield, J. C. Higginbotham and others. In 1967 he led his own band at the Garden Café in New York, and during the 70's he regularly worked with Brooks Kerr's trio. He continued to work until shortly before he died. During the Ellington band's residence at the Cotton Club (1927-31) Greer built up a huge amount of percussion equipment which he used to great effects during the "jungle" numbers. Later on he developed a more rhytmically subtle technique which perfectly blended with Ellington's orchestrations.

NAT CONELLA

English trumpeter and singer Nathaniel Charles "Nat" Gonella (1908-1998) started out on trumpet as a teenager. He grew up in London, and after stints with Billy Cotton, Roy Fox, Ray Noble and Lew Stone, he formed his own band, the Georgians, in 1934 which after the war was expanded to a big band. He then formed a bebop band for a short while, but in 1959 he returned to the dixieland format with his New Georgians. From the early 80's he ceased playing trumpet but still performed as a singer up to 1996. Gonella played in a style patterned after Louis Armstrong, and he inspired fellow musicians Kenny Ball and Humphrey Lyttelton.

BUDDY GRECO

Pianist and singer Armando "Buddy" Greco (1926-) entered the music business already at the age of five appearing as a singer on his father's radio shows. He was born in Philadelphia, Pennsylvania, and studied to become a pianist, and from 1944-49 he had his own trio in his home town. Here Benny Goodman heard him, and from 1949-51 Greco was with Goodman as both pianist, singer and arranger. In 1951 Greco formed his own trio, with which he has since played countless nightclubs in USA and England.

FREDDIE GREEN

Guitarist Frederick William "Freddie" Green (1911-1987) was born in Charleston, South Carolina, and began playing banjo from the age of twelve. In 1930 he moved to New York to finish school, and a little later on he changed to the guitar which he has always played unamplified. In 1936 he played at the Black Cat in Greenwich Village with a quintet which included trumpeter Bobby Moore and drummer Kenny Clarke, and here Count Basie heard them in early 1937 and hired both Moore and Green. For the next five decades Green was with the Basie band, except for minor absences. As part of the All American Rhythm Section with bassist Walter Page and drummer Jo Jones his light and rhythmically precise strumming of the chords perfectly complemented the relaxed, driving pulse of the Basie band. Green's playing was highly esteemed by fellow musicians, and he recorded prolifically with others.

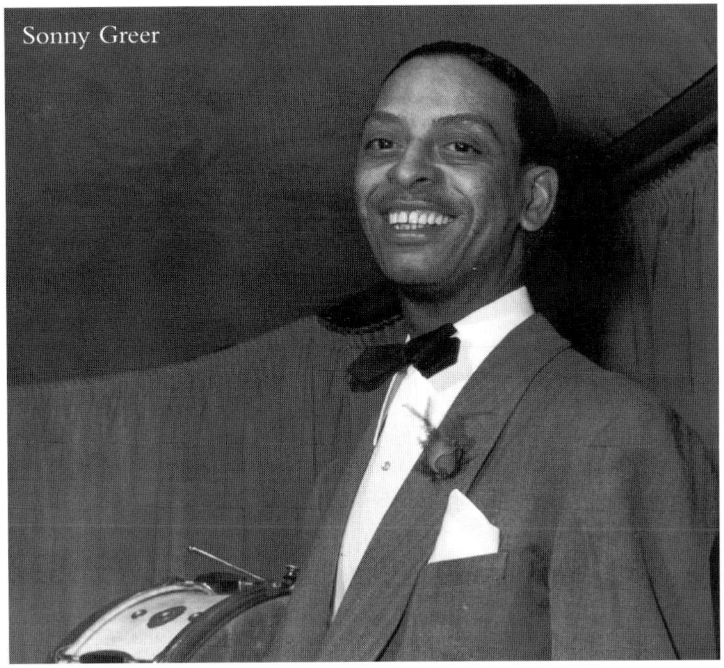
Sonny Greer

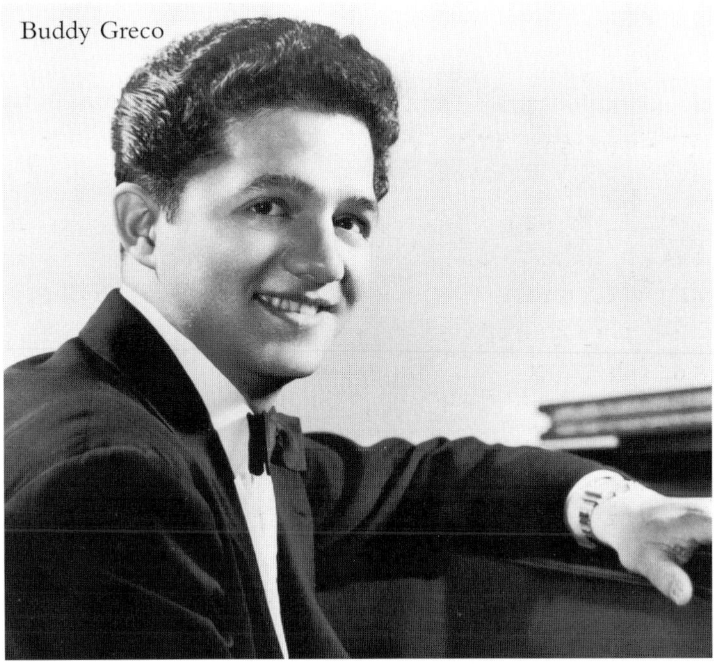
Buddy Greco

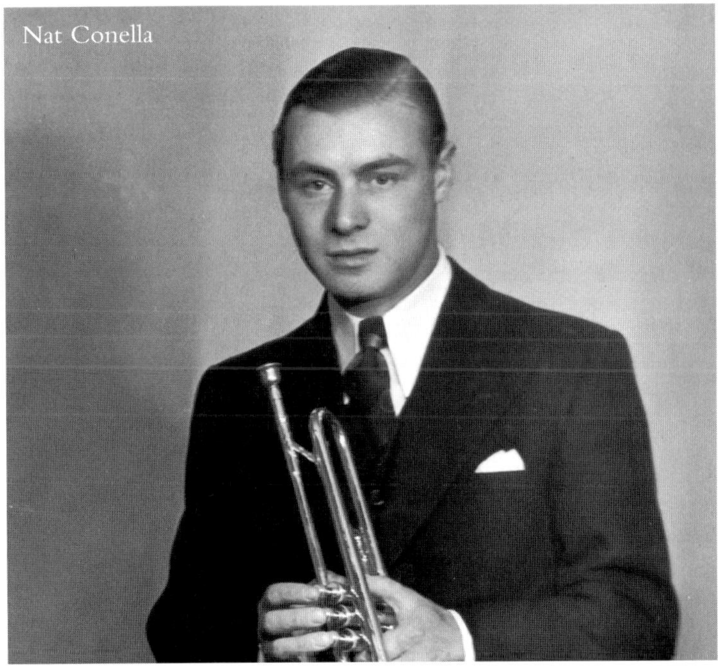
Nat Conella

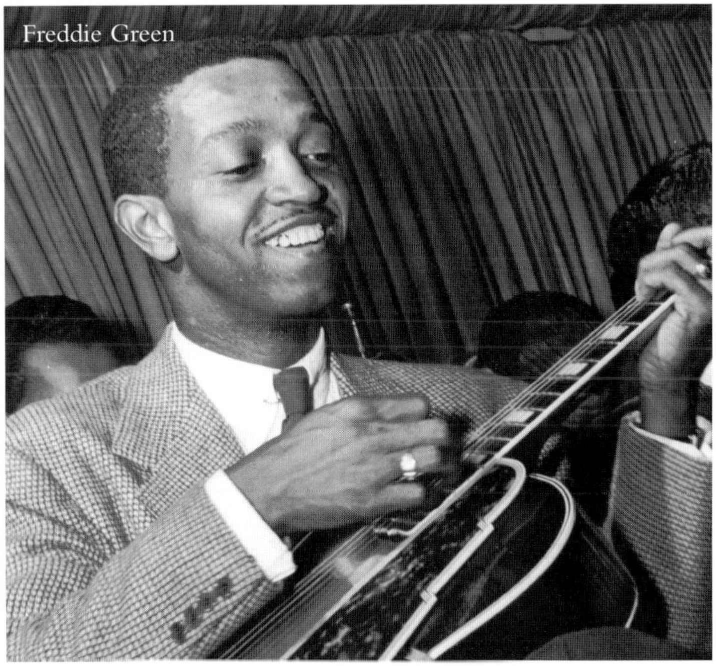
Freddie Green

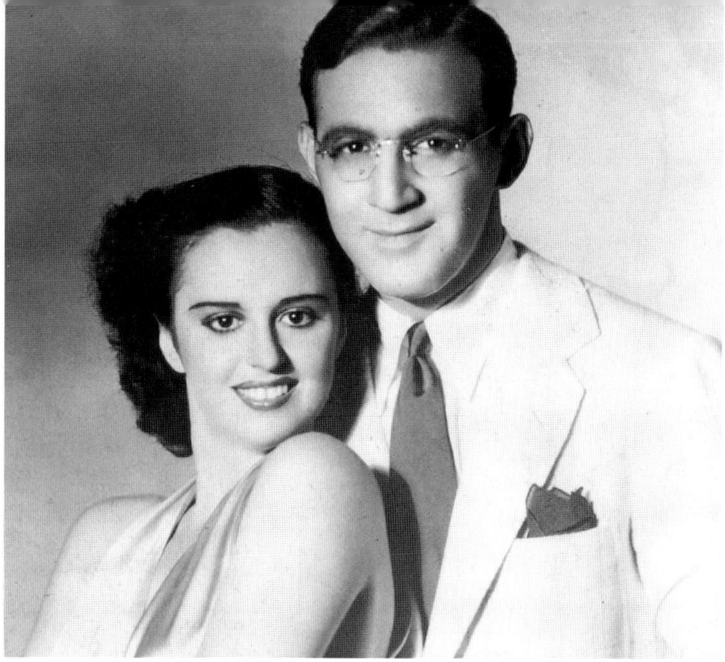

Benny Goodman with Helen Ward, his vocalist 1935-36.

Benny Goodman

Clarinetist Benjamin David "Benny" Goodman (1909-1986) was one of the most important white bandleaders of the swing era, and also one of the first to feature black musicians. He was a perfectionist who always expected the best from other musicians, and his flawless, easy flowing style on the clarinet set new standards for perfection. He was born in Chicago, and worked professionally from the age of thirteen. During the late 20's he was with Ben Pollack, after which he worked in Broadway shows and recording studios. In 1934 he formed his own band, which went on its first national tour in 1935 and became known nationally as well as internationally. Throughout the rest of his career Goodman continued touring with his own bands, small groups as well as big bands, and he also performed with classical ensembles as a clarinetist soloist.

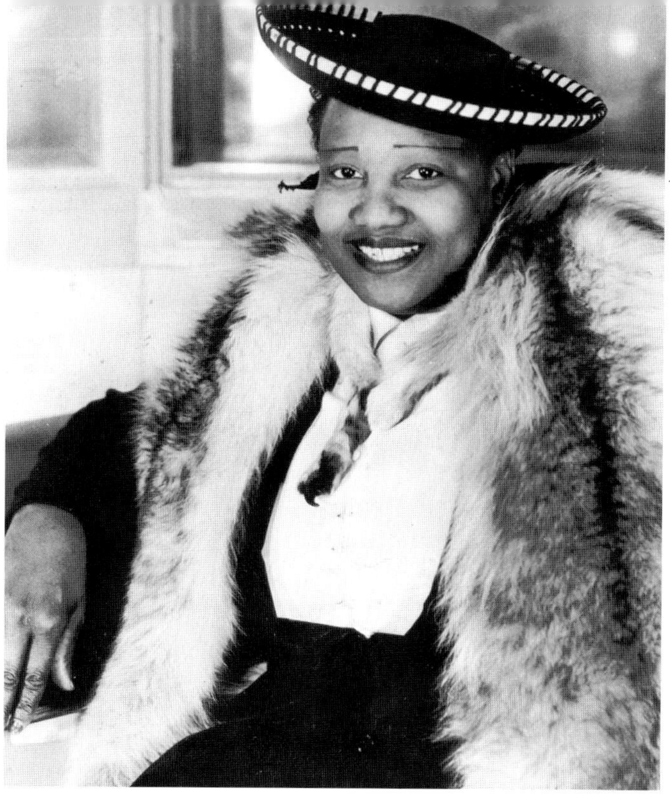

Lil Green

Singer Lil Green (1919-1954) came from Mississippi but grew up in Chicago. From the mid-30's she appeared at night clubs and began recording with Big Bill Broonzy and others. In the early 40's she toured with Tiny Bradshaw and Luis Russell, but she never really broke away from performing on the black theatre circuit which she had confined herself to, and therefore never achieved a national breakthrough. She composed several well-known songs herself, among them "Romance In The Dark", which has been recorded by many other singers, such as Mary Ann McCall and Billie Holiday. She didn't enjoy good health, and died all too soon at the age of 34.

Glen Gray and the Casa Loma Orchestra

This photo dates from a 1938 engagement at New York's Paramount Theater. The brass section is from the left, Billy Rauch and Pee Wee Hunt (tb), Grady Watts, Frank Zullo, and Sunny Dunham (tp). The rhythm section consists of drummer Tony Briglia, guitarist Jack Blanchette, bassist Stanley Dennis, and pianist Howard Hall. The saxophone section consists of Pat Davis, Murray McEachern, who also played trombone, Clarence Hutchenrider, Art Ralston, and Dan D'Andrea. Kenny Sargent, standing behind Glen Gray, performed as vocalist, but was also proficient as a saxophonist. Playing with a precise and polished ensemble work due to endless rehearsals led by arranger Gene Gifford and trombonist Billy Rauch, the band attained great success among the college crowds during the 30's.

Fred Guy

Banjoist and guitarist Fred Guy (1897-1971) was born in Burkesville, Georgia, but grew up in New York where he began his career in Joseph Smith's band. After the experience of leading his own band he joined Duke Ellington in 1925 and stayed with him until 1949. In 1934 he switched to guitar after having received tuition from Eddie Lang. When he left Ellington, he also left full-time music and moved to Chicago to become a dance hall manager. His last years were dominated by long periods of illnes and eventually he took his own life.

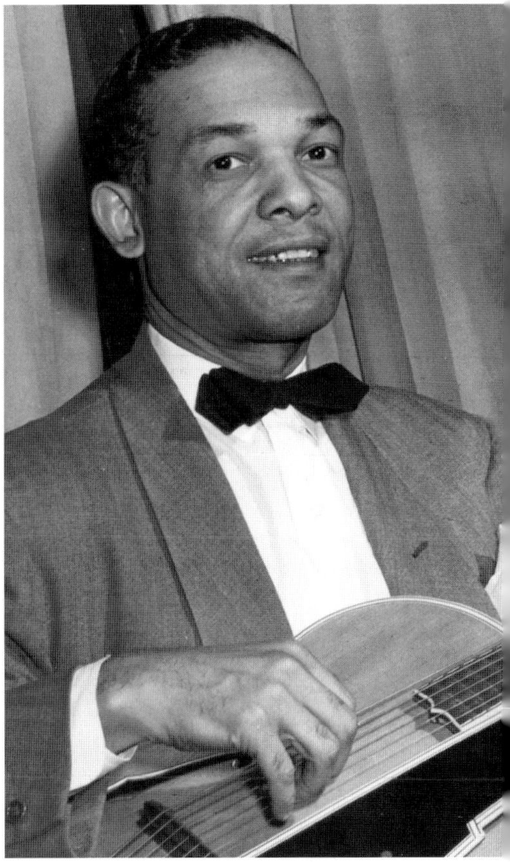

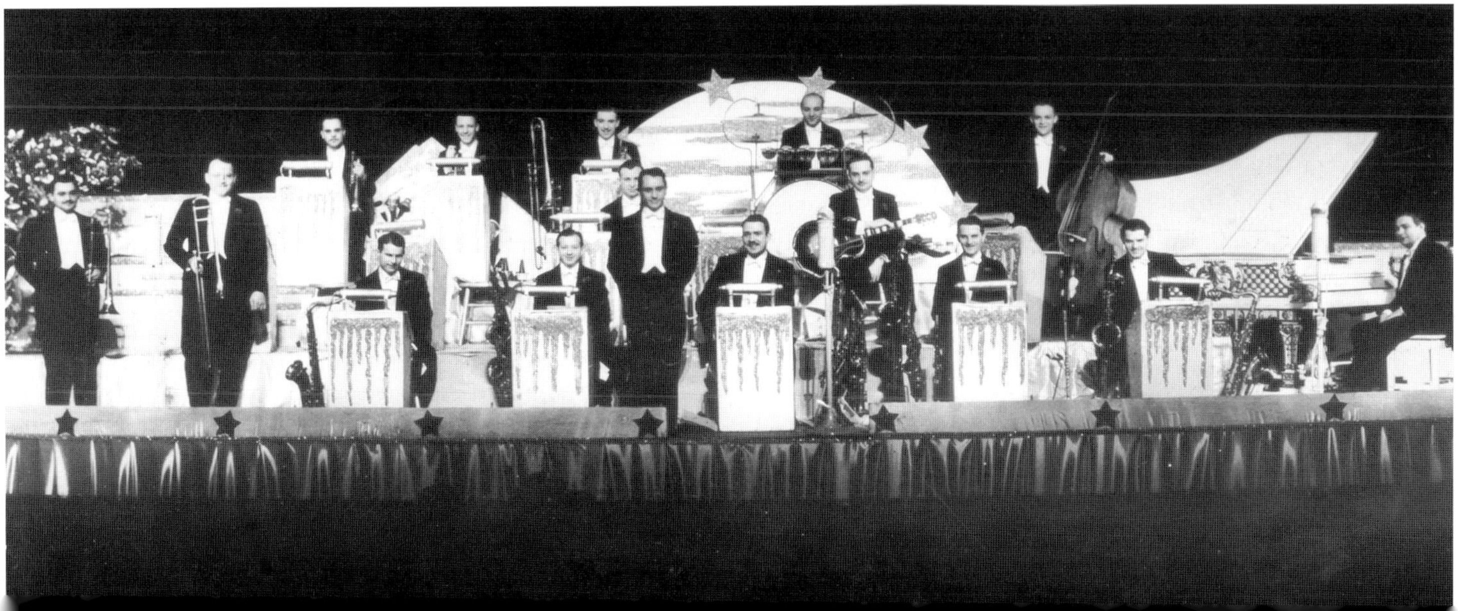

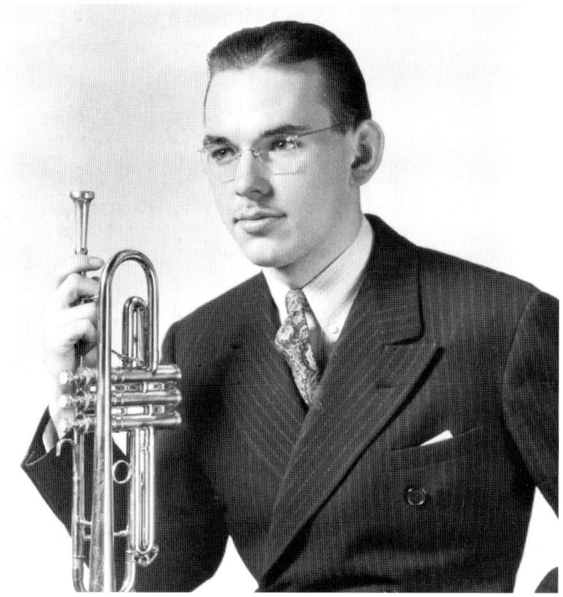

CHRIS GRIFFIN

Gordon "Chris" Griffin (1915-) came from Birmingham, New York, and from 1930 played trumpet in a taxi-dance hall in New York. From 1933-35 he was with Charlie Barnet, and after a spell at the CBS Studios he joined Benny Goodman whith whom he stayed until 1940, completing the legendary trumpet section of Harry James and Ziggy Elman. The following 30 years he worked as a studio musician for CBS only interrupted by a brief stay with Tommy Dorsey in 1940. With Pee Wee Erwin he ran a trumpet school in New York during the 60's and the 70's, and from 1981 he has played with Warren Vaché Senior's small group as well as leading his own Chris Griffin All Stars.

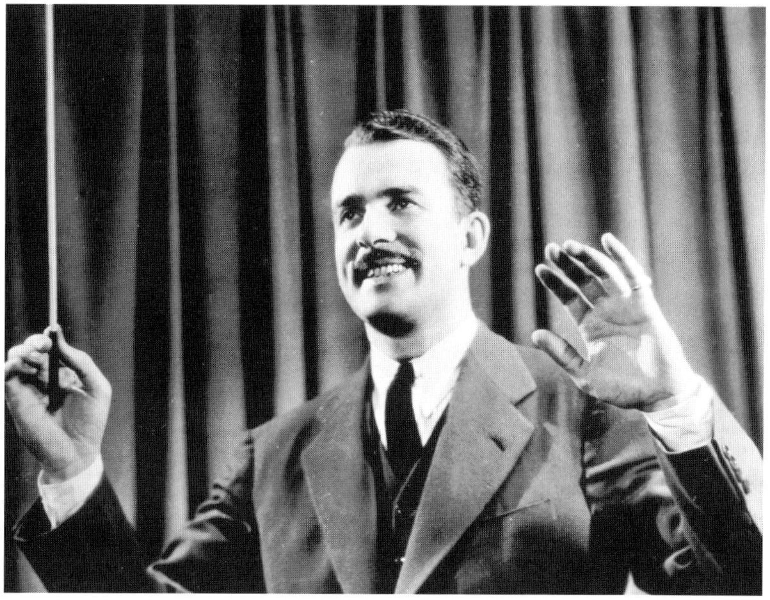

GLEN GRAY

Alto saxophonist and bandleader Glen Gray "Spike" Knoblaugh (1906-63) was a native of Roanoke, Illinois, and played in Detroit towards the end of the 20's with one of Jean Goldkette's band units, the Orange Blossoms. When Goldkette dissolved his bands, the Orange Blossoms continued as the Casa Loma Orchestra, named after its 1927 stay at a Toronto hotel. The band played ballrooms and hotels throughout the East as a co-operative unit with Gray elected as leader. Gray continued to play in the saxophone section until 1937, when he took over as the front man and renamed the band Glen Gray and His Casa Loma Orchestra. When the band folded in 1950 Gray left the music business, but returned in 1956 to lead studio orchestras playing the hits of the swing era, including old arrangements of the Casa Loma Orchestra

BOBBY HACKETT

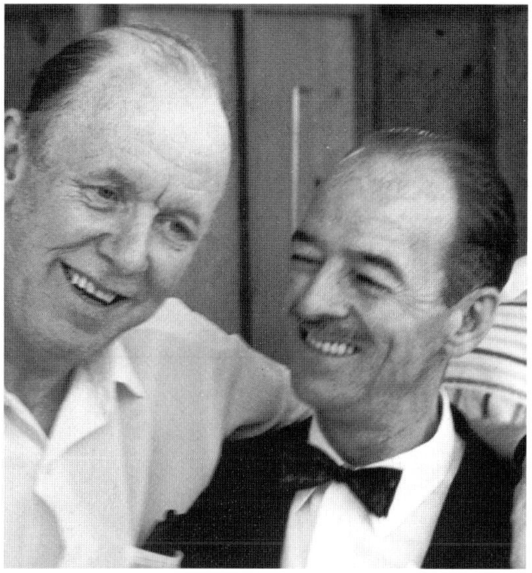

Bobby Hackett at the Newport Jazz Festival 1966 in a happy reunion with Rosenkrantz.

Robert Leo "Bobby" Hackett (1915-1976) started out on ukulele and guitar in local bands around his home town Providence, Rhode Island, before he specialized on the cornet. He moved to New York in 1937 to play with Joe Marsala, and led both small bands and a big band before he joined Glenn Miller's orchestra (1941-42). After a couple of years as a studio musician for NBC, he played in Glen Gray's Casa Loma Orchestra followed by a long period as a staff musician at ABC but concurrently also played clubs and led his own groups. In the late 60's he co-led a quintet with Vic Dickenson, after which he toured with George Wein and Dick Sudhalter before he died of diabetes. Hackett played in a lyrical, elegant way, inspired by both Bix Beiderbecke and Louis Armstrong. His tone was always attractive and easily recognizable, and in his solos he used to twist the harmonies in a very personal way.

JOE HAYMES

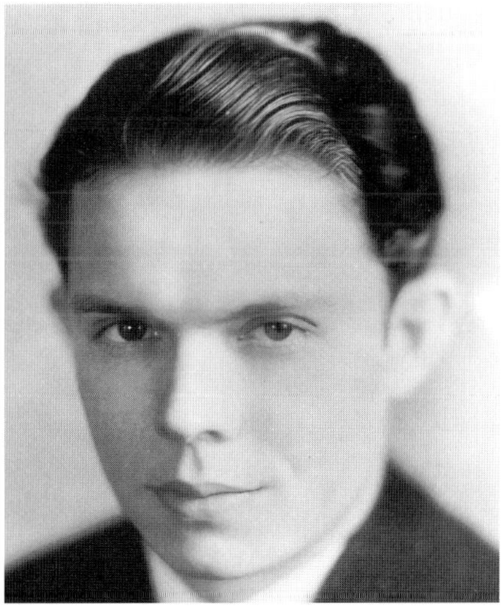

Pianist, arranger and bandleader Joe Haymes (1908-64) always seemed to spend most of the 30's in the wrong places at the wrong times. He was born in Marshfield, Missouri, and started out as a trapeze artist in circus. He was more interested in music though, and taught himself the fundamentals. In the early 30's he formed his own band with many outstanding musicians with whom he went to New York. The band broke up but he formed another one which was so great that Tommy Dorsey took it over in 1935 after his split with his brother Jimmy. Haymes continued to lead various good bands with little success throughout the 30's and eventually gave up as a bandleader and went to Hollywood as a staff arranger for Paramount. In the early 60's he moved to Dallas, where he wrote scores for various band leaders, including Jack Teagarden. Haymes was a very talented arranger who always wrote good music but unfortunately did not understand how to market himself. His bands were either taken over by others or broke up due to poor management.

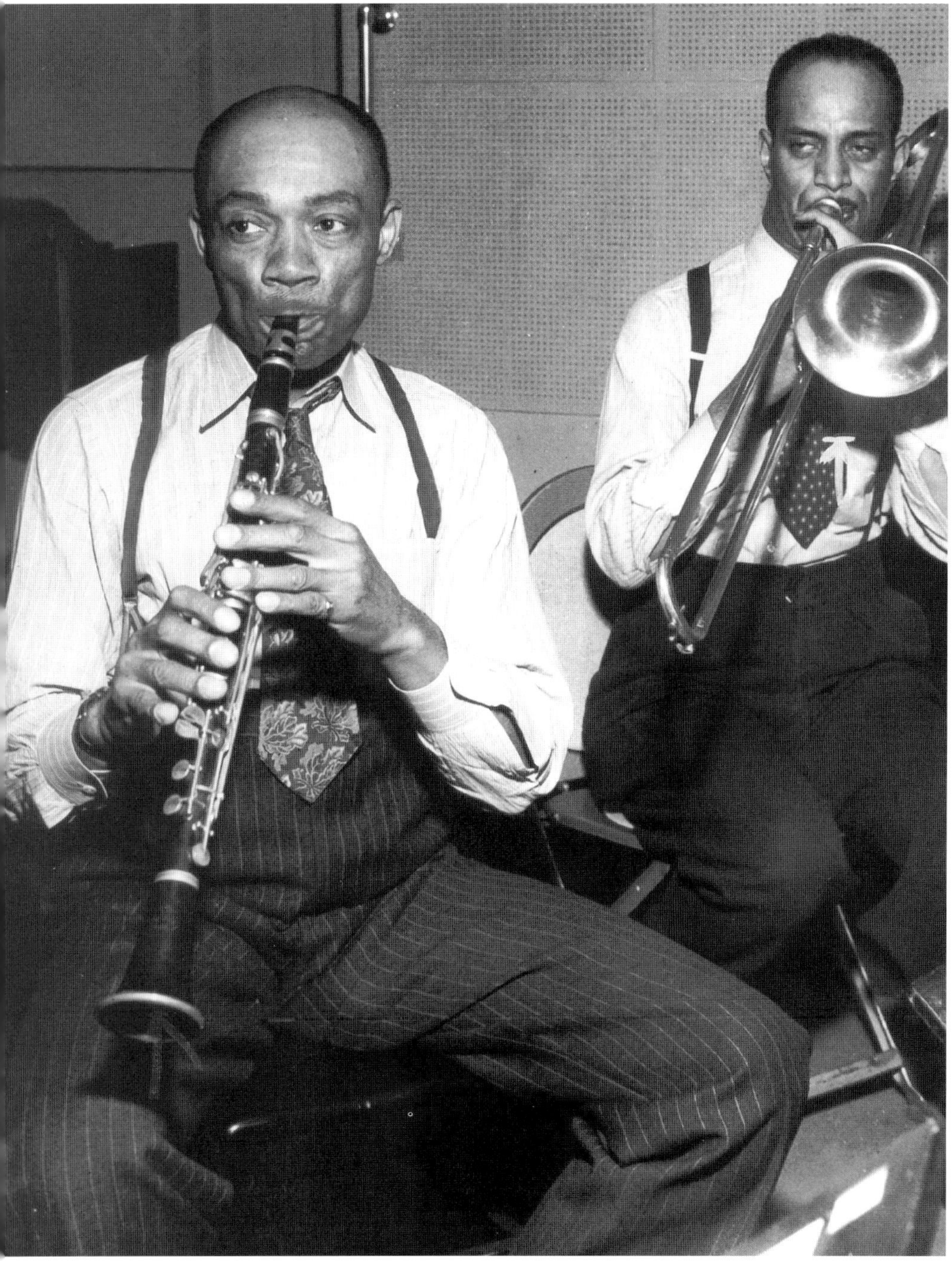

EDMOND HALL

Clarinetist Edmond Hall (1901-1967) was born in New Orleans into a musical family. His father played the clarinet too, like two of his other brothers, Robert and Herbie, while the third one, Clarence, played the tenor saxophone. Edmond Hall worked with various bands in New Orleans before he came to New York in 1928. From 1929-35 he was with Claude Hopkins' big band doubling on alto and baritone saxophone after which he played in small groups for the rest of his life. 1944-46 he led his own band at both New York's Café Society clubs, and 1950-55 he worked with Eddie Condon before he replaced Barney Bigard in Louis Armstrong's All Stars until 1958. Tired of the worldwide touring with Armstrong he settled in Ghana for a while but returned after a year to New York to freelance. He died of a heart attack after shovelling snow from his driveway. Hall was instantly recognizable by his vocal tone and a broad vibrato. He was one of the outstanding clarinetists of the swing era, playing a marvelous blend between the New Orleans style and the more polished swing style as executed by Goodman or Shaw.

Edmond Hall at a Blue Note recording session June 1944 with Art Hodes as the leader. Vic Dickenson is sitting behind him

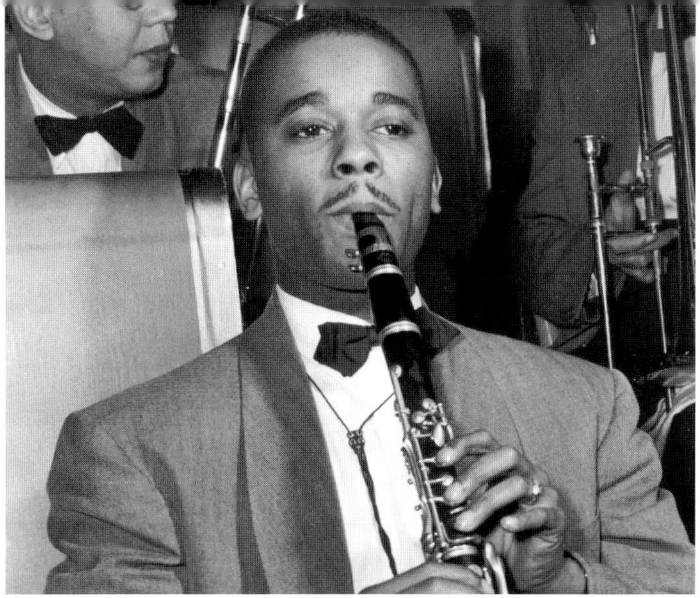

Jimmy Hamilton during a concert with Ellington around 1944 with Juan Tizol in the background.

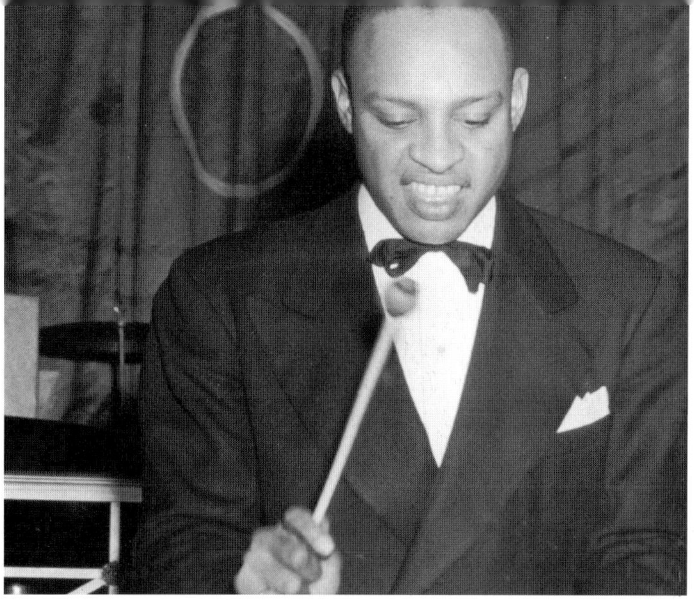

Lionel Hampton during his stay with Goodman, at the time where he also made a series of small-group recordings which belong to the very best of the swing era.

Jimmy Hamilton

A native of Dillon, South Carolina, James "Jimmy" Hamilton (1917-1994) was brought up in Philadelphia where he first studied piano and different brass instruments while playing in local bands. In the late 30's he switched to clarinet and saxophone and played with Lucky Millinder, Jimmy Mundy and Teddy Wilson before joining Duke Ellington in 1943 with whom he stayed for 25 years. He then moved to St. Croix to teach and freelance, but he also toured occasionally with Mercer Ellington, John Carter and his own groups. Hamilton's playing on the clarinet was very fluent but displayed an air of academic correctness with his almost vibratoless tone and lack of passion. By contrast his playing on the tenor saxophone was much in the vein of the rhythm-and-blues players.

Lionel Hampton

Vibraphonist, drummer and bandleader Lionel Hampton (1909-) was born in Louisville, Kentucky, but moved to Chicago with his family as a child. He played drums in local bands before moving to Los Angeles to play at the Cotton Club with Les Hite in the late 20's. During that period he began doubling on the vibraphone, and soon became the leading jazz performer on the instrument. In 1936 he had his own band at the Paradise Café in L.A., and when Benny Goodman heard him there he asked him to join his orchestra. In 1940 Hampton left to form his own big band with which he has performed successfully ever since. Hampton's showmanship is considerable, and his band has always played a happy form of jazz emphasizing high energy combined with great swing.

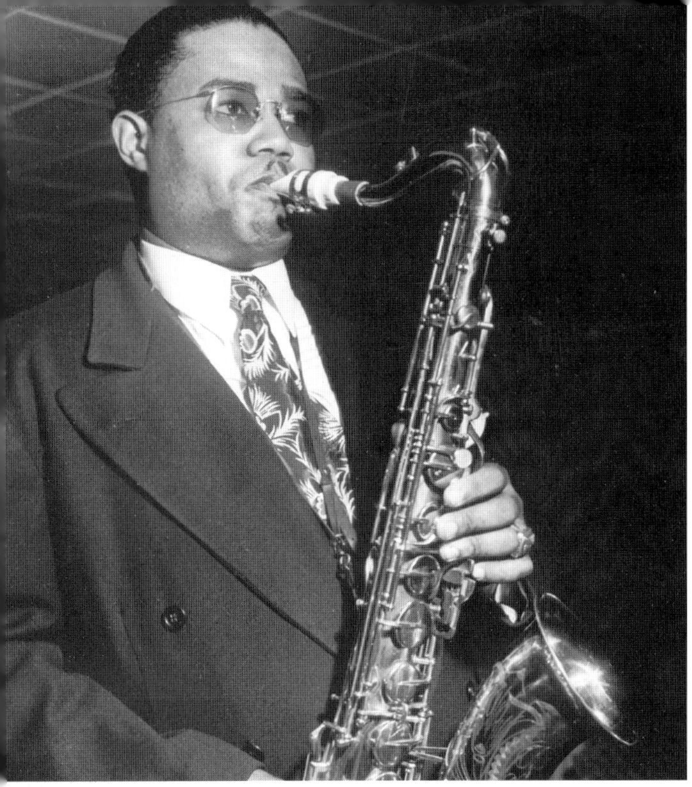

John Hardee

John Hardee (1918-1984) was born into a musical family in Corsicana, Texas. He played piano and mellophone before he tried out several members of the saxophone family until he finally chose the tenor. During his studies at Bishop College he also toured with Don Albert's band, and after his graduation in 1941 he became a band director. He served in the Army with the Signal Corps Band near New York, after which he remained in New York for some time playing with Tiny Grimes and leading his own bands. In 1949 Hardee returned to his home state settling in Dallas where he became a school band director. He also found the time to lead his own bands at local clubs until late 1974, when he quit playing for a while. But in 1975 he resumed his playing and appeared at the jazz festival in Nice that same year.

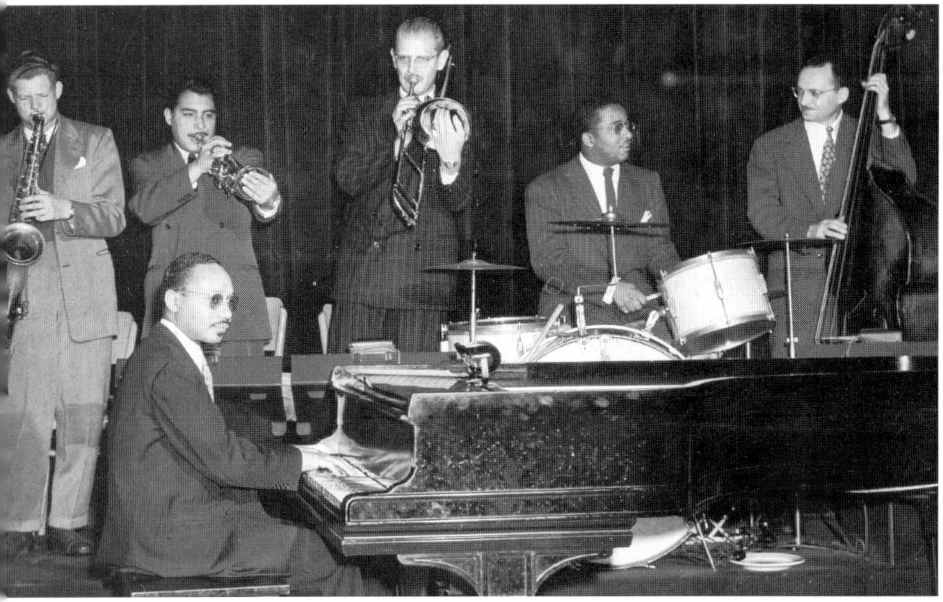

Clyde Hart at a jam session in New York around 1943 with, from the left, Zoot Sims, Sonny Berman, Bill Harris, Kenny Clarke and Sid Weiss.

Clyde Hart

One of the first pianists to adapt his style to the language of bop was Clyde Hart (1910-1945). He was born in Baltimore, Maryland, and played from the early 30's in bands led by Jap Allen, Blanche Calloway, and briefly with McKinney's Cotton Pickers. In 1936 he settled in New York where he played with Stuff Smith, Roy Eldridge, Lester Young and Frankie Newton before joining John Kirby. In 1944 he worked with Tiny Grimes but also led his own band, until he became too ill to perform. He died of tuberculosis. During the early 40's Hart was a regular at Minton's Playhouse, where the new bop took form, and also participated in several jam sessions elsewhere.

ÅKE HASSELGÅRD

Swedish clarinetist Åke Hasselgård (1922-1948) – or Stan Hasselgard as he called himself in the USA – was a native of Sundsvall. He studied music at Uppsala University and played with Arthur Österwall (1944-45) and Simon Brehm (1946-47). After his master's degree in the summer of 1947 he moved to New York where he sat in at various clubs along 52nd Street, introduced by Timme Rosenkrantz. In August he moved to Los Angeles to work with Johnny White, and also played concerts with Count Basie. In the spring of 1948 Benny Goodman heard him, brought him along to New York, and formed a new septet featuring himself with Hasselgård, Wardell Gray and Teddy Wilson. Due to very poor business, Goodman disbanded the group in October after which Hasselgård fronted a quintet with Max Roach. He was killed in a car accident outside Chicago. Hasselgård was a virtuoso clarinetist who started out as a lyrical Benny Goodman disciple but also became influenced by bop during his USA stay.

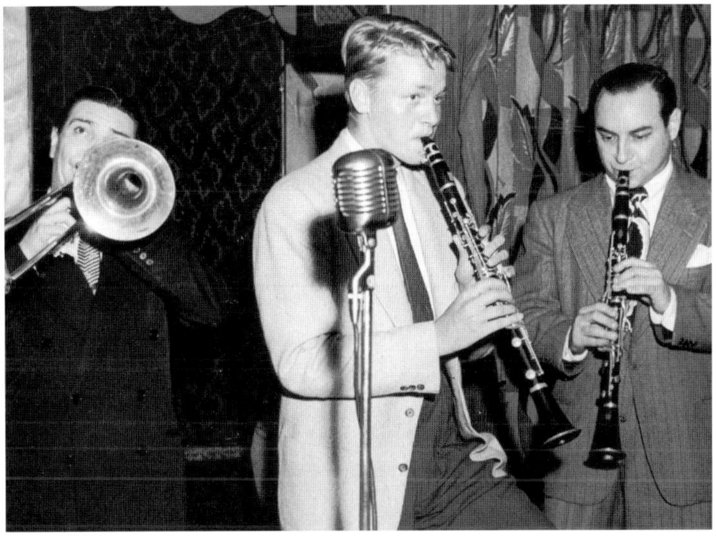

Jamsession at the Famous Door, 52nd Street, New York, July 1947. Hasselgård is between Jack Teagarden and Peanuts Hucko. Hasselgård used the photo as a letter to Nils Hellström, editor of the Swedish music magazine "Estrad"; on the back he has written (translated from Swedish): "I go to California today by car. How do you like that? Benny, Tommy D., King Cole are there just now. Wow! Regards, Åke."

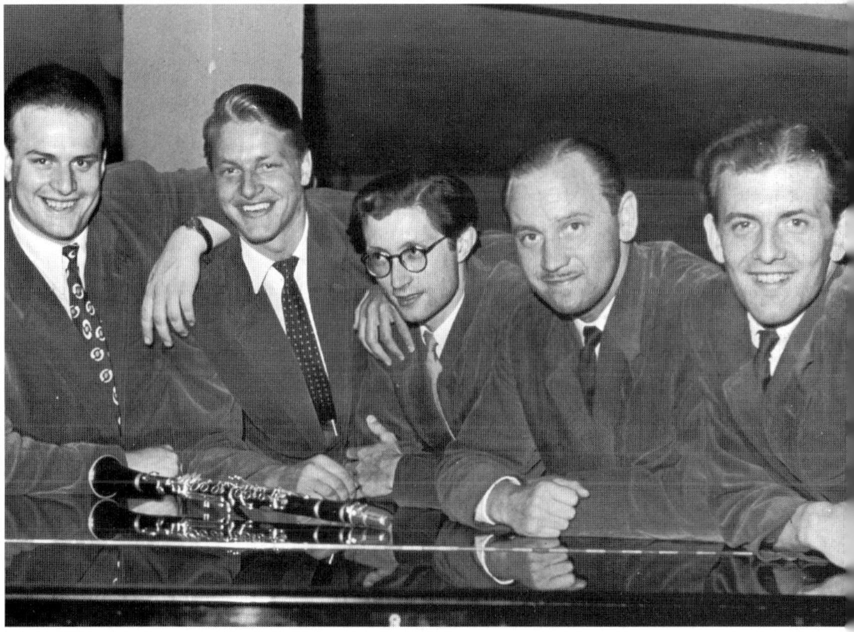

Hasselgård with Simon Brehm's Quintet at Berzelii-Terrassen in Stockholm, in the early Spring of 1946. From left Simon Brehm (b), Hasselgård, Per-Erik Sparrings (g), Thore Swanerud (vib), Bertil Frylmark (dr).

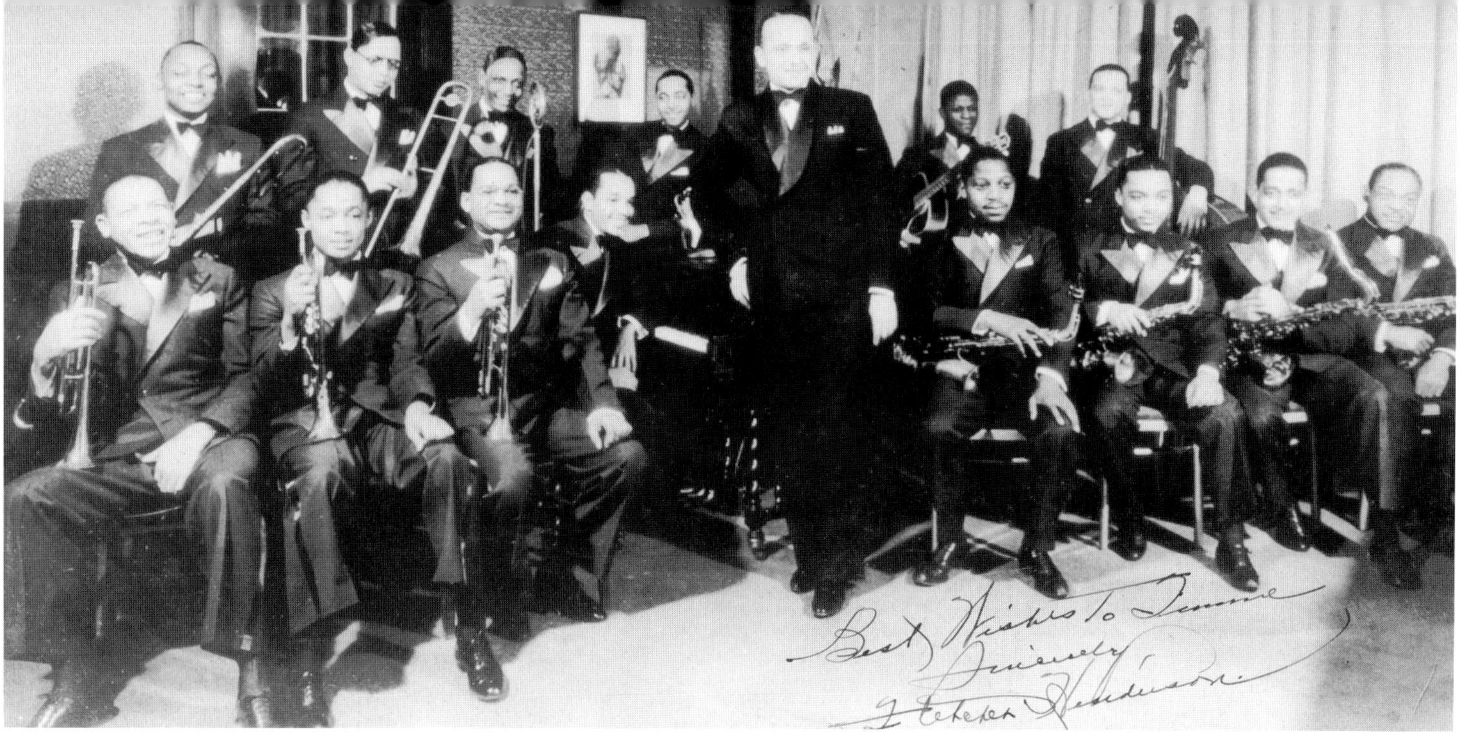

Fletcher Henderson's orchestra in late 1933. In the back row from left: Keg Johnson and Claude Jones (tb), Charles Holland (voc), Walter Johnson (dr), Bernard Addison (g) and John Kirby (b). In front: Henry "Red" Allen, Joe Thomas and Russell Smith (tp), Horace Henderson (p), Fletcher Henderson (standing), Hilton Jefferson, Russell Procope, Buster Bailey and Coleman Hawkins (reeds). *Best Wishes To Timme. Sincerely, Fletcher Hernderson.*

Fletcher Henderson

Pianist, composer, arranger and bandleader Fletcher Hamilton Henderson (1897-1952) was born in Cuthbert, Georgia. In his youth he studied classical music with his mother, who was a piano teacher, and graduated from Atlanta University with degrees in chemistry and mathematics. He then went to New York to find work in these fields, but being black this was impossible, so instead he was employed by the Pace-Handy Music Company as a song demonstrator. Around the same time, in the early 20's, he joined the Black Swan, the first black recording company, as its musical director, organizing recording sessions and also backing singers. This led to his forming his own band, and in 1924 he was offered to play permanently at New York's Roseland Ballroom, and he remained there the following decade. He continued to lead bands until 1939 when he joined Benny Goodman as a full-time arranger. From 1941 he occasionally led bands again, but in 1950 he suffered a severe stroke which left him partially paralyzed until his death. Henderson's was one of the most important of the pioneering big bands. It always had first-rate soloists, and the arrangements were generally of a high standard and very demanding, too, because he often used to write in difficult keys.

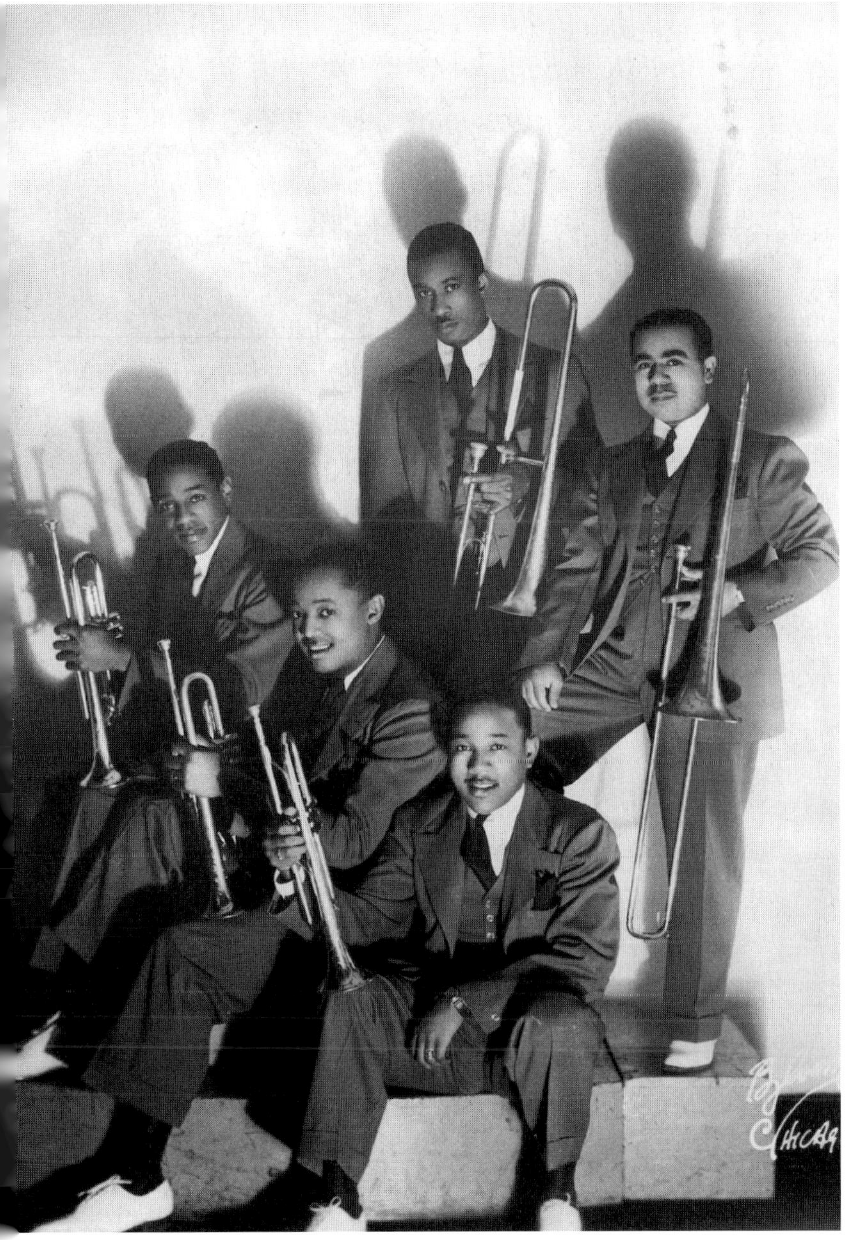

Fletcher Henderson's brass section 1936: Dick Vance, Joe Thomas and Roy Eldridge (tp), Ed Cuffee and Fernando Arbello (tb).

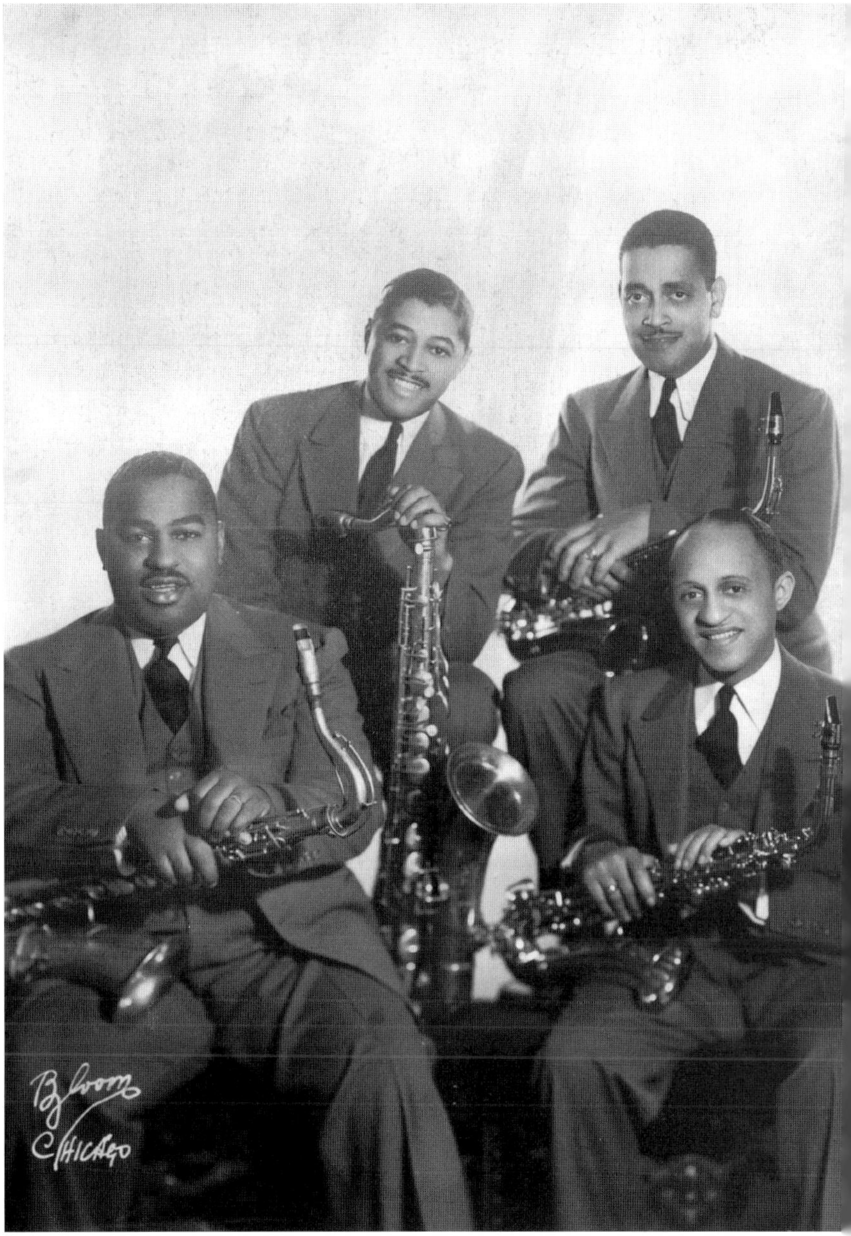

Fletcher Henderson's reed section 1936: Leon "Chu" Berry and Elmer Williams (ts), Buster Bailey and Don Pasquall (as).

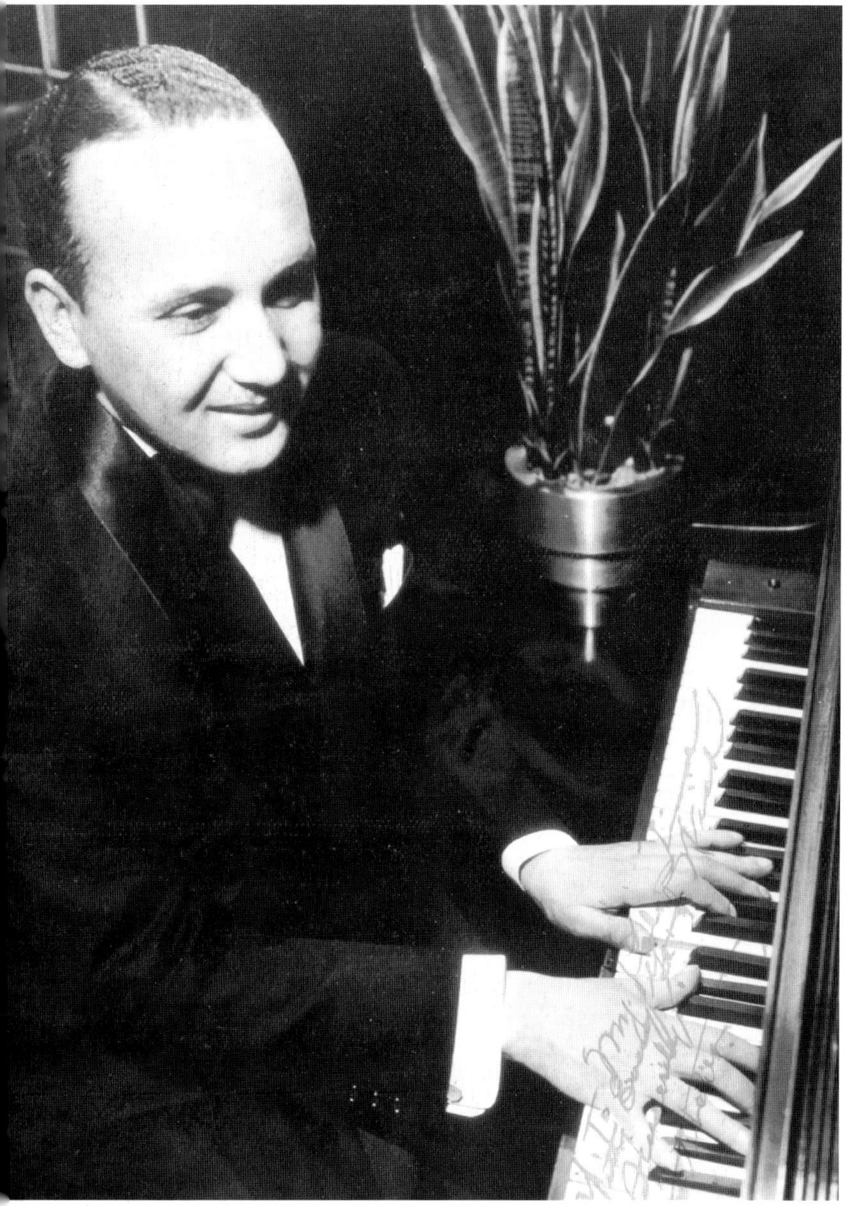

Publicity shot of Fletcher Henderson 1934. Up until this time he had been his own manager, but from 1934-39 he was managed by the Moe Gale Agency. *My Pal Timme With Every Good Wish. Sincerely, Fletcher.*

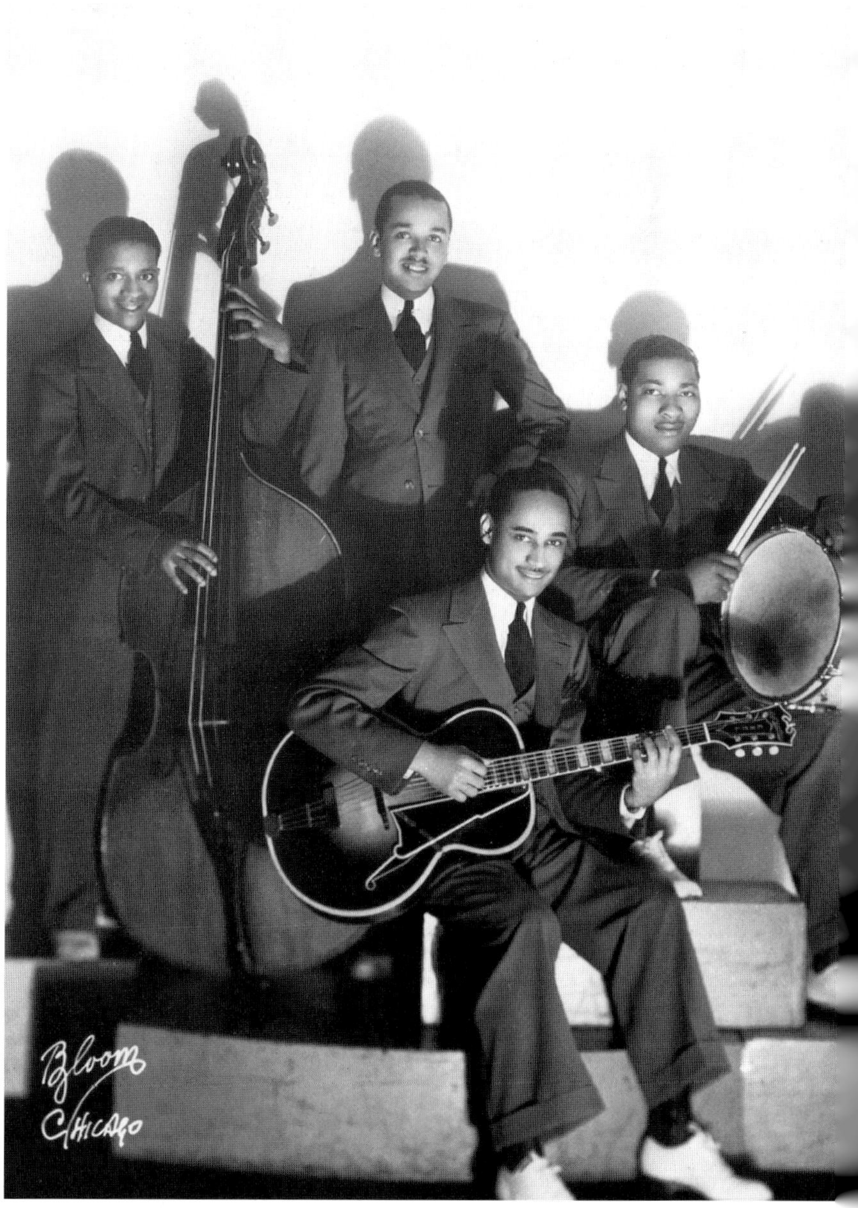

Fletcher Henderson's rhythm section 1936: Israel Crosby (b), Horace Henderson (p), Bob Lessey (g) and Sidney Catlett (dr).

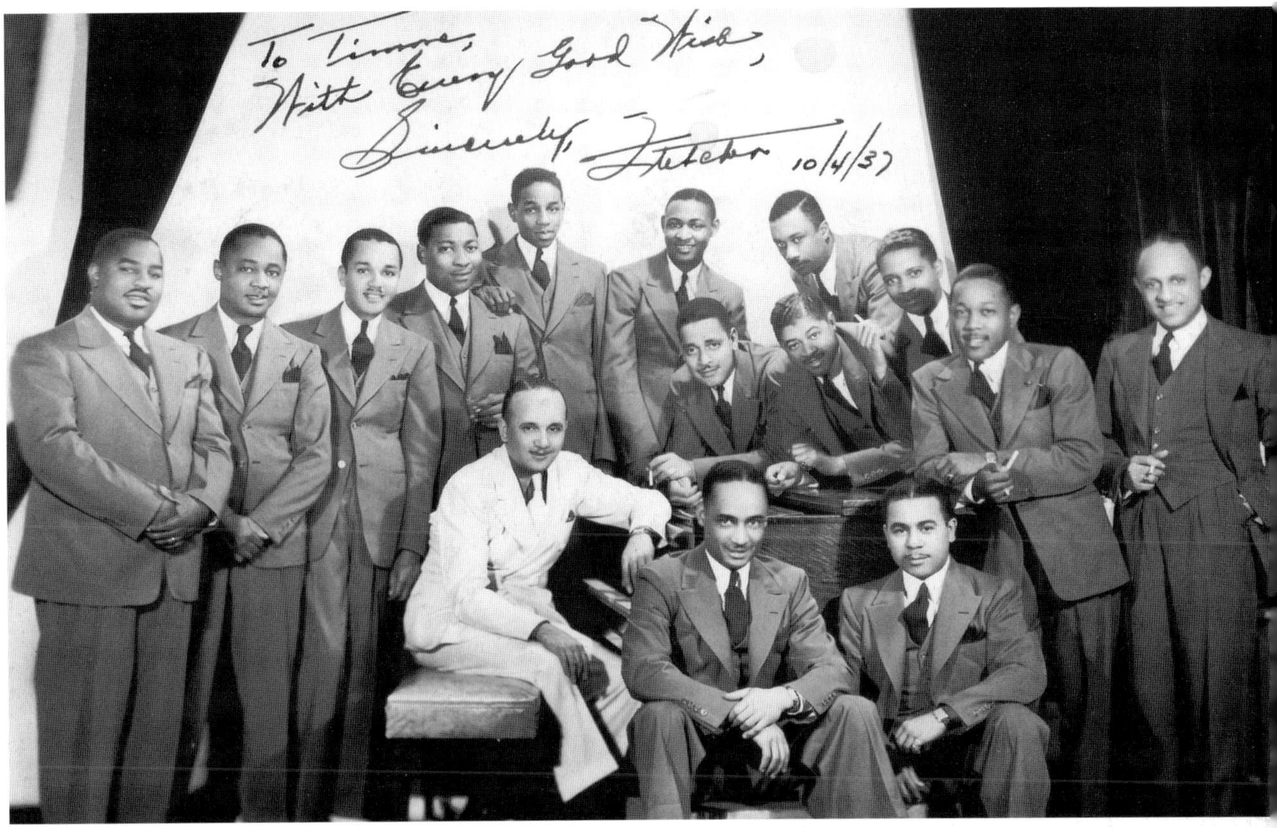

Fletcher Henderson's orchestra in 1936, at the time where they played at the Grand Terrace Café in Chicago. From left: Leon "Chu" Berry (ts), Joe Thomas (tp), Horace Henderson (p), Sidney Catlett (dr), Dick Vance (tp), Teddy Lewis (voc), Buster Bailey (cl, as) at the piano, Ed Cuffee (tb), Elmer Williams (ts) at the piano, Israel Crosby (b), Roy Eldridge (tp) at the piano, Don Pasquall (as). In the front row: Fletcher Henderson (p), Bob Lessey (g), Fernando Arbello (tb). *To Timme, With Every Good Wish, Sincerely, Fletcher. 10/4/37.*

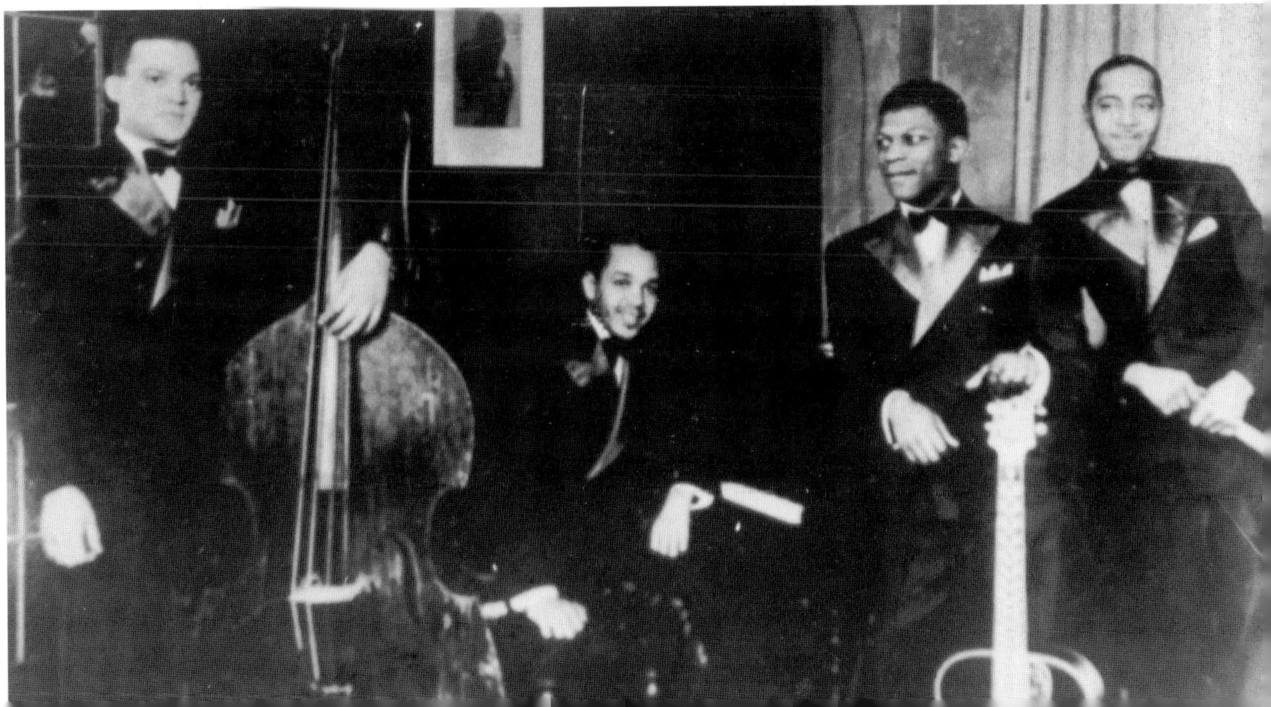

The Fletcher Henderson rhythm section 1933-34. From left: John Kirby (b), Horace Henderson (p), Bernard Addison (g), Walter Johnson (dr).

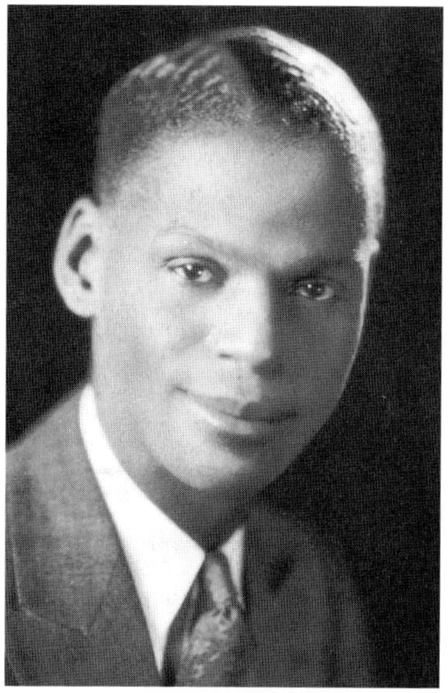

EARL HINES

Pianist and bandleader Earl Kenneth Hines (1903-1983) first studied trumpet with his father and then piano with his mother. He was born in Duquesne, Pennsylvania and played professionally from 1918. In 1923 he moved to Chicago where he played with several leading bands, such as those led by Sammy Stewart, Erskine Tate and Carroll Dickerson. In 1928 he formed his own band to play at the Grand Terrace where he stayed for the following decade. He continued to lead big bands until 1948 when he joined Louis Armstrong's All-Stars. From 1951 he led his own groups, and despite bouts of illness worked right up until the weekend before he died. Hines was one of the greatest pianists after Tatum and a stylist who strongly influenced jazz piano playing.

Earl Hines in 1928 at the Grand Terrace in Chicago at the time he formed his own band.

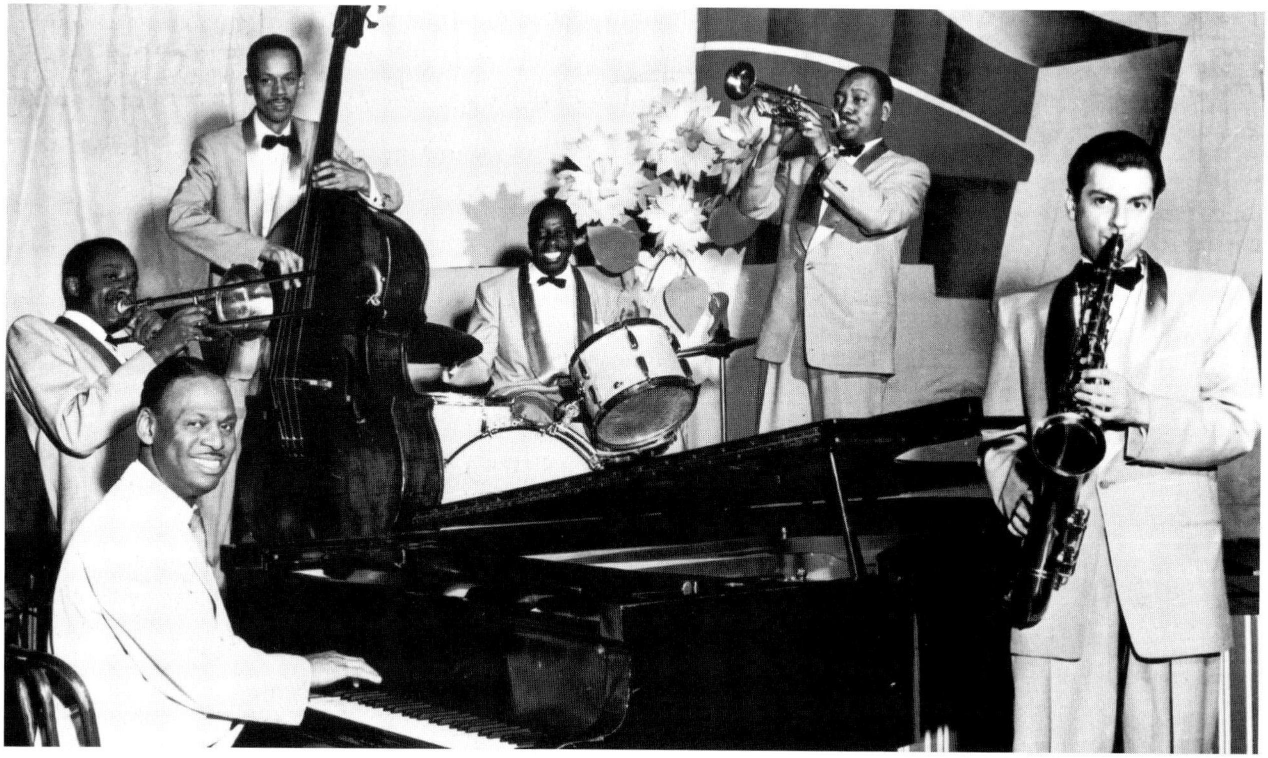

Earl Hines and His All-Stars in Hollywood 1953. This sextet included Benny Green (tb), Tommy Potter (b), Osie Johnson (dr), Jonah Jones (tp) and Aaron Sachs (ts).

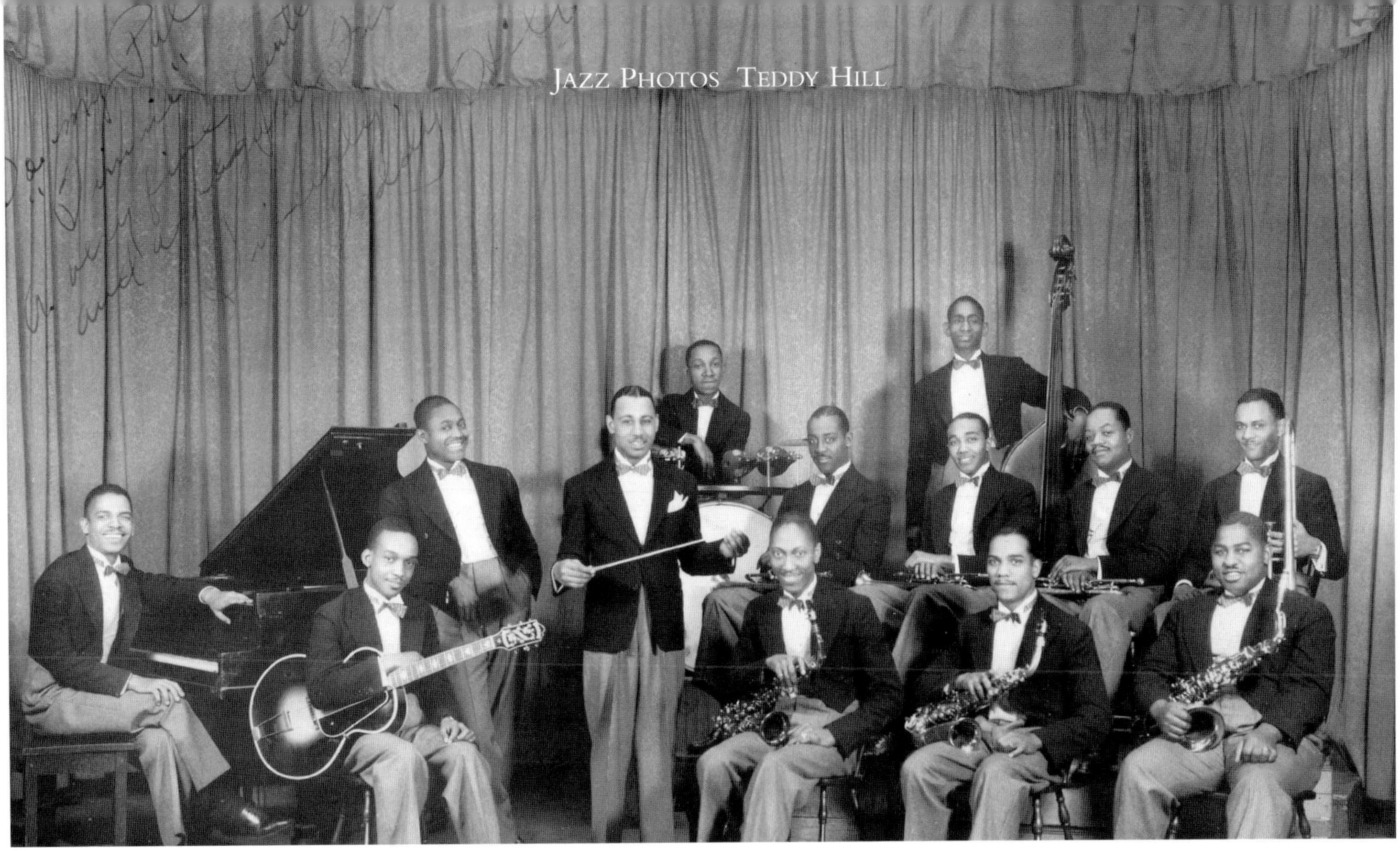

On this 1935 publicity photo of the Teddy Hill Orchestra the personel is Sam Allen (p), John W. Smith (g), Bill Beason (dr), Richard Fullbright (b), Shad Collins, Bill Dillard, Frankie Newton (tp), Joe Britton (tb), Howard Johnson and Russell Procope (as), and Chu Berry (ts). Teddy Hill holds the baton, and the man leaning against the piano is unidentified but probably the band's vocalist. *To my Pal "Timmie". A very fine Gentleman and a regular fellow. Sincerely, Teddy Hill.*

Teddy Hill

Born in Birmingham, Alabama tenor saxophonist Teddy Hill (1909-78) came to New York in 1927. During the next years he played with George Howe, Luis Russell, and James P. Johnson before organizing his own big band in 1932. The band was successful due to Hill's good management and clever sidemen, who over the years numbered such great soloists as Roy Eldridge, Bill Coleman, Frankie Newton, Shad Collins and Dizzy Gillespie (trumpets), Chu Berry, Russell Procope, Cecil Scott (saxes), and Dicky Wells (trombone). The band played regularly at the Savoy Ballroom and toured England and France (1937). In 1940 Hill broke up his band to become manager of Minton's Playhouse in Harlem, which, due to Hill's encouragement of jam sessions over the following years, gave the club a reputation as the birthplace of bop.

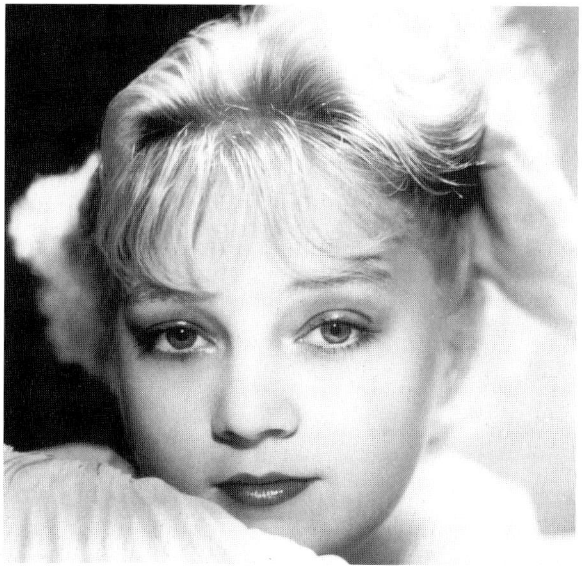

INA RAY HUTTON

Singer and bandleader Odessa Cowan "Ina Ray Hutton" (1916-1984) was born in Chicago into a musical family; her mother played piano professionally. As a teenager Hutton sang and danced in several productions in Broadway theatres until manager Irving Mills signed her to front an all-girl swing band in 1934, billed as Ina Ray Hutton and Her Melodears. The band became extremely popular and she continued to lead it through the 30's. From 1940 she led a male big band but had to disband in 1944. She married trumpeter Randy Brooks and moved to the West Coast, after which she sang as a solo act and only sporadically organized other bands. She retired from showbusiness in the late 50's.

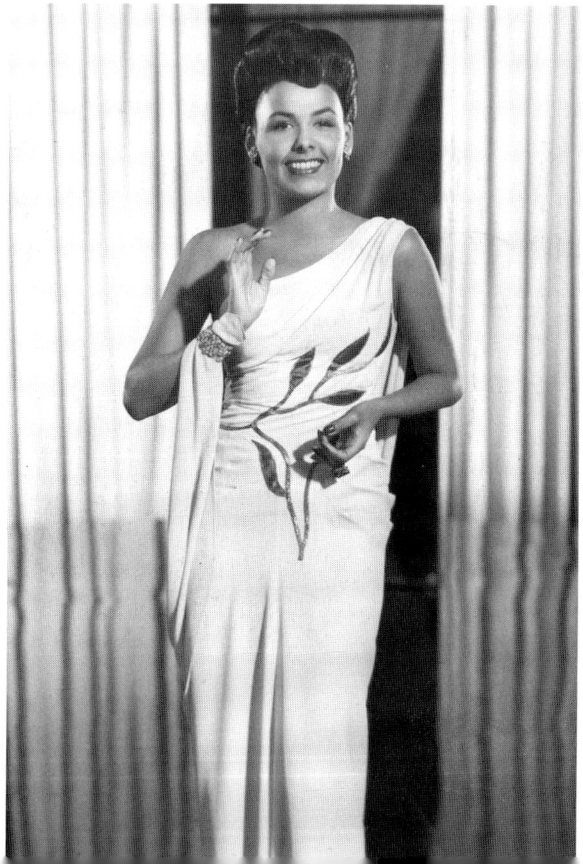

LENA HORNE

Lena Horne (1917-) was born in Brooklyn, N.Y. and started her career as a dancer at the Cotton Club in 1934. In 1935 she joined Noble Sissle's orchestra as a singer, and the winter 1940-41 she was with Artie Shaw, after which she became very popular at the Café Society in New York. From the early 40's she began appearing in movies, starring in "Cabin in the Sky", "Two Girls and a Sailor", and "Ziegfeld Follies". In 1947 she married her musical director Lennie Hayton, and henceforth she became an international star appearing at the best concert halls and clubs in America and in Europe. In 1957-59 she appeared in the Broadway musical "Jamaica", and she had a one-woman show on Broadway for more than a year in the early 70's. Although she has recorded with many jazz musicians and her voice has many jazz qualities, she is a popular rather than a jazz singer.

LES HITE

The best known and most successful of the West Coast bands in the 30's is probably that of Les Hite (1903-62). Hite was born in DuQuoin, Illinois but came to California in 1925 with a show. His big break came in 1930 when he formed his Californian Syncopators to play at Frank Sebastian's New Cotton Club in Culver City. It became his base for several years, and his band would often back guest stars like Louis Armstrong and Fats Waller. In 1939 Hite broke up his band and took over Floyd Turnham's adding a couple of new men, but in 1945 he gave up music to organize his own successful booking agency. During the years many great musicians played in Les Hite's orchestra, among others Lionel Hampton, Lawrence Brown, Marshal Royal, Dizzy Gillespie, Britt Woodman, Joe Wilder, and Al Morgan.

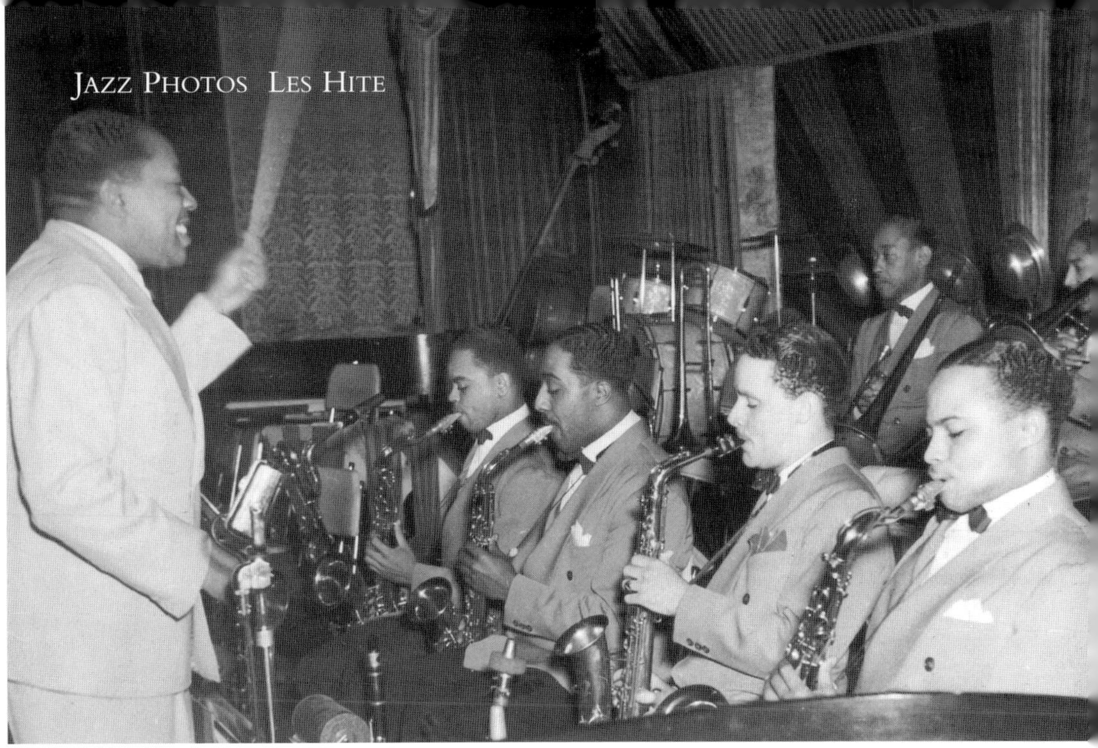

This picture was taken while Les Hite and His Orchestra guested New York in June 1940. Hite is conducting, and in the sax sextion is from left, Sol Moore, Floyd Turnham, Quedellis Martyn and Rodgers Hurd, while the two trombonists are Allen Durham and Britt Woodman.

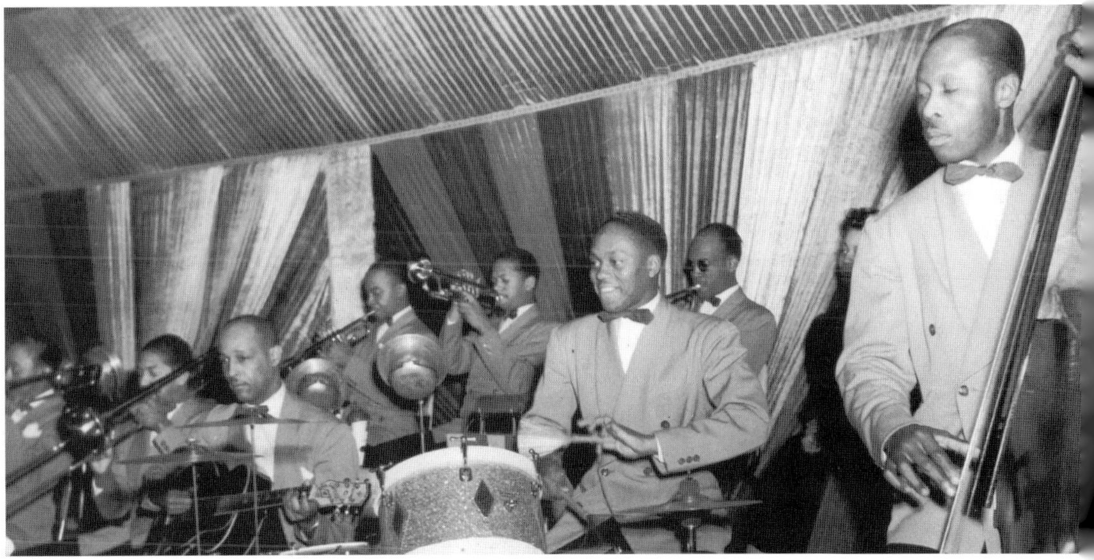

Another photo from the same evening showing the rest of the Les Hite band. From left: Allen Durham and Britt Woodman (tb), Frank Pashley (g), Walter Williams, Forrest Powell (tp), Oscar Bradley (dr), Paul Campbell (tp) and Al Morgan (b).

CLAUDE HOPKINS

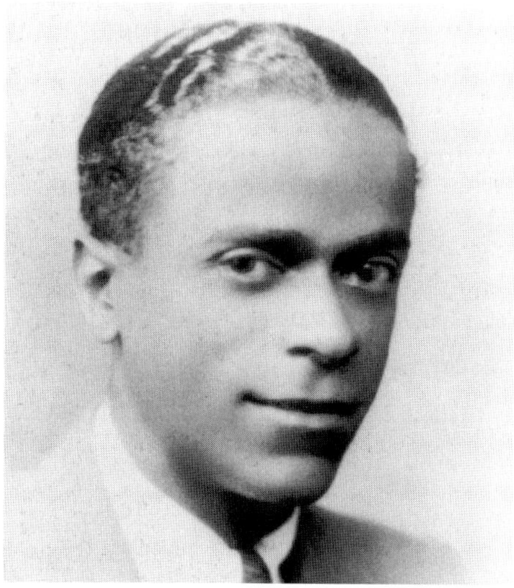

Claude Hopkins around 1932 when he began recording for Columbia.

Pianist, composer, arranger and bandleader Claude Driskett Hopkins (1903-1984) led one of the most popular black bands of the 30's: He was born in Alexandria, Virginia and studied medicine and music at Howard University in Washington. He led his own bands from the early 20's, and in 1925 toured Europe with the Revue Nègre (with Josephine Baker and Sidney Bechet and others). Back in the USA he continued leading his own groups, which enjoyed extended engagements at New York's Savoy Ballroom, Roseland Ballrom, and Cotton Club. In 1947 he disbanded his big band and continued leading small groups, but he also appeared as a sideman with Henry "Red" Allen, Herman Autrey, and Wild Bill Davison. He continued to perform into the 80's, touring Europe and appearing at several festivals. Hopkins played in an easy, flowing, gracious style, covering the jazz piano from Fats Waller's stride to Count Basie's spare delicacy.

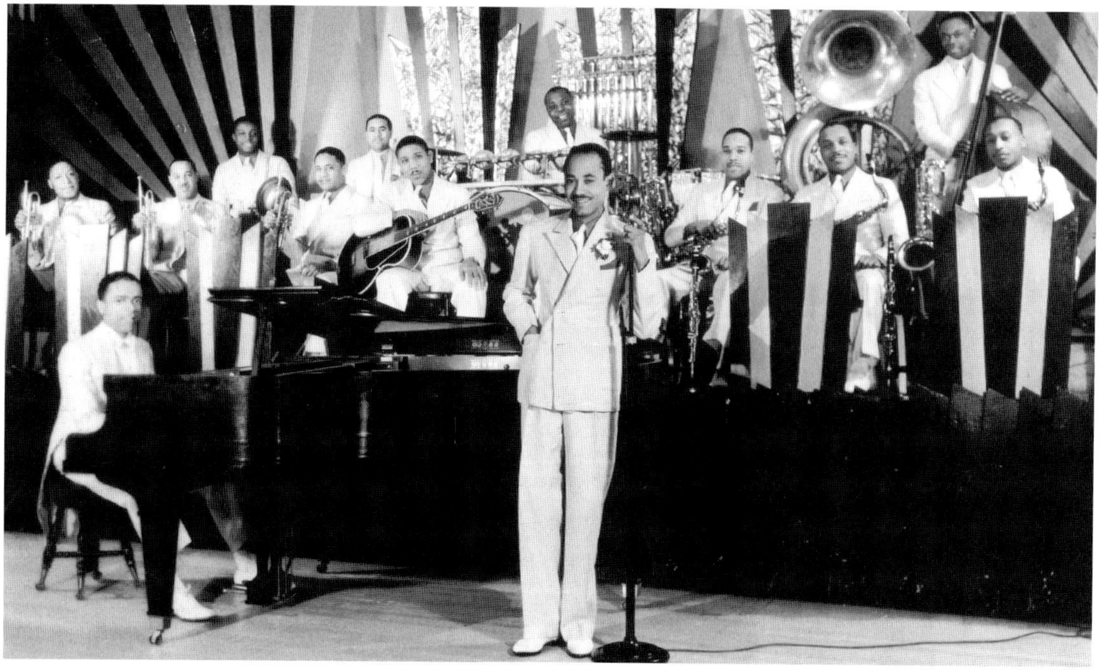

Claude Hopkins and His Orchestra at its peak 1933-34, probably during one of its film appearances. In the backrow from the left: Fred Norman and Fernando Arbello (tb), Pete Jacobs (dr) and Henry Turner (tu, b). In the front row: Albert Snaer, Sylvester Lewis and Ovie Alston (tp), Walter Jones (g), Gene Johnson (as, cl), Bobby Sands (ts, cl) and Edmond Hall (as, bars, cl). On the floor, Claude Hopkins at the piano and singer Orlando Robeson at the microphone

Billie Holiday performing at a concert, probably in the late 40's.

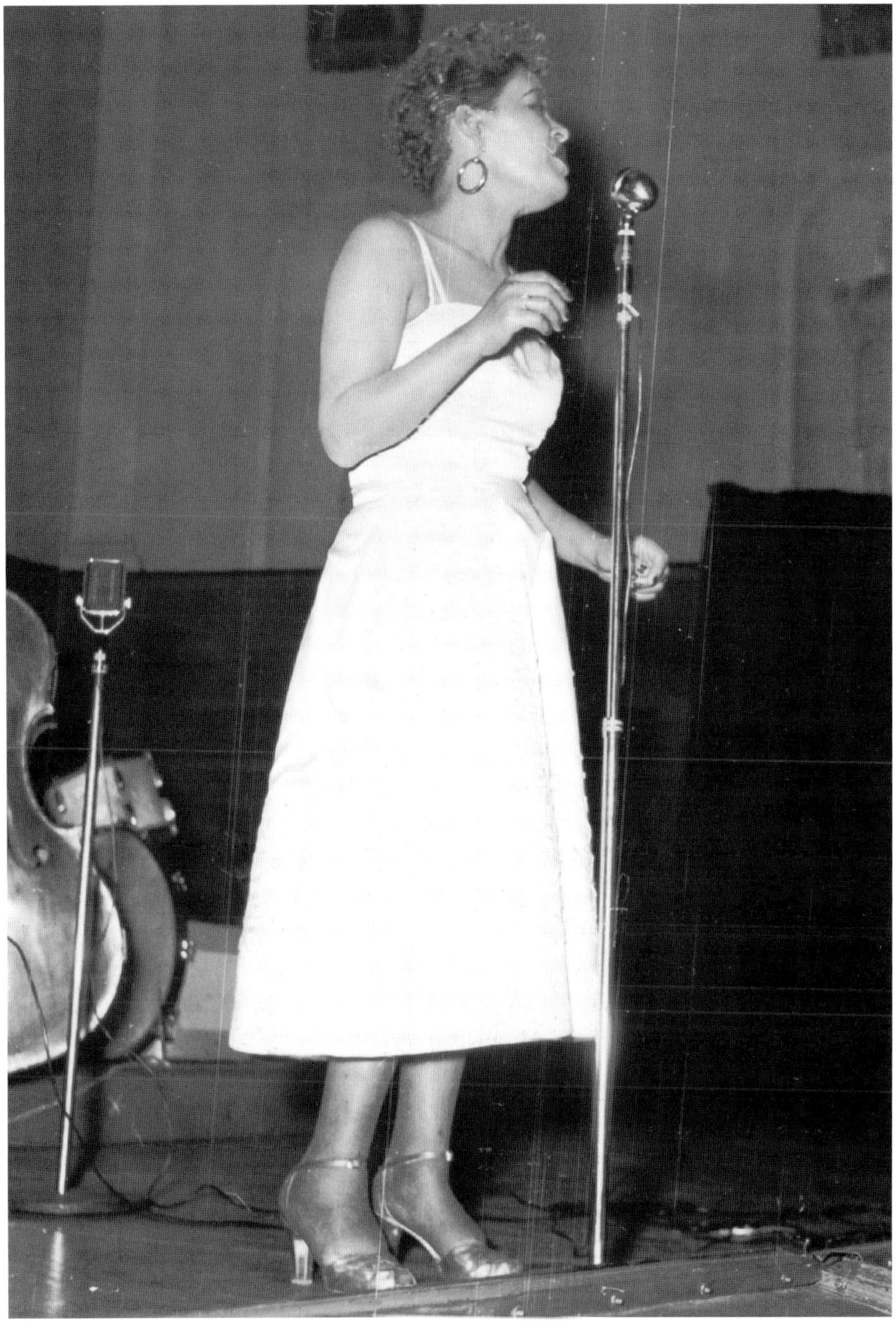

BILLIE HOLIDAY

Singer Eleonora Fagan "Billie" Holiday (1915-1959) is one of the greatest of all jazz singers, a unique interpreter who understood how to create gems out of otherwise unremarkable popular songs by rephrasing them like a jazz musician. She was born in Baltimore, Maryland but moved to New York in 1928 and began singing in clubs. She soon began to gain a reputation, and in 1933 she made her first recordings with Benny Goodman. In 1937 she was with Count Basie, and in 1938 with Artie Shaw, but from1939 she became a solo act working with her own trio. Personal problems and insecurity gave her a drug habit and drinking problems, and she was arrested several times during the 40's and 50's, spent time in prisons and also took cures at sanatoriums. She made her final public appearance at the Phoenix Theater in New York six weeks before she died. During her performances she knew how to create many moods, and her hard life gave her the experiences which she conveyed through her songs to the audience. She sang what she lived.

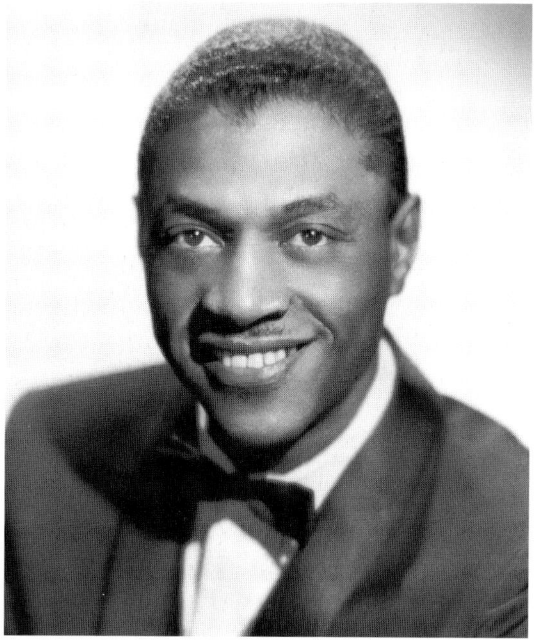

EDDIE HEYWOOD

Pianist, arranger and bandleader Edward "Eddie" Heywood (1915-1989) was born into a musical family in Atlanta Georgia. His father played several instruments and was musical director for the vaudeville team Butterbeans and Susie. Eddie Heywood played professionally from the age of 14, often substituting for his father, and in 1934 he joined Clarence Love's orchestra with whom he came to New York in 1937. After freelancing for awhile he was with Benny Carter 1939-40, and from 1941-47 he led his own successful sextet at various venues in New York – Village Vanguard, Café Society Downtown, the Three Deuces and others – and also worked in California. In 1947 arthritic paralysis forced him to quit playing but he recovered and had his own trio from 1950. During the late 60's he suffered another attack, but he recovered and up through the 80's played in clubs in New York and New England.

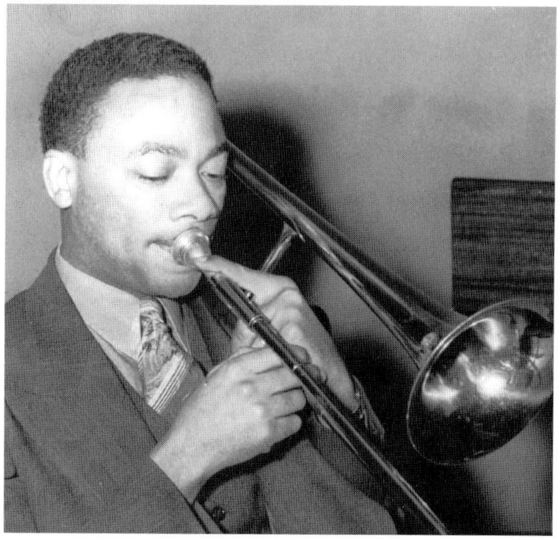

J.C. Higginbotham in New York, probably at a recording session in the early 40's.

J.C. HIGGINBOTHAM

Jack "J.C." Higginbotham (1906-1973) was one of the best of the swing trombonists. He was born in Social Circle, near Atlanta, Georgia, and worked in many southern and midwestern bands before coming to New York in the late 20's. From 1928 to 1931 he played with Luis Russell, and for the rest of the 30's he was with other leading bands, such as those led by Chick Webb, Fletcher Henderson, Benny Carter, Lucky Millinder and Louis Armstrong. From the 40's he played in small groups in New York, often with Henry "Red" Allen, and in the mid-50's he led his own band in Cleveland. From 1956 he again played in New York clubs, but illness forced him to quit playing in 1971. Higginbotham played in a legato style modelled after Jimmy Harrison, but more extrovert with a forceful tone and a temperamental attack.

JACK HYLTON

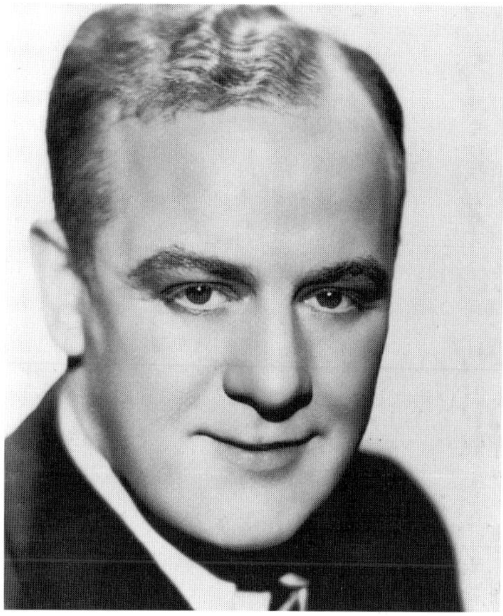

Pianist and bandleader Jack Hylton (1892-1965) led one of the most successful British bands between the two world wars. He was born in Great Lever near Bolton, and worked from his teenage years in pantomime, in cinemas and as a freelance musician in various clubs. From 1921 he led his own band which, becoming full-sized in 1924, achieved a huge commercial success equivalent to that of Paul Whiteman's show band. Hylton made several annual tours of the continent until the outbreak of World War II, and also in 1935-36 organized a band in the USA. From 1940, after disbanding his band, Hylton worked as a theatrical producer of various London stage shows. Though Hylton only flirted with jazz – his bands played mostly popular-oriented music – he was responsible for the visits of Duke Ellington (1933) and Coleman Hawkins (1934) to England.

WOODY HERMAN

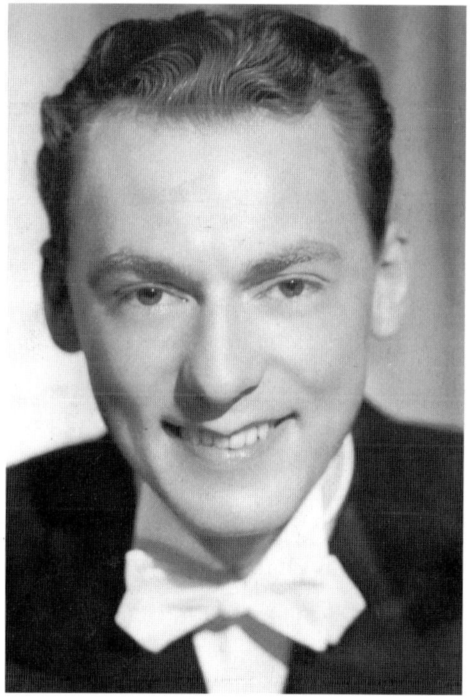

Clarinetist, saxophonist, singer and bandleader Woodrow Charles "Woody" Herman (1913-1987) was a native of Milwaukee, Wisconsin and began in show business as a child singer in vaudeville. From the age of eleven he took up the saxophone, which he played in numerous touring bands from the age of fifteen. From 1934-36 he was with Isham Jones after which he led his own bands for the rest of his life. Herman was one of the very few bandleaders who managed to survive the big band decline in the 40's and who was also capable of following the stylistic developments through the decades. Coming from the swing era, his band played bop charts in the late 40's, several tunes by Horace Silver in the 50's, pieces by Monk, Mingus and Herbie Hancock in the 60's, and Coltrane compositions and jazz-rock numbers in the 70's. He was also a great talent scout who over the years employed a long list of outstanding musicians. Though the style of the band changed, Herman's own playing was always rooted in the swing style.

SPIKE HUGHES

English composer, bass player and writer Patrick Cairns "Spike" Hughes (1908-1987). He was a Londoner, classically trained, and extremely busy from the late 20's, composing, writing arrangements, playing and touring. 1931-32 he was with Jack Hylton, and in 1933 he went to New York, writing songs and recording several masterpieces with Benny Carter, Coleman Hawkins, Henry "Red" Allen and Chu Berry. He returned to England in 1934 to concentrate on classical music and writing criticism, and never dealt with jazz again. Among his larger works are "A Harlem Symphony" and the jazz ballet "High Yellow", in which classical musicians and jazz musicians are matched.

ART HODES

Ukrainian born pianist Arthur W. "Art" Hodes (1904-1993) came to the USA as an infant. He grew up in Chicago where he received musical training, and from the early 20's played as a soloist at the Rainbow Café as well as with the Wolverines, Wingy Manone and others. In 1938 he moved to New York, and from 1941 he led his own bands. He also taught the old jazz, becoming a lecturer at schools and colleges, had weekly radio programs, edited the magazine "The Jazz Record" and in 1946 founded a record label of the same name. In 1950 he returned to Chicago where he lived for the rest of his life, playing solo, leading bands, hosting TV series, and teaching piano. He continued to tour internationally right up to the year of his death.

HORACE HENDERSON

Pianist, arranger and bandleader Horace W. Henderson (1904-1988) was, like his brother Fletcher, born in Cuthbert, Georgia. He organized his first band in the 20's while still studying at Wilberforce University, and he continued to lead bands into the 70's. In between he worked as a sideman in other bands, most notably that of his brother, for whom he played and wrote arrangements from 1931 to 1947. His arrangements were often used by other great bandleaders, such as Benny Goodman, Charlie Barnett, Tommy Dorsey, Earl Hines and Jimmie Lunceford and the Casa Loma Orchestra. *To Timmie With My Best Wishes. Horace Henderson.*

ALBERTA HUNTER

Alberta Hunter (1895-1984) was born in Memphis, Tennessee. 11 years old she ran away to Chicago and began singing professionally in nightclubs and cabarets from the age of 14. In 1921 she went to New York appearing at theatres and recording with some of the best musicians available, such as Louis Armstrong, Sidney Bechet, Fats Waller and Fletcher Henderson. Between 1927 and 1937 she was in Europe most of the time, and from 1944 to 1953 she toured all over the world for USO. In 1956 she graduated as a nurse after which she worked at the Goldwater Memorial Hospital on Welfare Island in New York. From 1977 she worked full-time as a musician again, singing regularly at the Cookery in Greenwich Village until a couple of months before her death.

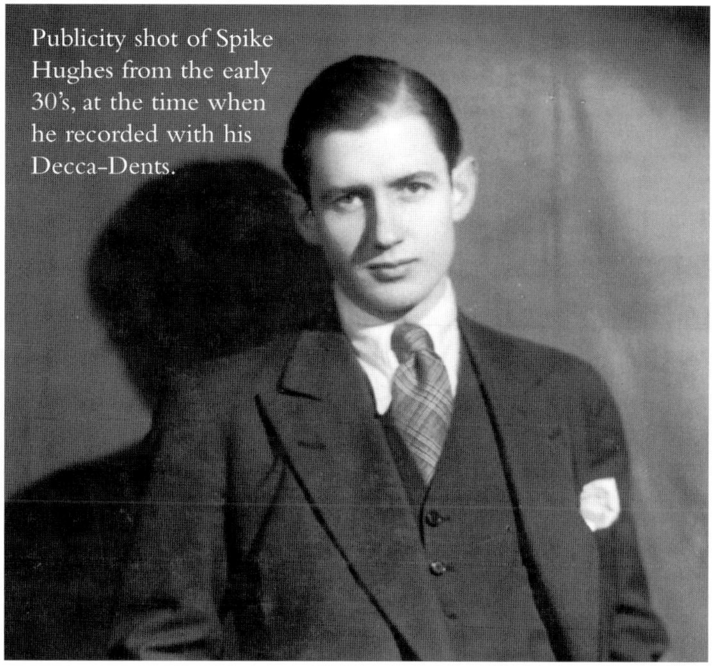

Publicity shot of Spike Hughes from the early 30's, at the time when he recorded with his Decca-Dents.

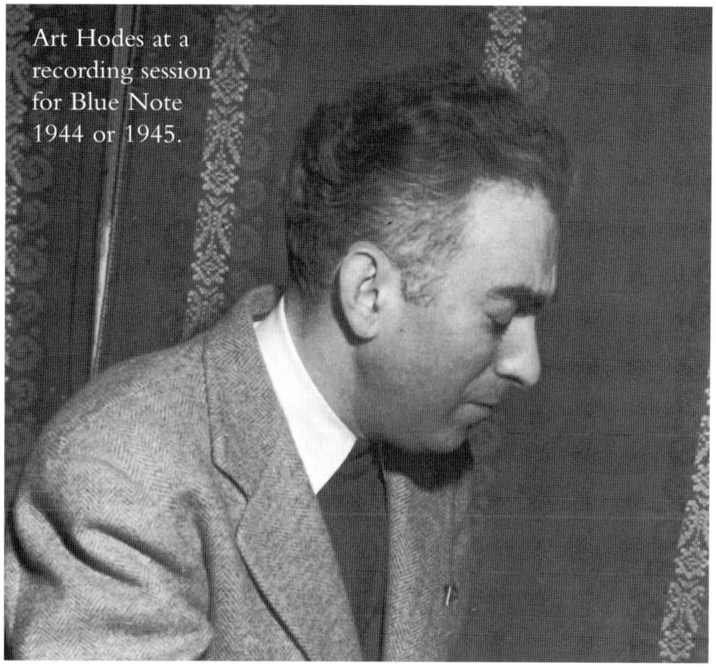

Art Hodes at a recording session for Blue Note 1944 or 1945.

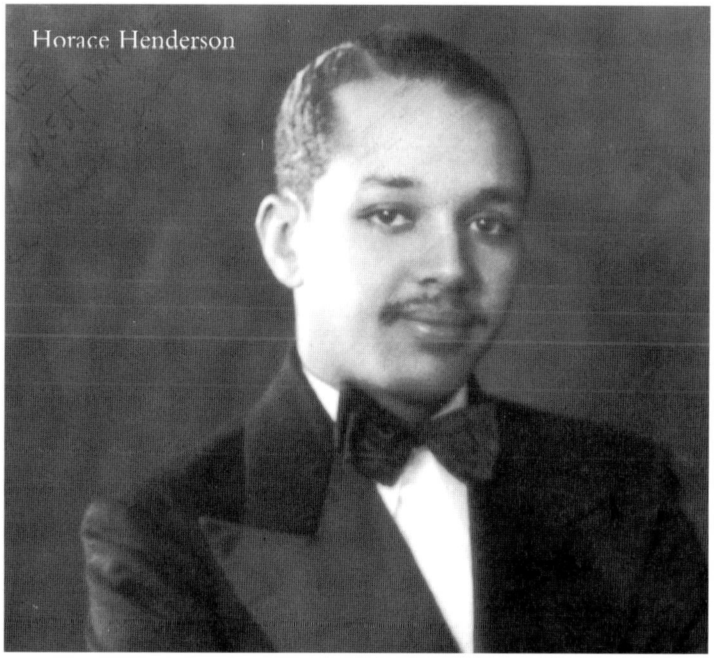

Horace Henderson

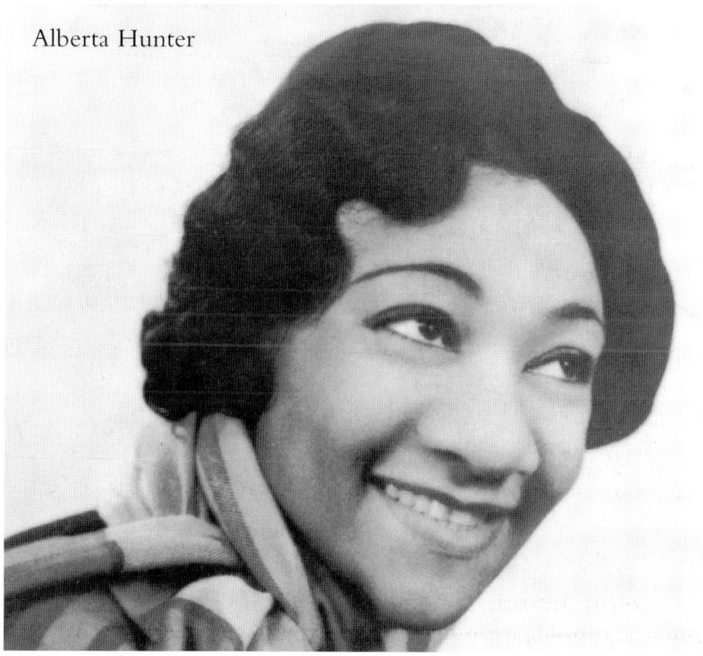

Alberta Hunter

ARNE HÜLPHERS

During the 30's Swedish pianist, composer and bandleader Arne Hülphers (1904-1978) led one of the best big bands in Sweden. He was born in Trollhättan and received early musical training on the piano, which he followed up with studies at the Musikaliska Akademien (the Academy of Music) in Stockholm. Already in 1924 he played professionally in dance orchestras, but in 1934 he organized a big band which became internationally renowned when touring Europe. The band consisted of some of the best Swedish jazz musicians at the time and the recordings are still regarded as belonging to the best of the period. In 1940 he had to disband but continued to lead dance bands and act as musical director of revues and for his wife vocalist and actress Zarah Leander. He died suddenly after an appearance at "Gröna Lund" in Stockholm.

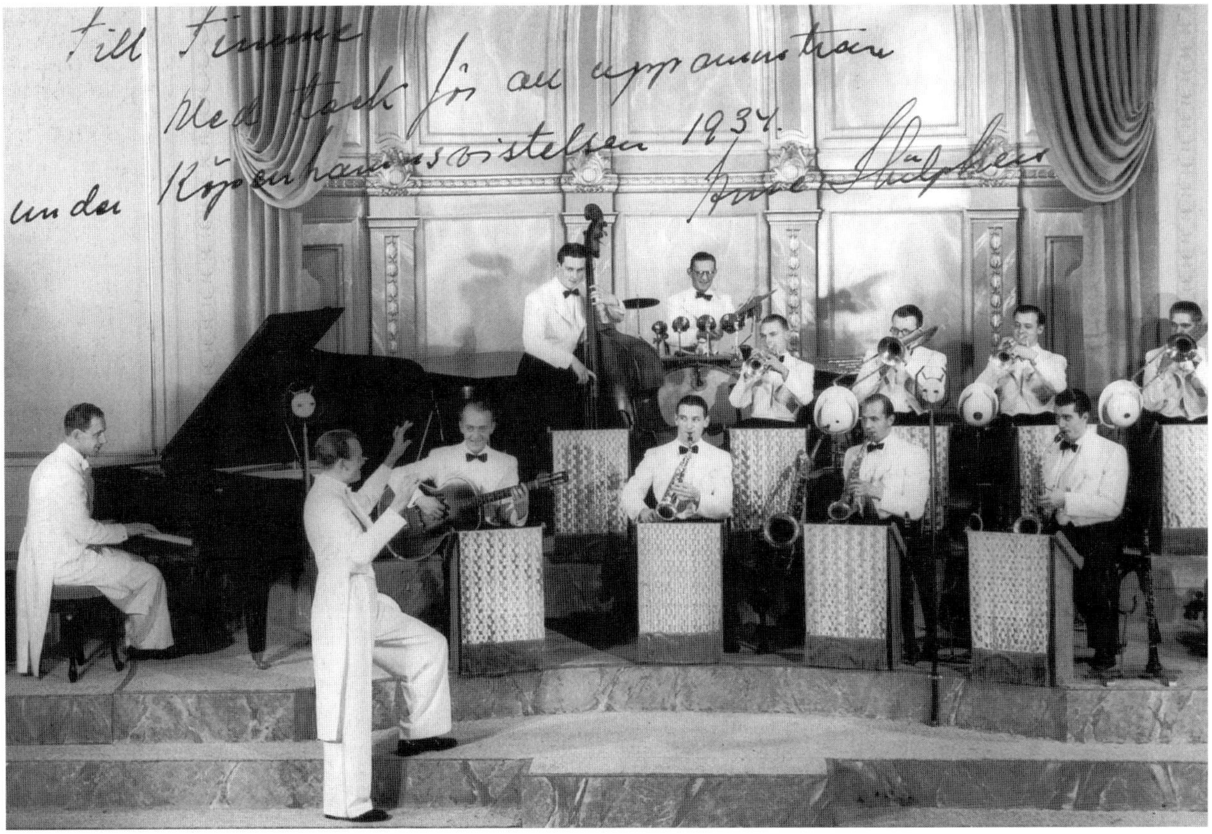

Arne Hülphers and His Orchestra in 1934. From the left, in the back row: Thore Jederby (b), Gösta Hedén (dr), Gösta "Smyget" Redlig (tp), Uno "Miff" Görling (tb), Gösta Petersson (tp) and Verner Karlsson (tb). In the front row: Arne Hülphers (p), Heintz von Vultée (cond), Charlie Hanson (g), Tony Mason (as), Eskil Wallberg (as) and Frank Vernon (ts). *Till Timme med tack för all uppmuntran under Köpenhamns-vistelsen 1934. Arne Hülphers.*

LENNIE HAYTON

New York born pianist, composer and arranger Leonard George "Lennie" Hayton (1908-1971) played many jobs as a pianist for several leading hotel bands in the late 20's. From 1928-30 he was with Paul Whiteman, and during this period he became associated with many of the famous white jazz musicians. He began recording and writing arrangements for Bix Beiderbecke, Joe Venuti, Red Nichols, Frankie Trumbauer, Miff Mole and others, and also led his own band. In the early 30's he moved to Hollywood to become musical director for Bing Crosby, and from 1941 until the early 50's he worked for MGM. In 1947 he married singer Lena Horne, and thereafter also served as her musical director, pianist and arranger.

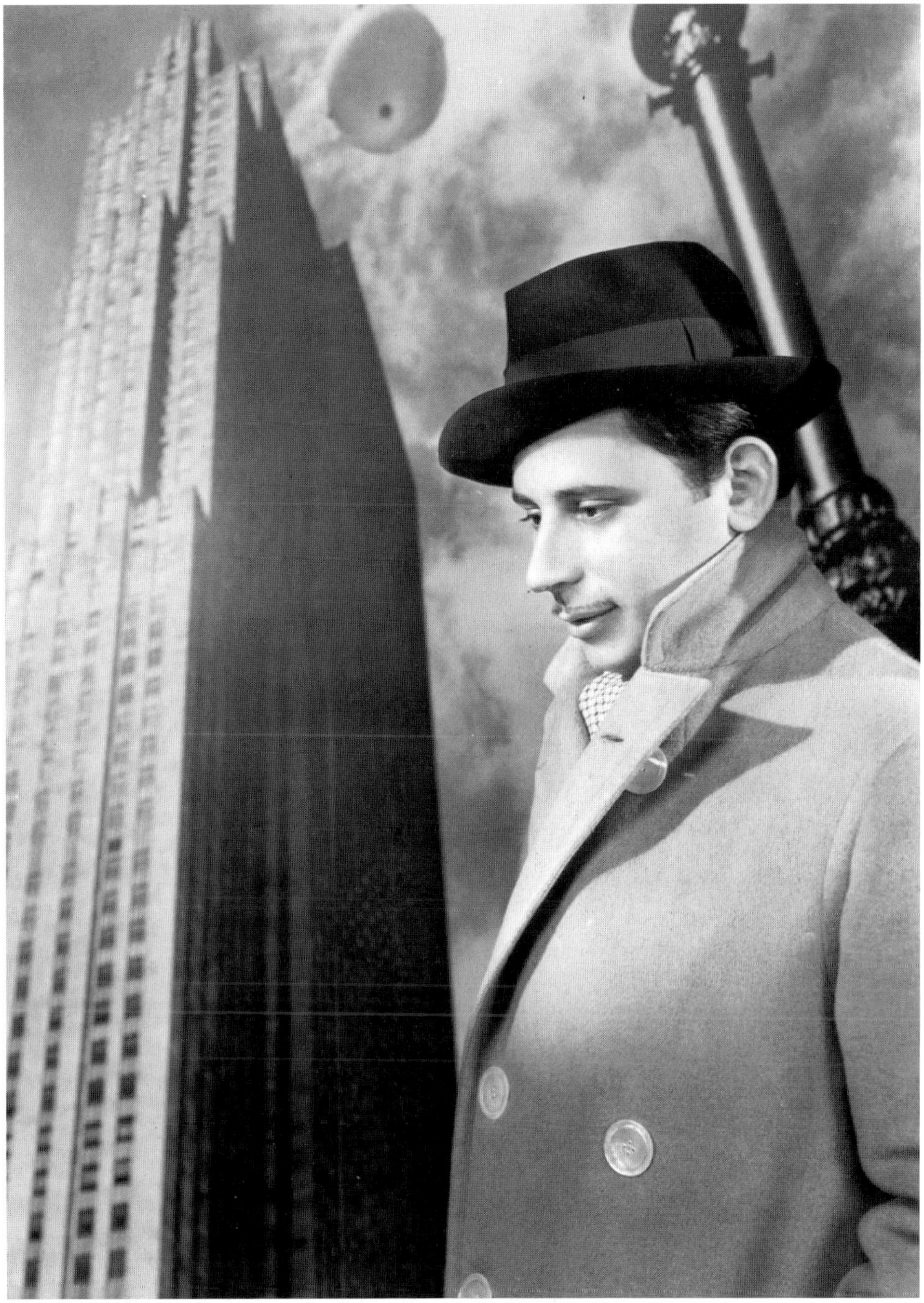

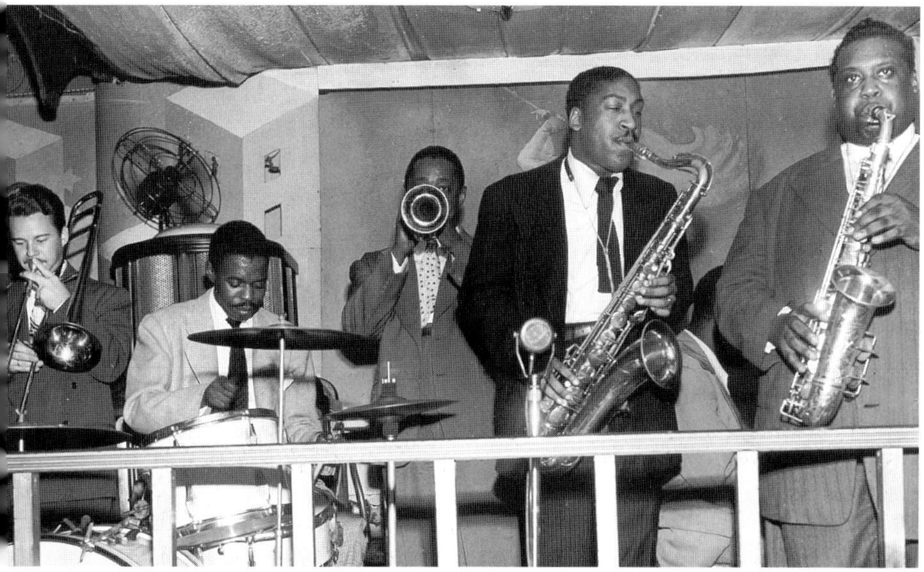

Jam sessions at Café Bohemia

In the fall of 1947 Timme Rosenkrantz arranged weekly jam sessions at the Café Bohemia in New York. These were held on Fridays from 10 p.m. and included musicians advertised beforehand plus guest musicians and a couple of surprises. Handbills advertising the jam sessions are in the Timme Rosenkrantz Collection.

From a jam session held on September 5; left: Eddie Bert, Denzil Best, Joe Thomas, Hal Singer, Jimmy Jones almost hidden, and Pete Brown.

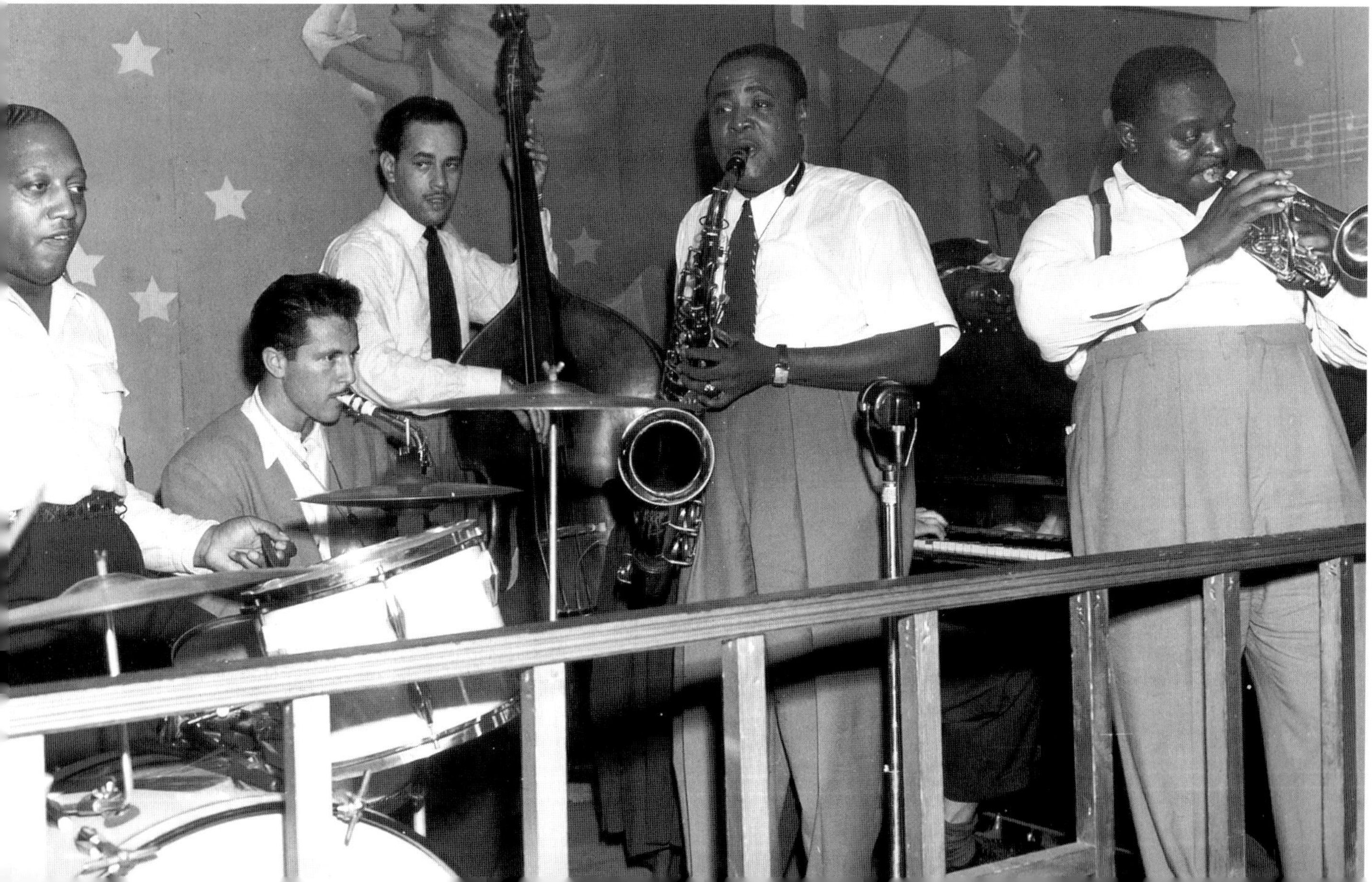

From a jam session held on September 12; from left: Jack "The Bear" Parker, Buddy DeFranco captured in an unusual setting blowing an alto saxophone, Lloyd Trotman, Gene Sedric, and Rex Stewart.

PETE JOHNSON

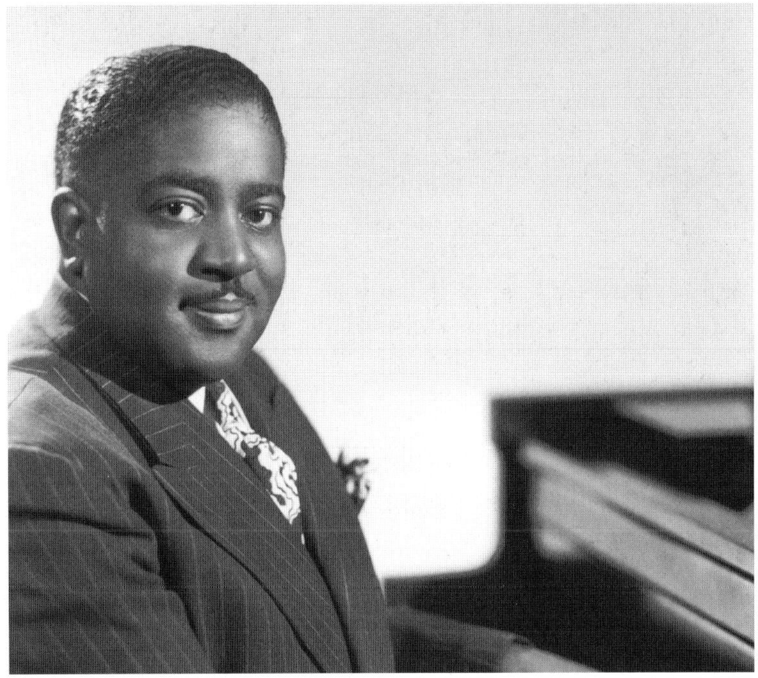

Kansas City born Peter "Pete" Johnson (1904-1967) started out on drums, but by 1926 he was playing piano at many of the Kansas City clubs, accompanying singer Joe Turner and others. In 1936 he came to New York, and from 1939 on performed successfully at the Café Society while teamed with pianists Meade Lux Lewis and Albert Ammons as "the Boogie Woogie Trio". During the 40's he worked regularly with Ammons as a duo act, and sometimes also with Lewis. In 1950 he moved to Buffalo, N.Y. where he performed as a soloist. In 1958 he suffered a stroke which left him partly paralyzed, but from 1960 he worked again at recording sessions, clubs and concerts until 1964 when he became too ill to perform.

TAFT JORDAN

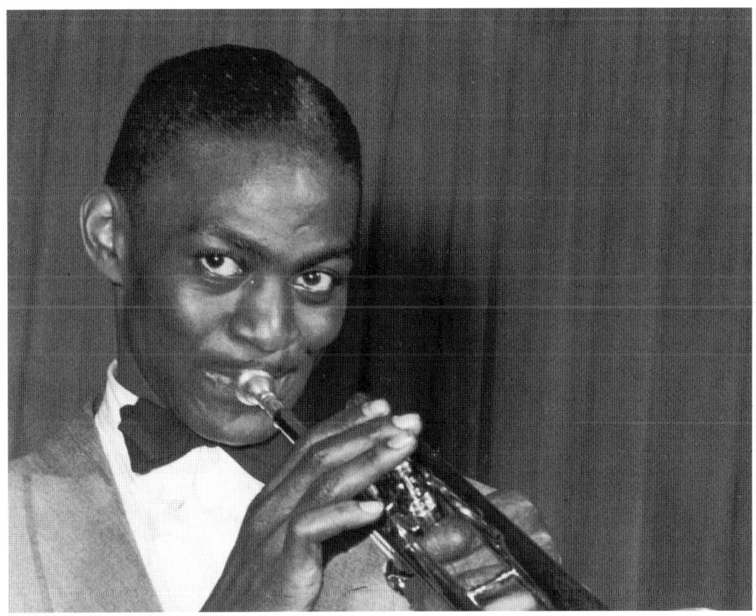

Louis Armstrong was a strong influence on many of the trumpet players born early in the century, and James Taft Jordan (1915-1981) was no exception. Born in Florence, South Carolina, he later moved to Philadelphia where he worked professionally from 1929 in a variety of bands. In 1933 he joined Chick Webb's orchestra in New York, remaining with the band until 1942 after which he joined Duke Ellington by 1943. From 1947 on he freelanced around New York, working with Lucille Dixon, Don Redman, Benny Goodman, and Earle Warren, played in Broadway shows, led his own bands and did studio work.

Jo Jones

Among the greatest drummers of all times, and the finest of the swing era, Jonathan "Jo" Jones (1911-1985) was a Chicagoan but grew up in Alabama and toured in carnival bands. From the late 20's he played in several mid-western territory bands, and moved in 1933 to Kansas City. After a spell in Minneapolis he returned to Kansas City and joined Count Basie in the autumn 1936. He remained with Basie until October 1944 when he was drafted into the Army. After military service he rejoined Count Basie for a couple of years after which he freelanced, playing with Lester Young, Joe Bushkin, leading his own groups etc. Jones was the first to move the basic pulse away from the bass drum and to stress each beat evenly so that the rhythm section became more subtle.

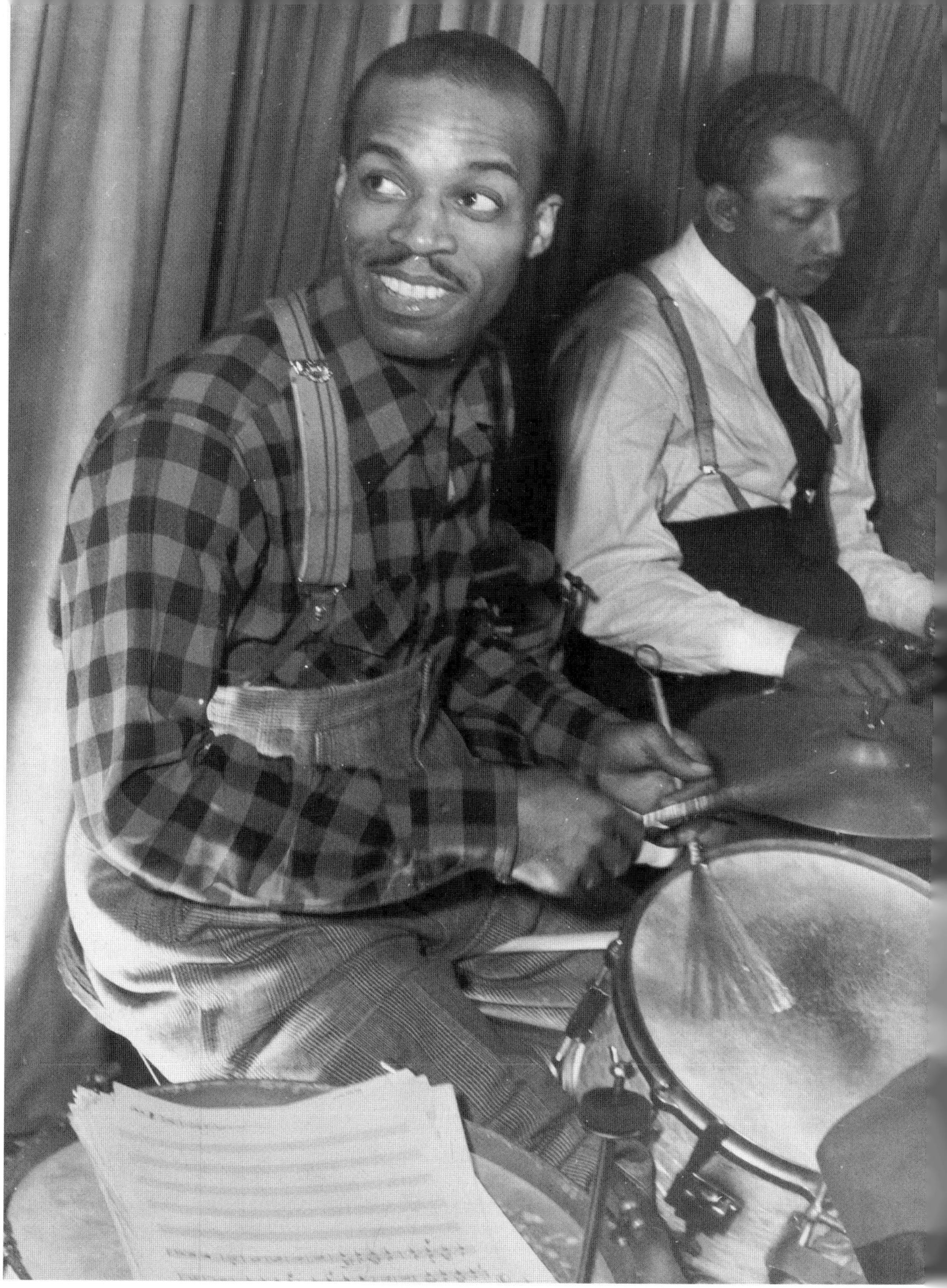

Jo Jones in the Basie band 1944 with trumpeter Joe Newman.

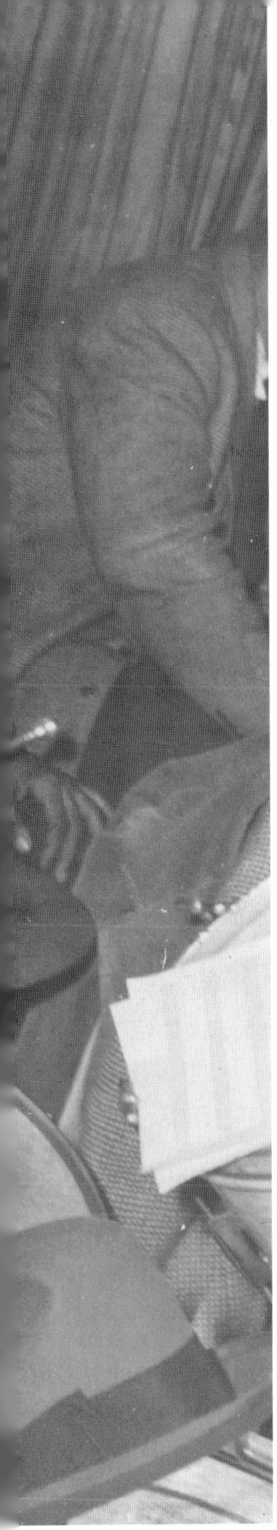

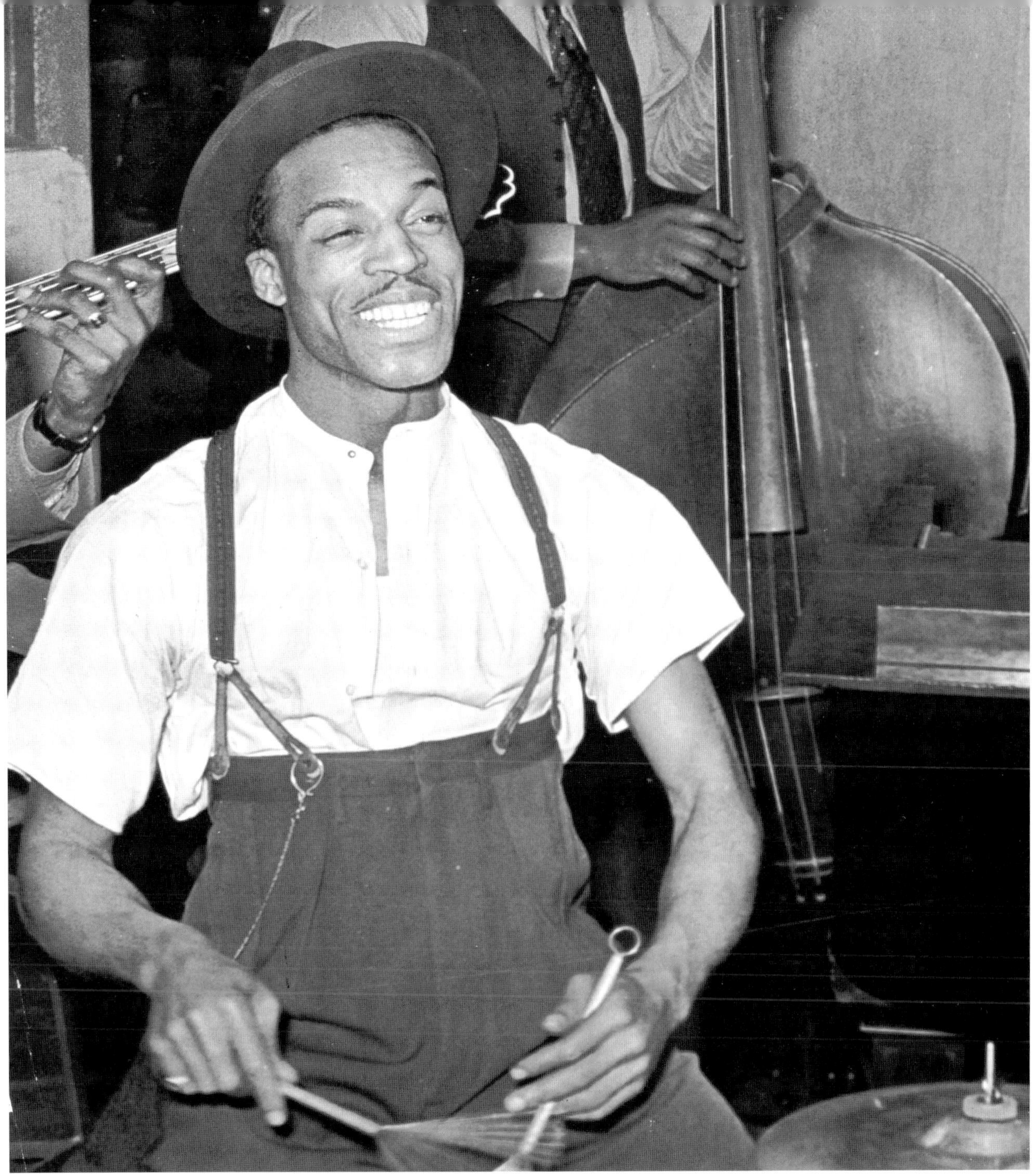

Jo Jones at a recording session with the Basie band for Decca in 1938. Guitarist Freddie Green and bassist Walter Page are behind him.

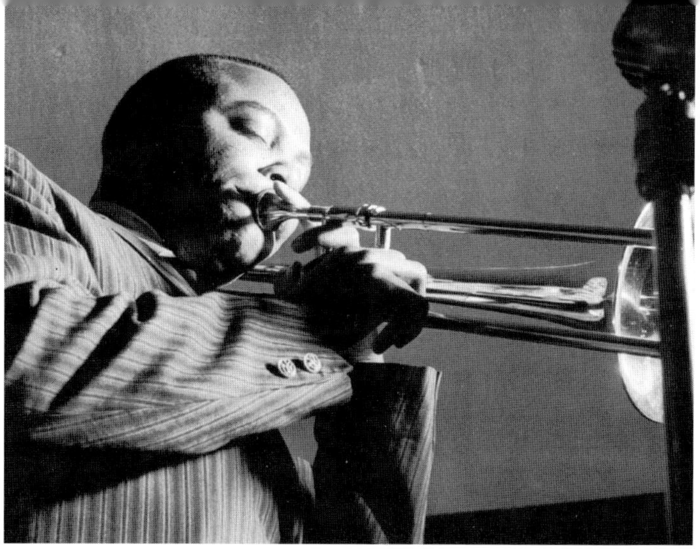

J.J. Johnson at a concert in Paris, probably during a European tour in the autumn 1958 when he was reunited with Kai Winding.

J.J. Johnson

James Louis "J.J." Johnson (1924-) was a stylist who influenced the modern way of trombone playing to the same degree as Dizzy Gillespie and Charlie Parker did trumpeters and saxophonists. He was born in Indianapolis and studied piano from the age of 9 before taking up the trombone five years later. Between 1941 and 1946 he played in various big bands led by Clarence Love, Benny Carter and Count Basie and others after which he settled in New York. Here he played in small groups with other young bop players, such as Bud Powell, Gillespie, Charlie Parker, Fats Navarro and Miles Davis. In 1952 he retired from music, but in 1954 he formed a quintet with trombonist Kai Winding – "Jay and Kai" – which toured extensively. The group disbanded two years later after which Johnson led his own groups. In 1970 he moved to Los Angeles to write scores for TV and films, but from 1987 he has been active as a player and bandleader again.

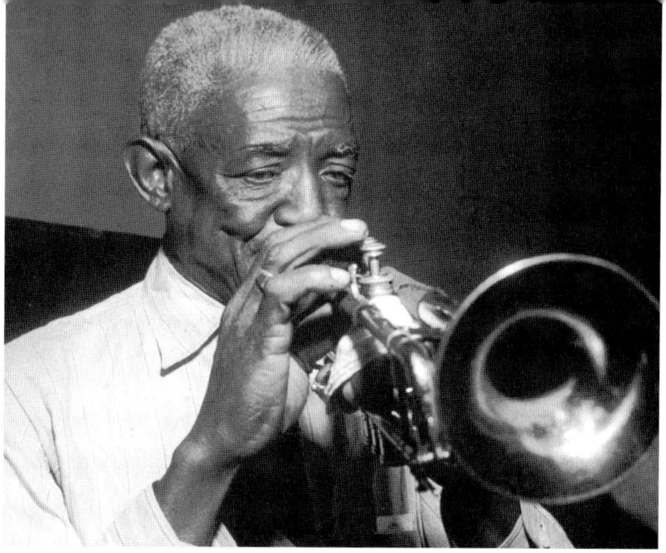

Bunk Johnson at a recording session with Sidney Bechet for Blue Note in March 1945.

Bunk Johnson

Trumpeter William Geary "Bunk" Johnson (1889-1949) is another legendary jazz musician. He was born in the Crescent City and performed from 1910 to 1914 with the Eagle Band after which he toured the South playing in theatres, clubs, and minstrel shows. In the early 30's he worked with Evan Thomas and His Black Eagle Band. When in 1932 the leader was stabbed to death on the band stand, and Johnson got his trumpet destroyed during a subsequent fight, he left show business and moved to New Iberia, Louisiana to work at various trades and to teach. He was rediscovered in 1939, got a trumpet, a new set of teeth and resumed playing. Apart from a period in 1945 when he played with Sidney Bechet in the Boston area, he led his own groups until 1948 when he retired to New Iberia.

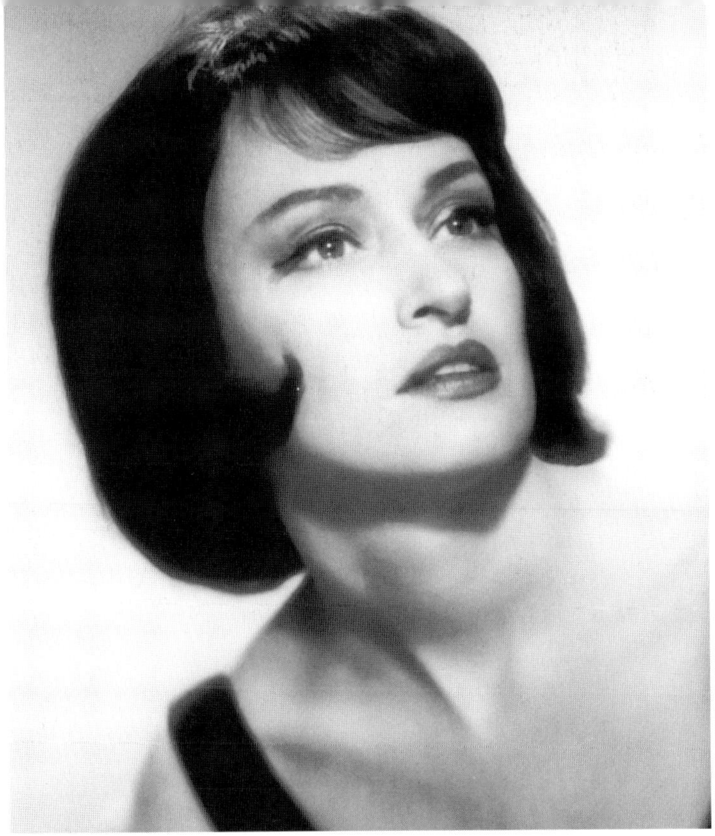

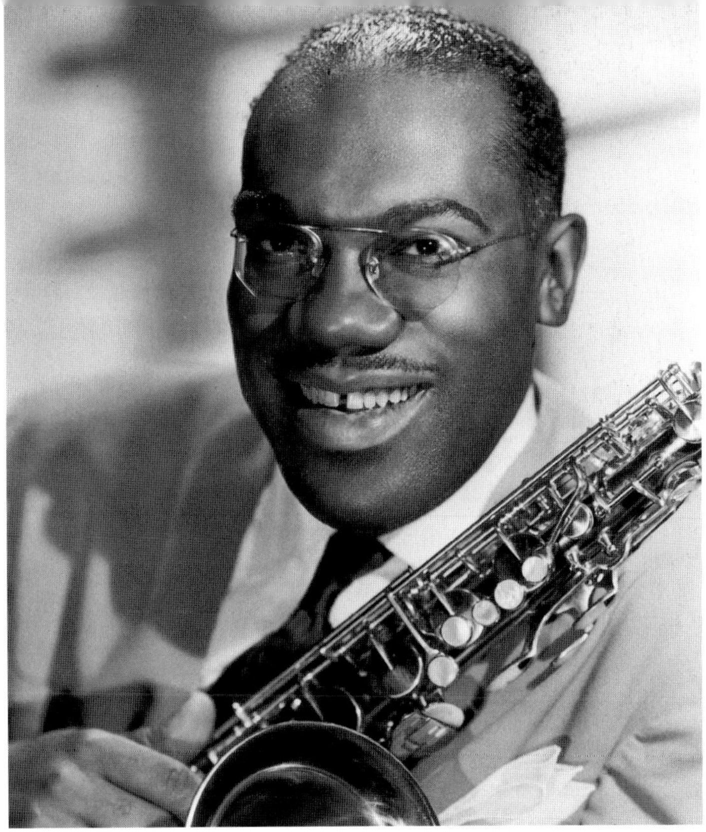

Sheila Jordan

Sheila Jeanette Jordan (1928-) resembles no other jazz singer. She is from Detroit, and began singing in her teens, deeply influenced by Charlie Parker. She moved to New York in 1951 to study with Lennie Tristano and Charlie Mingus, and in 1952 she married pianist Duke Jordan, her husband in the following decade. She performed in clubs, churches and concert halls, toured Europe in the 70's, collaborated with Carla Bley and Roswell Rudd, Steve Kuhn and Steve Swallow, and has led vocal workshops. Jordan is an uncompromising singer who is capable of making any song unique whether a well-known standard or new material.

Bull Moose Jackson

Cleveland, Ohio born singer, tenor saxophonist and band leader Benjamin Clarence "Bull Moose" Jackson (1919-1989) sang in church choirs as a child, and later studied the violin before he switched to the tenor saxophone while still in high school. He played in local bands led by Freddy Webster before joining Lucky Millinder (1944-45). Afterwards he organized his own group, the Buffalo Bearcats. With this outfit he toured nationwide and recorded a number of successful rhythm-and-blues singles until the early 50's, when he joined Tiny Bradshaw's band. In 1958 he retired from full-time playing and opened a bar in Philadelphia.

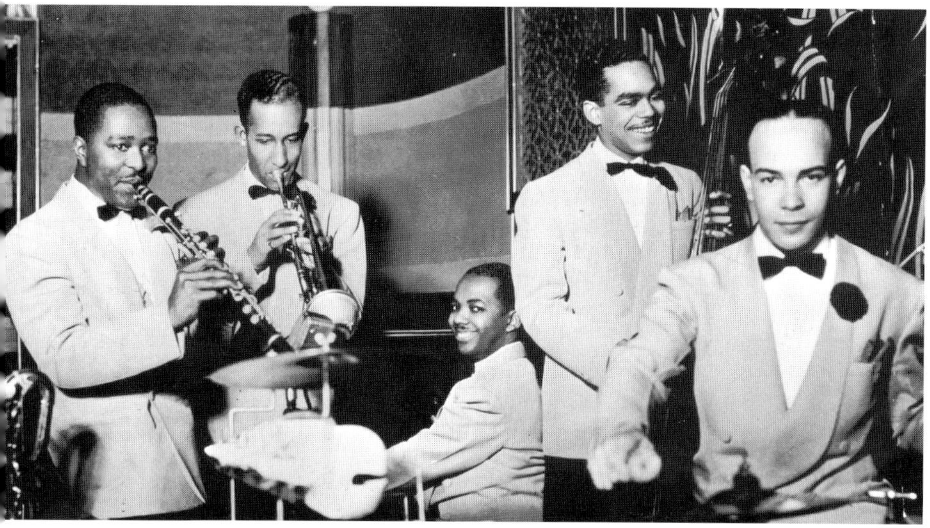

The photo dates from 1939-40 and shows an early version of the Tympany Five. From the left: Louis Jordan (cl), Courtney Williams (tp), Clarence Johnson (p), Charlie Drayton (b), and Walter Martin (dr).

LOUIS JORDAN

The Tympany Five led by saxophonist, clarinetist and singer Louis Jordan (1908-1975) was one of the most popular small groups of the 40's and 50's. Jordan was born in Brinkley, Arkansas, and worked in many territory bands, before he joined Charlie Gaines in 1933 and went with him to New York. Here he played with Chick Webb (1936-38), after which he formed a quintet which later was named the Tympany Five. He led this group for many years, only interrupted 1951-52 when he briefly led a big band. The Tympany Five became influential in the rhythm-and-blues field, and Jordan himself was a great showman, singing with wit and humour.

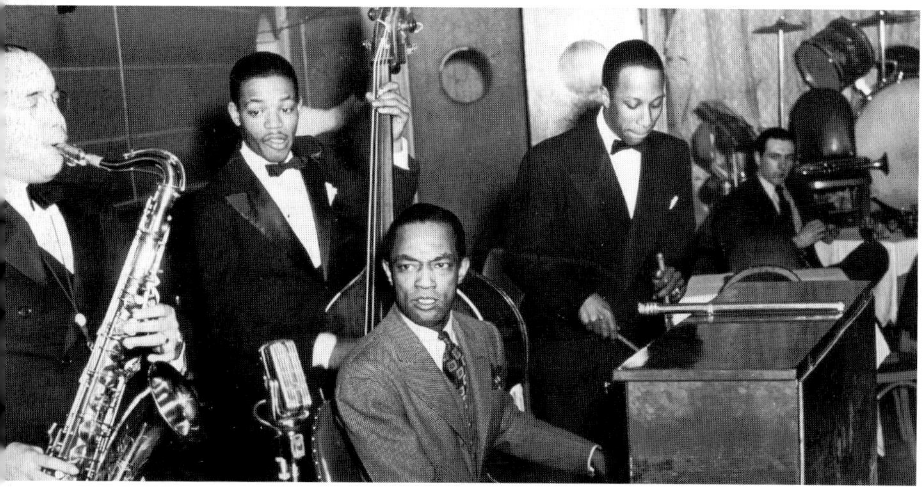

Buddy Johnson during the early 40's rehearsing his small band, which include Kenneth Hollon (ts) and probably Frank Clarke (b). The drummer standing at the piano is unidentified.

BUDDY JOHNSON

Pianist, arranger, composer, singer and band leader Woodrow Wilson "Buddy" Johnson (1915-1977) was another musician who achieved great success in the rhythm-an-blues market. He was born in Darlington, South Carolina, and came to New York in the late 30's playing in small night clubs. From 1939 he led his own small band, but in 1944 he organized a big band which played long residencies at the Savoy Ballroom. He also became a big rhythm-and-blues attraction in the South. In the 60's he returned to leading a small band and was also active in church welfare work.

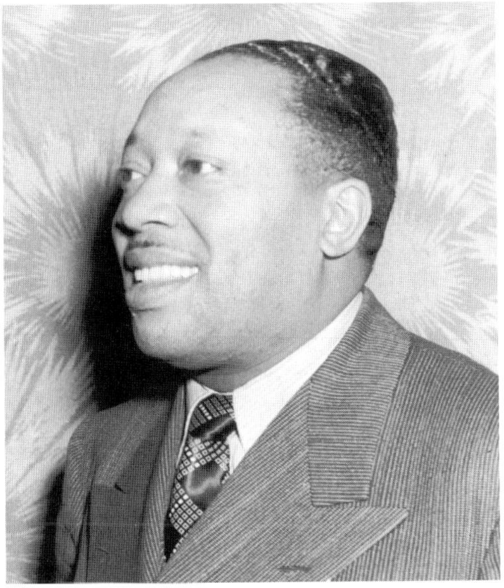

JAMES P. JOHNSON

Pianist and composer James Price "James P." Johnson (18994-1955) was the "father of the stride piano". He came from New Brunswick, New Jersey, but moved in 1908 to New York with his family. He took lessons with Eubie Blake, and from 1913 he worked in clubs. In 1917 he recorded the first of his piano rolls and also published the first of his 200 songs. From the 20's his career really took off. He recorded frequently with Bessie Smith and Ethel Waters and toured England with the "Plantation Revue". He began composing extended works, and during the 30's wrote several stage works for Broadway. From 1939 he played regularly again, but from 1951 he was inactive due to a severe stroke. Johnson's influence on the early jazz piano was unique. He taught Fats Waller, and perfected the style known as stride piano.

JIMMY JONES

Pianist, composer and arranger James Henry "Jimmy" Jones (1918-1982) was born in Memphis, Tennessee, but grew up in Chicago where he learned to play the guitar. As a teenager he switched to piano, and later on studied music at Kentucky State College. He joined Stuff Smith in 1943 and went with him to New York where he also made several home recordings for Timme Rosenkrantz. He played with J.C. Heard 1946-47 after which he accompanied Sarah Vaughan the following decade, except for a two year period of illness. In the 60's and the 70's he devoted much of his time to composing and arranging. He also worked for Ellington, conducting his show "My People". After a couple of years as accompanist for Ella Fitzgerald, he moved to Los Angeles in 1969 to write for TV and films.

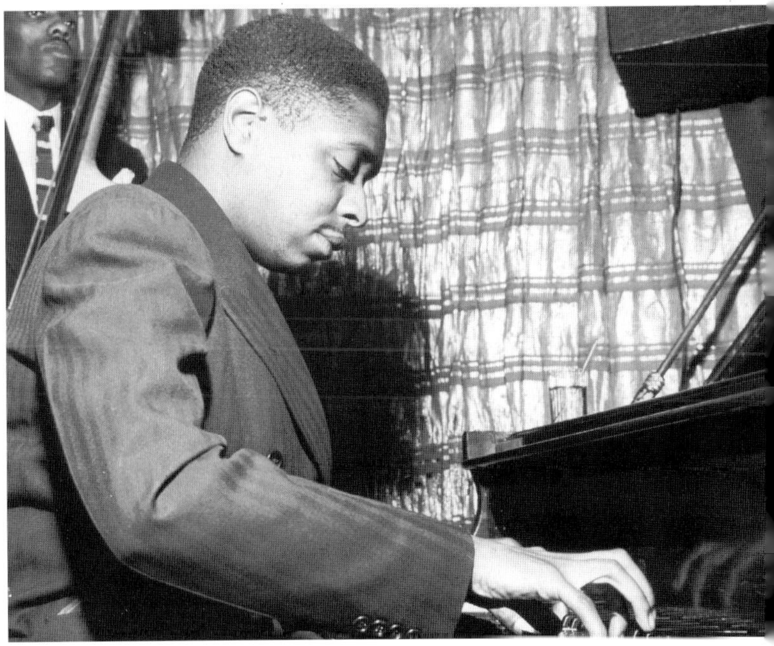

ANDY KIRK

One of the most popular among the mid-western territory bands was the Clouds Of Joy led by saxophonist Andrew Dewey "Andy" Kirk (1898-1992). Born in Newport, Kentucky, Kirk spent his childhood in Denver where he learned to play several instruments, singing and music theory. He began playing bass saxophone and tuba in 1918 with George Morrison, and in 1925 he moved to Dallas joining Terrence Holder's Dark Clouds Of Joy. In 1929 Kirk took over the band, renamed it, and led it until 1948 when the group disbanded. Kirk went then into hotel management, real estate, and also served as an official of the Musicians' Union in New York. The Clouds Of Joy had strong arrangements by pianist Mary Lou Williams, and a string of good soloists through the years, besides Williams herself, Dick Wilson, Don Byas, Shorty Baker, Howard McGhee, and Kenney Kersey.

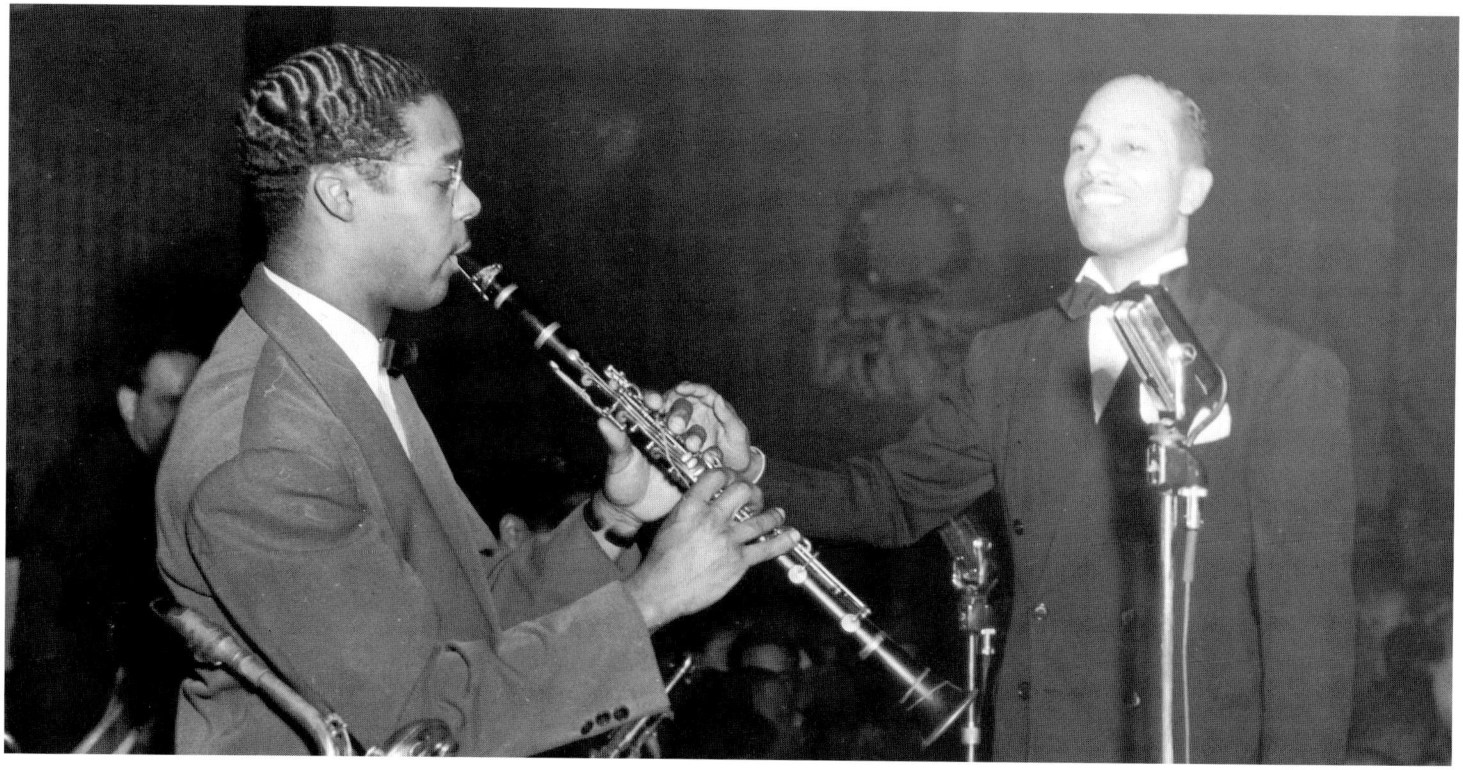

Andy Kirk conducts his band during a concert in 1940. Rudy Rutherford is soloing on the clarinet.

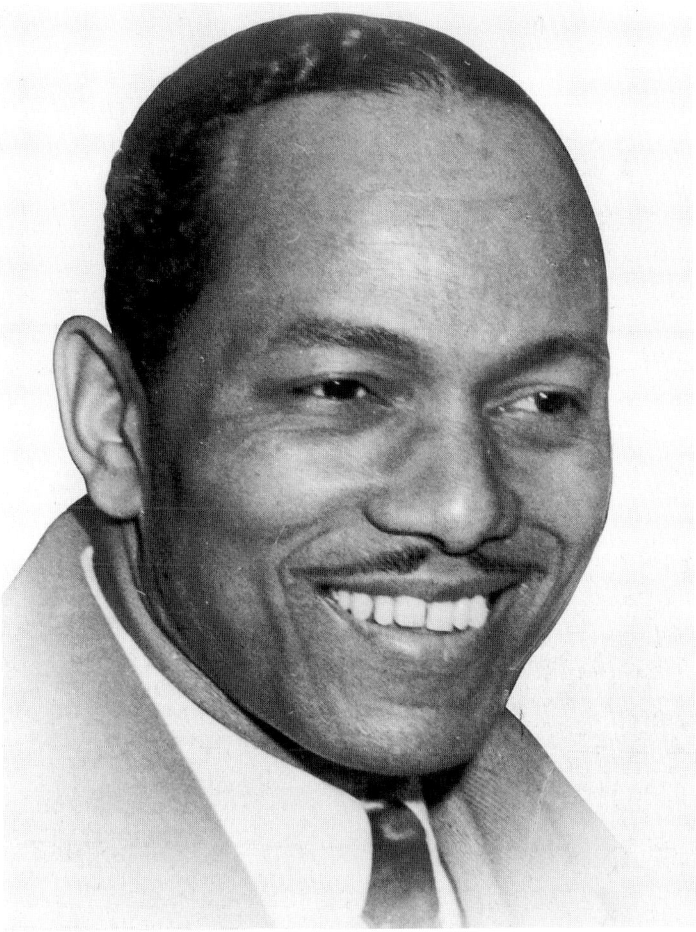

Publicity photo of Andy Kirk, probably from the 40's.

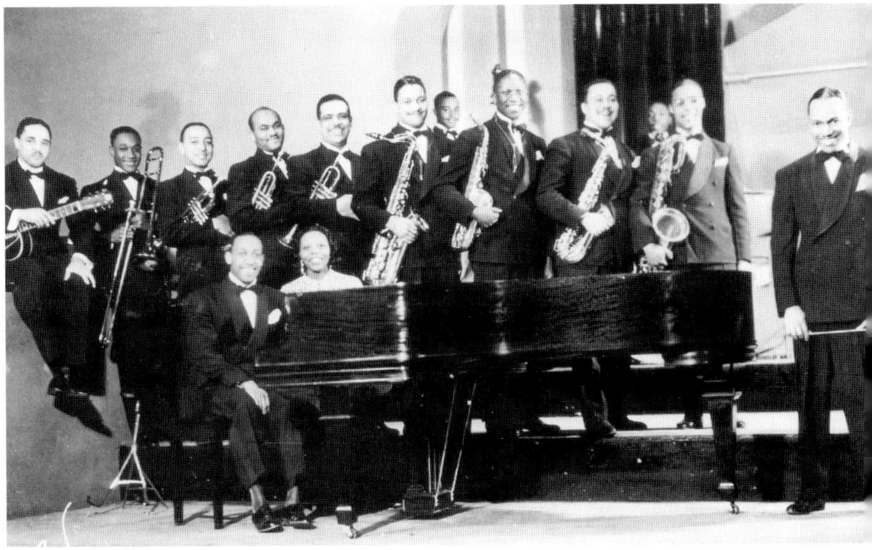

Top right:
Andy Kirk and the Clouds Of Joy 1937. In the background, Booker Collins (b) and Ben Thigpen (dr). Next, from the left: Ted Brinson (g), Theodore "Ted" Donnelly (tb), Earl Thompson, Paul King and Harry "Big Jim" Lawson (tp), Dick Wilson (ts), John Williams and John Harrington (as), Earl Miller (bars) and Kirk. Sitting at the piano are singer Pha Terrell and pianist, composer and arranger Mary Lou Williams.

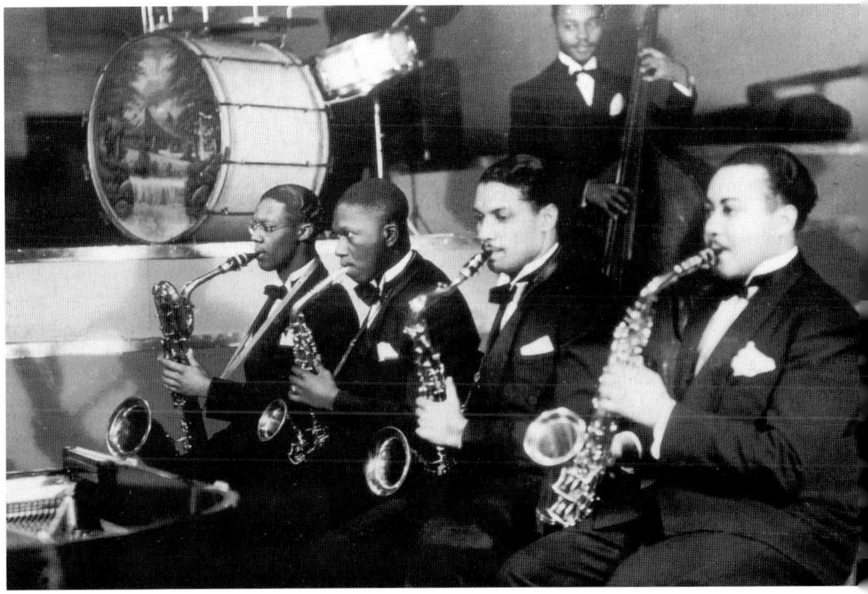

Andy Kirk's saxophone section in 1937: Earl Miller, John Williams, Dick Wilson and John Harrington. Booker Collins is playing the bass.

JOHN KIRBY

Bassist John Kirby (1908-1952) led a sophisticated, popular sextet from 1938-42, billed as "the Biggest Little Band in the Land". Kirby was from Baltimore, Maryland and began his musical career on trombone. He soon switched to tuba, and in 1930 joined Fletcher Henderson and stayed until 1934. During that time he began doubling on string bass and soon abandoned the tuba. From 1934-37 he was with Chick Webb, Lucky Millinder and Charlie Barnet, after which he assembled a small group to play at the Onyx Club on New York's 52nd Street. This sextet became the talk of the street with its precise, chamber-like ensemble playing in brilliant arrangements mostly supplied by trumpeter Charlie Shavers, and often with Kirby's wife, singer Maxine Sullivan, added to the group. Kirby disbanded the sextet right after the war, after which he moved to the West Coast. There he died of diabetes at the age of 43.

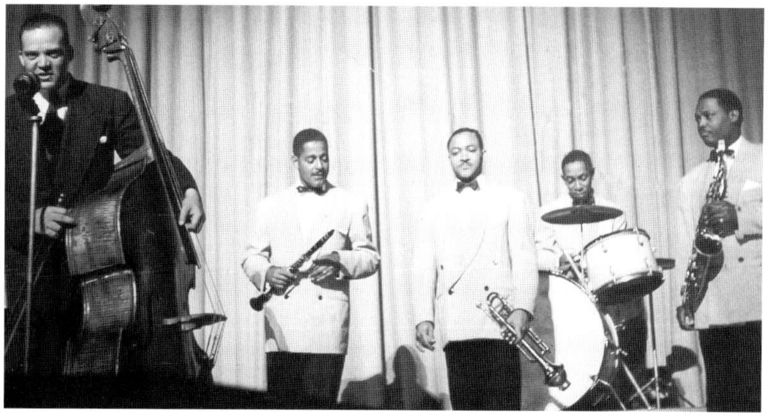

The John Kirby Sextet captured at a concert around 1940 with Kirby (b), Buster Bailey (cl), Charlie Shavers (tp), O'Neil Spencer (dr) and Russell Procope (as).

MANNIE KLEIN

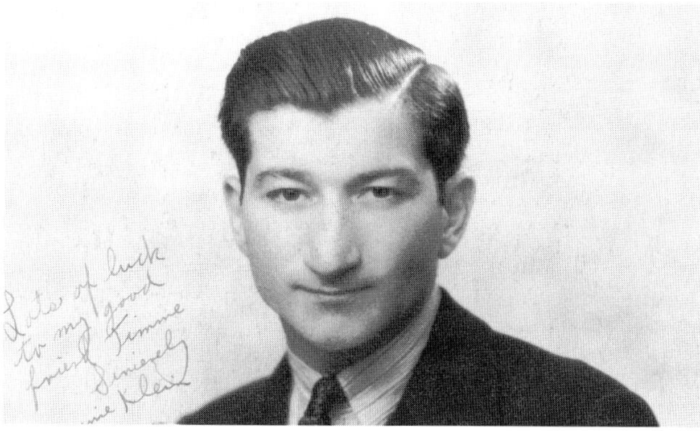

One of the most versatile of trumpet players, and a first rate musician, Emmanuel "Mannie" Klein (1908-1994) was a New Yorker and began playing professionally as a teenager. His talent soon made him one of the busiest freelance musicians in New York, recording with practically every white name band, such as those led by Paul Whiteman, Benny Goodman, the Dorsey Brothers, Red Nichols, Roger Wolfe Kahn and others. In 1937 he moved to Los Angeles where he was a studio musician for the rest of his life, except for a period in 1938 when he co-led a band with Frankie Trumbauer. Despite a stroke in 1973 which made him unable to read music, he continued to perform, playing perfectly until he retired in the early 90's. Klein was not only a good soloist, he was also one of the best lead trumpet players around, and equally good as a soloist in the classical repertoire. *Lots of luck to my good friend Timme. Sincerely Mannie Klein.*

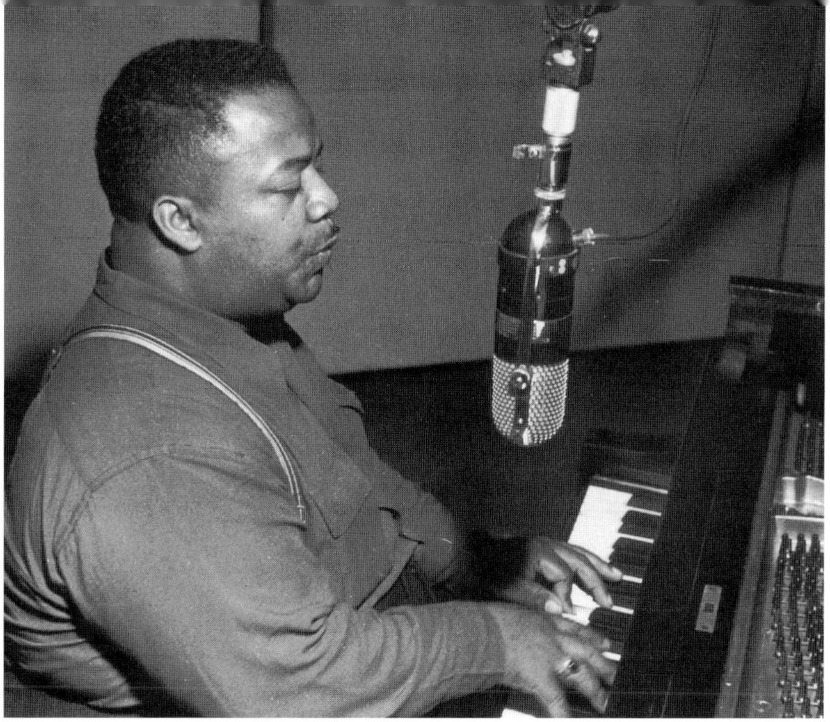

Meade Lux Lewis during a recording session for Blue Note, June 8, 1939, with Sidney Bechet.

Meade Lux Lewis

Meade "Lux" Anderson Lewis (1905-1964) was one of the most important figures among the boogie-woogie pianists, but one who also had much more than that to offer. He was first influenced by Fats Waller and Jimmy Yancey, and played from the mid-20's in bars and nightclubs in his hometown, Chicago. He left music for a while during the early 30's, making his living as a cab driver and a car washer, but from 1936 he was re-established as a full-time musician and shortly afterwards moved to New York. In 1938 he formed the Boogie Woogie Trio with Pete Johnson and Albert Ammons, but shortly afterwards he returned to work as a single act. From 1941 he lived in California as a celebrity, working along the West Coast and performing on radio and TV. He died in a car crash on his return to California after an engagement in Minneapolis.

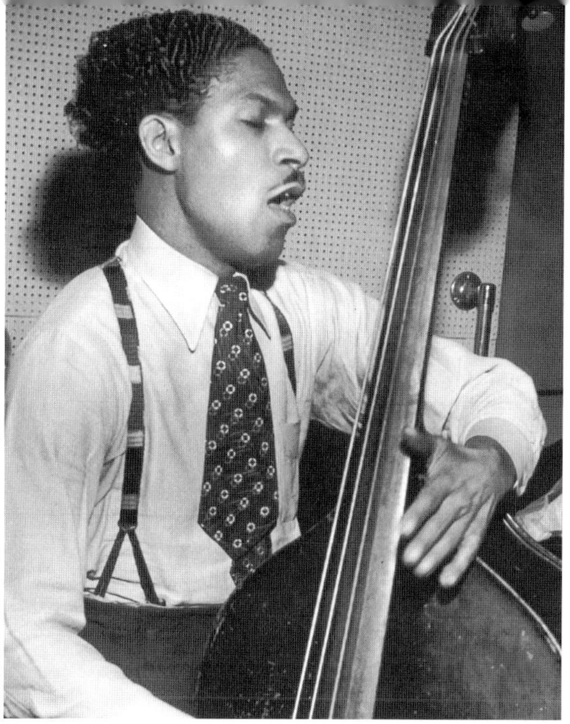

Al Lucas during a recording session for Blue Note with James P. Johnson in 1944.

Al Lucas

Born in Windsor, Ontario, Canada bassist Albert B. "Al" Lucas (1916-1983) moved to New York in 1933 where, after ten years with the Sunset Royal Orchestra, he played with many of the leading jazz musicians, such as Coleman Hawkins, Eddie Heywood, Duke Ellington, Ben Webster, Erroll Garner, Hot Lips Page, Mary Lou Williams, Illinois Jacquet, and Teddy Wilson. During the 60's and 70's he worked mostly as a studio musician but toured occasionally. Lucas played a style rooted in the swing idiom, but from the 40's his solos were influenced by Jimmy Blanton.

JIMMIE LUNCEFORD

James Melvin "Jimmie" Lunceford (1902-1947) led an outstanding big band, noted for its high standards of ensemble work, excellent arrangements and a distinctive two-beat rhythm. He was born in Fulton, Missouri, and learned to play several instruments as a child while growing up in Denver. After a degree in music from Fisk University he organized a band in Memphis in 1927, the Chickasaw Syncopators, which during the early 30's mainly played in Cleveland and Buffalo. In 1934 the band got an important engagement at New York's Cotton Club, which established its reputation as a prominent orchestra after which it became one of the most sought-after big bands, touring constantly. Lunceford died after collapsing in a music store where he was signing autographs.

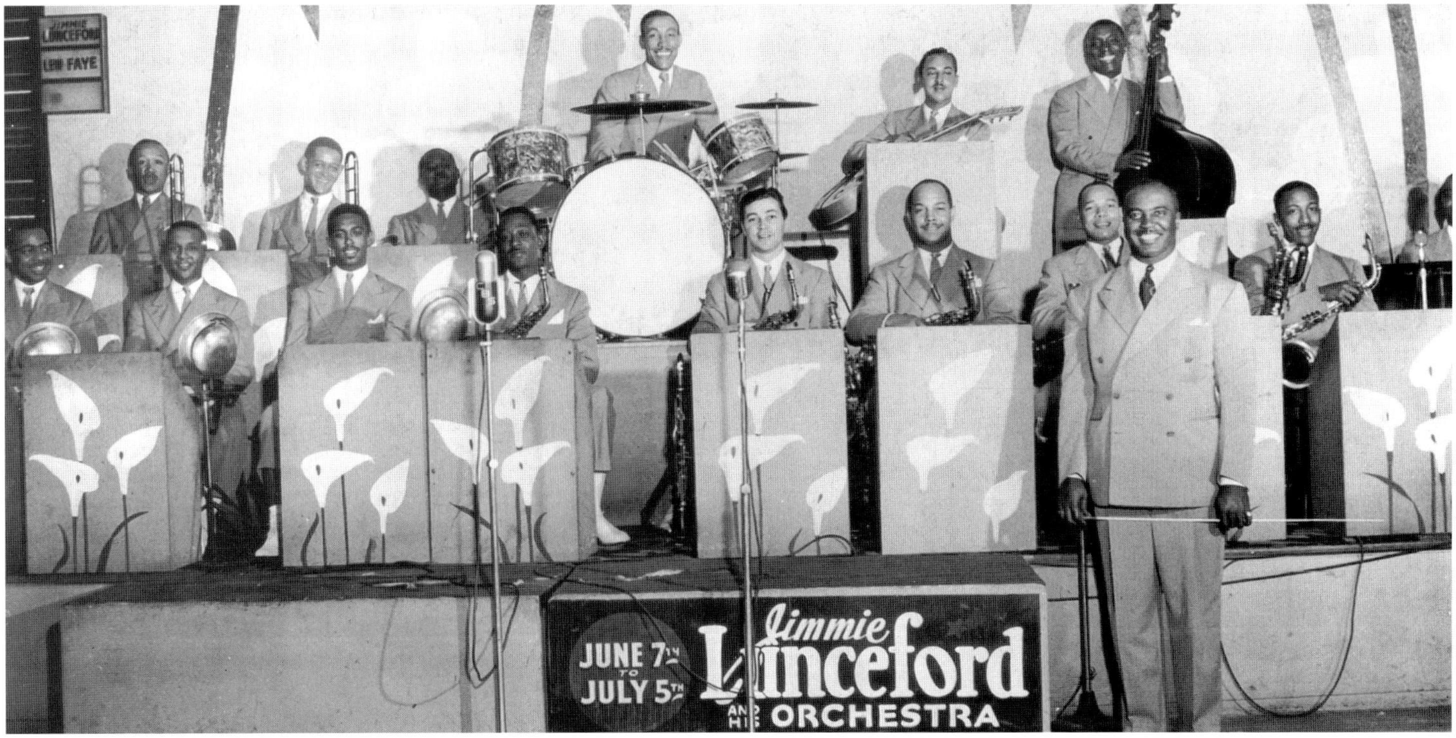

Jimmie Lunceford in front of his orchestra in 1941. In the back row from left: Russel Bowles, Trummy Young and Elmer Crumbley (tb), Jimmie Crawford (dr), Al Norris (g) and Moses Allen (b). In the front row from left: Paul Webster, Snooky Young and Gerald Wilson (tp), Joe Thomas, Willie Smith, Dan Grissom, Ted Buckner and Earl Carruthers (reeds), and Eddie Wilcox (p).

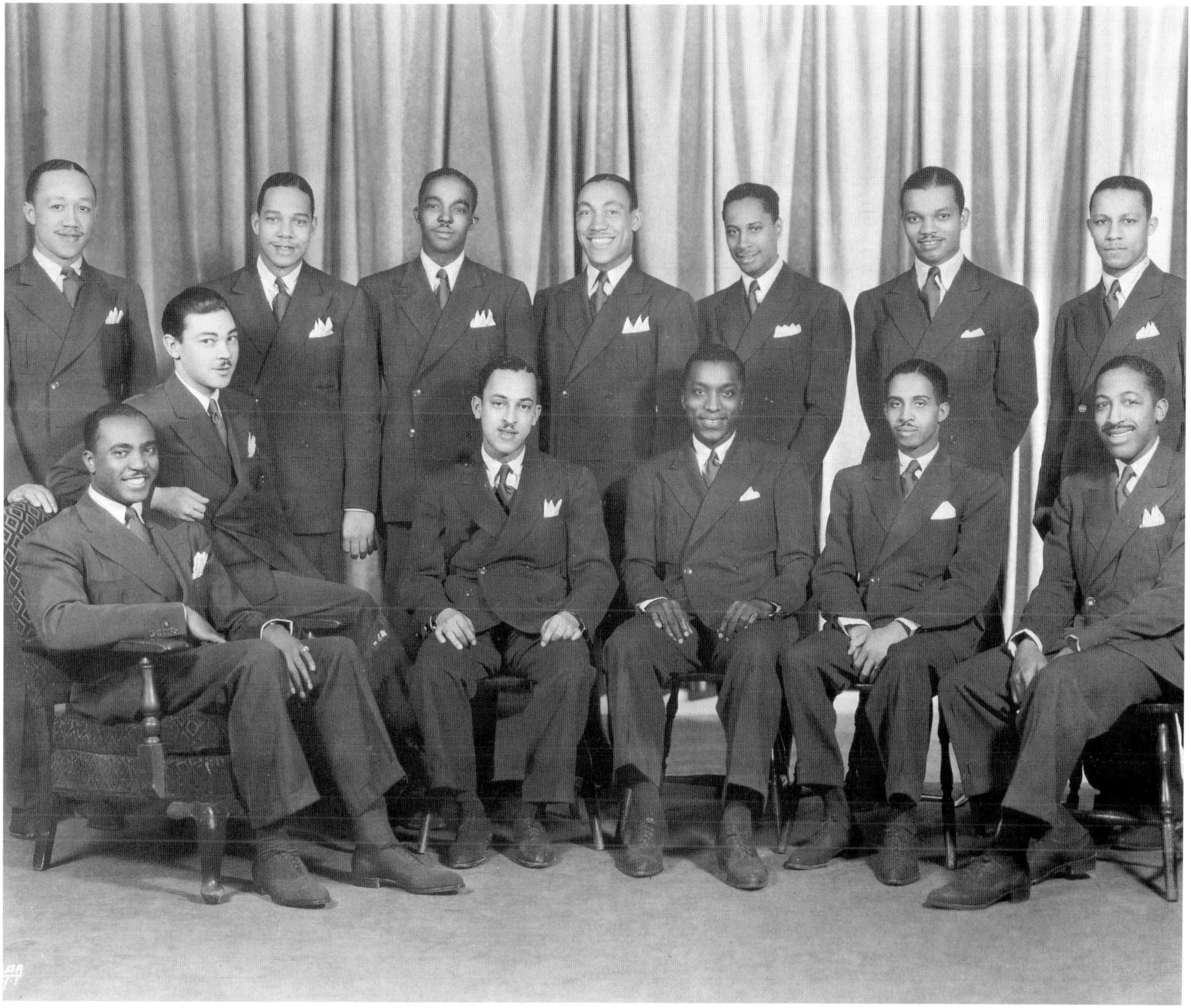

Jimmie Lunceford and His Orchestra, 1936. In the back row from left: Russell Bowles (tb), Eddie Wilcox (p), Moses Allen (b), Jimmie Crawford (dr), Eddie Durham (tb, arr.), Sy Oliver (tp, arr.), and Paul Webster (tp). Sitting in the front row from left: Jimmie Lunceford, Willie Smith (as), Al Norris (g), Joe Thomas (ts), Eddie Thompkins (tp), and Earl Carruthers (as, bars).

Guy Lafitte

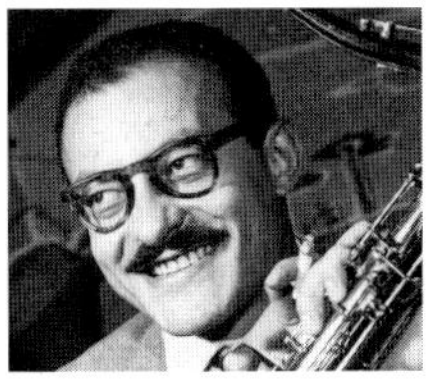

The French tenor saxophonist Guy Lafitte (1927-1998) was strongly influenced by Coleman Hawkins, and therefore a natural choice to accompany many of the guesting American swing musicians who toured in France after World War II. Lafitte was born in St.-Gaudens and played clarinet in gypsy bands in the south-western region of France near Toulouse. He took up the tenor saxophone in 1947, and from 1954 he was based in Paris where he led his own groups but also toured with Americans like Big Bill Broonzy, Mezz Mezzrow, Bill Coleman, Dicky Wells, Emmett Berry, Lionel Hampton, Buck Clayton, Milt Buckner, Arnett Cobb, Jimmy Woode, Wild Bill Davis and others. In 1954 he was awarded the first Prix Django Reinhardt.

Harlan Lattimore

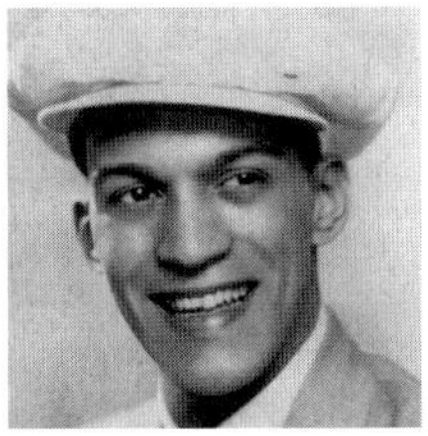

Born in Cincinnati, Ohio, singer Harlan Lattimore (1908-?) began his career performing on a local radio station. He later worked for a year at the Regal Theater in Chicago. Throughout the 30's he worked with Don Redman, but also recorded with Fletcher Henderson, Victor Young, Abe Lyman, Owen Fallon and under his own name. He served in the US Army during World War II, after which he moved to New York and left full-time music. Lattimore sang with a pleasant, light baritone and an easy swing.

Ed Lewis

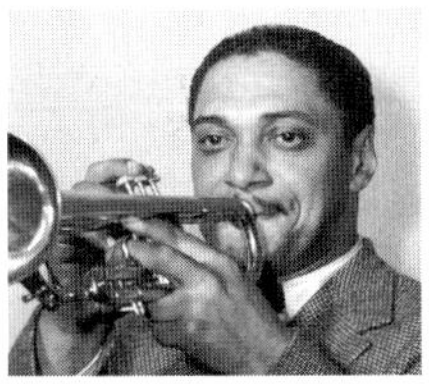

Trumpeter Edward "Ed" Lewis (1909-1985) was born in Eagle City, Oklahoma, but moved to Kansas City with his family while still a child. From 1926-31 he worked with Bennie Moten, whereafter he played with Thamon Hayes, Harlan Leonard and with Jay McShann before joining Count Basie in 1937. He stayed with Basie for eleven years, then left music to become a cab driver and a motorman on New York's subway. In 1954 he resumed playing, leading his own band in and around New York, and in 1983 toured Europe with the Countsmen. He worked right up to his death. In the early 30's Lewis was a featured soloist, influenced by Joe Smith, Red Nichols and Bix Beiderbecke, but in the Basie band he became a lead trumpeter, and henceforth was seldom heard soloing.

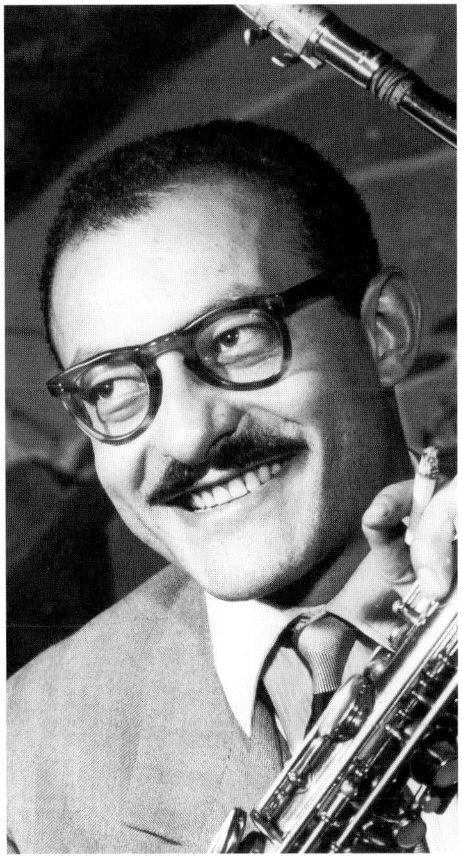

Guy Lafitte.

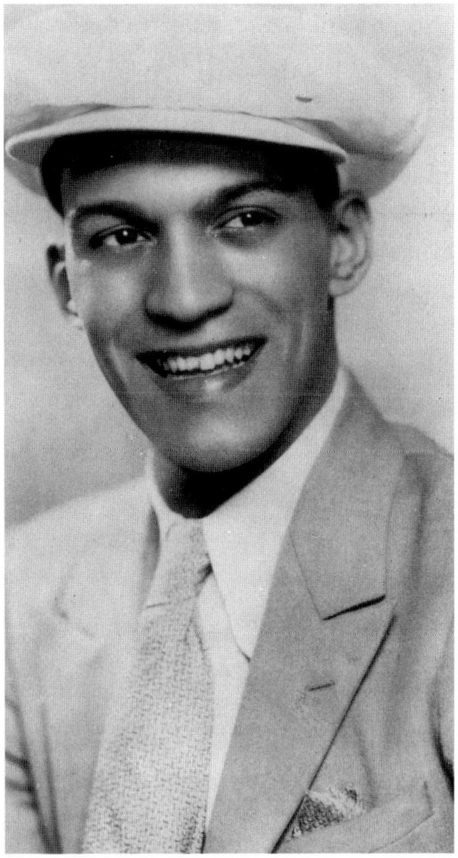

Harlan Lattimore.

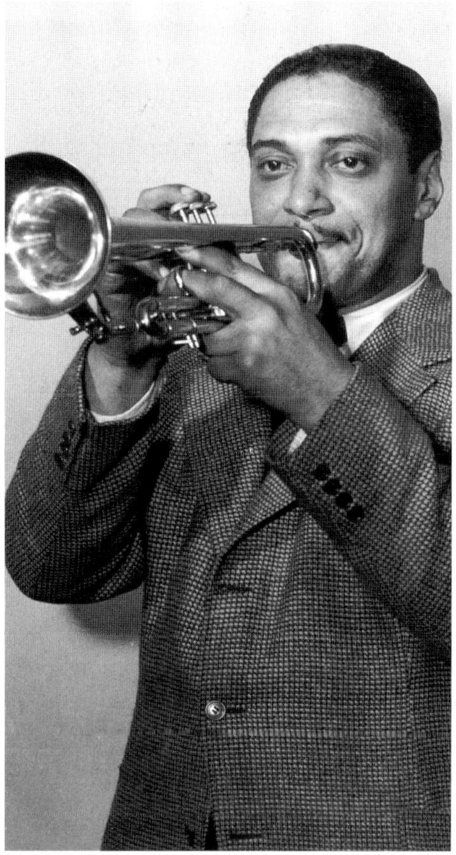

Ed Lewis.

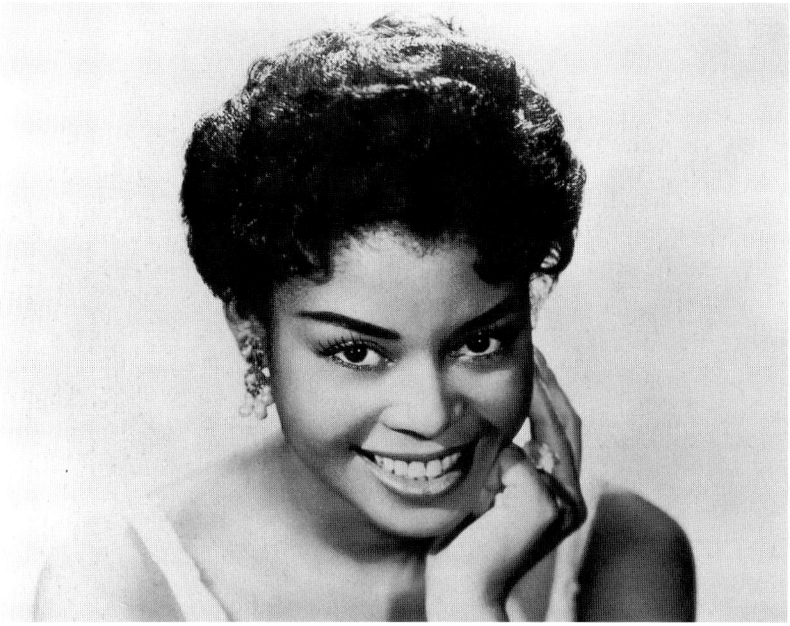

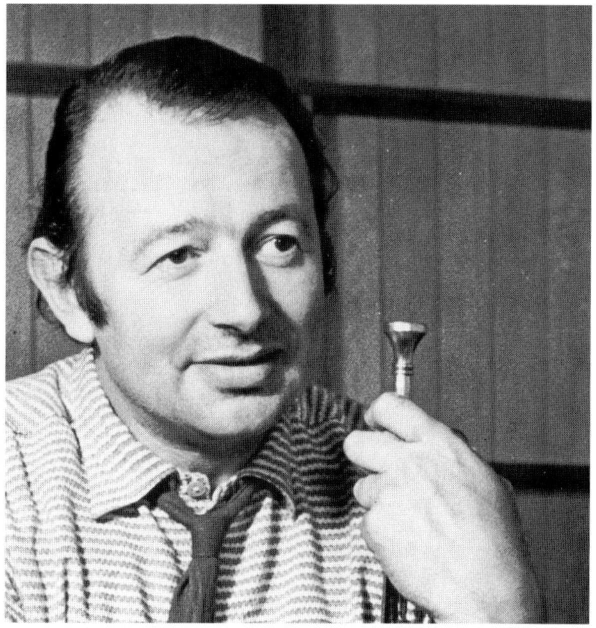

ABBEY LINCOLN

Singer and composer Abbey Lincoln (1930-) has used much of her time and efforts writing songs and singing about social and political matters inspired by her sometime husband, drummer Max Roach. She was born in Chicago as one of twelve children and was brought up on a farm in Michigan. She began to perform professionally in the early 50's using several pseudonyms, but in 1956 she chose her current name. From the late 50's she also worked as an actress, appearing in several movies. During the 80's and 90's she has enjoyed a rising career and tours now constantly. From the energetic, bitter, and at times aggressive style she used during the 60's and 70's in her political repertoire, she has returned to a warmer and gentler mode as well as to the more conventional ballads and love songs that characterized her earlier work.

HUMPHREY LYTTELTON

Born at Eton College, trumpeter, clarinetist and bandleader Humphrey R.A. Lyttelton (1921-) learned to play jazz while still a school boy. After military service he began playing professionally in 1947, and from 1948 he had his own bands. At first his bands played in the New Orleans style, but as Lyttelton's playing became more influenced by swing trumpeters like Buck Clayton and Roy Eldridge the band style became more mainstream. In addition to his talents as a trumpeter, Lyttelton is also a critic, a writer and a broadcaster, and is now considered England's senior jazz ambassador.

MILLS BLUE RHYTHM BAND

This band was formed in late 1929 by drummer Willie Lynch and called the Blue Rhythm Band. In 1931 manager Irving Mills took over and changed the name to Mills Blue Rhythm Band. When Lynch left the band Baron Lee was chosen to front it, and from 1934 Lucky Millinder was the leader until the group disbanded in 1938.

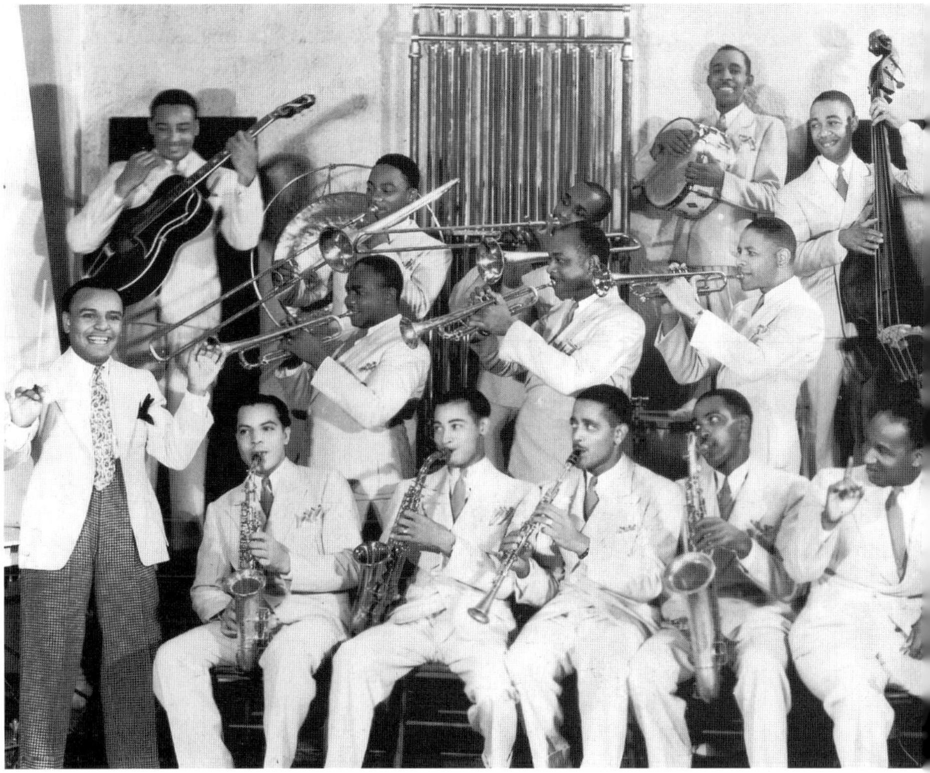

Mills Blue Rhythm Band in 1934-35. In the back row, from left: Lawrence Lucie (g), J.C. Higginbotham and George Washington (tb), O'Neil Spencer (dr) and Elmer James (b). In the middle row: Shelton Hemphill, Wardell "The Preacher" Jones and Henry "Red" Allen (tp). Sitting in the front row are Crawford Wethington and Eugene Mikell (as), Buster Bailey (metal cl), Joe Garland (ts) and pianist Edgar Hayes. Lucky Millinder is conducting.

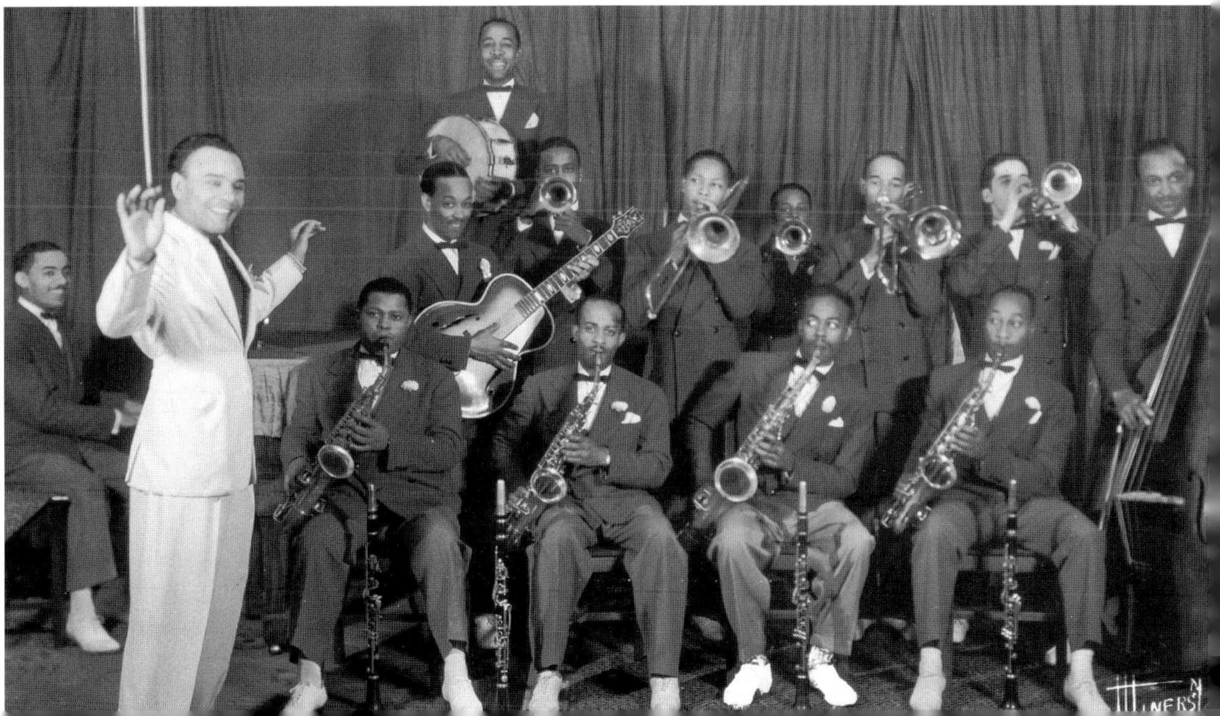

Mills Blue Rhythm Band 1937. The pianist is Billy Kyle and the drummer Lester "Sonny" Nichols. Standing in the back row, from left: Danny Barker (g), Harry "Sweets" Edison (tp), Wilbur De Paris (tb), Charlie Shavers (tp), Sandy Weston (tb), Carl Warwick (tp) and Johnny Williams (b). Sitting from left: Tab Smith and Eddie Williams (as), Ronald Haynes and Harold Arnold (ts). Lucky Millinder is conducting.

Leo Mathisen

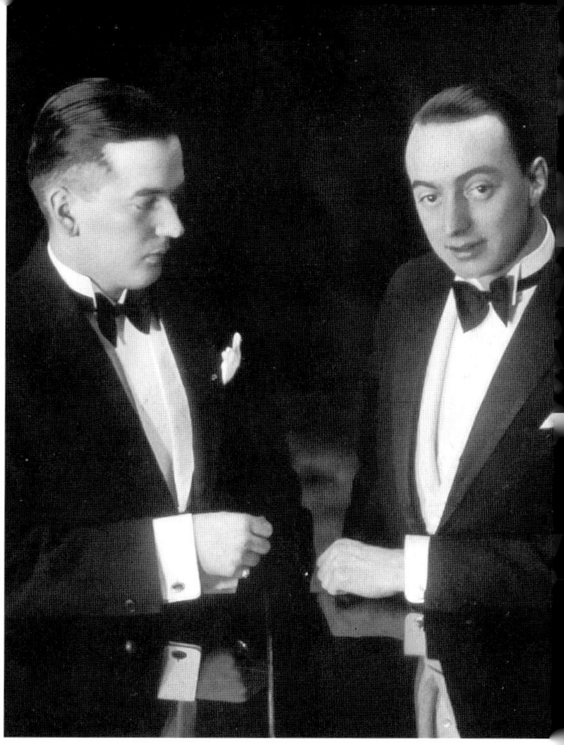

The Danish pianist, singer and bandleader Leo Mathisen (1906-1969) was a major force on the local jazz scene during the 30's and the 40's. He was born in Copenhagen and got his first professional job in 1927 as an intermission pianist at a dance hall, Arena, after which he became a member of the multiinstrumental group We Three, which played the same venue during the winter 1927-28. Mathisen then toured Germany and Sweden with Max Lefko and others from 1928 to 1931 after which he returned to Copenhagen. Here he played with Kaj Julian before joining Erik Tuxen in 1932. From 1936 he led his own bands, but 1951-53 he performed as a solo pianist after which he was forced to retire due to illness. Mathisen was extremely popular during the 40's, and one of the best Danish soloists at the time, strongly influenced by Fats Waller, both as pianist, singer and showman.

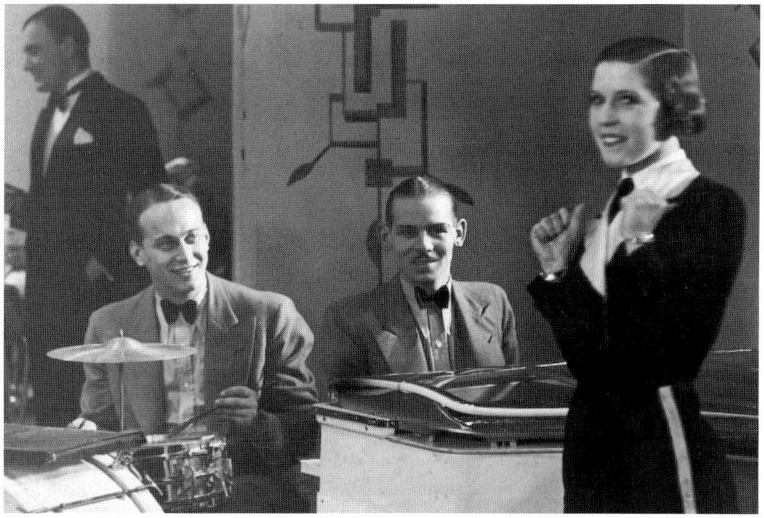

This photo was taken during the shooting of the movie "5 Raske Piger" ("Five Jolly Girls") in 1933. On the left an extra is acting as a servant, Erik "Spjæt" Kragh is on drums, Leo Mathisen at a piano designed by Danish architect Poul Henningsen; right the Norwegian actress Nanna Stenersen.

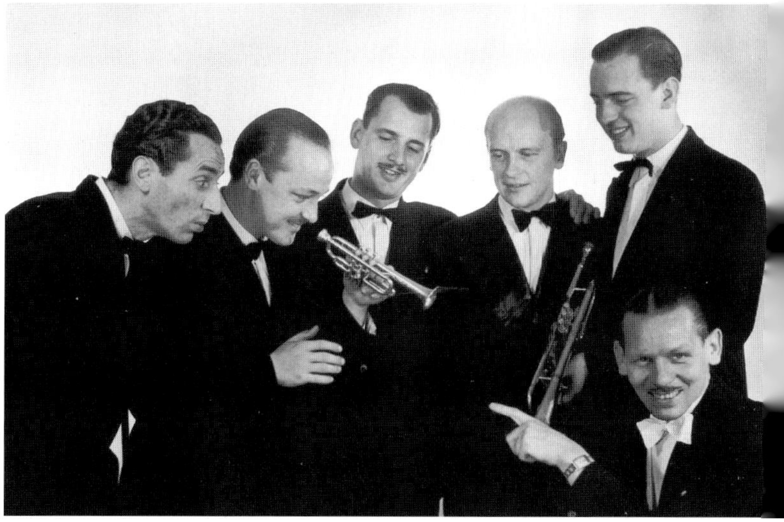

Leo Mathisen with his 1945 band. From the left: Knut Knutssøn (ts) , Leif Johansen (tp), John Steffensen (dr), Carlo Jensen (b), Paul Thaulow (tp) and Leo Mathisen.

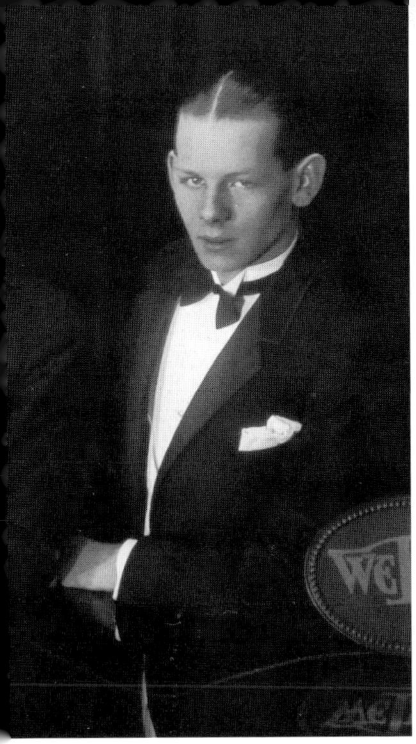

We Three in 1927. From the left: Otto Lington (violin and guitar), Anker Skjoldborg (drums, clarinet, soprano, tenor and bass saxophones) and Leo Mathisen (piano, accordion and goofus).

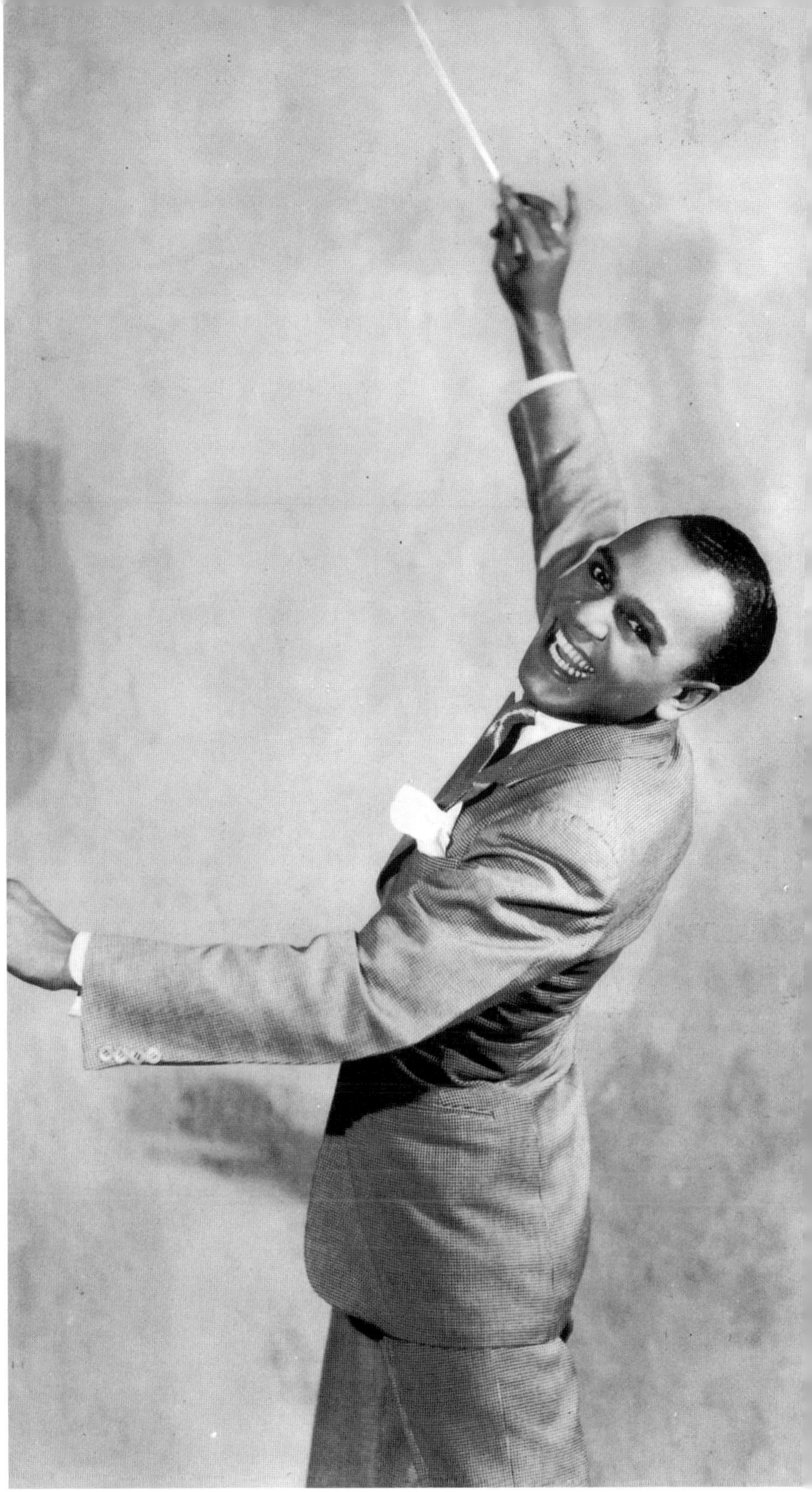

LUCKY MILLINDER

Although Lucius Venable "Lucky" Millinder (1900-1966) couldn't read music at all, he became a successful bandleader during the 30's. He was born in Anniston, Alabama, but grew up in Chicago working as a dancer and master of ceremonies in numerous cabarets, ballrooms and nightclubs. In 1932 he moved to New York where two years later he was chosen to front the Mills Blue Rhythm Band for an engagement at the Cotton Club in Harlem. Millinder stayed with the band until 1938, and in 1940 he formed a new band, which remained active until 1952 when he left full-time music. After this time he worked as a liquor salesman and a disc jockey and only occasionally fronted a band again. Millinder was a gifted showman with an ebullient personality, and he had a big ear which enabled him to conduct a score after one hearing.

MEZZ MEZZROW

A great admirer of black musicians, clarinetist Milton Mesirow "Mezz Mezzrow" (1899-1972) made his greatest contributions to jazz as an organizer of recording sessions with prominent musicians like Frankie Newton, Tommy Ladnier and Sidney Bechet. He was born into a Jewish family in Chicago and played briefly with members of the Austin High School Gang after which he moved to New York and freelanced. During the 30's and 40's he organized several recording sessions, and also in 1937 put together one of the first interracial jazz bands. He settled in France in the 50's and helped assemble American musicians for European tours. Never a great soloist, Mezzrow's playing was earthy, and had a deep feeling for the blues which can be heard especially on recordings with Sidney Bechet.

JOHNNY MERCER

John Herndon "Johnny" Mercer (1909-1976) was one of the greatest lyricists of all times and a successful singer as well. He was born in Savannah, Georgia, but came to New York in 1927 as a member of an acting troupe. From 1932 he worked with Paul Whiteman and later on he worked in radio and television. In 1942 he founded Capitol Records, but left after a few years to concentrate on writing lyrics and music. As a singer he performed in an engaging, relaxed manner, emphazising his southern accent. As a song writer he wrote the lyrics to hundreds of songs, many of which became standards, such as "Jeepers Creepers", "Blues in the Night", "Skylark", "That Old Black Magic", "Moon River", "I Thought About You", "Too Marvelous For Words", and "The Days of Wine and Roses".

MILLS BROTHERS

A vocal quartet formed by brothers John Mills (1911-1936), who sang bass and played guitar, Herbert Mills (1912-1989), Harry Mills (1913-1982) and Donald Mills (1915-). They were born in Piqua, Ohio, and began singing in vaudeville and tent shows in the late 20's. The following decade they became a great commercial success, touring everywhere, performing in clubs, theaters, on radio and TV and in many films. When John died in 1936 his place was taken by their father, John Sr. (1889-1967), who toured with the quartet until his retirement in 1957. The quartet was famous for its smooth four-part harmony combined with their ability to imitate different instruments, especially trumpet and trombone.

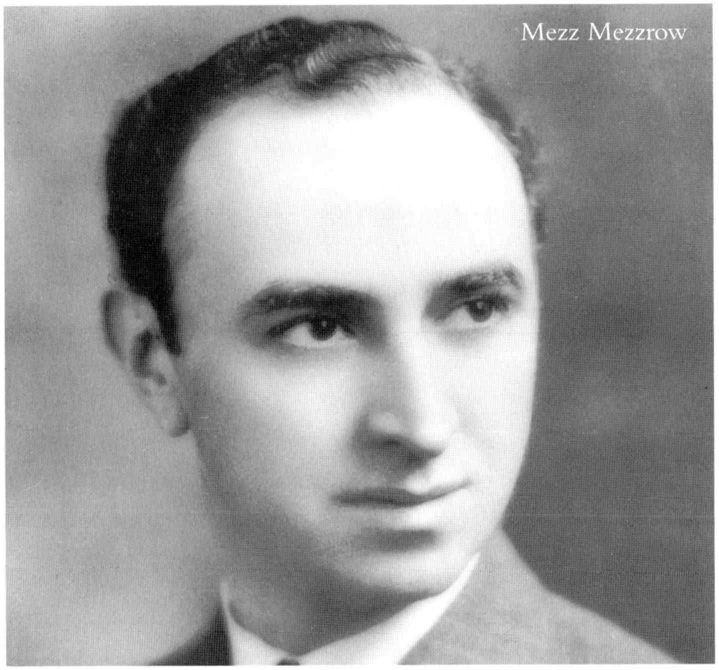

Mezz Mezzrow

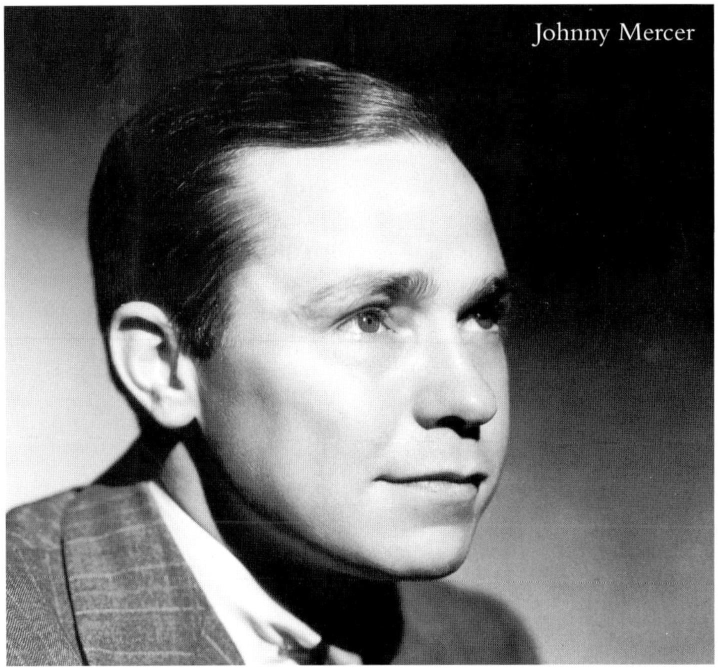

Johnny Mercer

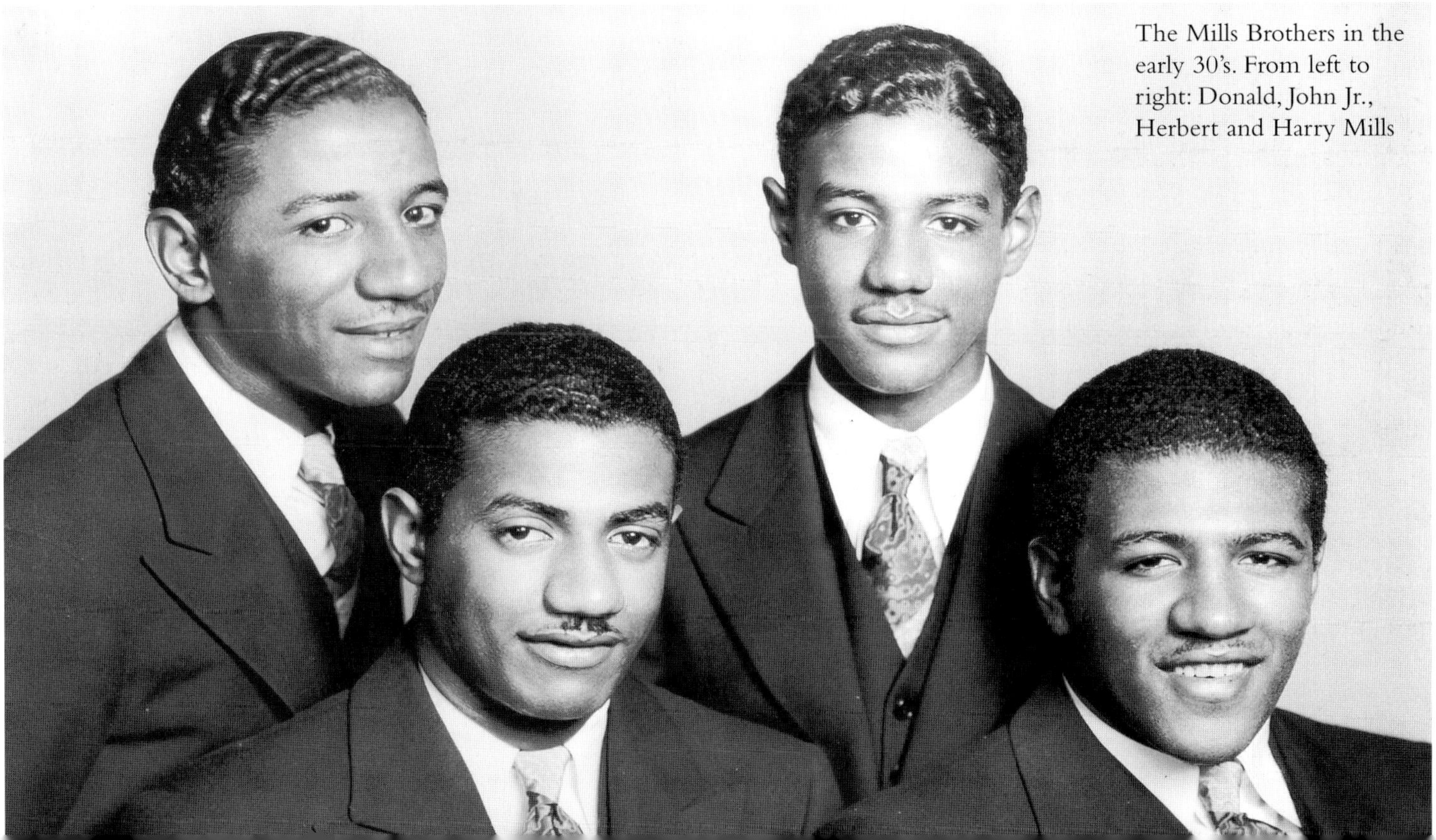

The Mills Brothers in the early 30's. From left to right: Donald, John Jr., Herbert and Harry Mills

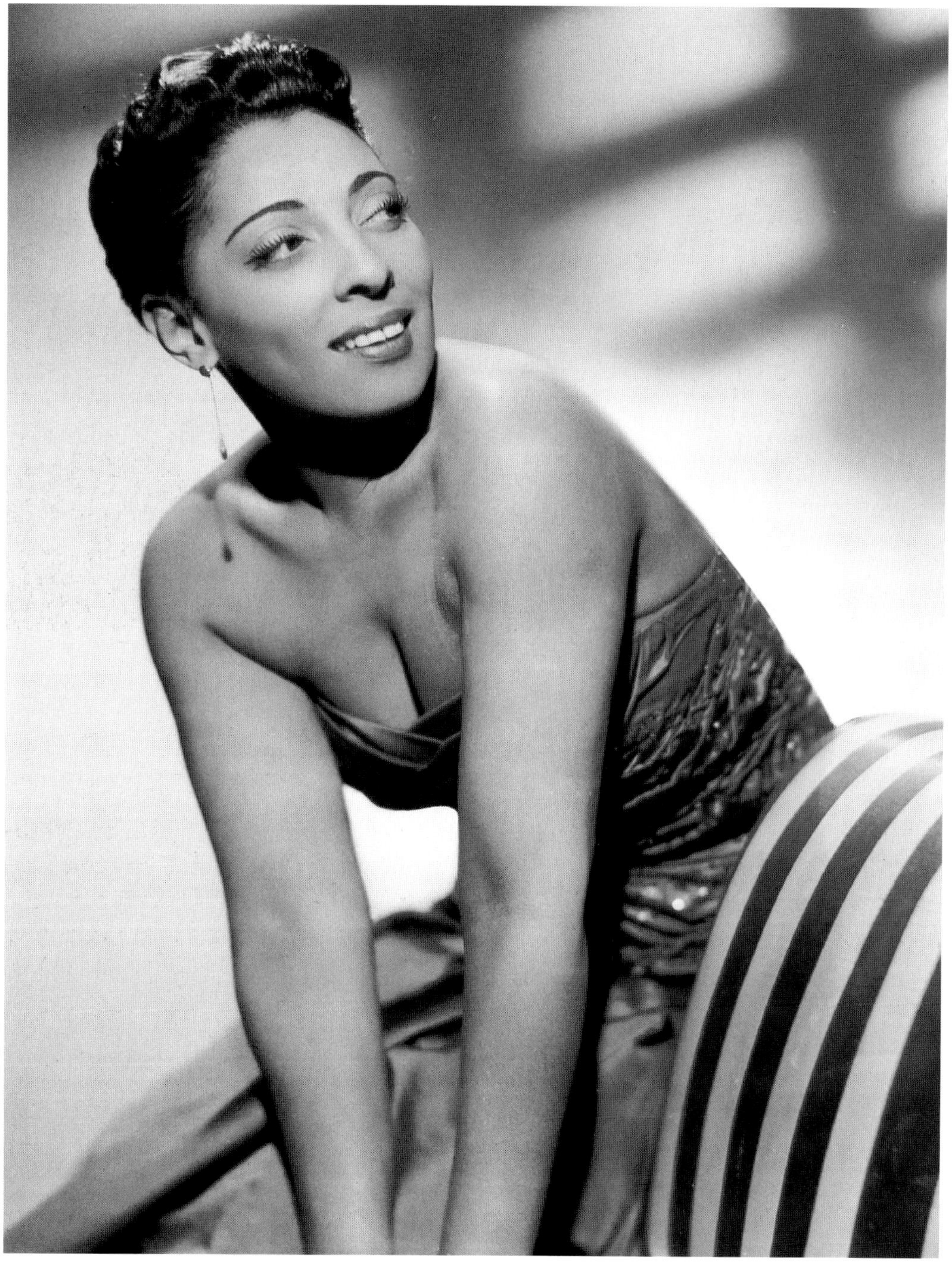

Carmen McRae

Born in New York, singer and pianist Carmen McRae (1920-1994) was first influenced by Billie Holiday. She began her career as a member of Benny Carter's band in 1944, after which she worked the following three years with Count Basie and Mercer Ellington. By 1947 she was singing in Minton's Playhouse and other New York clubs, absorbing the new sounds of bop. From the 50's she was very active on the national and the international jazz scene, touring Japan and Europe several times. She was married to drummer Kenny Clarke 1940-56. McRae developed into a great performer, emphazising the interpretation of the lyrics with deep feeling. She was also an inventive scat singer and a competent pianist who used to accompany herself once or twice during a set.

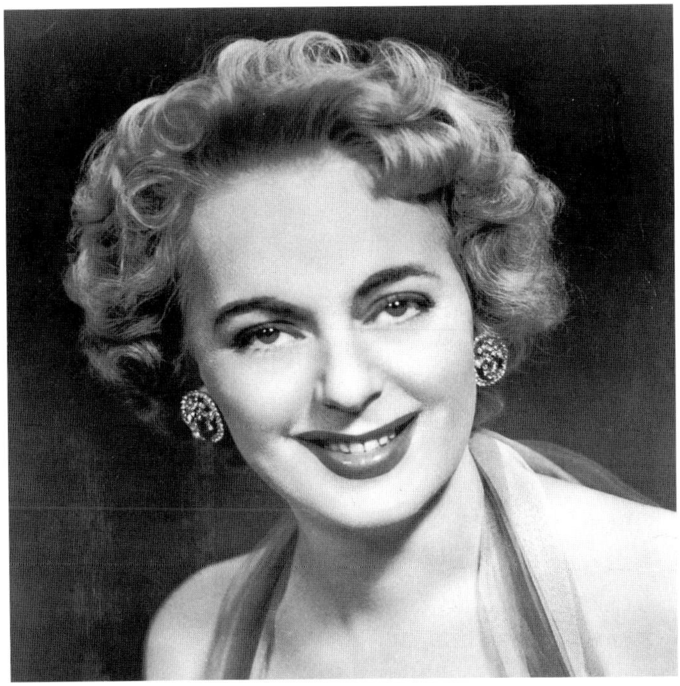

MARIAN MCPARTLAND

Born in Windsor, English pianist Marian Margaret McPartland (1920-) in 1945 settled in New York after having married American trumpeter Jimmy McPartland. She first played as a solo pianist, but in 1950 she established an excellent trio with Bill Crow and Joe Morello who played for years at the Hickory House, New York. From the 70's she has hosted a "Jazz Piano" programme for NBC, and she is still busy playing and recording jazz, as well as doing classical piano concertos which she brought into her repertoire in the 80's. McPartland has a remarkable technique and performs in an elegant, modern style.

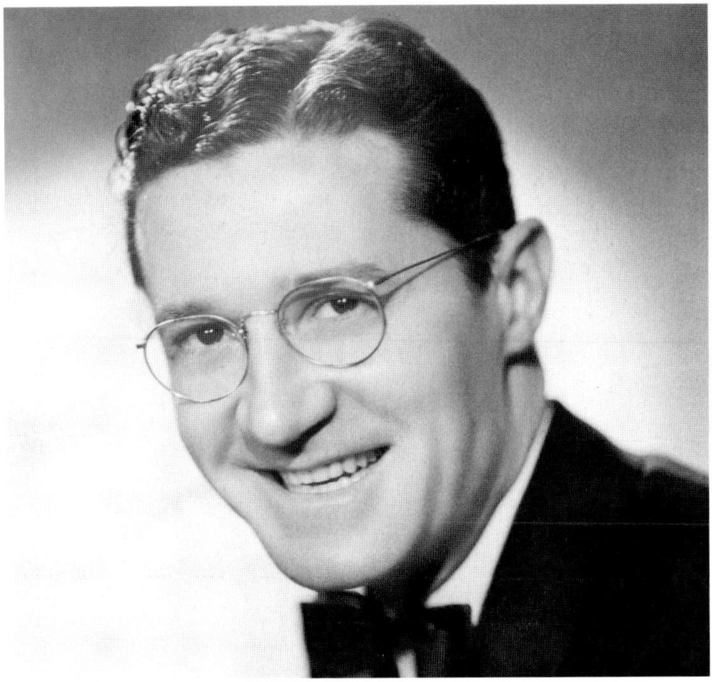

RAY MCKINLEY

Texan Raymond Frederick "Ray" McKinley (1910-1995) was a swinging and tasteful drummer, who was also a good singer. He was born in Fort Worth, and played first professional jobs in territory bands, before joining the Dorsey Brothers' Orchestra in 1934. When the brothers split the following year, McKinley stayed with Jimmy Dorsey until 1939 when he formed a big band with Will Bradley. After disbanding in 1942 he joined Glenn Miller, and after Miller's death in 1944 he led the band for a while until he formed his own band in 1946. Between 1956 and 1978 he led the Glenn Miller tribute bands touring all over the world. He was active right up to his death.

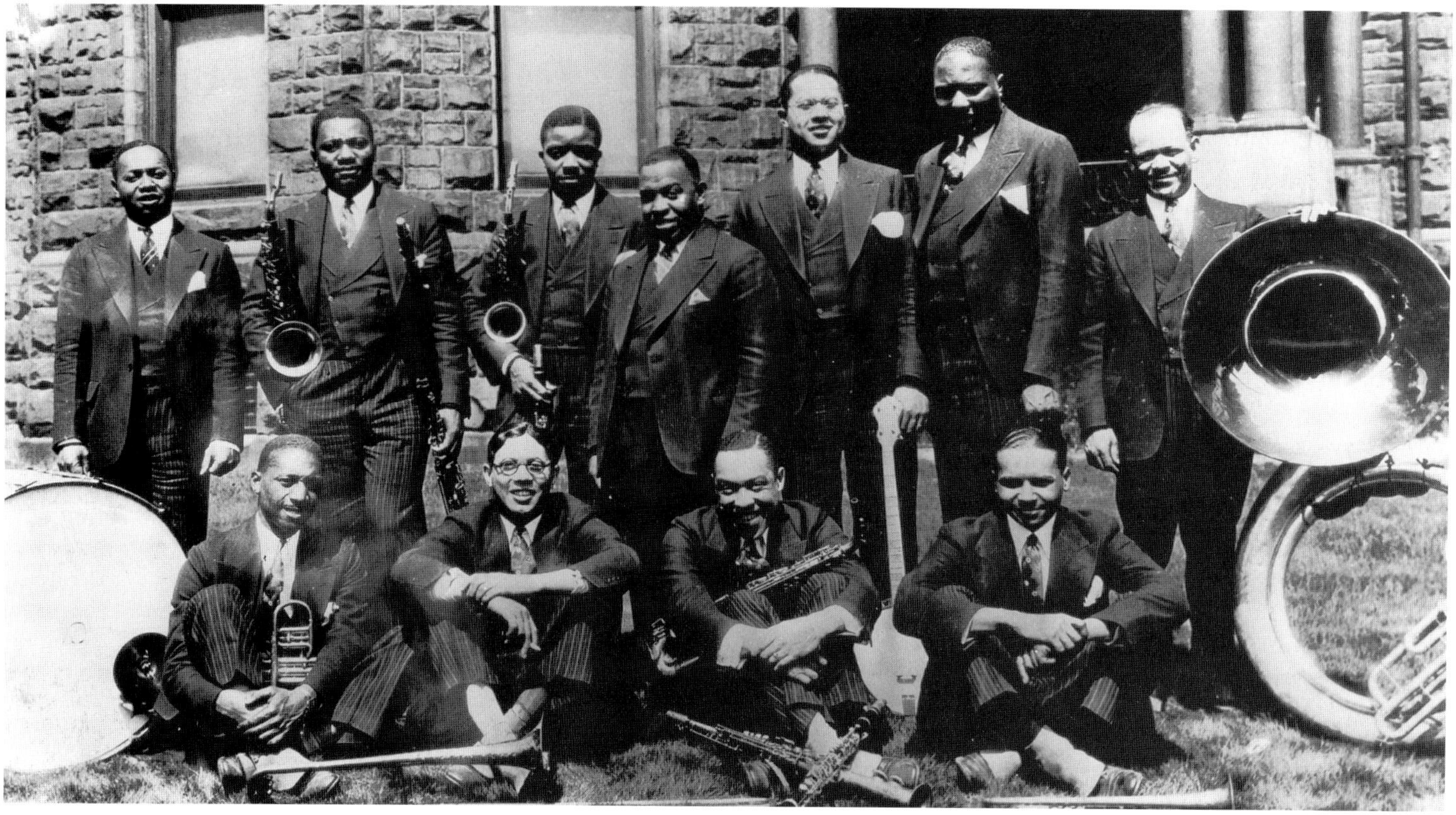

McKinney's Cotton Pickers in 1928: From left: Cuba Austin (dr), Prince Robinson (ts), George "Fathead" Thomas (as, voc.), Don Redman (arr.), David Wilborn (bj), Todd Rhodes (p), and Ralph Escudero (tu). Sitting, from left: John Nesbit (tp), Claude Jones (tb), Milton Senior (as), and Langston Curl (tp).

McKINNEY'S COTTON PICKERS

Drummer Wiliam "Bill" McKinney (1895-1969) led a band in Springfield, Ohio, The Synco Jazz Band, which in 1926 performed in Detroit. Here Jean Goldkette booked them into his Graystone Ballroom and changed the name to McKinney's Cotton Pickers. McKinney, who had ceased playing drums in 1923, was at that time conductor and manager. The Cotton Pickers made Detroit their home base the following years, but also toured extensively until the band broke up in 1934. The following year McKinney reformed the band and managed it until the early 40's when he left the music business.

VIDO MUSSO

Tenor saxophonist Vido William Musso (1913-1982) was born in Carrini, Sicilly, but his family emigrated to the USA in 1920, settling in Detroit. Here Musso took up the clarinet and later on specialized on the tenor saxophone. In 1930 he moved to California where he played in several local bands, often with Stan Kenton with whom he founded a big band in 1936. He left after a while to play with Benny Goodman, Gene Krupa and to form his own band. During the 40's he worked with several bandleaders, such as Benny Goodman again, Harry James, Woody Herman, Tommy Dorsey and Stan Kenton. After leaving Kenton in 1947 Musso played in California, and by 1957 he was working in Las Vegas. Musso had a big tone and played in an aggressive style which made him a crowd pleaser during the 30's and 40's.

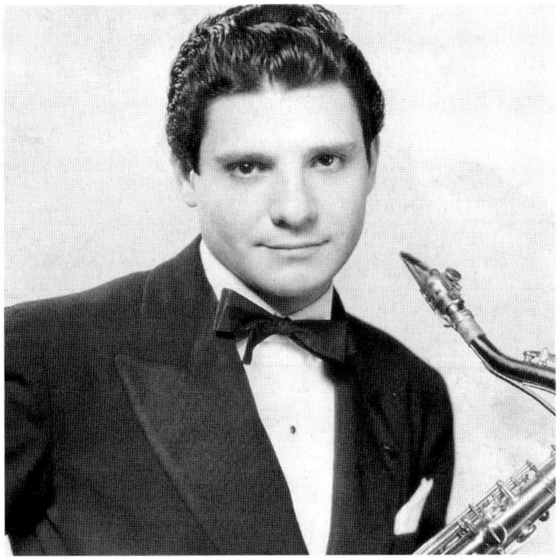

Vido Musso in 1937 with his brand new Conn saxophone.

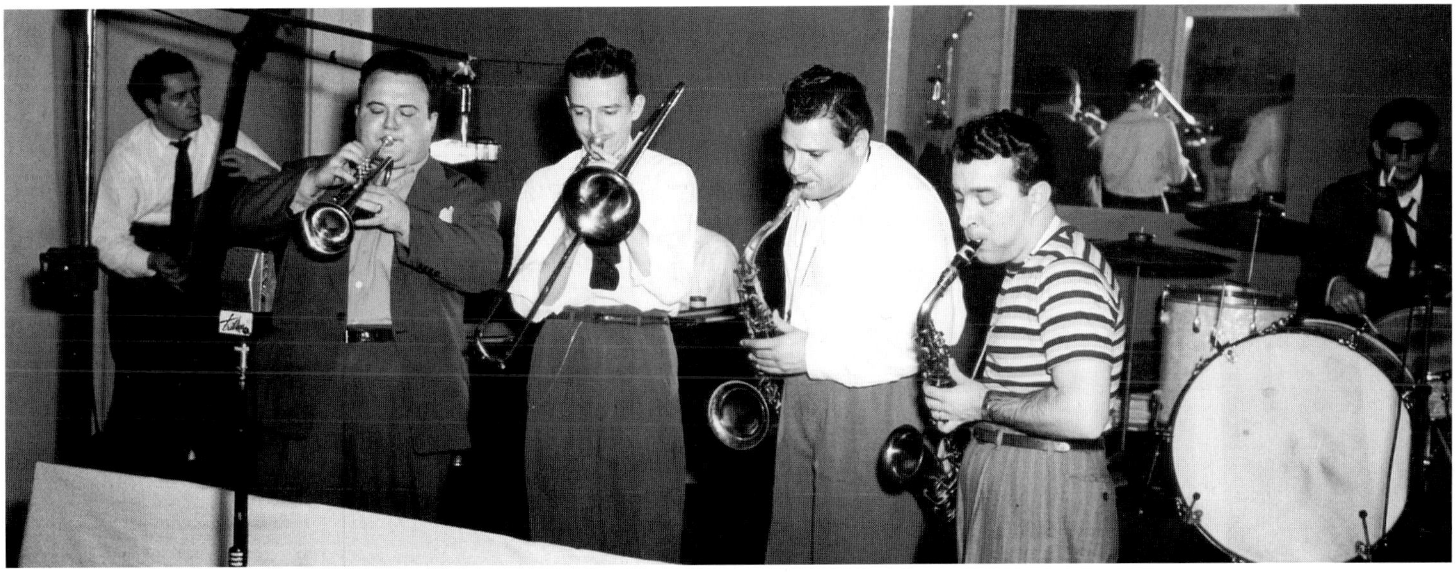

Vido Musso and His Orchestra – in fact members of the Stan Kenton orchestra – recording for Trilon in Los Angeles in June 1946. From left: Eddie Safranski (b), Ray Wetzel (tp), Kai Winding (tb), Vido Musso (ts), Boots Mussulli (as), Shelly Manne (dr). Halfway hidden behind Winding is pianist Pete Rugolo.

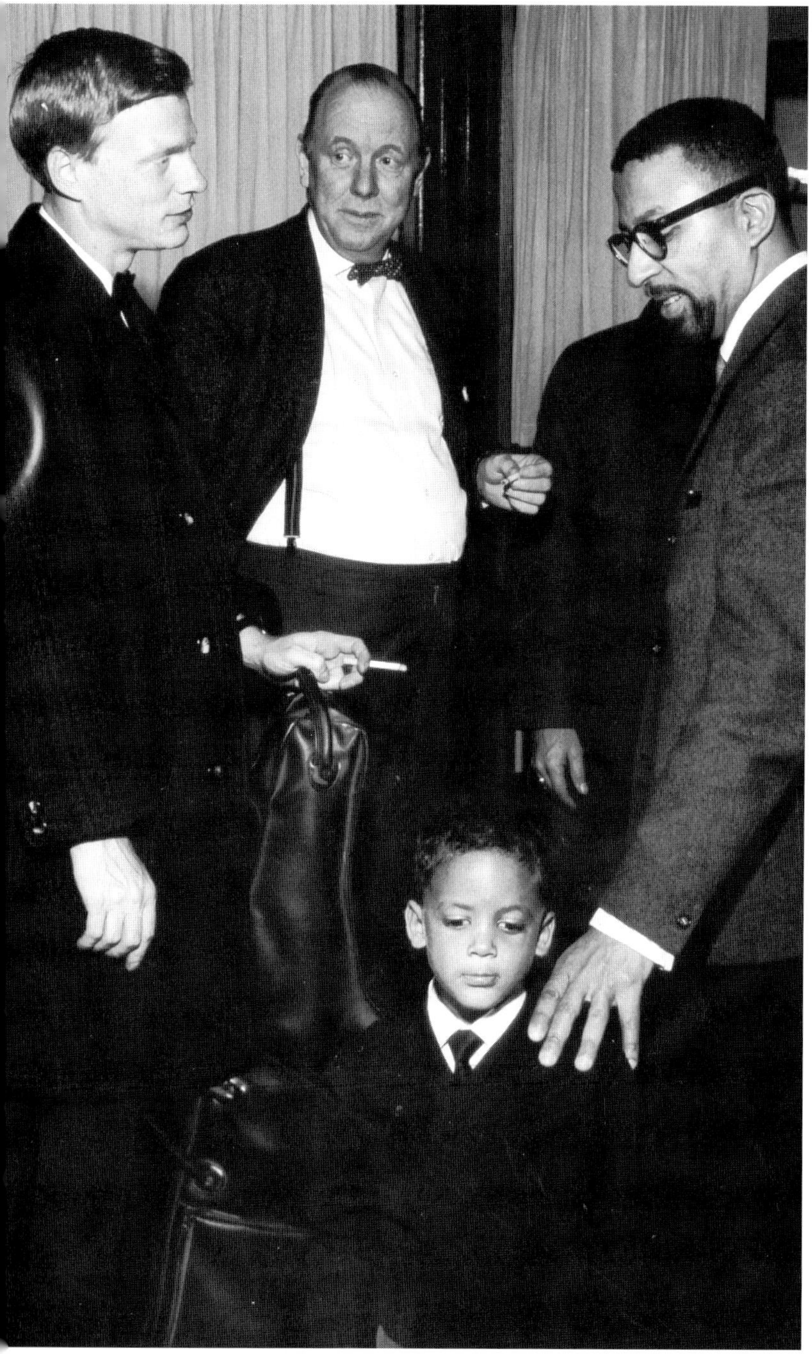

GERRY MULLIGAN

"The Zoot Sims of the baritone" is a suitable description of the playing of Gerald Joseph "Gerry" Mulligan (1927-1996). A New Yorker raised in Philadelphia, Mulligan was first known as an arranger for a local radio band, but in 1946 he moved to New York and became a staff arranger for Gene Krupa. Later on he worked for Claude Thornhill, Elliot Lawrence and Stan Kenton, and wrote for and took part in the famous nonet recordings with Miles Davis (1949-50). By 1952 he was in California where he formed a quartet with Chet Baker, after which he freelanced or led bands of various sizes. Mulligan was a versatile instrumentalist, equally at home in a dixieland setting or in more modern surroundings. With his light phrasing and an unusual talent for improvised countermelody he became the most important baritone saxophonist after Harry Carney. His writing was characterized by intricate innner parts and a light-textured feeling.

This photo was taking after a concert at the Tivoli Gardens Concert Hall in Copenhagen with the Gerry Mulligan Quartet, October 1962. Mulligan is talking with instrument-colleague Sahib Shihab who keeps an eye and a hand on his son, while Rosenkrantz gives Mulligan a quizzical look.

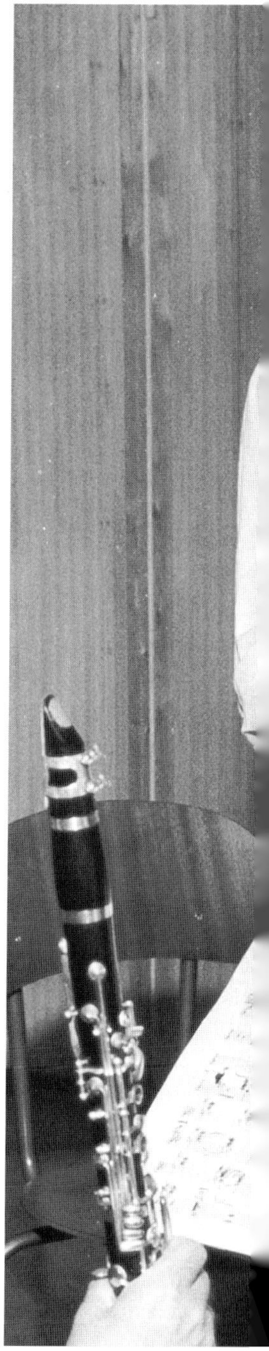

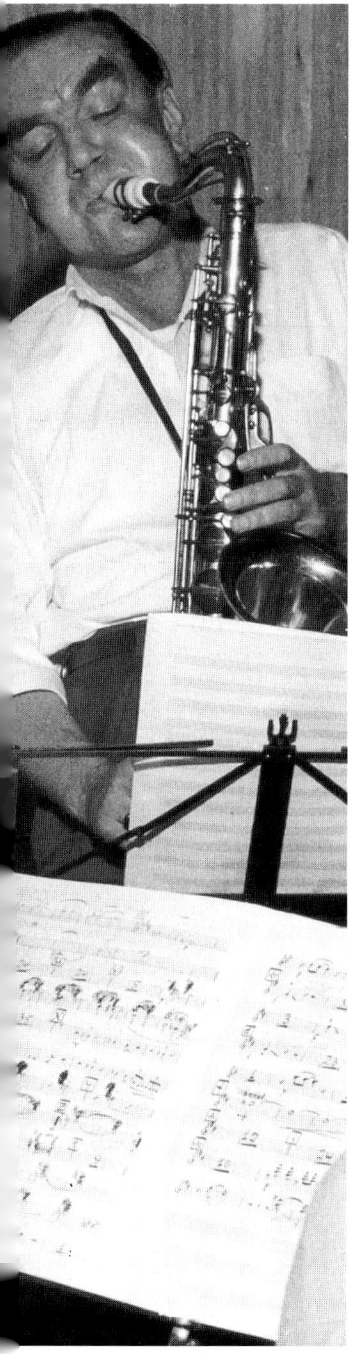

BREW MOORE

Milton Aubrey "Brew" Moore (1924-1973) was without a doubt Lester Young's most devoted disciple. He is the author of the famous tag: "Anyone who doesn't play like Lester is wrong!" Moore came from Indianola, Mississippi, and played several instruments from the age of 12 before he changed to the tenor saxophone while at high school. He played in New Orleans and Memphis before moving to New York in 1948 and getting a job with Claude Thornhill. From 1949 he played with Gerry Mulligan, Machito, Kai Winding, and Cal Tjader, besides leading his own groups. In 1961 he went to France to play with Kenny Clarke after which he settled in Copenhagen and only intermittently visited the USA again. He died from a fall down a flight of stairs at the Chinese Tower Restaurant in Copenhagen's Tivoli Gardens.

Brew Moore during a recording of "Blues Suite" at the Metronome Studios in Copenhagen, August 30, 1962 with the Danish Radio Jazz Group conducted by Erik Moseholm.

TOOTS MONDELLO

Alto saxophonist Nuncio "Toots" Mondello (1912-1992) came from Boston, Massachusetts. He played for six years with Mal Hallett who had a popular dance band, after which he played lead with Benny Goodman 1934-35. After stints with Joe Haymes and Ray Noble he led his own band after which he once more joined Goodman until 1940. After this time he went into studio work and freelanced. Mondello was not only a highly skilled lead saxophonist, but also a fine and intelligent soloist.

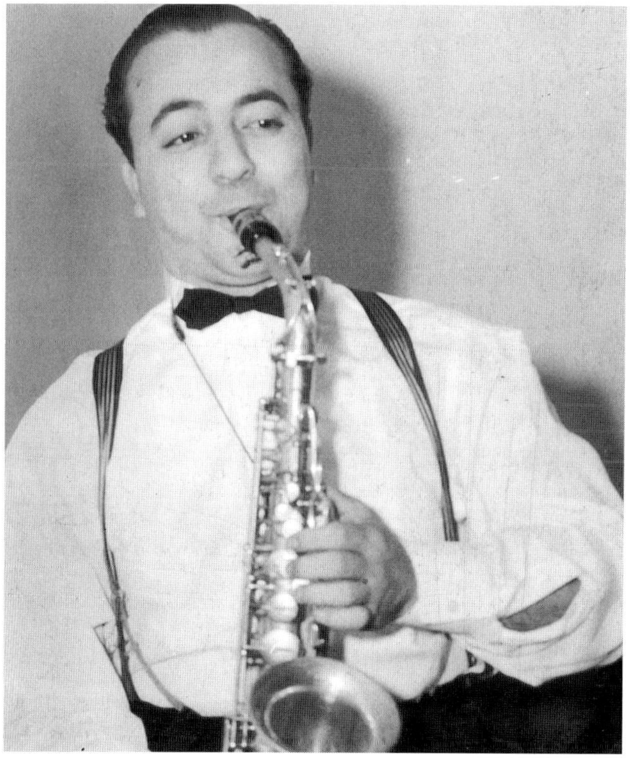

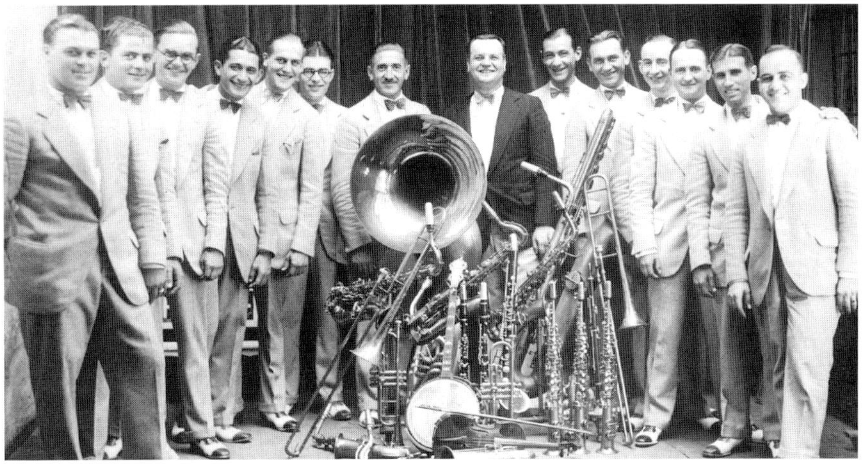

Ray Miller and His Orchestra in 1924. From the left: Ward Archer (dr), Charles Rocco (tp), Miff Mole (tb), Danny Yates (vl), Roy Johnston (tp), Tom Satterfield (p), Louis Chassagne (tu), Ray Miller (leader), Frankie Trumbauer (C-melody sax), Andy Sindelar (tb), Rube Bloom (p), Billy Richards (ts), Frank DiPrima (bj), Andy Sannella (as).

RAY MILLER

Bandleader Ray Miller formed a 6-piece band in New York called "Ray Miller's Black and White Melody Boys", which around 1920 played in many musical productions on Broadway. During the early 20's he expanded it to a full-scale dance band which over the years featured many excellent musicians, and played many of the best dance halls in and around New York, such as the Arcadia Ballroom and the New York Hippodrome. By the early 30's Miller was forced to disband, after which he went out of business.

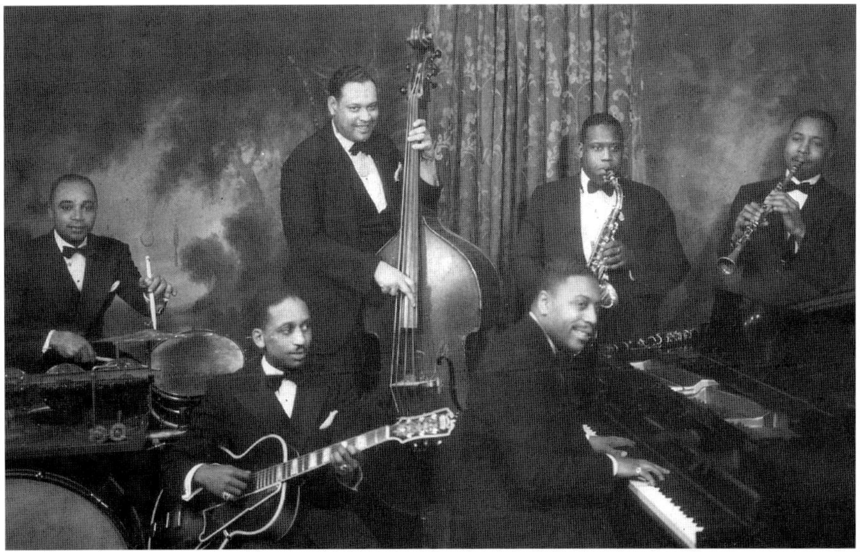

Freddie Moore and His Melody Boys with Don Frye (p) and Pete Brown (as) at the Victoria Café in Harlem 1937.

FREDDIE MOORE

Born in Washington, North Carolina, Freddie Moore (1900-1992) began to play drums as a child, and in his teens travelled with tent shows throughout the southern states. In the late 20's he played with Charlie Creath and Wilbur Sweatman, after which he joined King Oliver. 1933-37 he led his own band in New York after which he was much in demand, freelancing with Art Hodes, Sidney Bechet, Sammy Price, Emmett Berry, Toni Parenti, Roy Eldridge and others. Due to ill health he concentrated on playing washboard from the mid-80's.

GLENN MILLER

A perfectionist and leader of one of the most popular big bands of the swing era, Alton Glenn Miller (1904-1944), was also a great arranger whose works for big band are easily recognized by the doubling of the melody on saxophone with a clarinet an octave higher. Miller was born in Clarinda, Indiana, but grew up in Fort Morgan, Colorado where he studied music. He gained experience in territory bands in the early 20's, and in 1926 he joined Ben Pollack's band on the West Coast. He left Pollack in New York two years later, after which he freelanced for several years, working with Red Nichols, the Dorsey's and others. In 1937 he formed his own big band but had to disband it due to failing success. The following year he organized another one which gradually gained popularity, and after a couple of years became one of the highest paid bands in the USA. In 1942 Miller disbanded to join the Army where he assembled a military band with which he travelled to England in 1944. During a trip to Paris to arrange an appearance for his band his plane disappeared over the Channel, and no trace of it has ever been found.

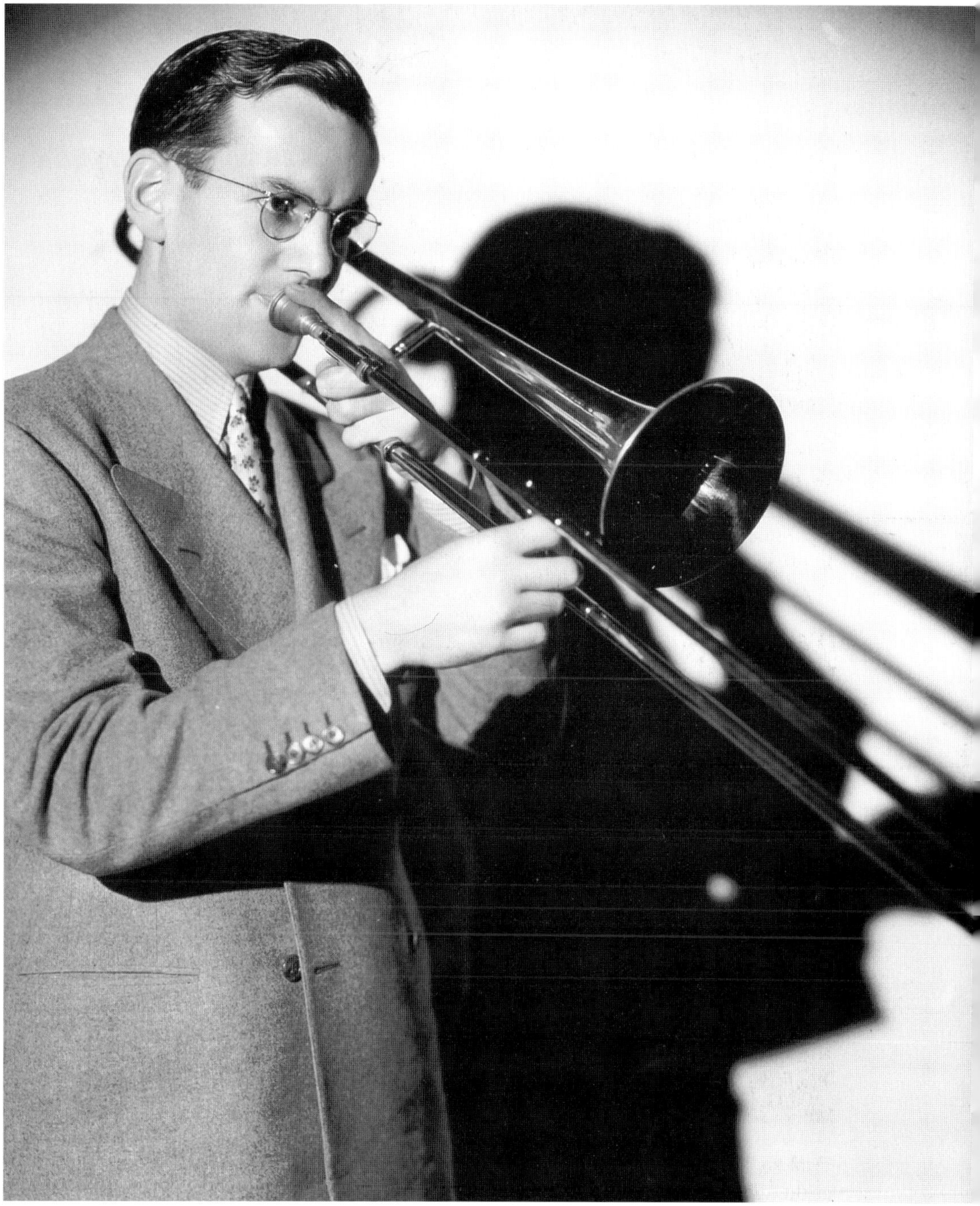

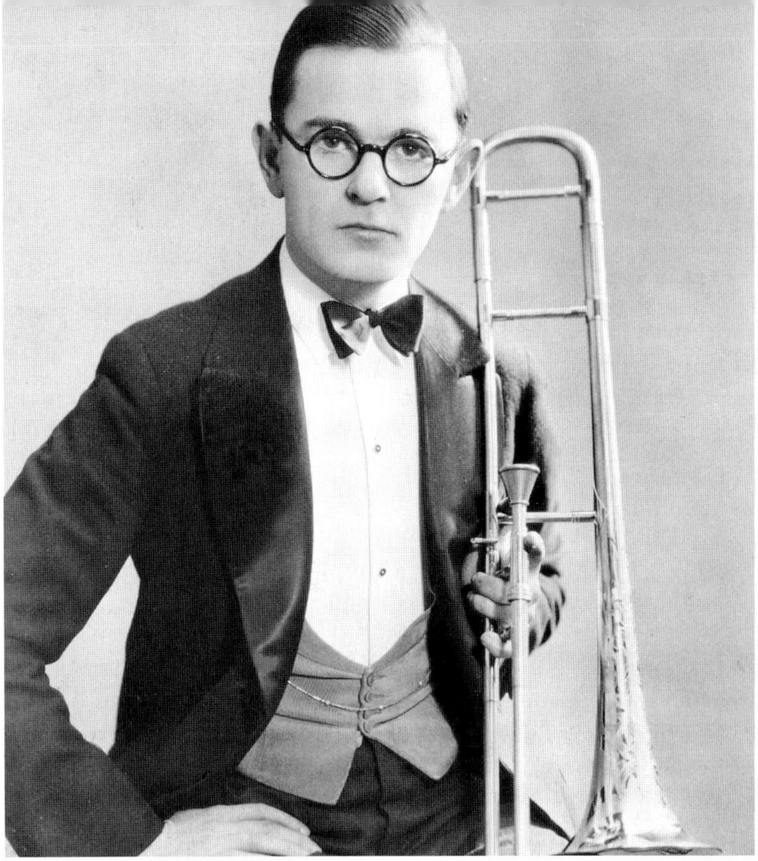

Miff Mole

Irving Milfred "Miff" Mole (1898-1961) was one of the first to form a solo style on the trombone free from New Orleans tailgate playing. He was born in Roosevelt, New York, and played several instruments before he took up the trombone. With Phil Napoleon's Original Memphis Five and with Red Nichols he recorded hundreds of records in the 20's which were influential and showed his clean, quick technique and precise intonation. From 1929 and into the following decade he played in the NBC radio orchestra, and 1938-40 he was with Paul Whiteman. In 1943 he returned to freelance with small groups, but also led his own bands. From the mid-50's he only played sporadically due to illness.

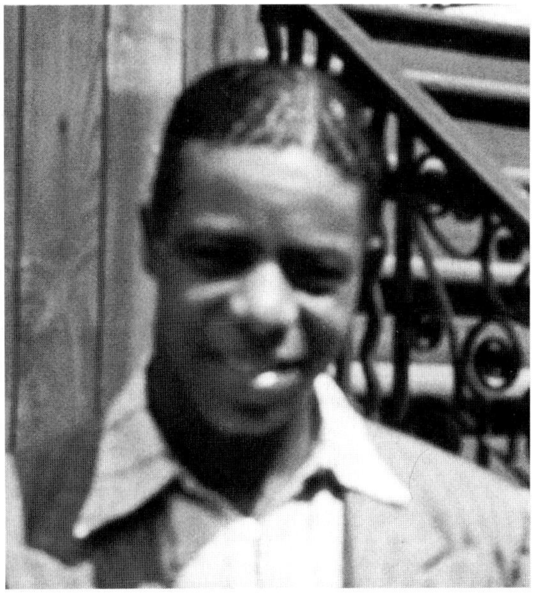

Benny Morton

Trombonist Henry Sterling "Benny" Morton (1907-1985) was a New Yorker who gained a lot of experience working in big bands during the 20's and 30', such as those led by Fletcher Henderson, Chick Webb, Don Redman and Count Basie. Between 1940 and 1946 he played in small groups followed by a long period working in pit bands for Broadway shows. From the 60's he freelanced, playing with Henry "Red" Allen, the Saints and Sinners, Wild Bill Davison, Sy Oliver, the World's Greatest Jazzband and others. Morton was not a great virtuoso on his instrument but always played meaningful solos presented with feeling and an exquisite tone.

Benny Morton photographed by Rosenkrantz in 1938 in New York.

FRANKIE NEWTON

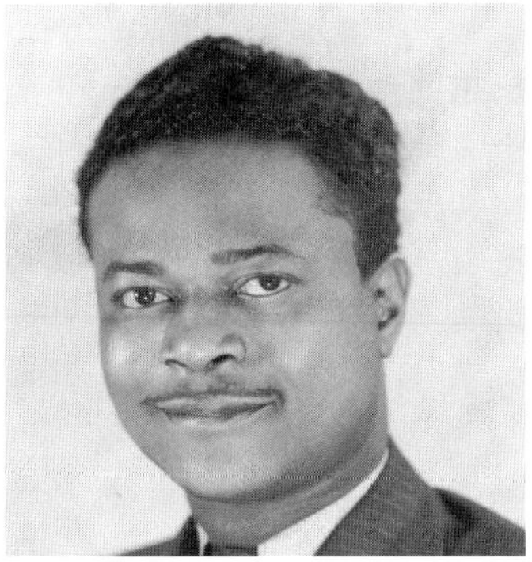

Born in Emory, Virginia trumpeter William Frank "Frankie" Newton (1906-1954) came to New York with drummer Lloyd Scott in 1929. In the following decade he played in a variety of bands, including those led by Chick Webb, Elmer Snowden, Charlie Johnson, Teddy Hill, John Kirby and Lucky Millinder. In 1939 he formed his own band, and during the 40's he commuted regularly between New York and Boston. Due to ill health he did little playing after 1951, devoting most of his time to painting and politics. Newton was an inventive and highly original soloist, playing with a warm tone and executing his ideas with precision and accuracy.

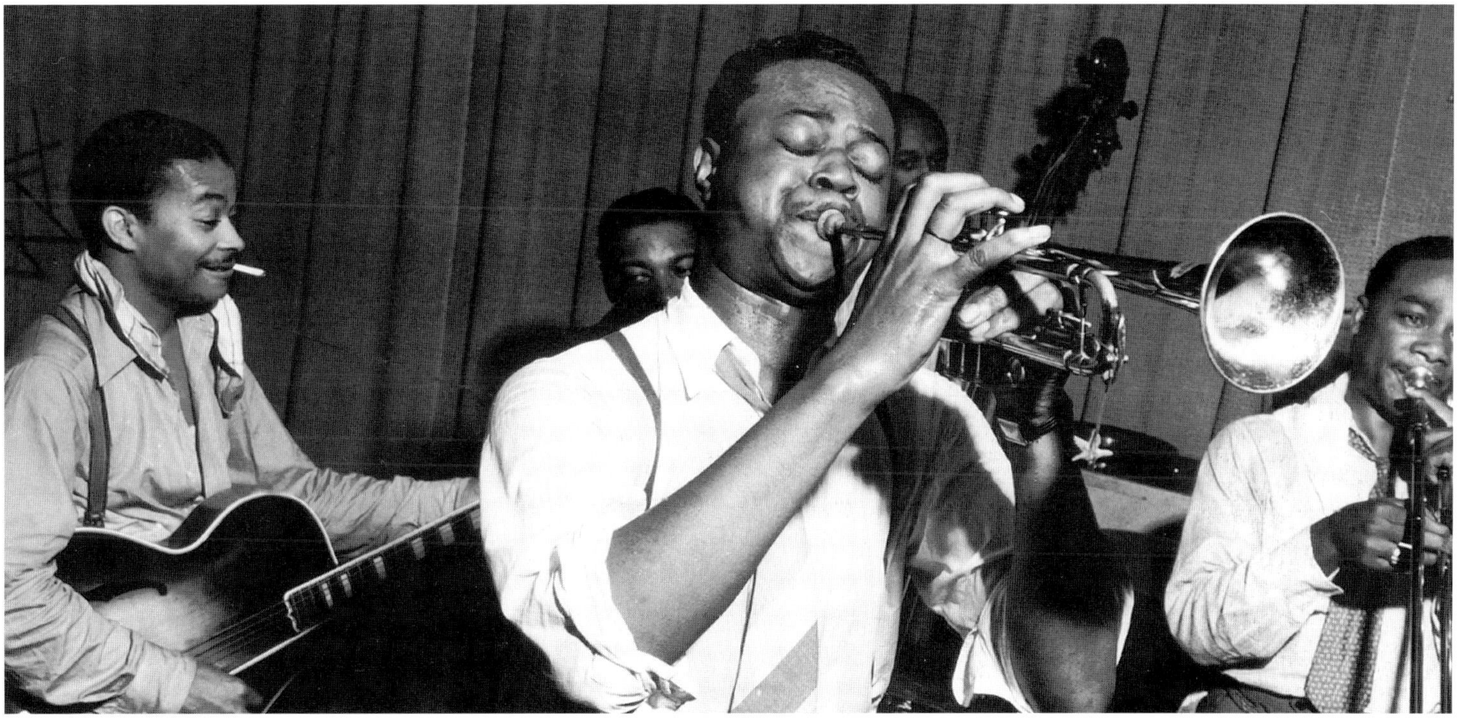

Newton at a recording session for Blue Note June 8, 1939 with the Port of Harlem Jazzmen under the leadership of Sidney Bechet. Newton is surrounded by Teddy Bunn (g), Sidney Catlett (dr), Johnny Williams (b) and J.C. Higginbotham (tb).

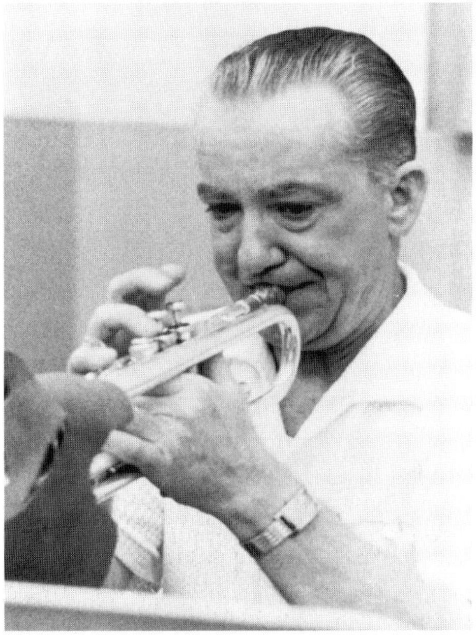

Red Nichols recording in the 50's.

RED NICHOLS

Cornetist and bandleader Ernest Loring "Red" Nichols (1905-1965) was taught by his father, who was a college music teacher. In 1923 he moved from Ogden, Utah, to New York where he soon became much in demand as a sideman, playing Broadway shows and leading his own groups. During the 20's he made numerous recordings with his own studio groups called the Five Pennies, the California Redheads, the Charleston Chasers, the Louisiana Rhythm Kings, the Arkansas Travellers and others, and was the most recorded white bandleader of the period. Nichols led his own big band from 1930, and was on network radio, conducting orchestras for Bob Hope and Ruth Etting. But from the mid-30's he returned to small-group jazz. Except for 1942-44, when he was out of business, he was busy throughout the rest of his life recording, leading his own bands, appearing on TV and radio, and touring. He died from a heart attack in his Las Vegas hotel room. Nichols' recordings of the late 20's are regarded as being among the best white jazz of the period.

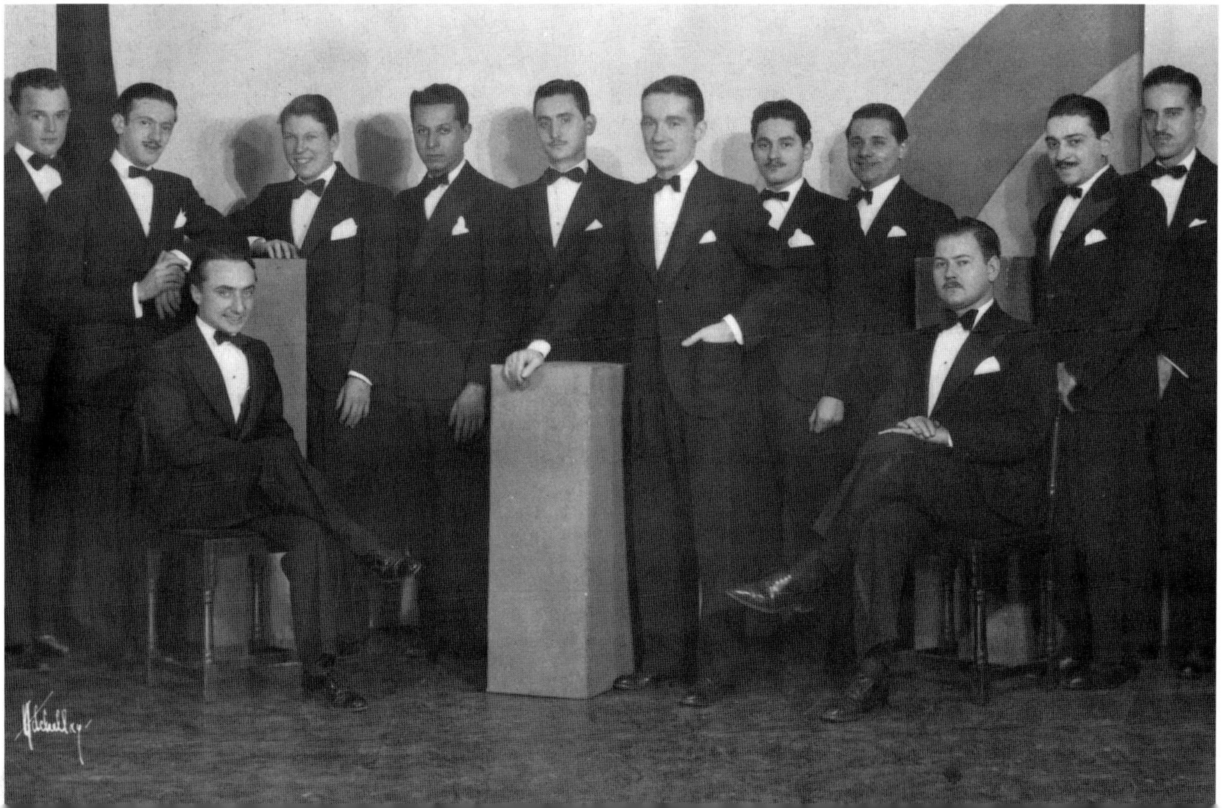

Red Nichols and His Orchestra 1931. From the left, Will Bradley (tb), Eddie Bergman (vl), Fulton McGrath (p), Johnny Davis (tp), Artie Bernstein (b), Frank Salto (sax), Red Nichols (cnt), Babe Russin (ts), Tony Socco (g), Don Moore (tp), Victor Engle (dr), Fred Morrow (sax).

ALBERT NICHOLAS

Albert Nicholas (1900-1973) was one of the outstanding clarinetists born in New Orleans. He took lessons with Lorenzo Tio and played in many of the name bands while still in his teens, such as those of Buddy Petit, King Oliver, and Manuel Perez. After three years in the US Navy he led his own band in New Orleans followed by two years with King Oliver in Chicago. Then he toured the Far East with Jack Carter, spent a year in Cairo, Alexandria and Paris, and returned in 1928 to New York to a chair in Luis Russell's band. From 1933 and the following two decades he played with Chick Webb, John Kirby, Louis Armstrong and Rex Stewart, but in 1953 he settled in France and toured Europe for the rest of his life. Nicholas played with a full, rich sound, favoring the low – chalumeau – register of the clarinet.

Albert Nicholas at a recording session for RCA with Jelly Roll Morton on September 14, 1939. Producer Harry Lim has his arm around tenor saxophonist Happy Caldwell, with drummer Zutty Singleton in the background.

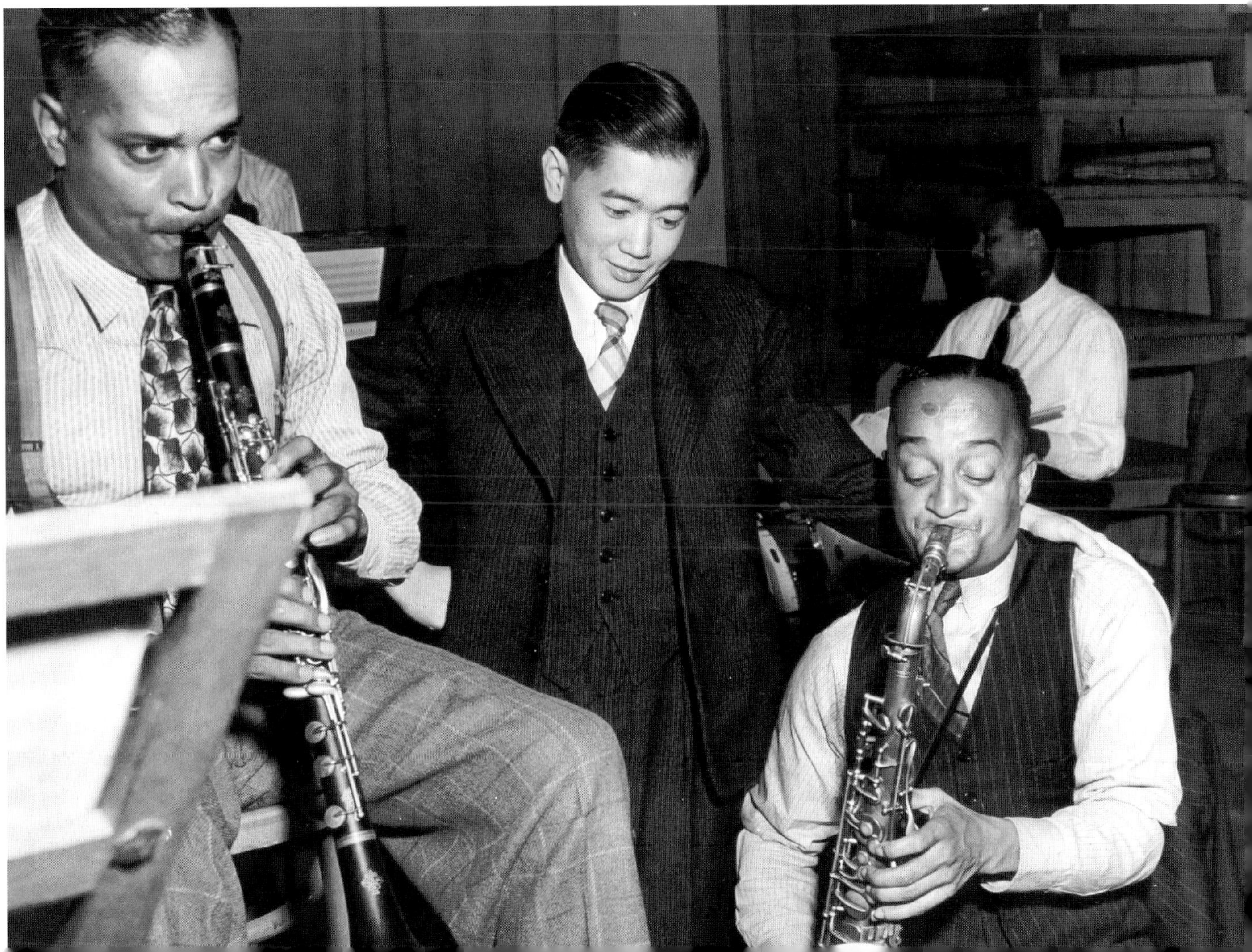

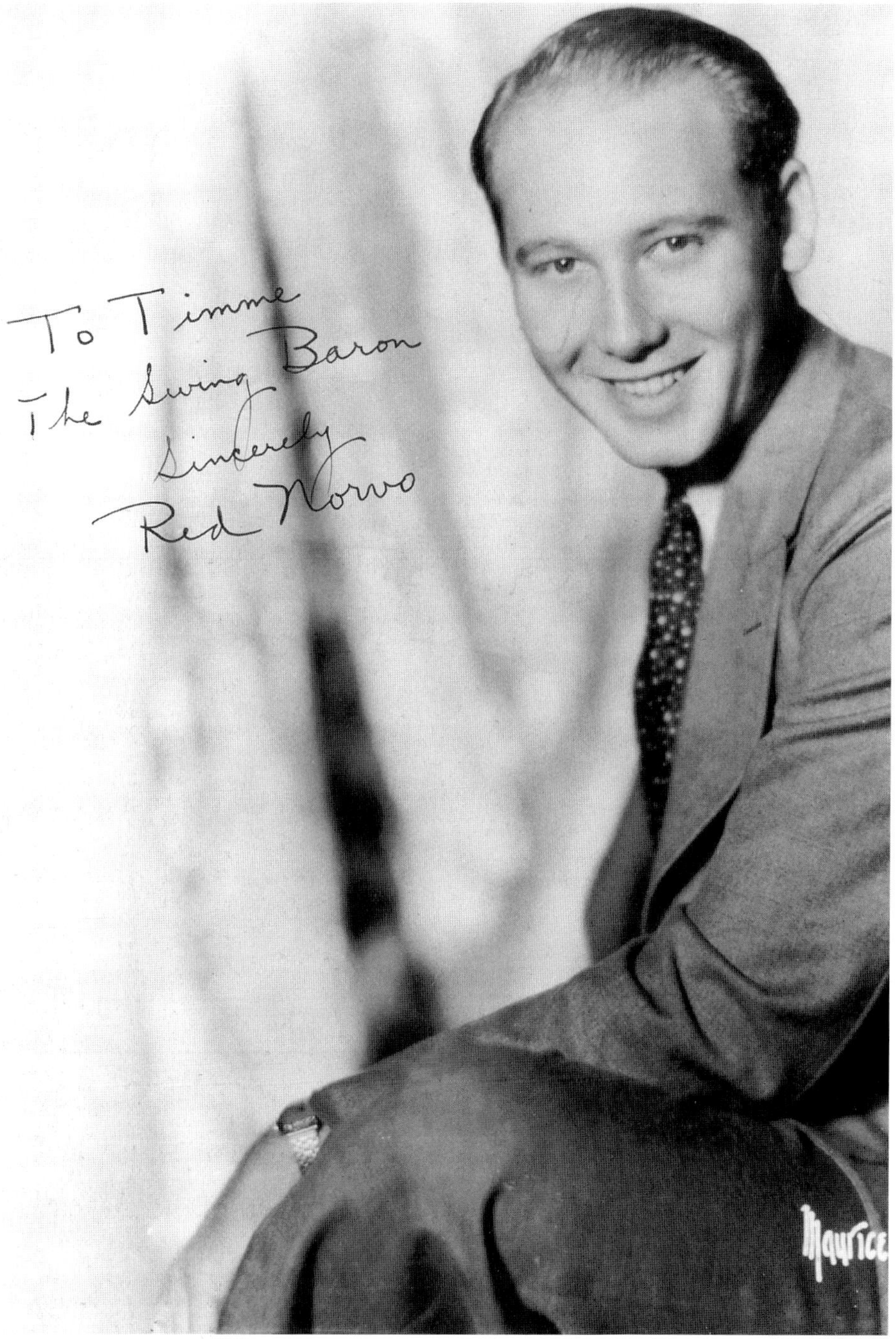

RED NORVO

Kenneth Norville "Red Norvo" (1908-1999) came from Beardstown, Illionois, and took up the marimba in his teens. In the late 20's he toured with a marimba band after which he joined Paul Whiteman's orchestra where he met his future wife Mildred Bailey. During this time he changed to the xylophone, and in 1933 he and Bailey left Whiteman to freelance in New York. From 1935 to 1944 he led his own band after which he joined Benny Goodman. During the 50's he led trios with guitar and bass, of which the first one with Tal Farlow and Charlie Mingus was the most outstanding. Except for occasionnally touring in Europe, Norvo worked mostly in California and Las Vegas from the 60's, until his retirement in the late 80's. Norvo was an exceptional soloist, playing in a style influenced by pianists Jess Stacy and Teddy Wilson.

Publicity shot of Red Norvo from the mid-30's. *To Timme The Swing Baron. Sincerely Red Norvo.*

JOE "TRICKY SAM" NANTON

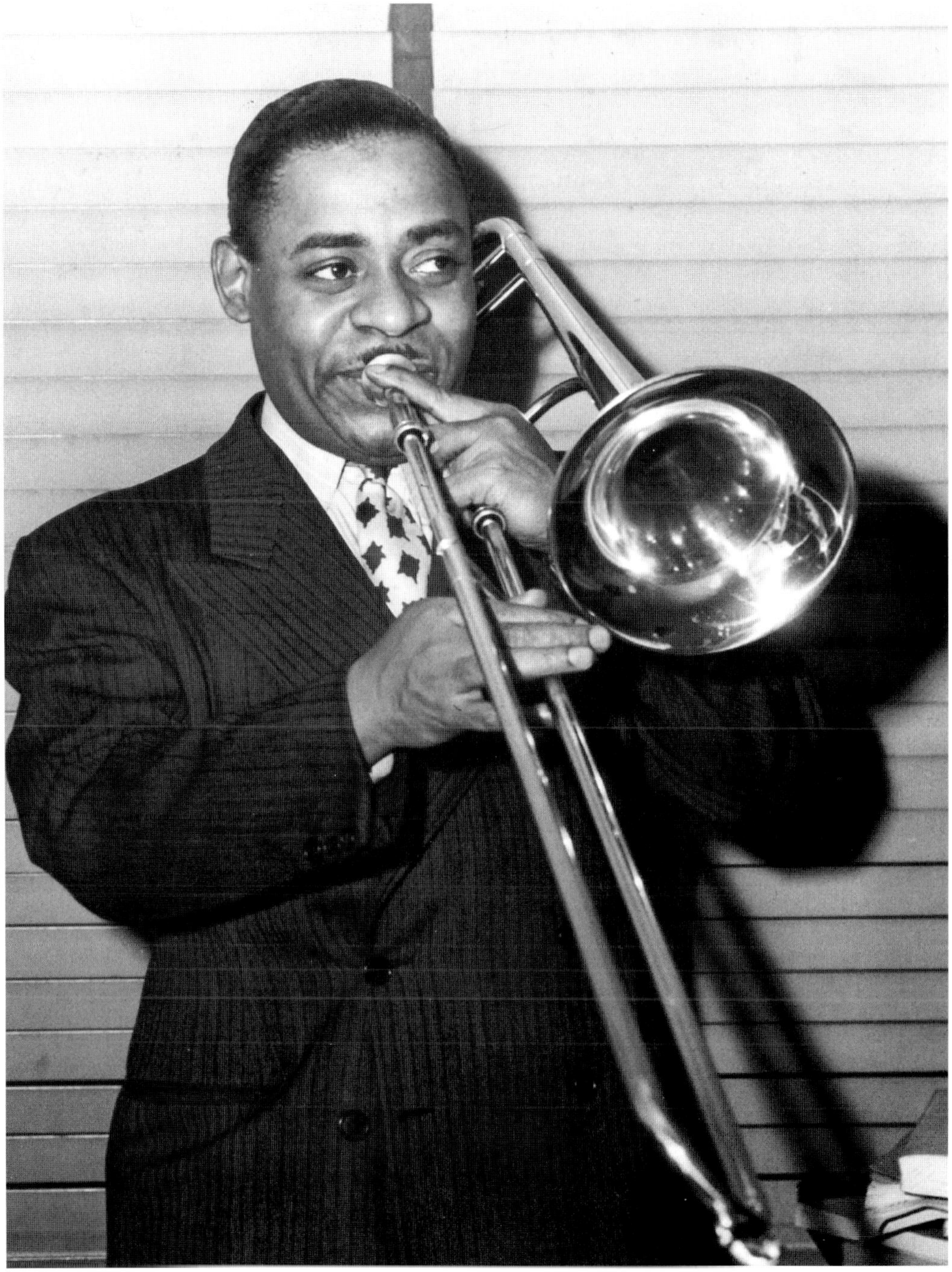

Trombonist Joseph Nanton Irish "Joe Tricky Sam" Nanton (1904-1946) was born in New York to West Indian parents. From the early 20's he worked in cabaret bands led by Clifford Jackson, Earl Frazier and Elmer Snowden before he joined Duke Ellington in 1926, with whom he stayed for the rest of his life. With Ellington he perfected the use of the rubber plunger mute, creating many effects from the sound of a tissue paper being torn to the roar of an enraged tiger. This speciality, for which Otto Hardwick nicknamed him, was effectly used in Ellington's "jungle" style music. Nanton suffered a stroke in late 1945, and half a year later he was found dead one morning in his hotel room in San Francisco while on tour with Ellington.

PHIL NAPOLEON

Born into a musical family trumpeter Filippo Napoli "Phil Napoleon" (1901-1990) received a solid musical education from an early age. Already in 1917 he founded the Original Memphis Five with pianist Frank Signorelli, which between 1921 and 1931 made hundreds of recordings of popular tunes, blues, and dixieland and New Orleans standards for dozens of labels all over the USA, thus making way for the popularity of jazz. In 1931 he broke up the group and went into studio work for NBC until 1949, only interrupted by short periods with his own big band in 1938 and a stint with Jimmy Dorsey in 1943. In 1949 he reformed the Original Memphis Five, with whom he stayed at Nick's in New York for seven years. Then he moved to Miami and opened his own club, Napoleon's Retreat, running a band there for the rest of his life. Napoleon played in a strong, solid and flexible style which influenced Red Nichols.

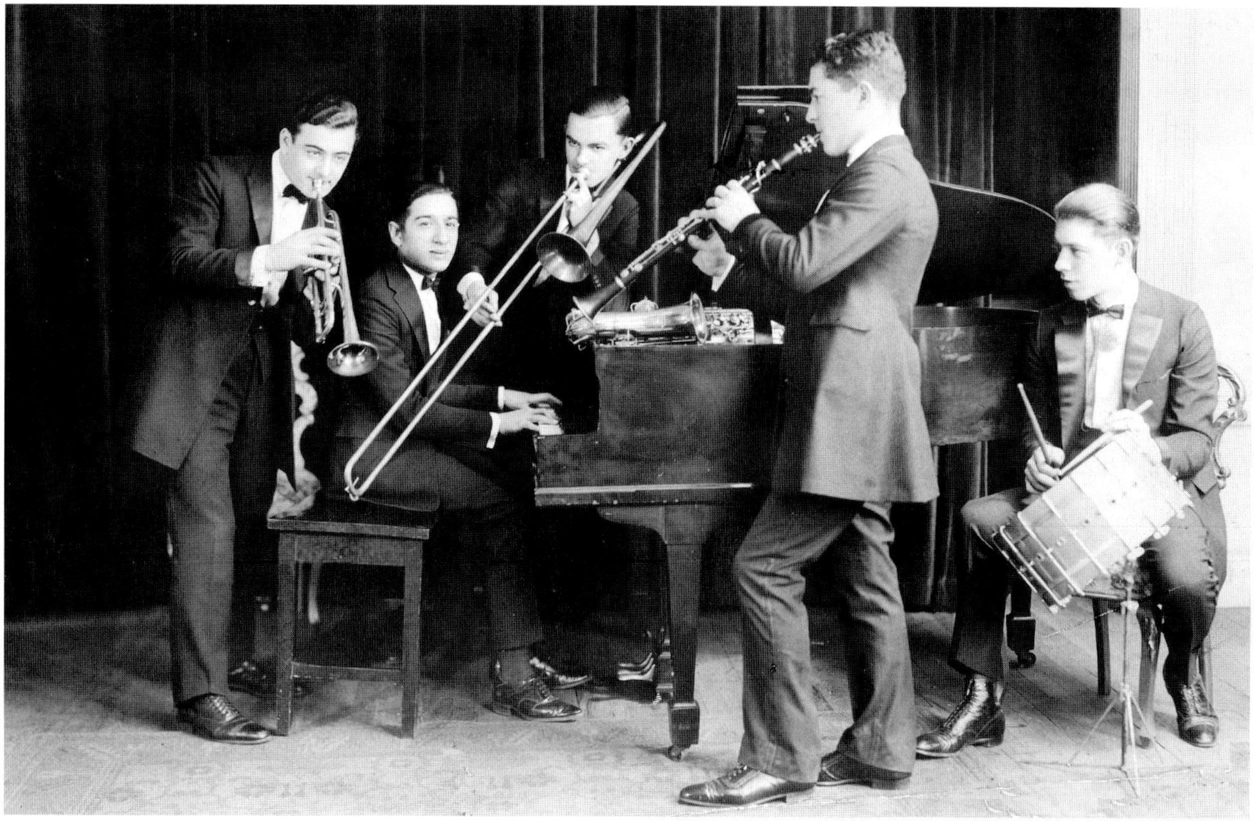

On this photo of the Original Memphis Five from ca. 1922 the personnel is Phil Napoleon (tp) Frank Signorelli (p), Miff Mole (tb), Jimmy Lytell (cl), and Jack Roth (dr).

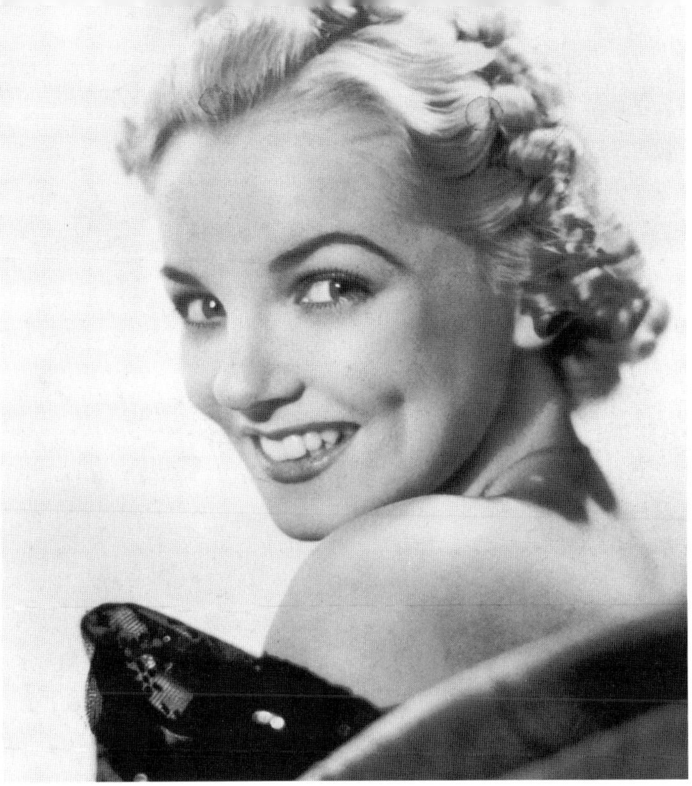

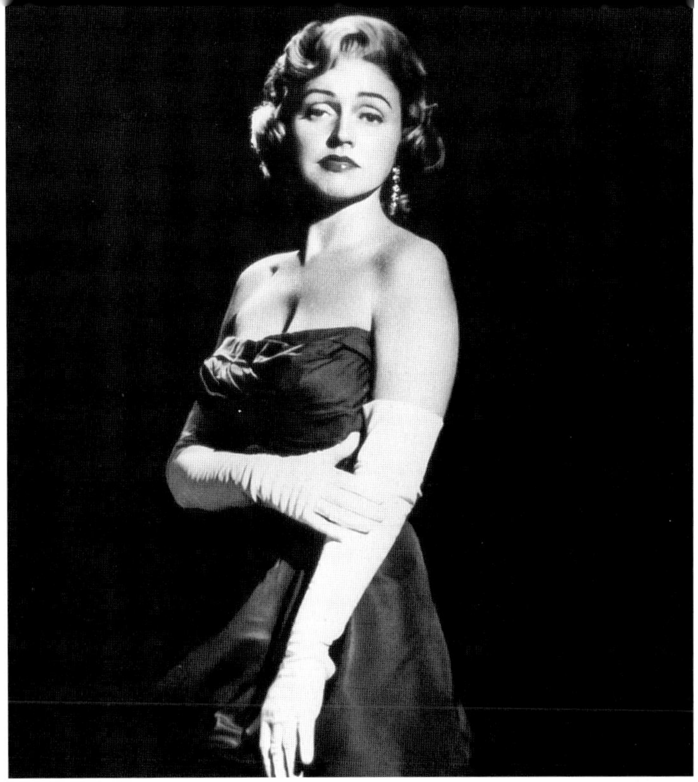

Helen O'Connell

Born in Lima, Ohio, Helen O'Connell (1920-1993) was educated in Toledo and sang on radio already as a youngster. From the mid-30's she worked with mid-western bands and in 1939 she was hired by Jimmy Dorsey. Teamed with Bob Eberly they became the most popular dance band singing couple. In 1943 she left Dorsey, married and sang on radio shows for a while after which she retired. She returned to show business in 1953, and was busy right up to her death of cancer, recording, appearing on radio and TV shows, and occasionaly touring with nostalgic big band shows. O'Connell sang with a sexily slurred delivery, in her early years often in part-talking style, but always emphasizing feeling, phrasing and personality.

Anita O'Day

Anita Belle Colton "Anita O'Day" (1919-) is from Chicago where she first performed in dance marathons, and during that time took the stage name O'Day. From the late 30's she sang with local groups, and in 1941 she was hired by Gene Krupa for his big band, and by Stan Kenton 1944 45. She then established herself as a soloist, recording and touring extensively. The hard life made her a drug addict for several years, and she nearly died from a collapse in 1966. Eventually she was cured, and has since then continued touring, singing in clubs, festivals and concerts all over the world. As a ballad singer she is somewhat reminiscent of Billie Holiday, while in up-tempo numbers she is more herself, performing with great rhythmic drive and swing.

KING OLIVER

Cornetist and bandleader Joe "King" Oliver (1885-1938) was one of the most important musicians of the New Orleans style. From around the turn of the century he played in brass bands, dance bands and small groups in bars and cabarets in New Orleans. In 1918 he moved to Chicago to join Bill Johnson's band, and from 1920 on he led his own bands, most notably his Creole Jazz Band (1922-24) with Louis Armstrong, Johnny and Baby Dodds and others. In 1924 he formed the Dixie Syncopators with whom he came to New York in 1927, and until 1936 he toured widely in the mid-western and southern states. He retired in 1936, troubled by pyorrhea, and worked in his last years as a janitor in a Savannah pool room.

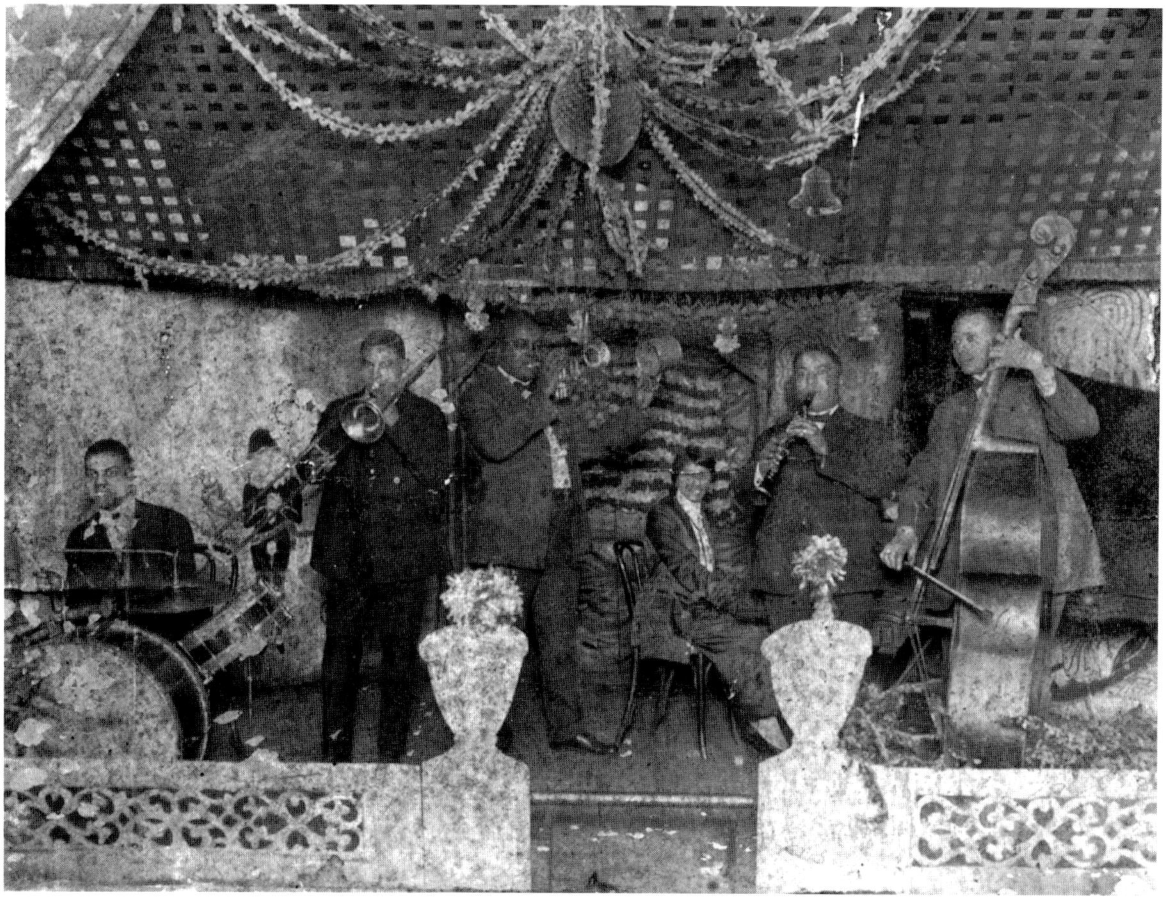

This extremely rare photo dates from 1918 when King Oliver played in Bill Johnson's band in Chicago, and it is the earliest photo of King Oliver in a band. In early 1918 Johnson was asked to form a band for a re-opening of the Royal Gardens Café, the biggest dance hall in Chicago at the time, and he assembled a group of primarily New Orleans musicians, Paul Barbarin (dr), Eddie Venson (tb) – whose name also has been spelled Vinson or Vincent – King Oliver (cnt), Lottie Taylor (p), Jimmy Noone (cl) and Johnson (b). With this personnel the group played at the Royal Gardens throughout 1918.

Ben Pollack

Drummer, singer and bandleader Ben Pollack (1903-1971) is best known today for the jazz-oriented dance bands he led around 1930 in which many of the best white musicians gained early experience, such as Benny Goodman, Jack Teagarden, Eddie Miller, Ray Bauduc, Bud Freeman, Glenn Miller and Harry James. Pollack was from Palm Springs, California, and played from 1923 with the New Orleans Rhythm Kings. In 1926 he formed his own band, which was highly regarded by contemporary musicians, but in 1934 he disbanded, mostly due to bad business. Pollack then settled in California and ran a succesful agency and recording company, but during the 50's he also led a sextet at his own club. Later on he opened a restaurant in Palm Springs, but depressed by a developing bad heart condition he hanged himself in his bathroom.

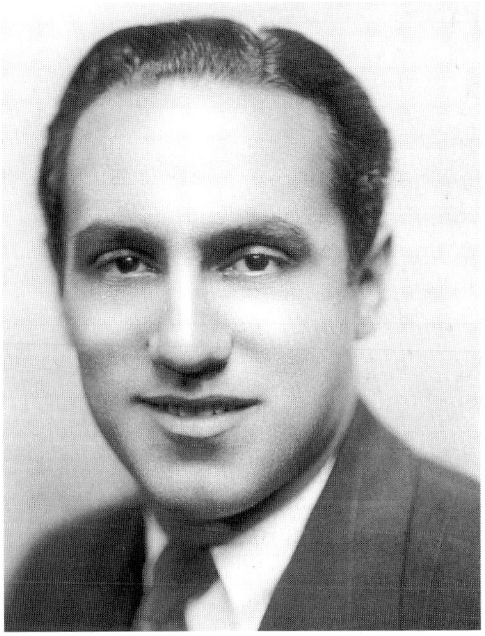

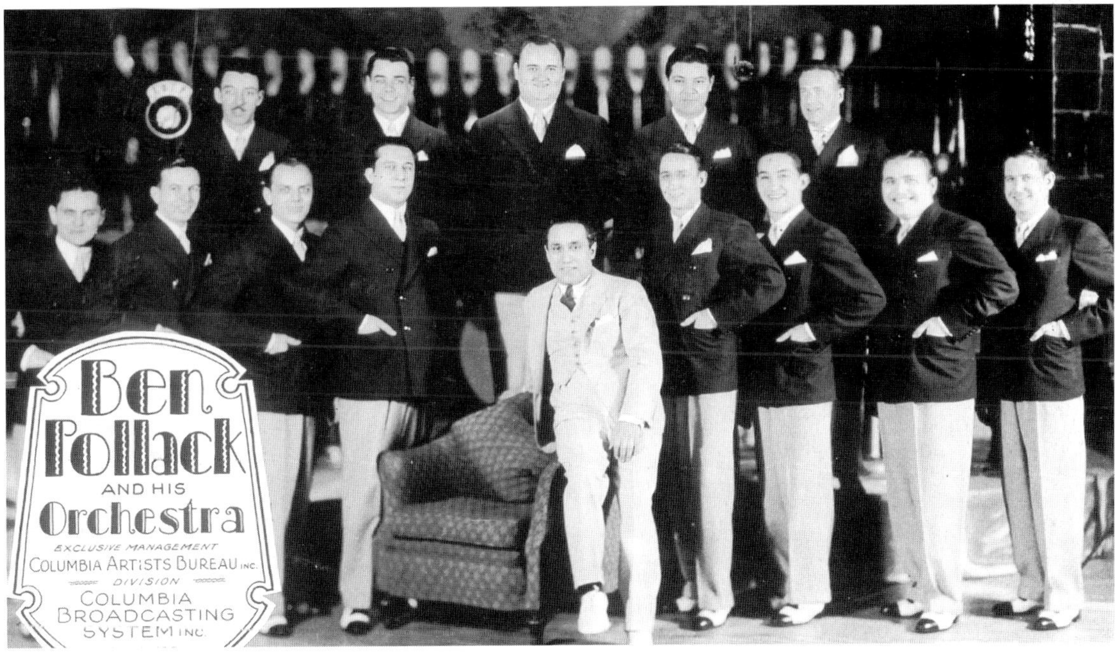

Ben Pollack and His Orchestra 1932. In the back row, from left: Ray Bauduc (dr), Gil Bowers (p), Ralph Copsey and Jack Teagarden (tb), Gil Rodin (cl, as). In the front row, from left: Al Beller (vl), Nappy Lamare (g), Jerry Johnson (b), Ruby Weinstein (tp), Ben Pollack (voc, dir), Matty Matlock (cl, as), Eddie Miller (ts), Charlie Spivak and Sterling Bose (tp).

OSCAR PETTIFORD

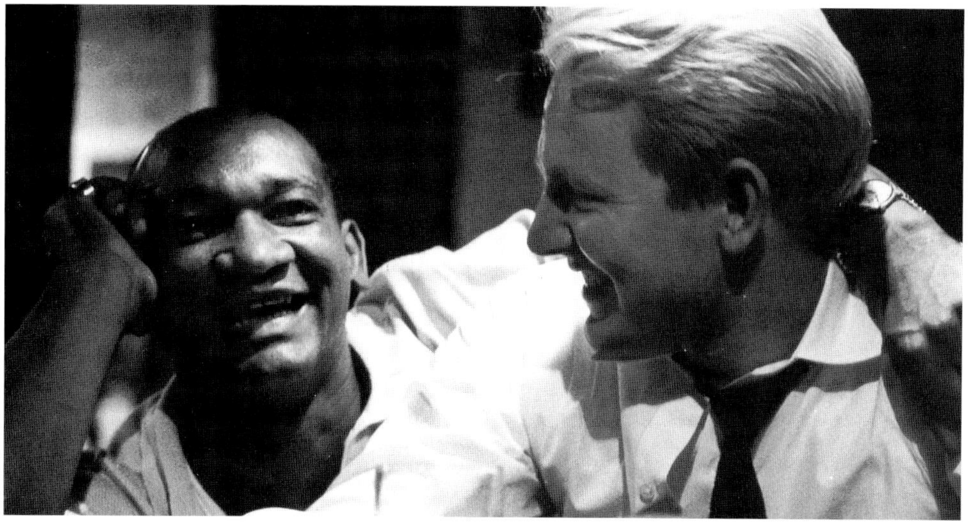

Oscar Pettiford at the Café Montmartre in 1959 with owner Anders Dyrup.

The first bass player to adapt the innovations of Jimmy Blanton to the bop language was Oscar Pettiford (1922-1960), who was born in Okmulgee, Oklahoma into a highly musical family of mixed black and American-Indian origin. Pettiford came to New York in 1943 and worked there with Roy Eldridge and Dizzy Gillespie. Then he joined Duke Ellington followed by a stint with Woody Herman. In 1950 he toured with the Louie Bellson-Charlie Shavers band, and went on to lead his own groups, including a big band in 1956-57. In 1958 he came to Europe with the Jazz From Carnegie Hall package and remained in Europe, settling in Copenhagen the following summer. Here he played at the newly opened Café Montmartre with Stan Getz, Jan Johansson, Don Byas, Helen Merrill, Benny Bailey, Bud Powell and others, until he suddenly died from a polio-related virus. With his clear articulation, strong melodic lines and beautiful intonation and time Pettiford had a lasting influence on the development of the bass as a solo instrument, and was also the first jazz musician successfully to use the cello as a solo instrument.

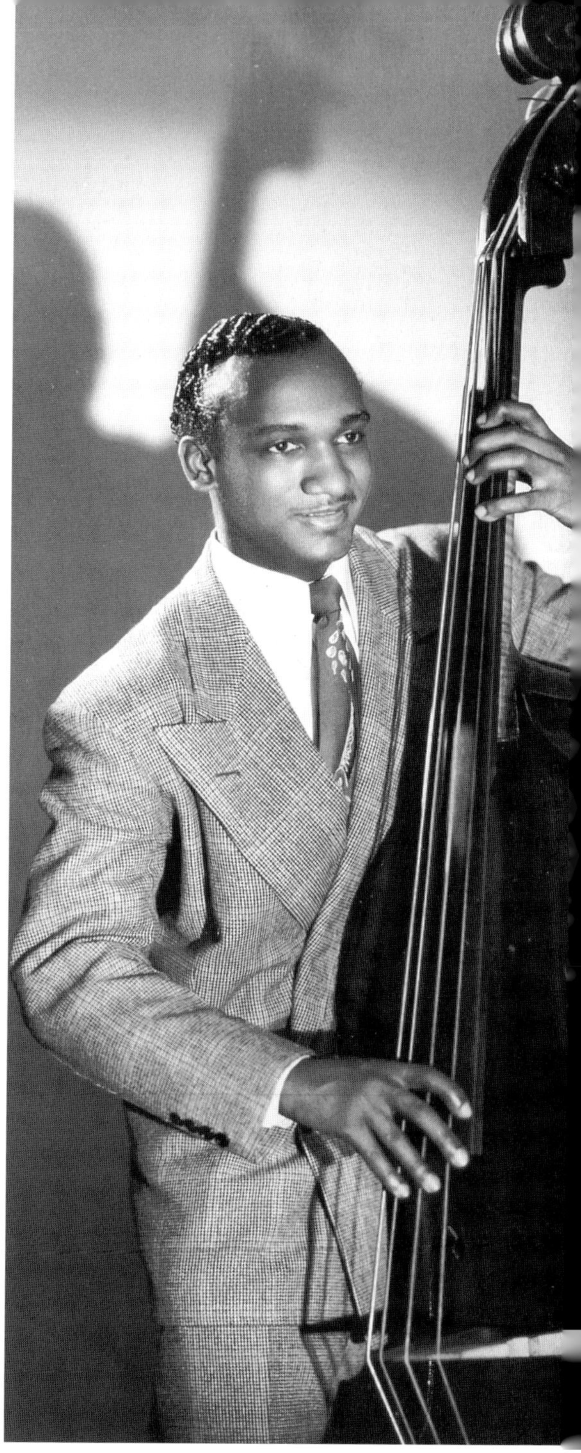

Publicity shot of Oscar Pettiford from the early 40's.

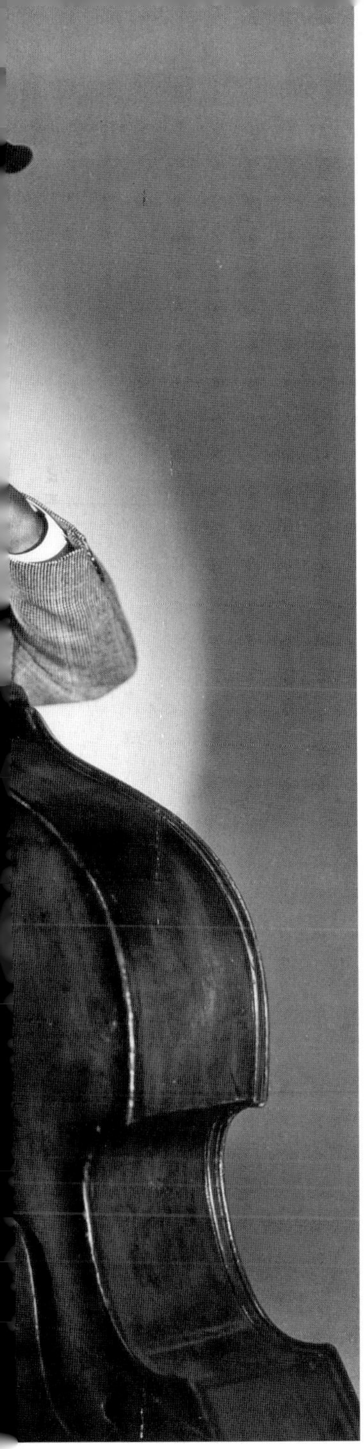

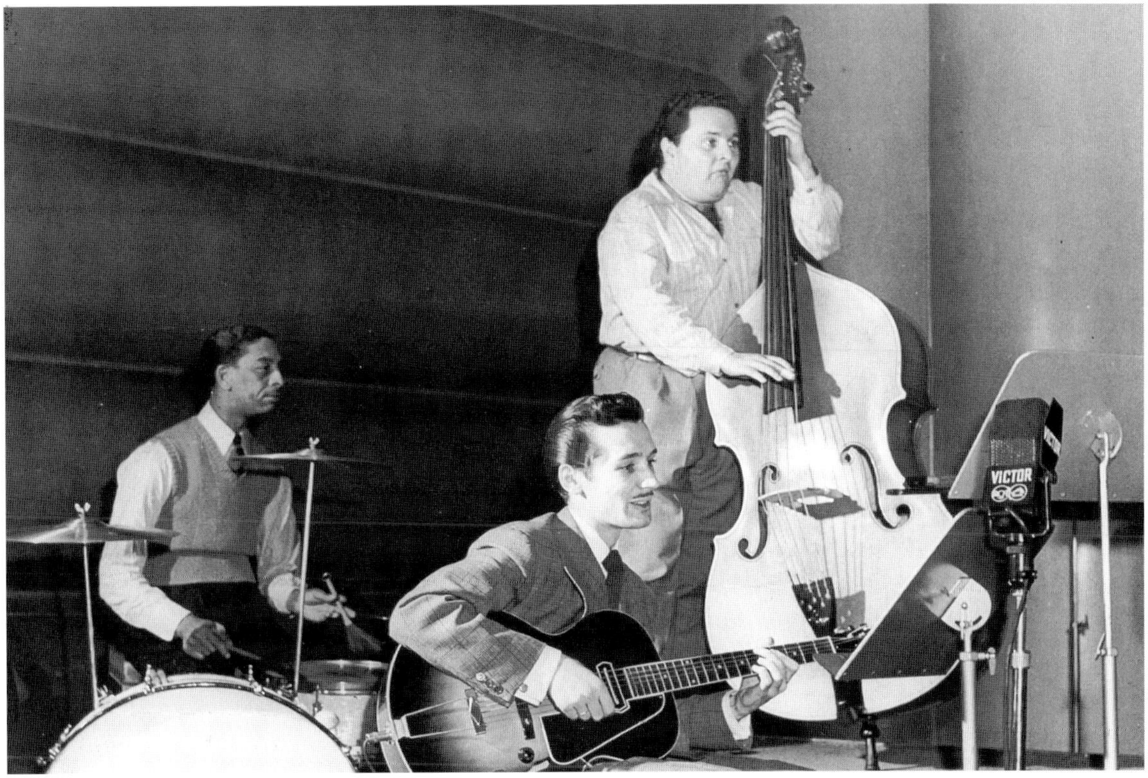

Remo Palmieri at a recording date for RCA on January 10, 1946 with Leonard Feather's Esquire All Americans. Sonny Greer is on drums, and Chubby Jackson on bass.

REMO PALMIERI

Guitarist Remo Palmieri – or Palmier – (1923-) is a New Yorker who began to play from the age of eleven. He originally played professionally to pay for art studies, but the music took over when he joined Nat Jaffe's trio in 1942. The following years he was with Coleman Hawkins, Red Norvo, Billie Holiday, Mildred Bailey, and Dizzy Gillespie, and in 1945 he joined CBS as a studio musician, remaining there until 1972. During the 70's he played jazz again with his own quartet and with Hank Jones, Bobby Hackett, Dick Hyman, and Benny Goodman, but after 1978 he resumed his career as a studio musician.

RUSSELL PROCOPE

Clarinetist and alto saxophonist Russell Procope (1908-1981) was born in New York into a musical family. After eight years studying violin, he took up clarinet and saxophone playing while in high school. He soon became a reliable musician, and from 1928 he played with Jelly Roll Morton, Benny Carter, Chick Webb, Fletcher Henderson, Tiny Bradshaw, Teddy Hill and Willie Bryant. In 1938 he joined John Kirby's Sextet, and remained until drafted into the US Army in 1943. In 1946 he subbed one night for Otto Hardwick in Duke Ellington's orchestra, and when Hardwick did not show up, he stayed 28 more years until Ellington's death. In the 70's he often worked with Brooks Kerr's trio. During his early career Procope was not much of a soloist, but he developed a warm, mellow, woody sound on the clarinet which was often featured by Ellington.

DANNY POLO

Although he always looked as if he wanted to do something else, Danny Polo (1901-1949) was an excellent clarinetist and saxophonist who played in a gentle, smooth and somewhat restrained style. Born in Toluca, Indiana, he grew up in Clinton, Indiana and received musical training from his clarinet playing father at an early age, and already from the age of eight he was playing in marching bands. By 1923 he was working in Chicago with Elmer Schoebel, after which he toured with bandleaders Ben Bernie, Gene Goldkette and Joe Venuti. In 1927 he went to Europe with George Carhart's band and remained there the following six years, playing first in France, then from 1929 in London where he was featured in Bert Ambrose's orchestra. After a period in the USA from 1935 to 1938 he once more went to Europe, then after his return in 1939 he played with Joe Sullivan at New York's Café Society. His last years were spent with Jack Teagarden and Claude Thornhill, but while touring with the latter he suddenly collapsed and died within two days.

DOC POMUS

Singer and song writer Jerome Felder "Doc Pomus" (1925-1991) was born in Brooklyn, New York. He contracted polio at the age of nine and had to use crutches since that time. At the age of fifteen he was performing in jazz and blues clubs. During this period he changed his name so his parents would not find out about his activities. But they did – a few years later! By the 50's he had begun writing songs, and some of his earliest efforts were recorded by Fabian and Ray Charles. 1958-65 he teamed with Mort Schuman, and together they wrote several great rock 'n' roll songs which were recorded by Elvis Presley, the Drifters, Bobby Darin, Andy Williams and others. From the late 60's to the late 70's Pomus kept a low profile, but in the 1980s he wrote for Dr. John, B.B. King and others and was also instrumental in assembling the Blues Brothers band.

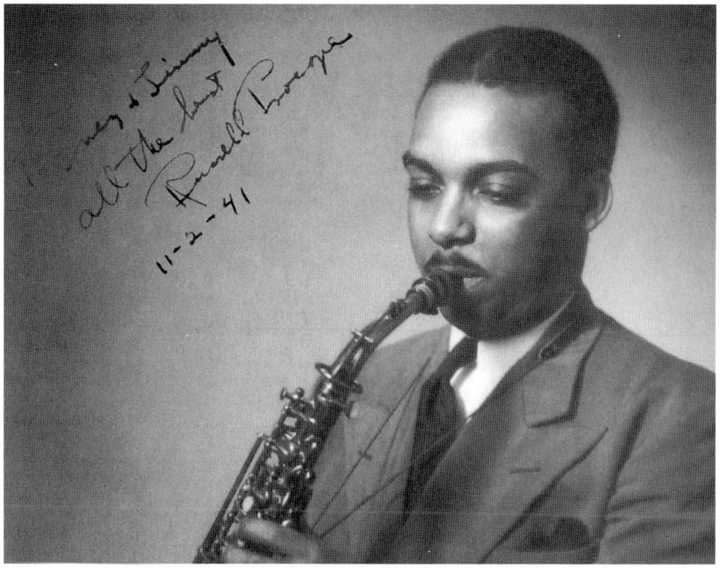

Publicity photo of Russell Procope from 1941. *To Inez + Timmy all the best Russell Procope. 11-2-41.*

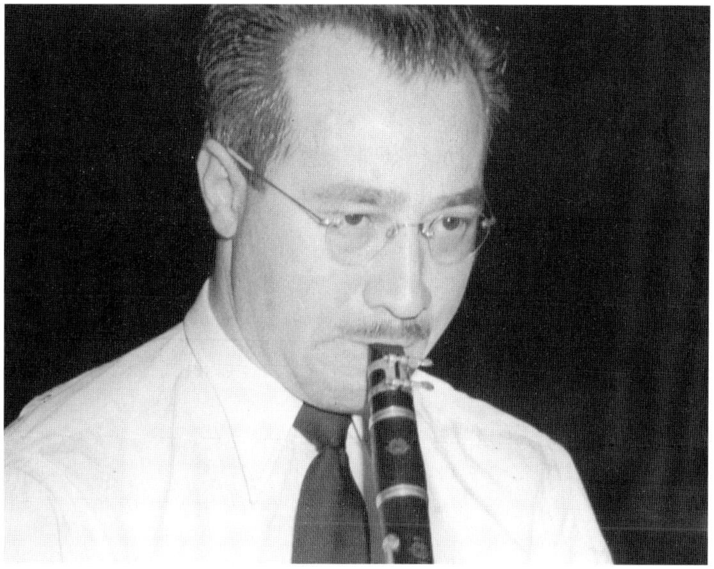

This photo of Danny Polo is probably taken during one of the two recording sessions with Benny Carter's Varsity Seven in 1939-40.

Doc Pomus at one of Timme Rosenkrantz's jam sessions autumn 1947 at Café Bohemia with Rex Stewart.

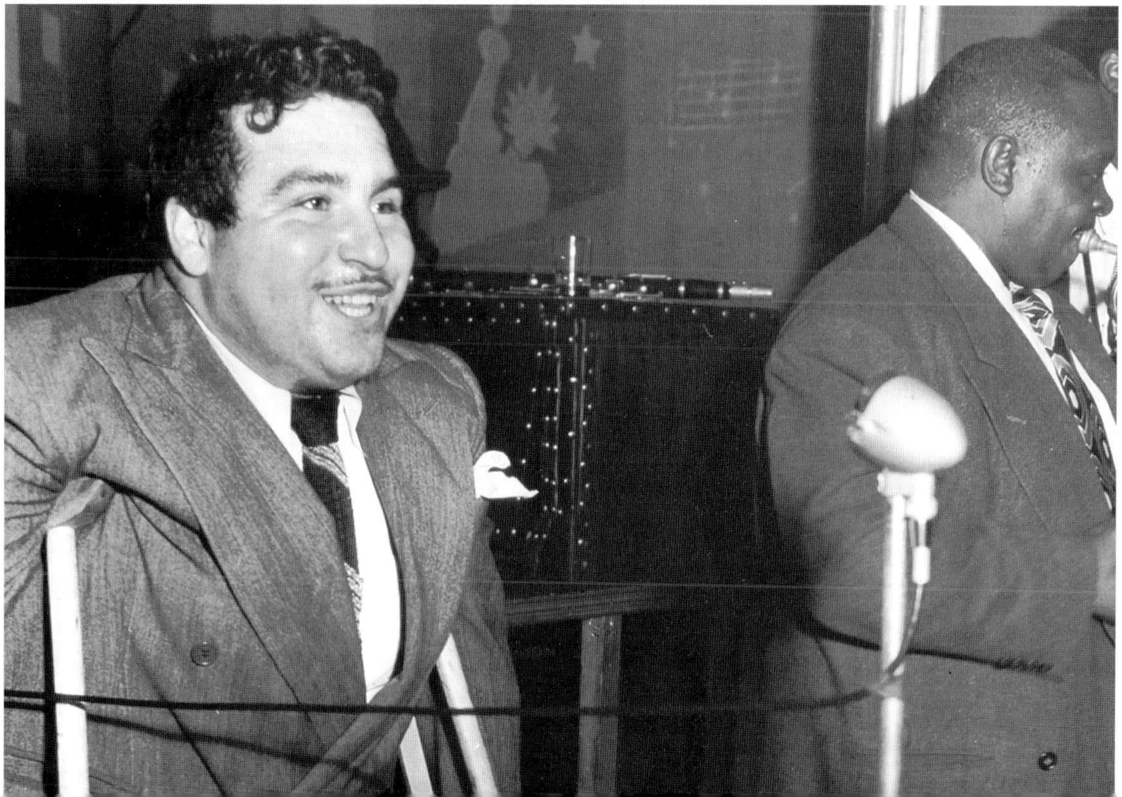

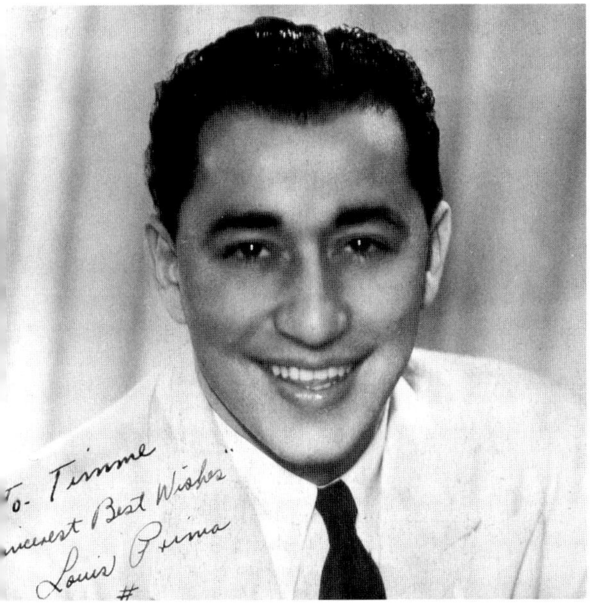

LOUIS PRIMA

One of the most successful trumpet playing and singing bandleaders was New Orleans born Louis Prima (1911-1978). He began playing the trumpet in 1925, and after leaving high-school he formed his own band which played in and around New Orleans until the early 30's. In 1934 he arrived in New York where he headlined at the Famous Door, after which he moved to California where he opened his own Famous Door club in Los Angeles. During the 40's and early 50's he led his own big band, after which he cut back to a small band format. During the 50's he was married to singer Keely Smith and together they achieved widespread commercial success for their cabaret-like style. Prima kept working long engagements in Las Vegas until he suffered a serious illness in 1975. Prima's trumpet playing and hoarse singing was modelled after Louis Armstrong, but from the 40's he became overtly commercial. *To – Timme. "Sincerest Best Wishes". Louis Prima.*

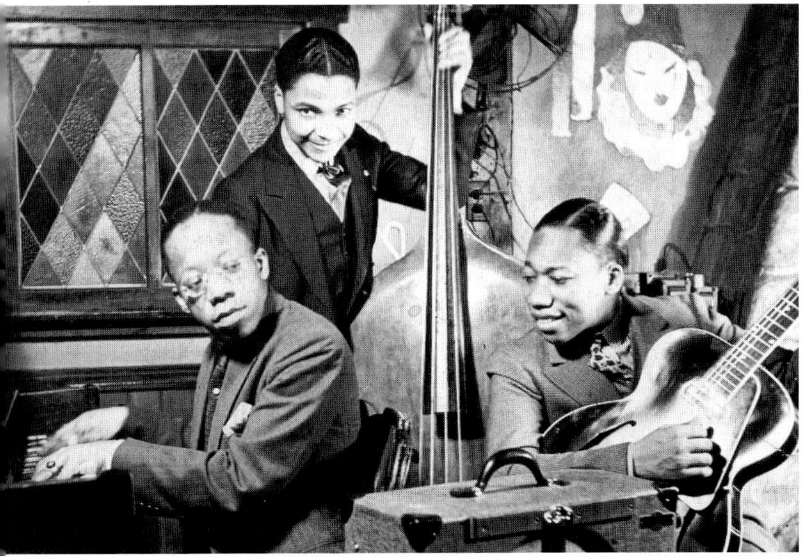

The Clarence Profit Trio at the Village Vanguard in 1940 with Benjamin Brown on bass and James Shirley on guitar.

CLARENCE PROFIT

Now virtually forgotten, but highly admired by Teddy Wilson and Oscar Peterson, pianist Clarence Profit (1912-1944) led an innovative trio of piano, guitar and bass, which later became popularized by Nat "King" Cole and Art Tatum. Profit was a New Yorker and played piano from the age of three. In his teens he led a big band which played New York clubs like the Bamboo Inn and the Alhambra. 1930-31 he played with Teddy Bunn, after which he moved to the West Indies playing in Antigua, Bermuda and elsewhere. In 1936 he returned to New York and formed a successful trio, with which he played for the rest of his life in clubs like George's Tavern, Cafe Society, Kelly's Stable, the Village Vanguard and others. Profit's playing had a delicate touch and was rich in harmonic and melodic ideas.

IKE QUEBEC

Born in Newark, New Jersey, Ike Abrams Quebec (1918-1963) began his career in show business as a pianist and dancer. In 1940 he changed to the tenor saxophone, playing in and around New York in small bands led by Benny Carter, Kenny Clarke, Coleman Hawkins, Roy Eldridge, Frankie Newton and others. From 1944 to 1951 he was with Cab Calloway after which he led his own small band. In the late 50's he left full-time music and made his living as a cab driver, but in 1959 he began performing again and also worked as assistant musical director for Blue Note Records until he had to retire a few years later due to illness. He died of lung cancer. Quebec's playing was modelled after Coleman Hawkins and Ben Webster. He was especially impressive as an interpreter of the blues.

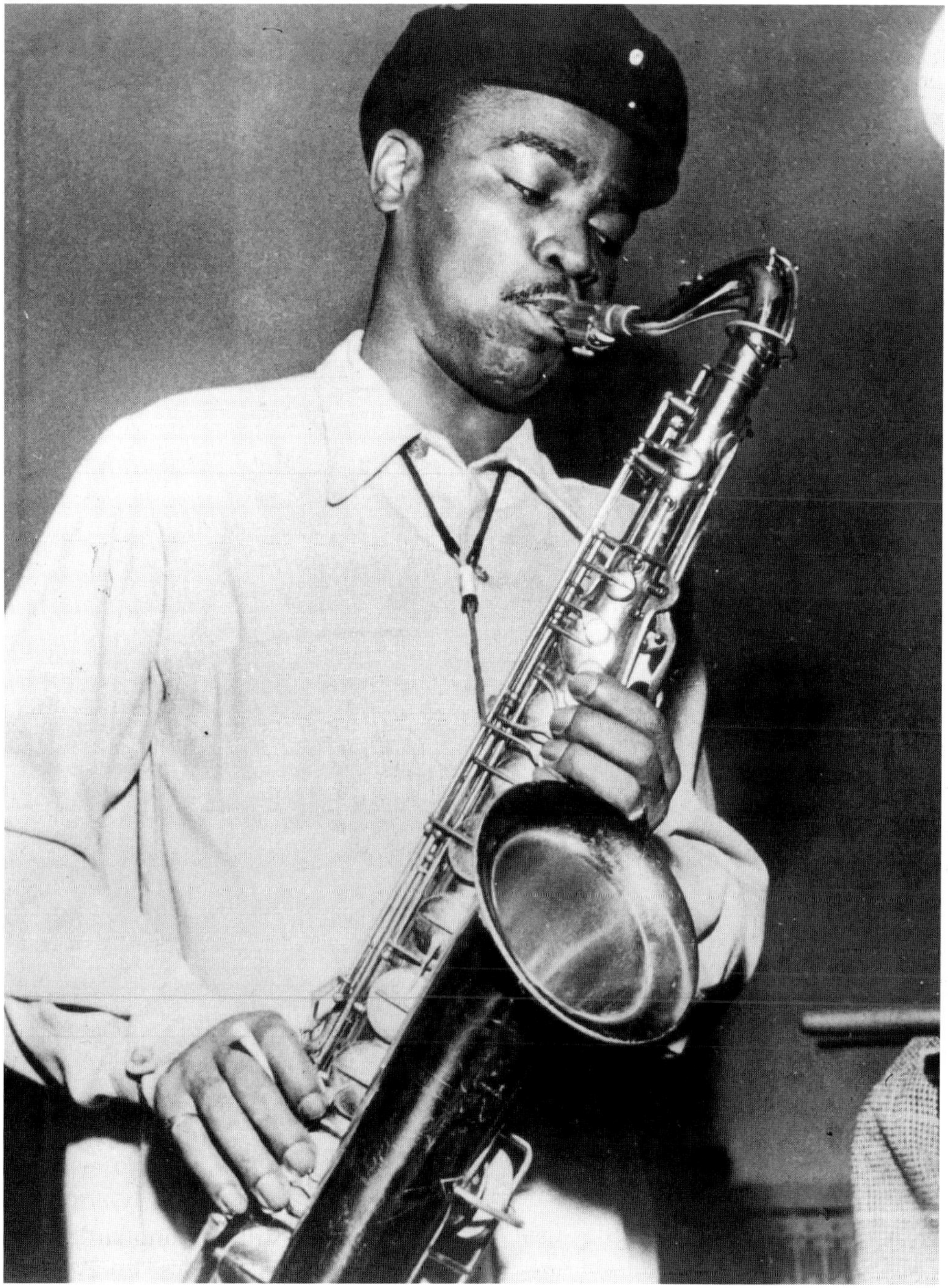

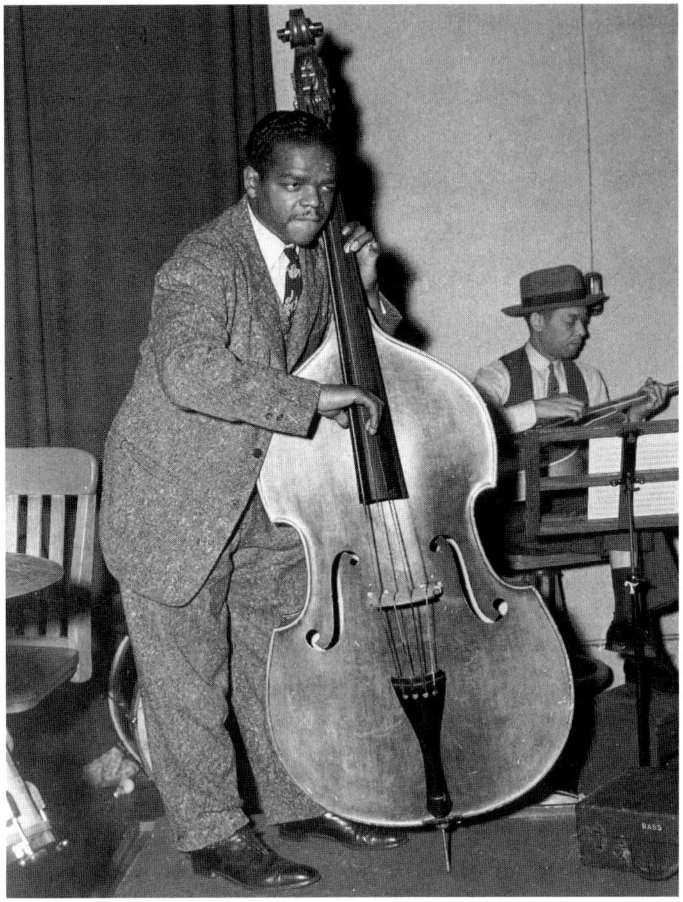

Junior Raglin at a rehearsal with the Ellington band in New York 1944 with guitarist Fred Guy.

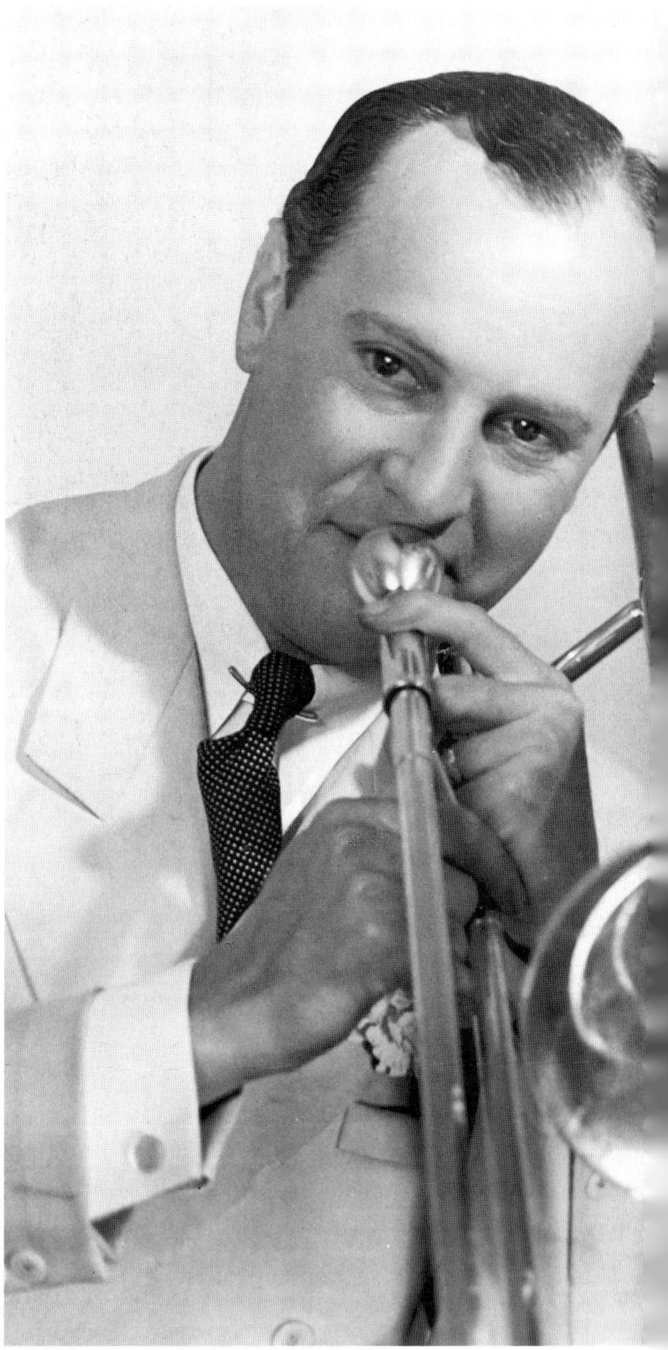

JUNIOR RAGLIN

Born in Omaha, Nebraska Alvin Redrick "Junior" Raglin (1917-1955) started out as a guitarist. 1938 he played the string bass with Gene Coy in Oregon, and in 1941 joined Duke Ellington in California, for a time doubling for Jimmy Blanton. In 1945 he left Ellington to lead his own small group in New York, followed by a stint in Dave Rivera's trio, after which he rejoined Ellington in 1946. Due to illness he retired the following year.

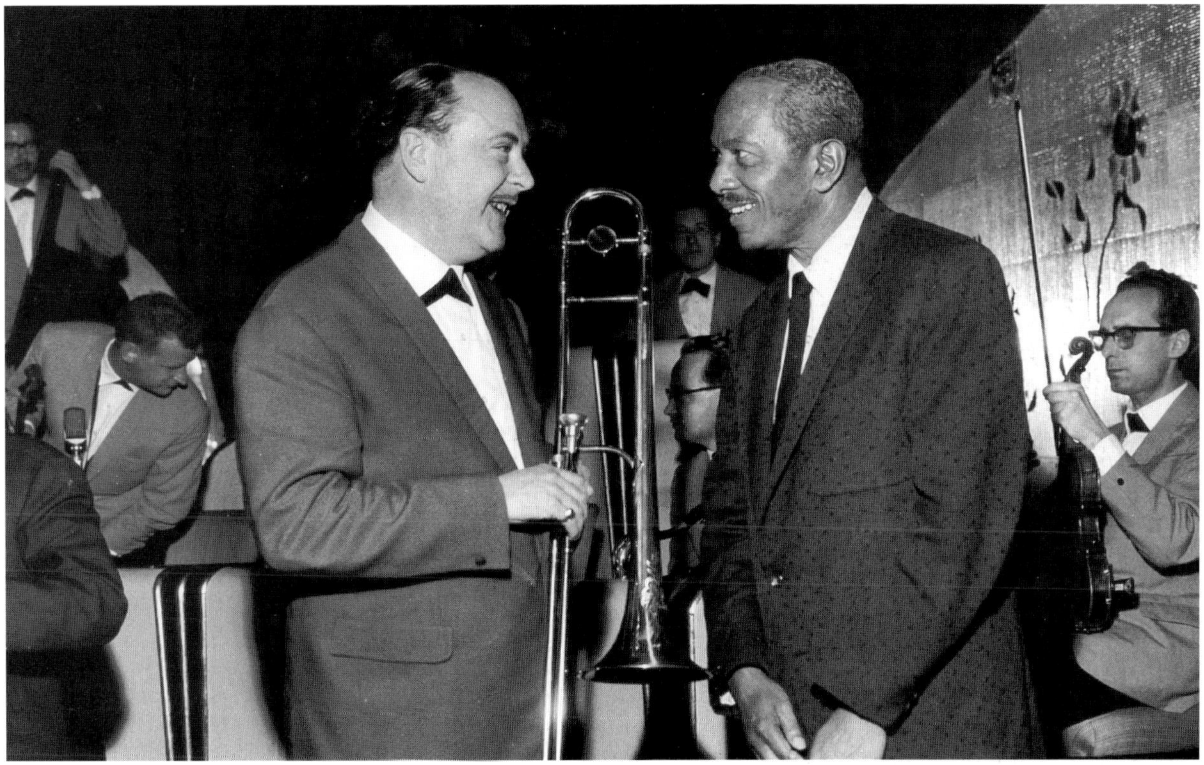

Peter Rasmussen in the concert hall of Danish Radio in the early 60's, talking with trumpeter Nelson Williams.

PETER RASMUSSEN

Danish trombonist Peter Christian Hans Rasmussen (1906-1992) was a legendary figure in Danish jazz and a most remarkable musician playing in a style inspired by Tommy Dorsey, although with more punch and imagination. Rasmussen played professionally from 1922, and in the following years he toured Europe and the USA where he took lessons with Miff Mole and Tommy Dorsey. From 1933 he was back in Denmark playing with Erik Tuxen (1933-36) and Kai Ewans (1936-43), after which he led his own bands, from the 50's usually commercial big bands. From the 60's he worked in Danish Radio as a producer and also had his own talkshows.

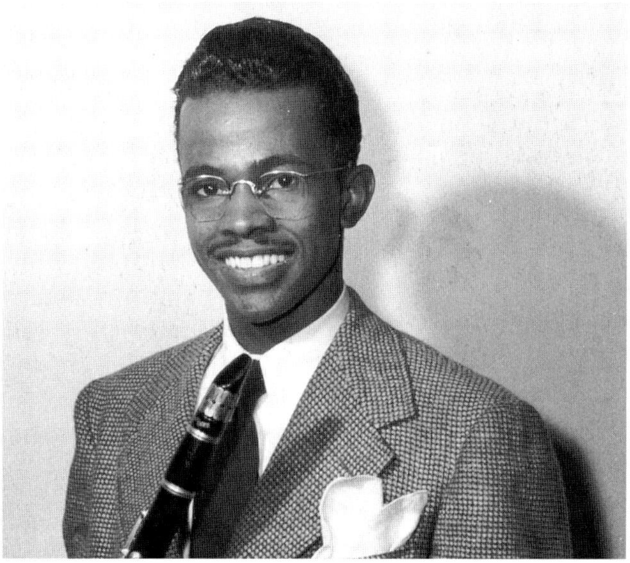

RUDY RUTHERFORD

Born in Detroit, Michigan, saxophonist and clarinetist Elman "Rudy" Rutherford (1912-) worked mainly in his home town before he joined Andy Kirk in 1940. After a short spell with Lionel Hampton he played with Count Basie 1944-47, after which he returned to Detroit to play with Teddy Buckner and leading his own small bands. From the 70's he worked mainly in New York with his own groups, but also played with Wilbur De Paris, Chuck Berry, Buddy Tate, Ram Ramirez, and Earl Hines. Rutherford was a solid section player on both the alto and the baritone saxophone, whereas as a soloist on the clarinet he displayed much verve and distinction.

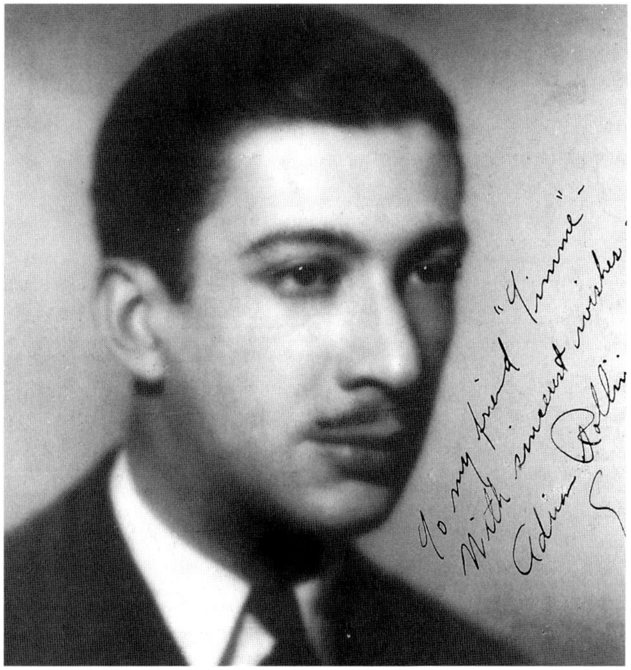

ADRIAN ROLLINI

The cumbersome bass saxophone was masterly played by Adrian Rollini (1904-1956). Born in New York he first took up the piano, and gave a Chopin recital at the Waldorf Astoria Hotel at the age of four. He led his own bands from the age of fourteen, and from 1922 he began playing the bass saxophone with the California Ramblers. From 1927 to 1929 he worked in London with Fred Elizalde after which he freelanced in New York, working in the studios and also playing with his own small groups in hotels. In 1935 he opened his own club, Adrian's Tap Room, after which he concentrated on playing the vibraphone. In the early 50's he moved to Florida and opened a hotel in Tavernier. He continued to play in various clubs in Miami until his death of pneumonia and complications following a liver complaint.
To my friend "Timme" – With sincerest wishes – Adrian Rollini.

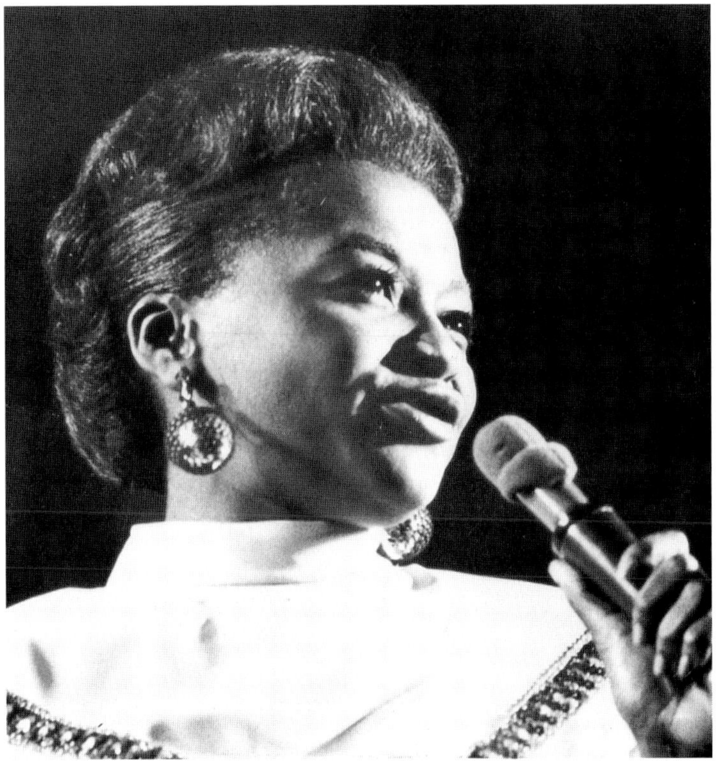

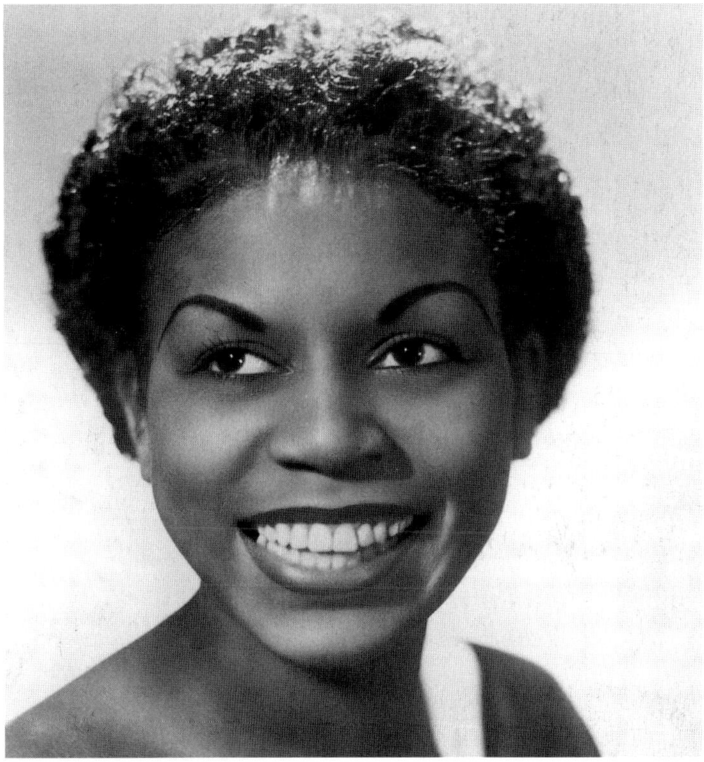

VI REDD

Singer and alto saxophonist Elvira "Vi" Redd (1928-) grew up in a musical family in Los Angeles. In the 60's she played with Earl Hines, Dizzy Gillespie, Max Roach, and Count Basie, and also led her own quartet with her husband, drummer Richie Goldberg. Throughout the 70's and the 80's she devoted most of her time to teaching but has since played and toured everywhere, often backed by her son Randall Goldberg on drums. Redd sings in a style deeply influenced by the blues and plays the saxophone in a Charlie Parker-inspired way.

BETTY ROCHÉ

Singer Mary Elizabeth "Betty" Roché (1920-99) was born in Wilmington, Delaware, and won an amateur contest at the Apollo Theatre in Harlem, after which she sang with the Savoy Sultans (1941-42). In 1943 she joined Duke Ellington, performing at his first Carnegie Hall concert in January, and the following year she was with Earl Hines, after which she disappeared from show business for a while. In 1952 she rejoined Ellington, but after a short solo career around 1960 she returned to obscurity. Roché performed in a warm and attractive style.

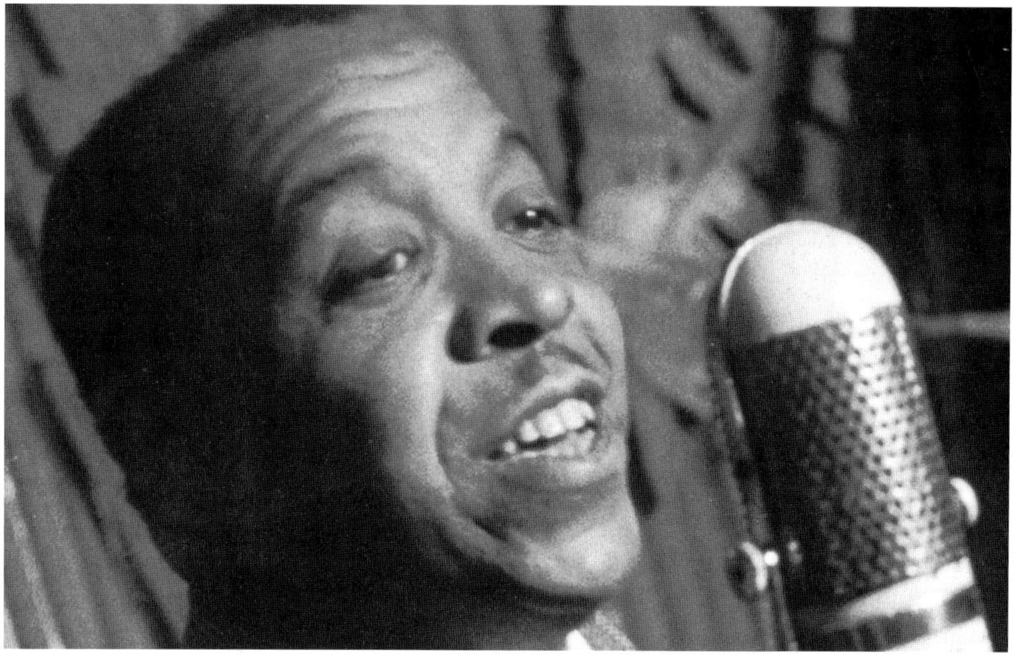

Don Redman caught during his concert in Copenhagen, September 15, 1946.

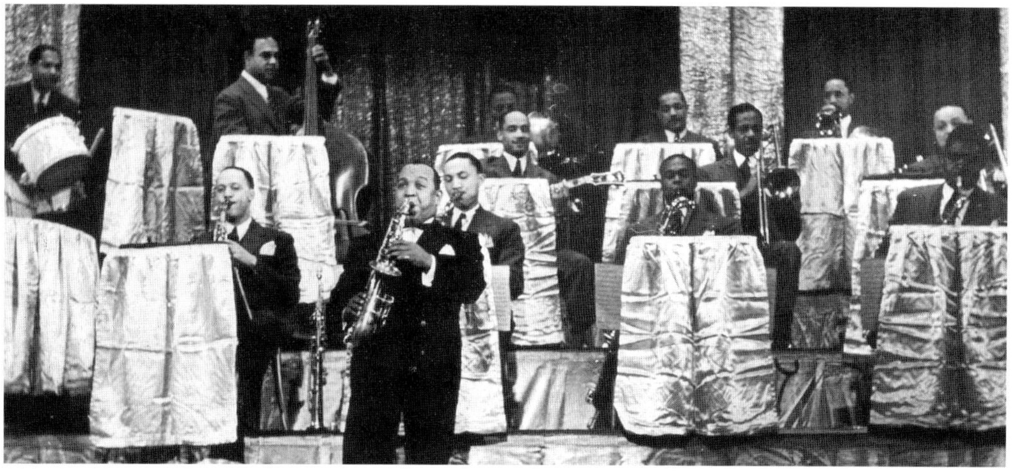

Don Redman fronting his band in 1938: Bill Beason (dr), Bob Ysaguirre (b), Carl Warwick, Mario Bauza, Reunald Jones (tp), Bob Lessey (g), Gene Simon, Quentin Jackson (tb), Eddie Barefield, Edward Inge, Pete Clark, Joe Garland (reeds).

DON REDMAN

Saxophonist and singer Donald Matthew "Don" Redman (1900-1964) was one of the most influential among the early jazz arrangers. He was born in Piedmont, West Virginia, into a musical family and could play all wind instruments by the age of 12. After a thorough musical education at the Chicago and Boston conservatories he joined Billy Paige's Broadway Syncopators with whom he came to New York. In 1923 he left to join Fletcher Henderson's newly formed band as a staff arranger and a saxophonist, and in 1927 he became musical director of McKinney's Cotton Pickers. Redman formed his own band in 1931 to play in New York at Connie's Inn, and after the band broke up in 1940 he concentrated on freelance arranging. He formed a big band in 1946 to tour Europe after which he worked for CBS. From 1951 he acted as musical director for Pearl Bailey.

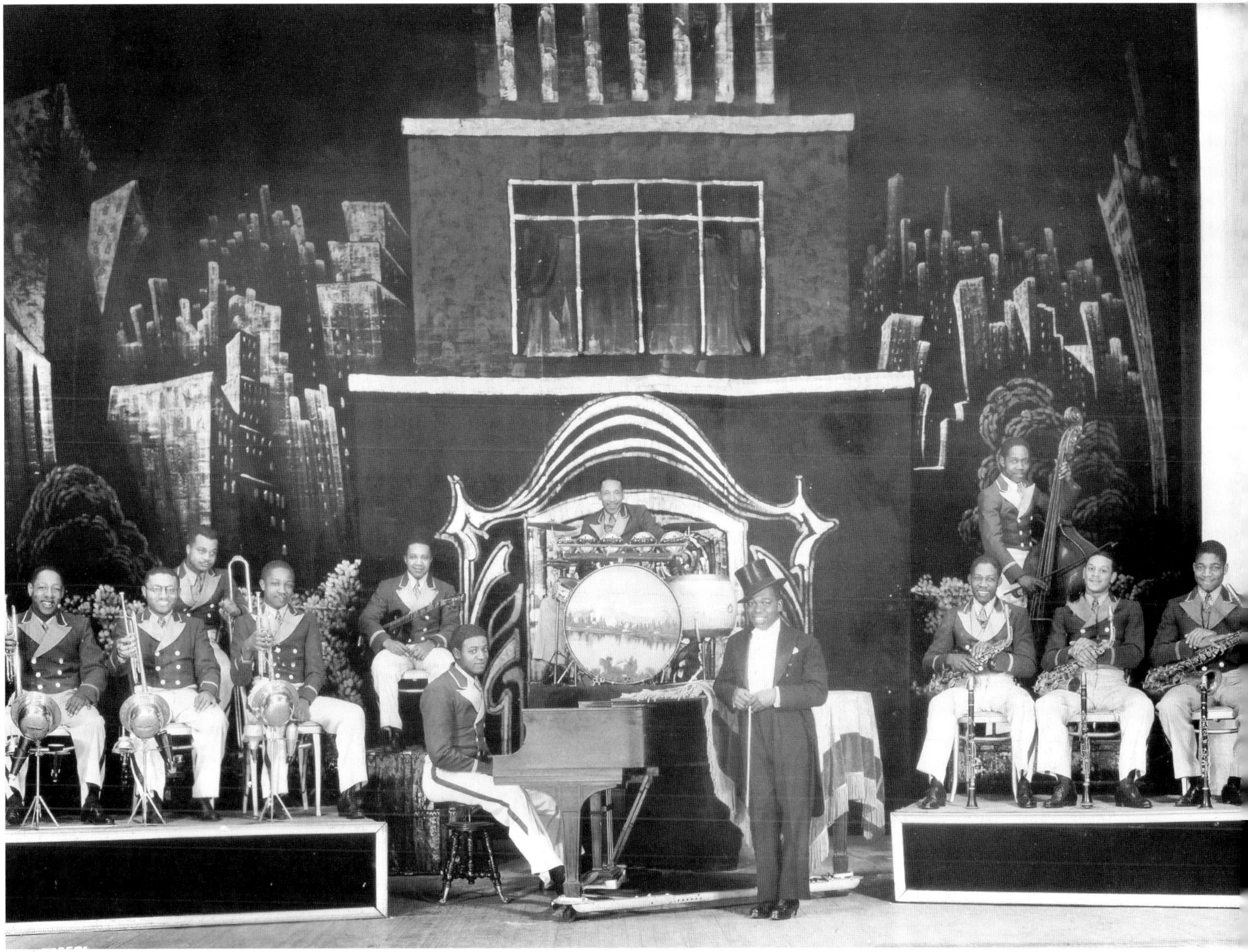

Don Redman & His Orchestra in the Vitaphone short film of the band of 1934. From left: Henry "Red" Allen, Sidney De Paris (tp), Gene Simon (tb), Shirley Clay (tp), Talcott Reeves (g), Horace Henderson (p), Manzie Johnson (dr), Don Redman (cond.) Rupert Cole (as), Bob Ysaguirre (b), Edward Inge (as), Robert Carroll (ts).

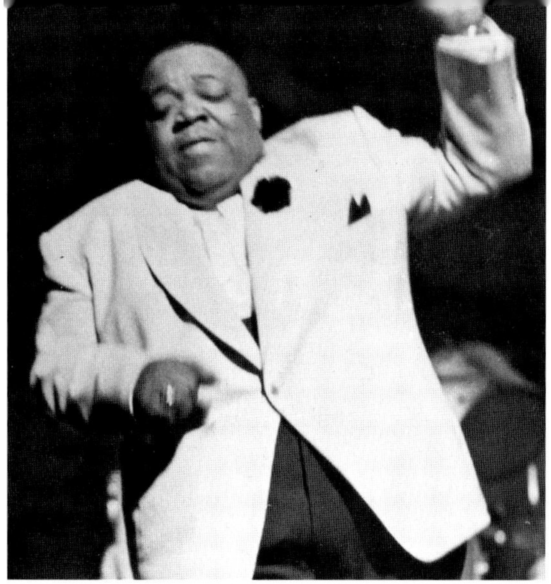

Jimmy Rushing dancing in front of the Count Basie Orchestra in the 40's.

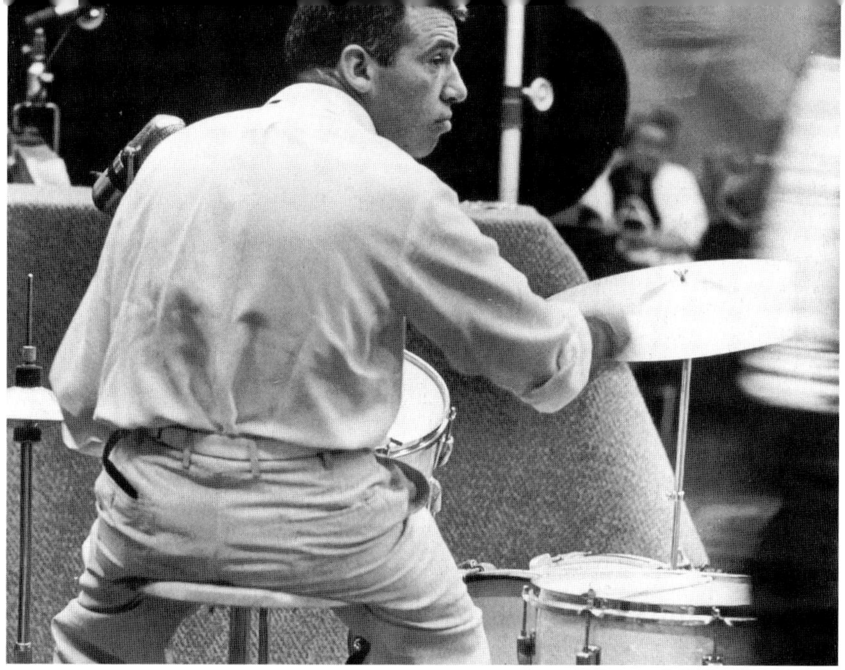

Jimmy Rushing

Oklahoma-born singer James Andrew "Jimmy" Rushing (1903-1972) had musical experience as a pianist from an early age. After a while he concentrated on singing, and from 1923 began touring the Midwest and California. In 1927 he was with Walter Page's Blue Devils, and from 1929 to 1935 he sang with Bennie Moten. He then joined Count Basie and remained until 1948 after which he formed his own small band and worked as a soloist, touring with Basie, Buck Clayton, Eddie Condon, Benny Goodman, Al Cohn, Zoot Sims and others. He died of leukaemia. Known as "Mr. Five-By-Five", Rushing was an outstanding singer, rooted in the blues, performing in an intense, dramatic voice.

Buddy Rich

Show business was part of the life of drummer and singer Bernard "Buddy" Rich (1917-1987) ever since he could walk. Before he was two he performed on stage in his parents' vaudeville act, and by the age of four he was singing and drumming on Broadway. At six he toured Australia and the USA, and by the age of eleven he had his own stage band. From the mid-30's he played with Art Shapiro, Hot Lips Page, Joe Marsala, Bunny Berigan, Harry James and Artie Shaw, after which he was with Tommy Dorsey 1939-42. After military service and another stint with Dorsey he formed his own band which he led until 1951. The following 15 years were divided between Harry James, Charlie Ventura, Jazz at the Philharmonic and his own small groups, after which he formed his own big band in 1966. Disbanding in 1974 he played with small groups in his own club in New York, Buddy's Place, after which he organized another successful big band, with which he toured until his death of a brain tumour. Rich was a phenomenal drummer with astonishing technical dexterity and speed.

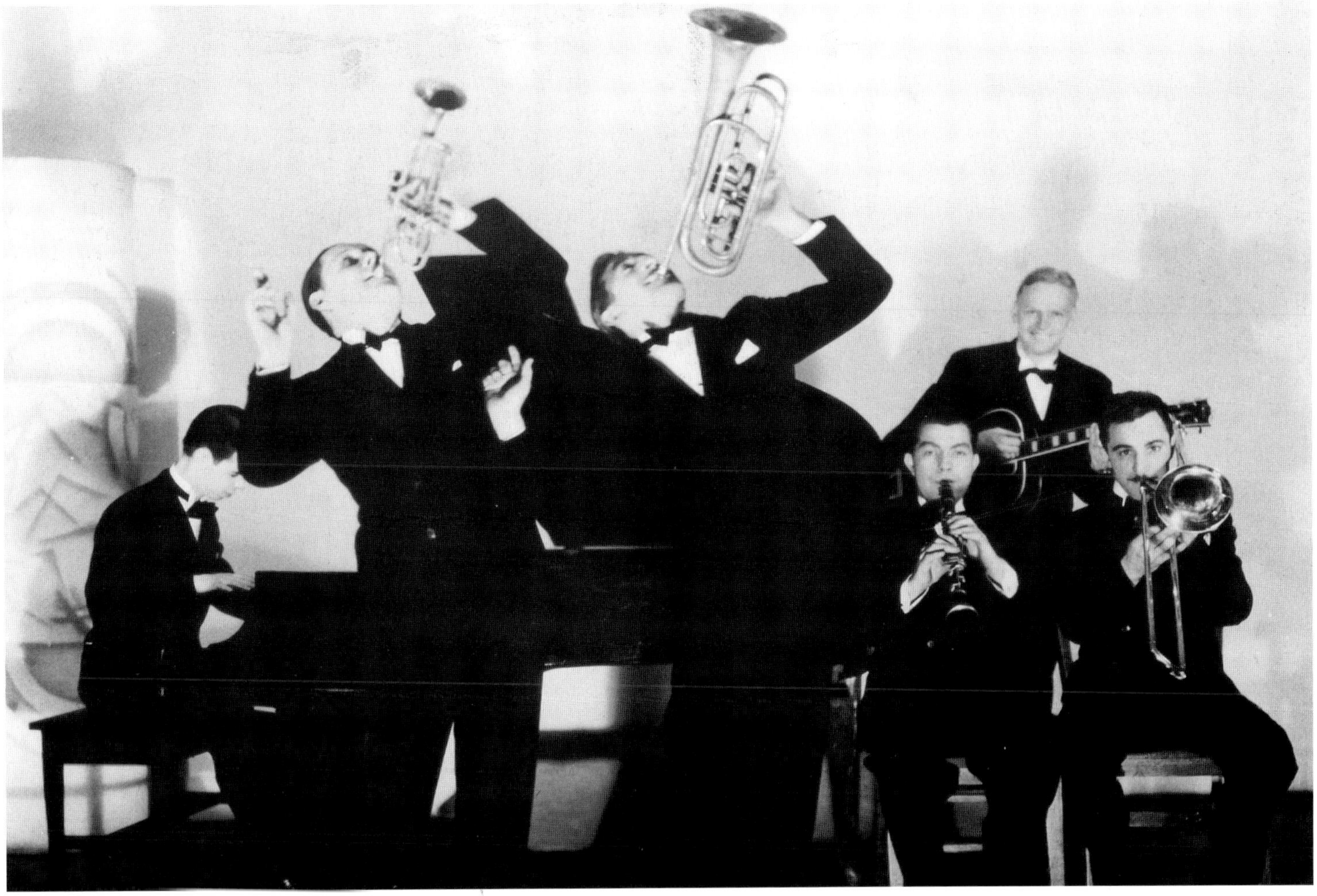

RILEY/FARLEY

Trombonist Mike Riley (1904-1984) and trumpeter Eddie Farley (1904-?) co-led a successful combo at the Onyx Club in New York 1935-36, aided by their hit record, "The Music Goes 'Round and Around". The public loved their on-stage antics, and after their separation both leaders led their own bands. This publicity photo from 1936 shows from left: Frank Froeba (p), Eddie Farley (tp), Mike Riley (mellophone), Frank Langone (cl), Arthur Ens (g) and an unidentifed trombonist.

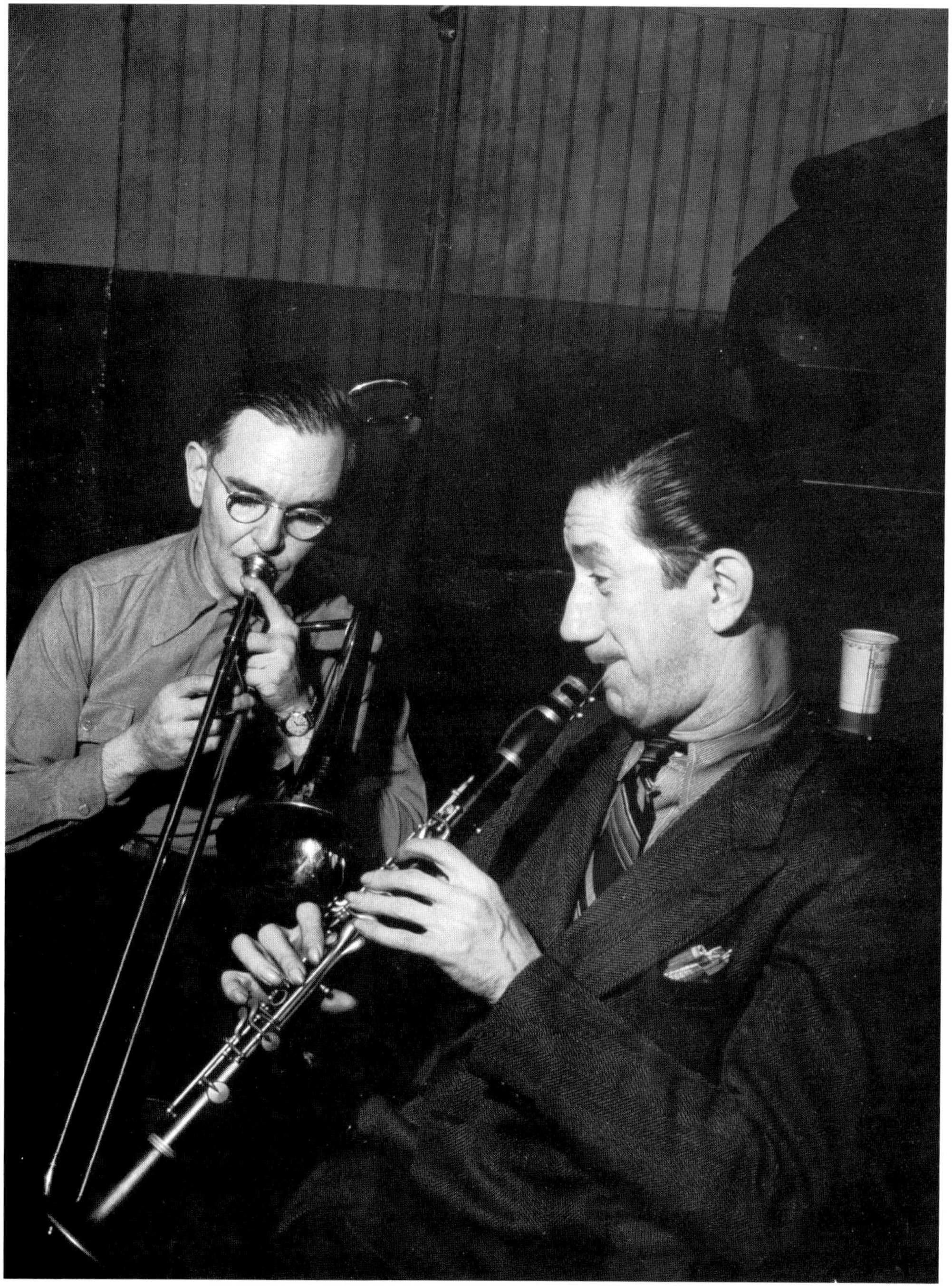

PEE WEE RUSSELL

Clarinetist Charles Ellsworth "Pee Wee" Russell (1906-1969) was a highly original voice in jazz. He was born in Maple Wood, Missouri, but moved in early childhood to Muskogee, Oklahoma. After studying several instruments he concentrated on the clarinet and played in several bands around St. Louis, until he settled in New York in 1927. Here he worked with Red Nichols, Ben Pollack, Louis Prima and others, and from 1937 was most of the time with Eddie Condon in dixieland clubs in New York, such as Nick's, Jimmy Ryan's, the Riviera Club, and Eddie Condon's. He also led his own small groups at the Village Vanguard, Jack Dempsey's and other venues, until he died of a liver complaint.

Pee Wee Russell and trombonist Miff Mole during the "Jam Session at Commodore" recording session for Eddie Condon at the Decca Studios in New York, March 23, 1940.

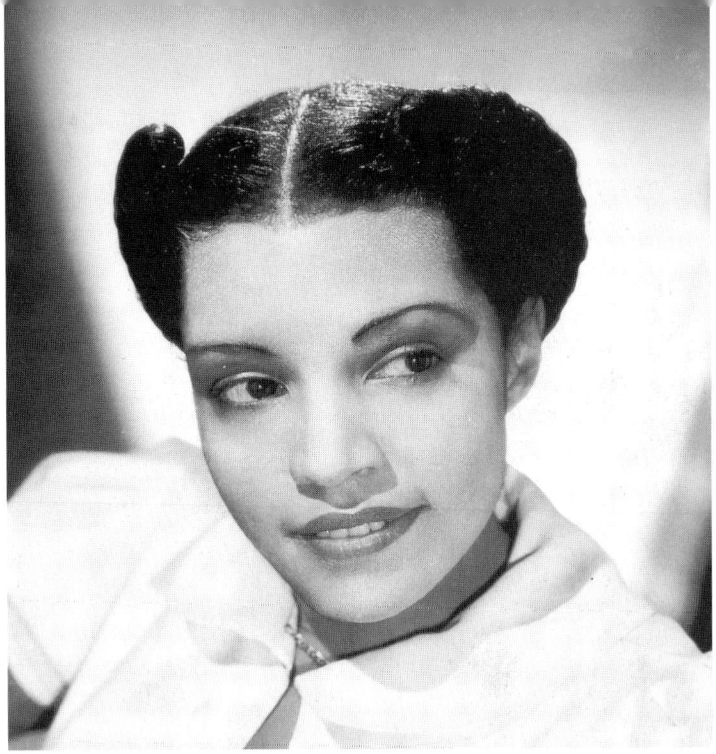

Maxine Sullivan in the late 30's.

Maxine Sullivan

A charming and delicate singer with a light swing, Marietta Williams "Maxine Sullivan" (1911-1987) became popular in the late 30's by doing swinging versions of folk and light-classical songs. She was born in Homestead, Pennsylvania, and worked in 1937 with Claude Thornhill, after which she joined John Kirby's new band, with whom she performed until 1942. She then pursued a solo career until the mid-50's when she retired to take up nursing, but she returned to show business in 1958, working with Clifford Jackson, Bob Wilber, the World's Greatest Jazzband, and Scott Hamilton. In addition to singing she also began playing valve trombone, fluegelhorn and pocket trumpet. She performed right up to the time of her death.

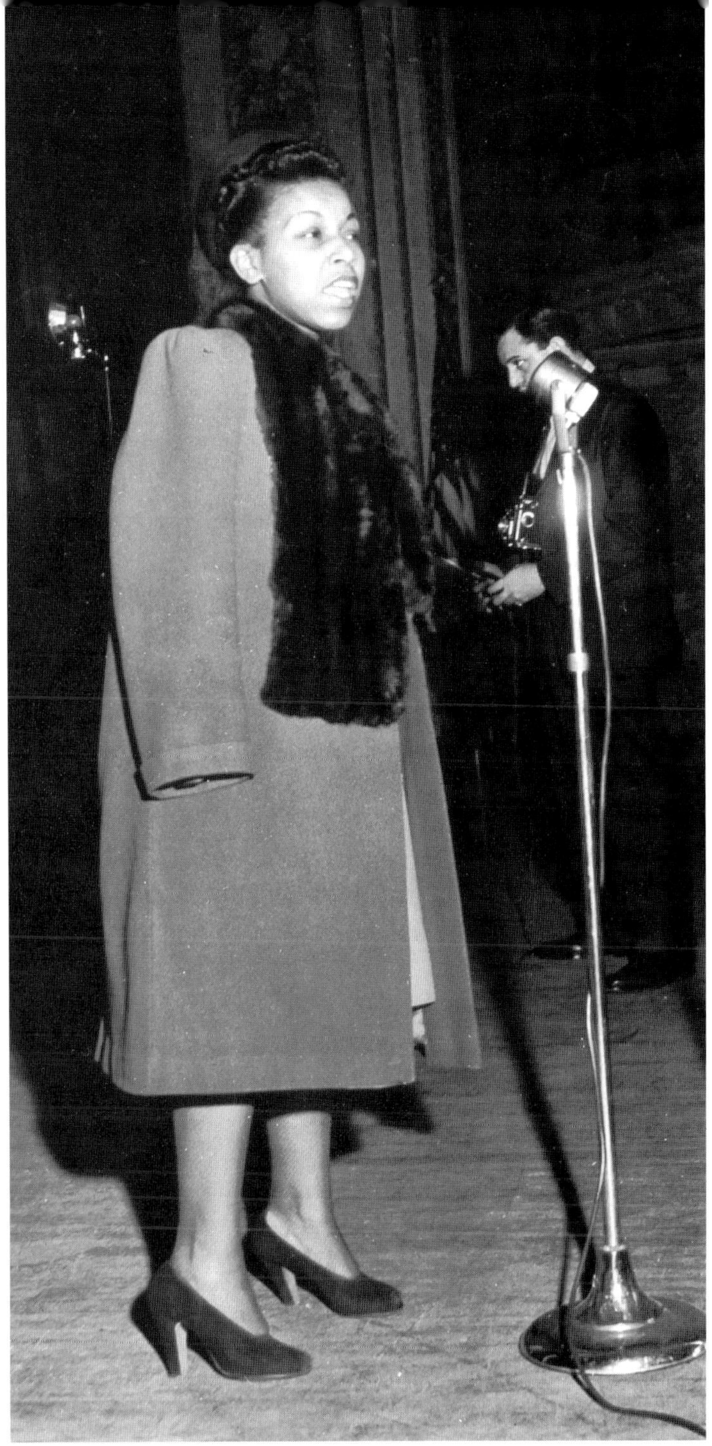

Maxine Sullivan caught during a rehearsal at Carnegie Hall in the late 40's.

Slam Stewart

An inventive and original bass player, Leroy Elliott "Slam" Stewart (1914-1987) came up with a new sound during the late 30's, when he began to sing along with his bowed solos. He was born in Englewood, New Jersey and studied at the Boston Conservatory. In 1937 he teamed with guitarist Slim Gaillard as the duo Slim and Slam, after which he played on 52nd Street in New York for several years, either with his own small groups, or with Art Tatum, Tiny Grimes, Erroll Garner, Beryl Booker, Roy Eldridge and others. By the late 50's he worked mainly with Rose Murphy, after which he led his own trios and also worked with Benny Goodman, Milt Buckner, Jo Jones, and Bucky Pizzarelli.

Arthur Schutt

Almost forgotten today but one of the finest white pianists of the 20's, Arthur Schutt (1902-1965) played in movie houses at the age of thirteen. He was born in Reading, Pennsylvania and was taught piano by his father. 1918-24 he was pianist and arranger for Paul Specht's orchestra after which he established himself in New York, playing with leading society bandleaders, such as Roger Wolfe Kahn, Don Voorhees and others. In the late 30's he led his own bands but moved to Hollywood around 1940 where he worked as a studio musician for M.G.M., Columbia and other studios until he was forced to retire in the early 60's, due to ill health. *To my dear friend and helpmate "Timmie". Arthur Schutt.*

Charlie Spivak

Born in Kiev, Ukraine, trumpeter and bandleader Charles "Charlie" Spivak (1907-1982) emigrated to the USA as a child with his parents, settling in New Haven, Connecticut. He learned the trumpet at the age of ten, and between 1924 and 1939 he was much in demand in bands and in studios, playing with Paul Specht, Ben Pollack, the Dorsey Brothers, Ray Noble, Bing Crosby, Jack Teagarden and others. From 1939 until the late 70's he led his own bands with considerable commercial success. Spivak's playing was famous for his wide range and sweetness of tone.

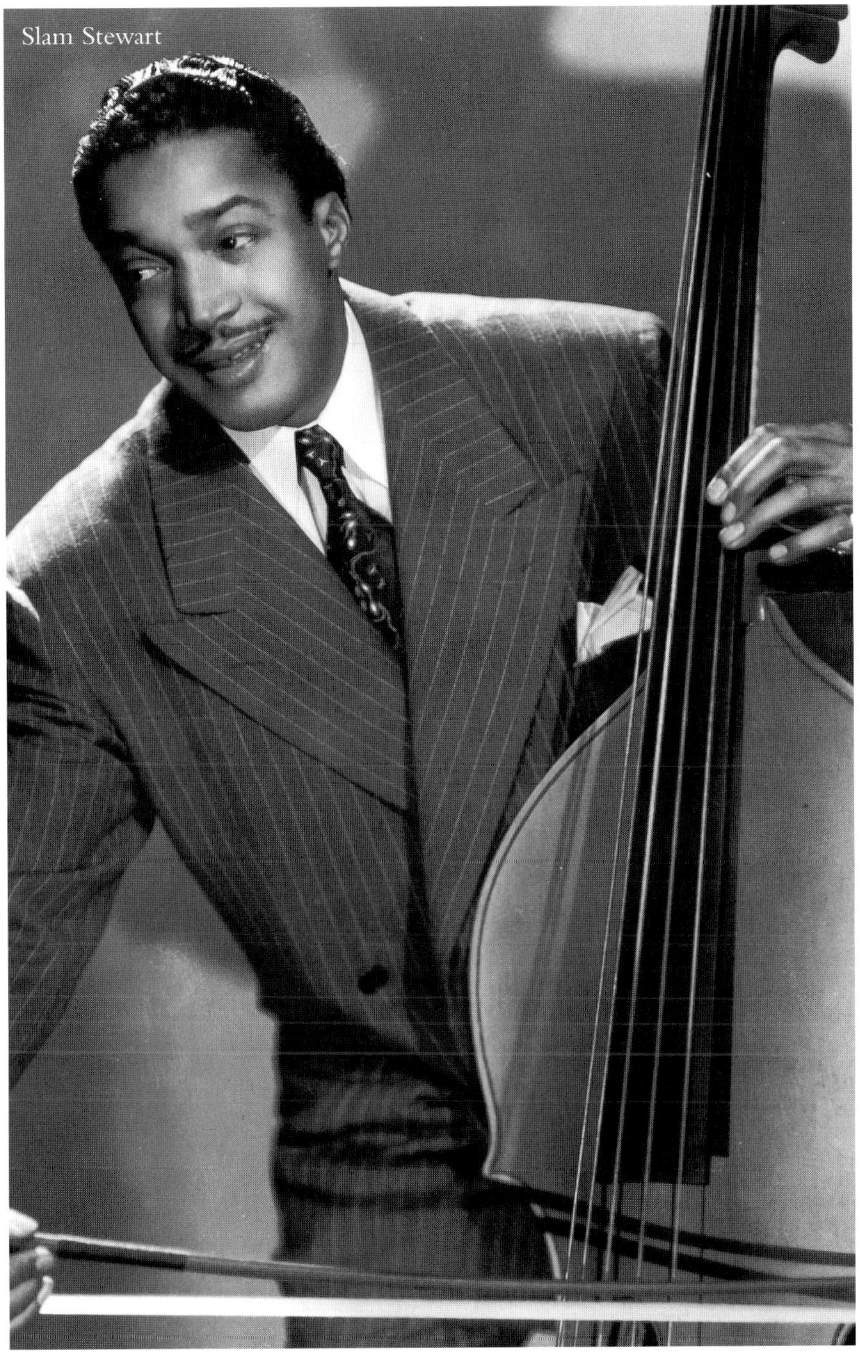
Slam Stewart

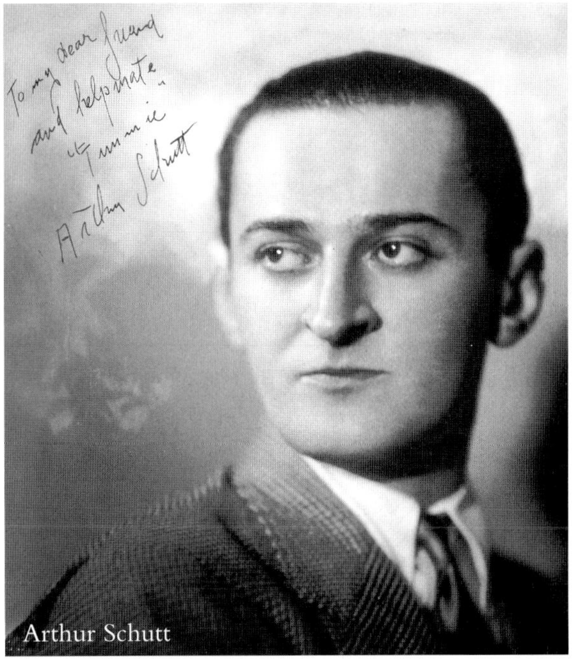

Arthur Schutt

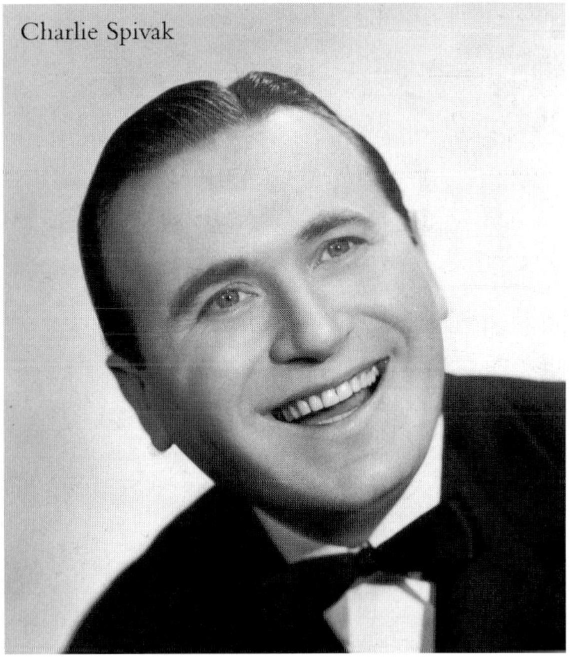
Charlie Spivak

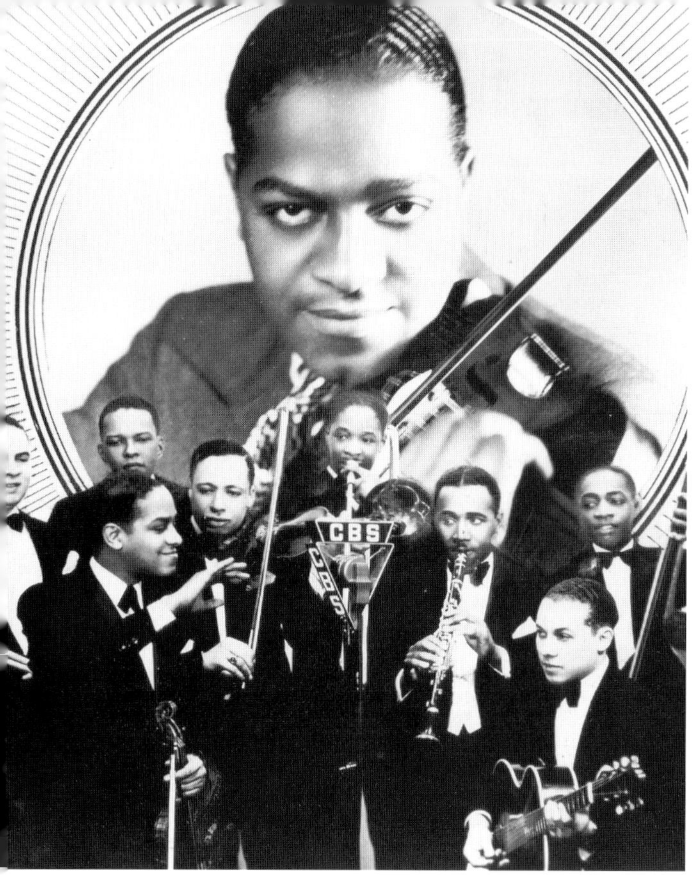

EDDIE SOUTH

Violinist Eddie South (1904-1962) received a thorough classical training, but being black there was no place for him on the concert stage in the 20's. He was born in Louisiana, Missouri, and after studies at the Chicago Musical College he worked with Jimmy Wade, Erskine Tate and others around Chicago. In 1928 he went to Europe where he became a popular figure the following three years, after which he returned to Chicago to lead his own band. 1937-38 he visited Europe once more. Back in the USA he formed his own groups, and during the 50's he also had his own radio and TV shows. South played with a warm tone, a powerful swing and a faultless technique, and his solos were always melodic and tasteful.

Eddie South and His Orchestra 1936. From the left: Jimmy Bertrand (dr), Zinky Cohn (p), South (cond.), Wright Smith (vl), Ed Burke (tb), Harold Scott (cl), Everett Barksdale (g), and Milt Hinton (b).

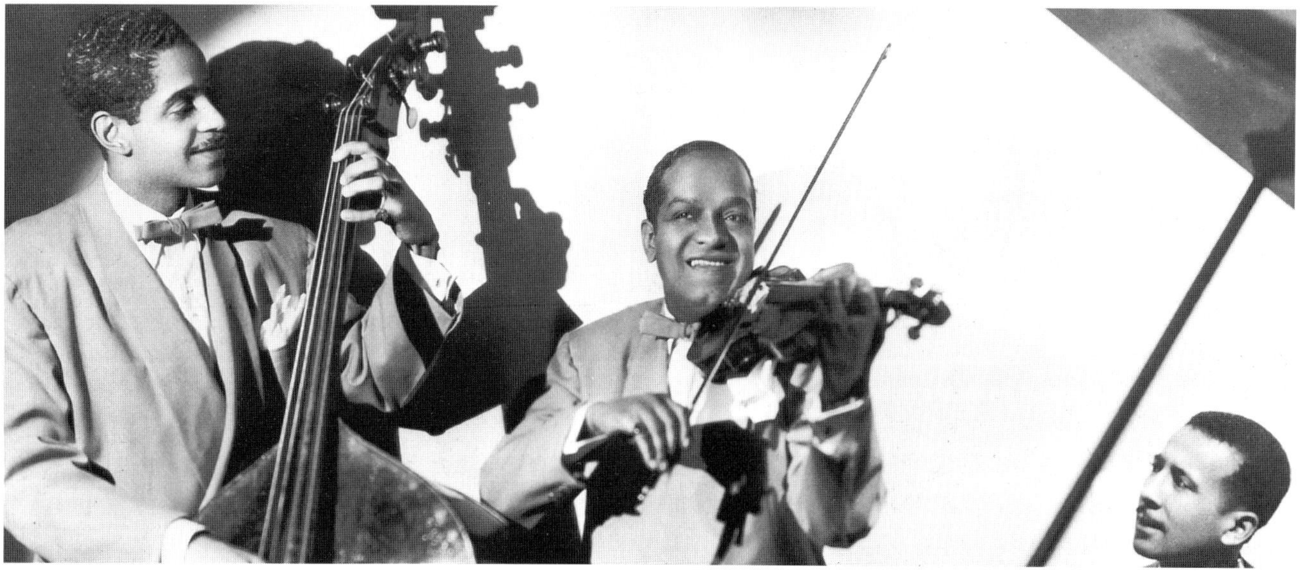

Eddie South and His Orchestra 1947 with Leonard Gaskin (b) and Don Abney (p).

JESS STACY

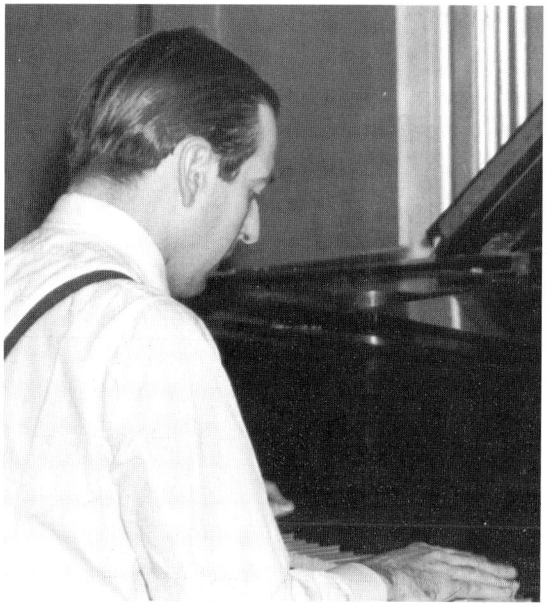

Pianist Jess Alexandria Stacy (1904-1994) was mainly self-taught. He was born in Bird's Point, Missouri, and played in his teens on riverboats. In the mid-20's he moved to Chicago where he was with numerous band leaders until he joined Benny Goodman in 1935. He was with Goodman on and off until 1947, in between playing with Bob Crosby, Tommy Dorsey and leading his own bands. From 1947 he freelanced in New York and California, until he left full-time music in 1963 to work as a salesman for Max Factor. In 1973 he was pursuaded to perform publicly again, after which he appeared regularly at festivals, on radio and TV. Stacy formed his own style after Earl Hines and Teddy Wilson, playing with inventiveness and rhythmical precision.

GENE SEDRIC

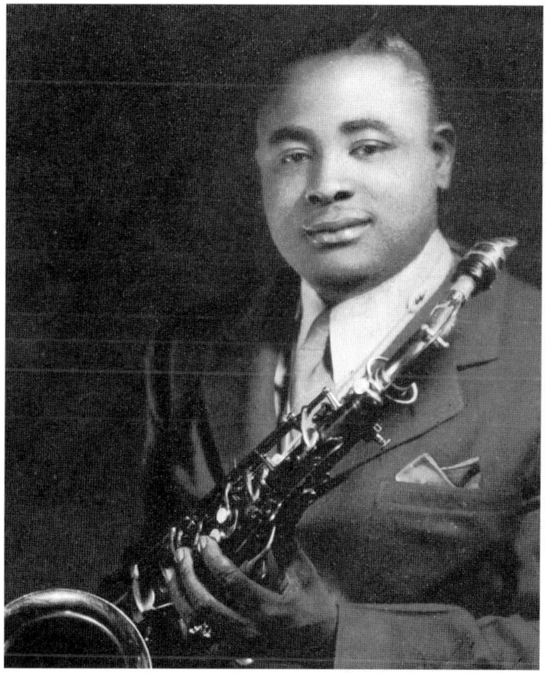

Clarinetist and tenor saxophonist Eugene "Gene" "Honey Bear" Sedric (1907-1963) was born in St. Louis and worked in his teens with the local Charlie Creath, and on the riverboats with Fate Marable and Dewey Jackson. In 1923 he came to New York and joined Sam Wooding with whom he toured extensively in USA, Latin America and Europe duing the following decade. After a short stint with Fletcher Henderson in 1934 he began a long association with Fats Waller. Upon Waller's death he formed his own bands, but played and toured also with other leaders, such as Jimmy McPartland, Bobby Hackett, Mezz Mezzrow, and Dick Wellstood. Today Sedric is mostly remembered for his countless recordings with Fats Waller, on which he was heavily featured, playing the clarinet beautifully in its chalumeau register, or the saxophone in a more forthright, easily recognizable way with plenty of swing. *To Timme and Inez with best wishes always. Eugene (Honey Bear) Sedric.*

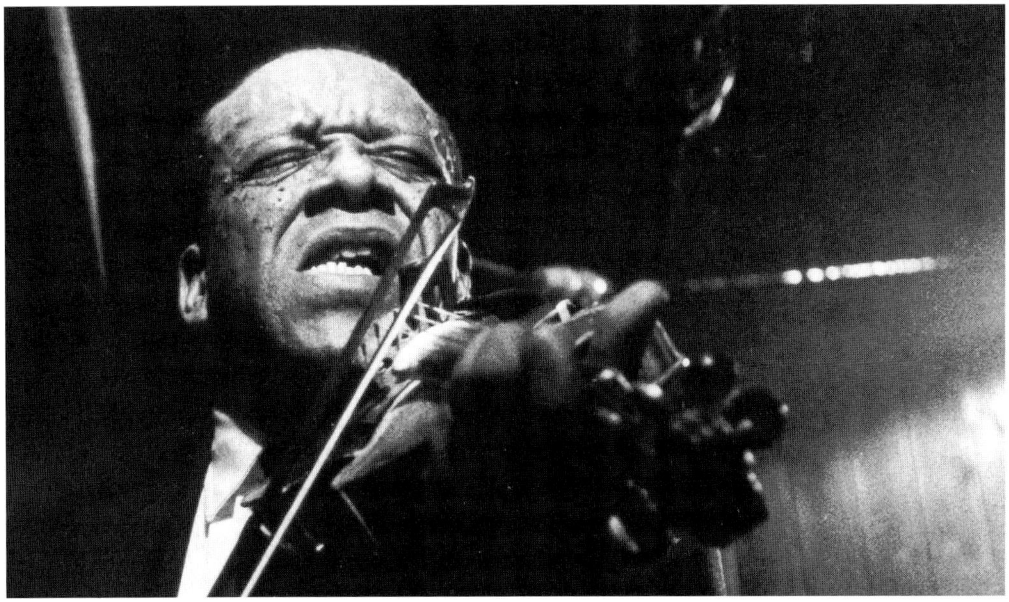

Stuff Smith at the Jazzhus Montmartre, Copenhagen, March 1965.

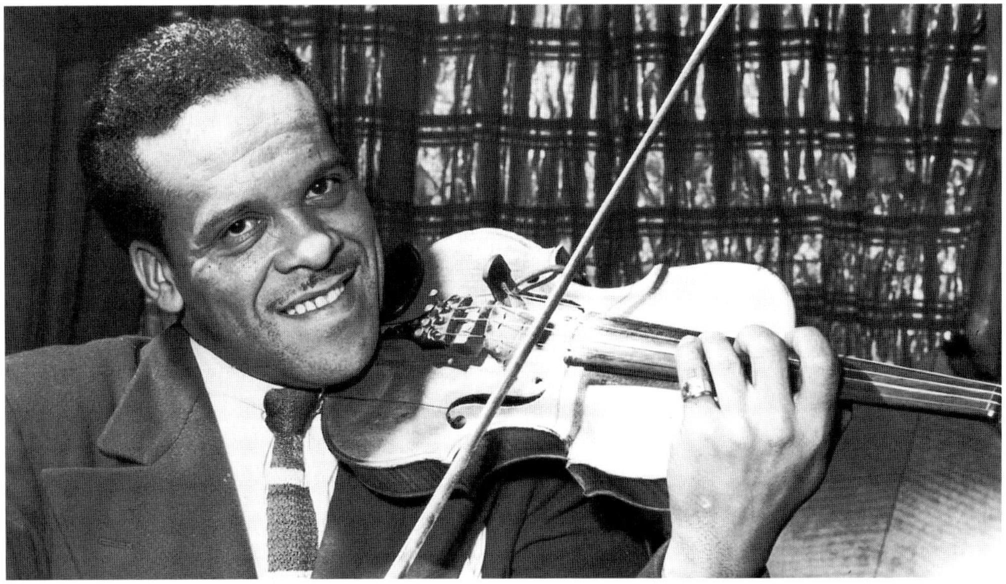

Stuff Smith at the Onyx Club in New York, 1944.

STUFF SMITH

Probably the hardest swinging violinist in jazz, and one of the great innovators on the instrument, Hezekiah Leroy Gordon "Stuff" Smith (1909-1967) received his first instrument at the age of seven, and five years later he was playing in his father's band. He was born in Portsmouth, Ohio, and from 1924 he toured with a revue for a few years. In 1926 he joined Alphonso Trent's band, and 1930 found him working in Buffalo. In 1936 he worked successfully at the Onyx Club in New York, after which he moved to California, and the following years he played in Chicago, New York, Milwaukee, Washington, and California. Throughout the 50's he was mostly on the West Coast, but in early 1965 he settled in Copenhagen, touring Europe successfully until his death. Smith played in a harmonically adventurous, uniquely infectious style of his own. He also sang in a hoarse, yet attractive voice.

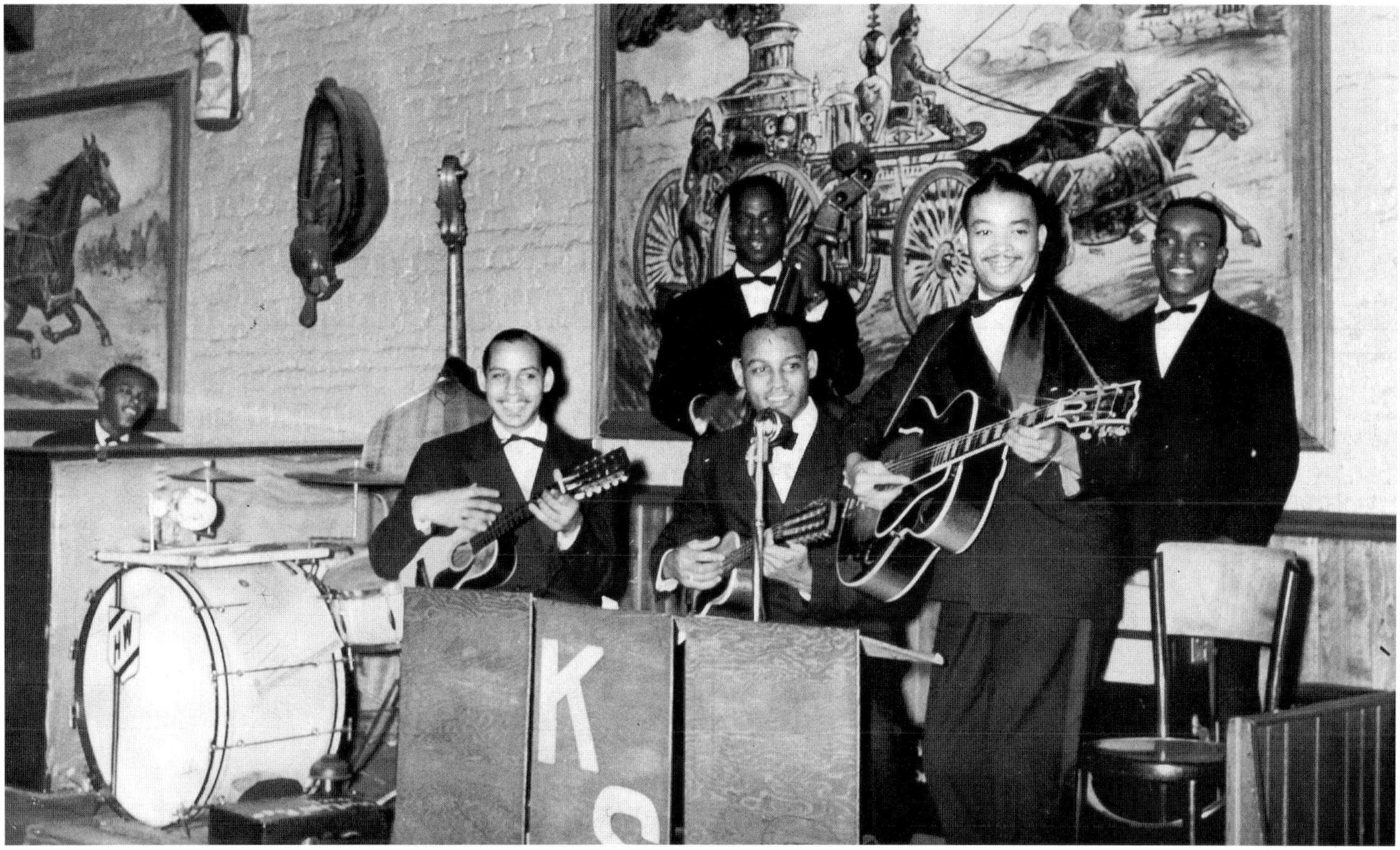

This photo of The Spirits of Rhythm dates from the early 40's, and shows from left: Wilbur Daniels (tiple), Wilson Myers (b), Douglas Daniels (tiple), Teddy Bunn (g) and Virgil Scroggins (various percussion instruments). The unidentified pianist belongs to an alternating band.

THE SPIRITS OF RHYTHM

One of the most influential string bands of the 30's, this novelty group was formed by Wilbur and Douglas Daniels in the late 20's, performing under various names. In 1929 singer Leo Watson was added, and from 1932, when guitarist Teddy Bunn joined, the group changed its name to the Spirits of Rhythm. In between Watson worked with others, and the group finally disbanded in 1946.

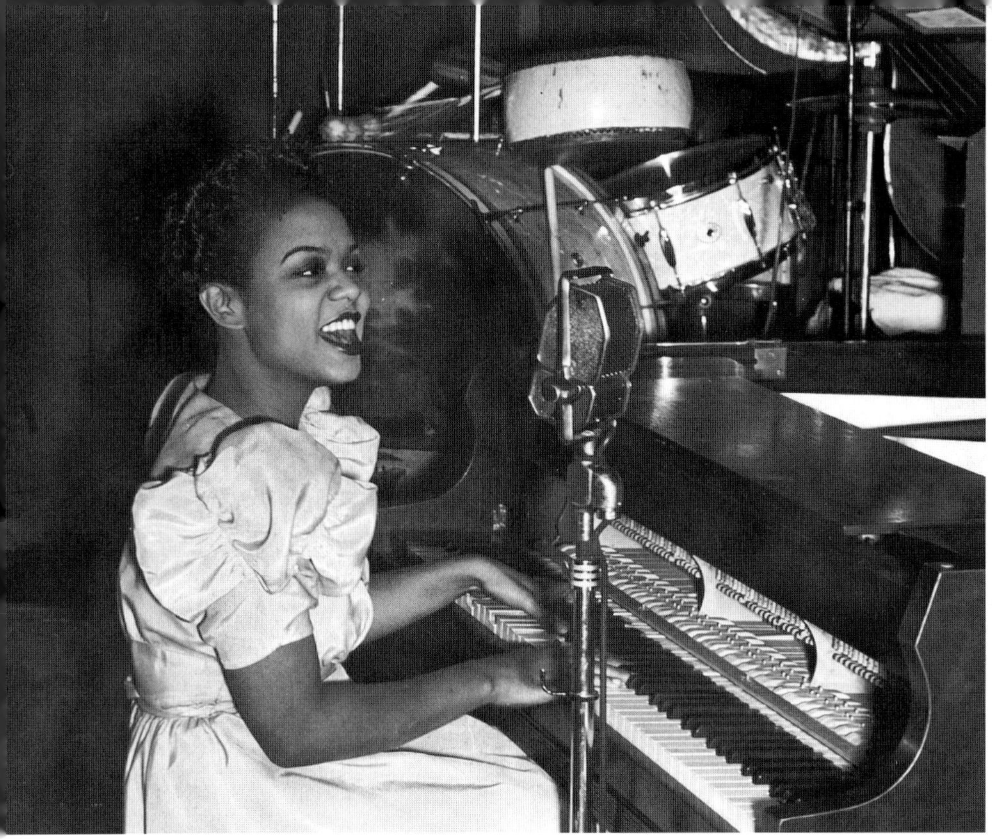

Hazel Scott during a performance at the Café Society around 1940.

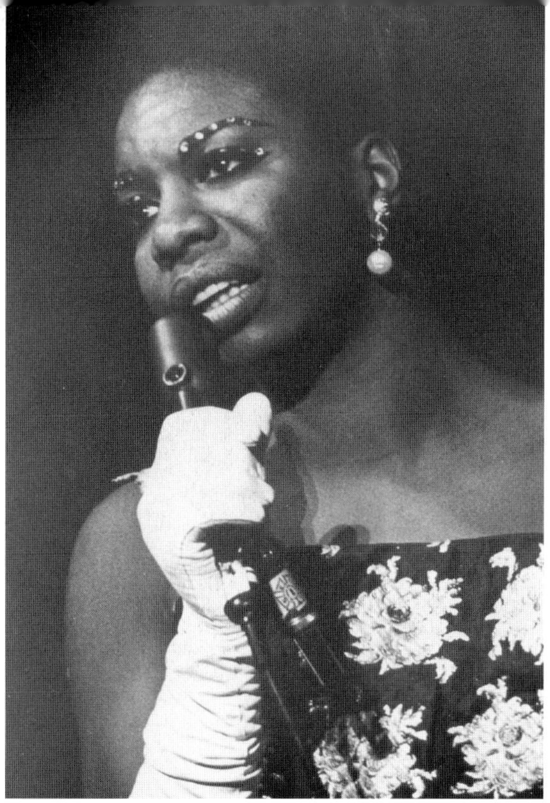

Nina Simone photographed by Rosenkrantz during a concert, probably in the mid-60's.

Hazel Scott

Pianist and singer Hazel Dorothy Scott (1920-1981) began playing at the age of two. She was born in Port of Spain, Trinidad, but moved to New York with her family a few years later. She studied at the Juilliard School of Music from the age of eight, and played jazz in night clubs and on the radio in the 30's. Between 1939 and 1943 she was an attraction at both Café Societies, and by the mid-40's she was leading her own groups. She was married to the prominent black politician Adam Clayton Powell. During the 50's her career drifted somewhat, but she continued to play clubs until the year she died. Scott sang with a pleasant voice, but she was best known for her swinging versions of popular classical pieces.

Nina Simone

Singer Eunice Waymon "Nina Simone" (1933-) is a striking, powerful performer and an uncompromising artist who has settled in France, tired of the social conditions of blacks in the USA. She was born in Tryon, North Carolina, and played piano from an early age. After studies at the Juilliard School of Music in New York she began a career as a singer which is still flourishing, incorporating elements of jazz, soul, blues and pop into her own unique interpretations.

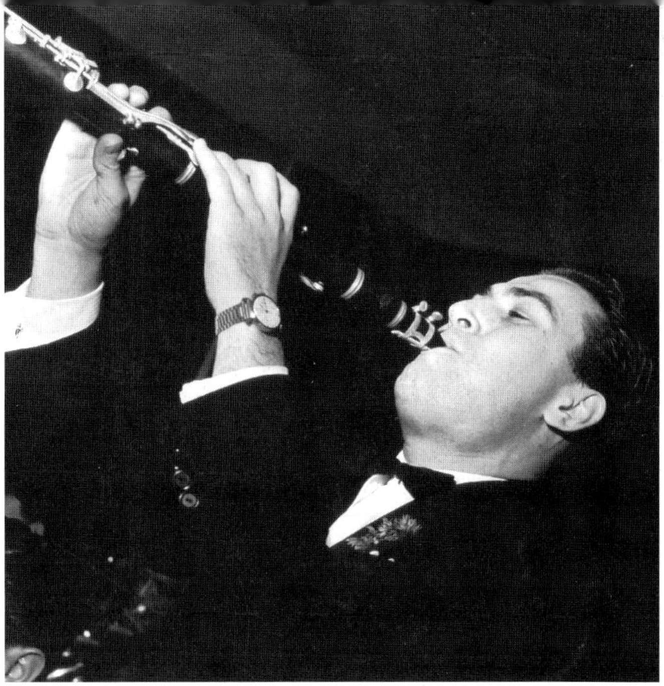

Artie Shaw and His Orchestra at the Blue Room, Lincoln Hotel in New York, December 1938.

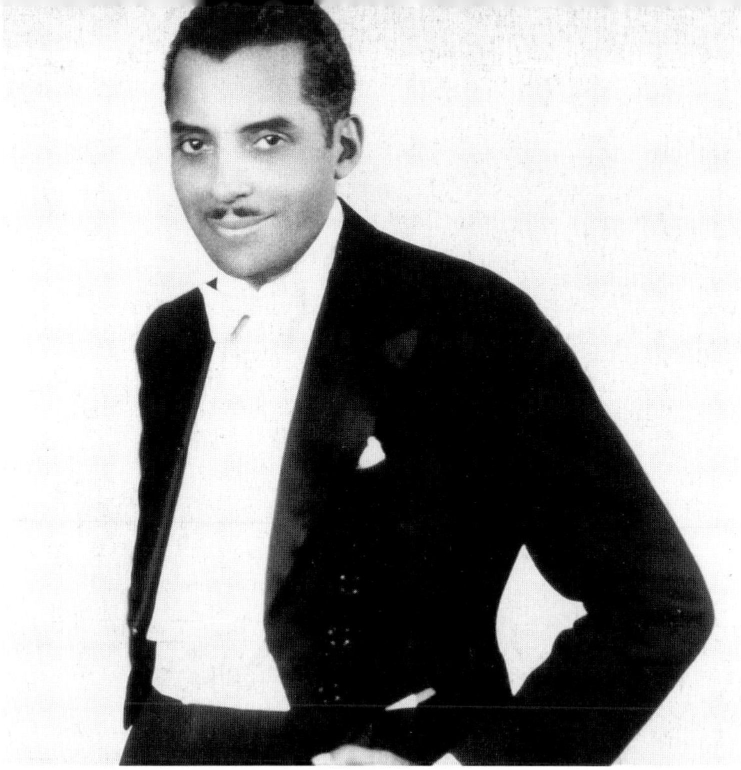

Artie Shaw

One of the leading clarinetists of the swing era was Arthur Jacob Arshawsky "Artie Shaw" (1910–). He was born in New York, but grew up in New Haven and played in local bands at the age of twelve. From 1926 he worked in Cleveland and Chicago. Coming to New York in 1929 he began playing with Willie "The Lion" Smith. Between 1931 and 1936 he freelanced as a studio musician, after which he formed his own band. The following years he formed and disbanded several big bands and small groups, often characterized by their unusual instrumentation. He retired in 1954 to launch a career as a writer, but from 1983 he has organized a band again, which he occasionally conducts.

Noble Sissle

Best known as a highly gifted composer and a lyricist in collaboration with Eubie Blake, Noble Lee Sissle (1889–1975) was an important figure in early jazz, leading a band with famous musicians during the 20's and singing with other bands. He was born in Indianapolis, Indiana, and formed his own band in 1914. In 1916 he was singing and playing with Jim Europe, and from 1919 he formed a successful duo with Eubie Blake with whom he composed and produced many Broadway shows in the following decade, including "Shuffle Along" and "Chocolate Dandies". Between 1926 and 1931 he toured Europe several times and led commercial bands that held long residencies in New York. From 1960 he managed his own night club and publishing company and occasionally led his own bands. He spent the last years of his life in Florida.

WILLIE "THE LION" SMITH

Alongside James P. Johnson and Fats Waller, William Henry Joseph Bonaparte Bertholoff, called Willie "The Lion" Smith (1897-1973), stands out as the most influential of the Harlem stride pianists. Born in Goshen, New York into a family of Jewish and black parentage, he grew up in Newark, New Jersey, and played the piano from the age of six. While still in his teens he began playing professionally in New York. After military service in World War I he returned to New York and played clubs and toured with blues singers for example Mamie Smith. From the mid-30's he became more known to the public and came to lead his own bands. He toured Europe and Canada as a soloist to the end of his days.

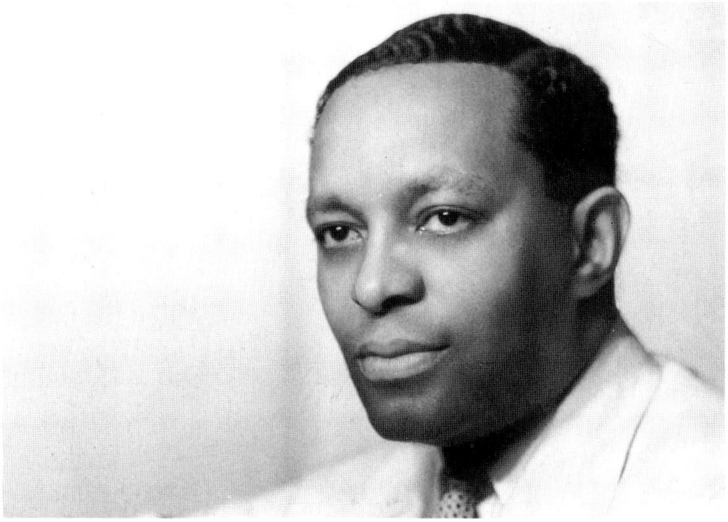

This publicity photo of Willie "The Lion" Smith from the 30's is remarkable because of the lack of both his charateristics: a derby and a cigar.

SAHIB SHIHAB

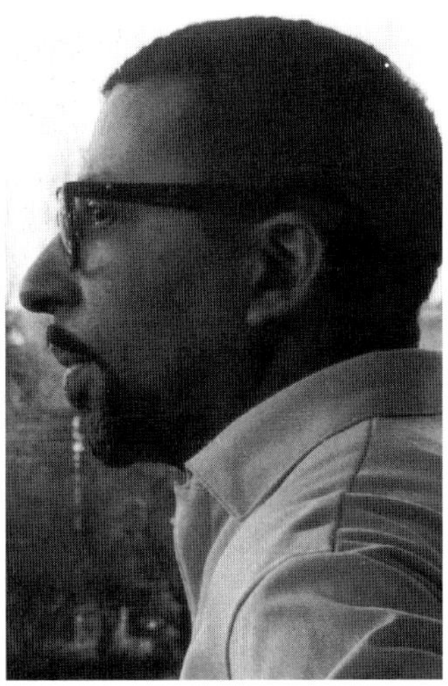

Sahib Shihab at his home in Copenhagen around 1963.

Born in Savannah, Georgia, saxophonist and flutist Edmund Gregory (1925-1989) played in various territory bands at the age of thirteen before studying music in Boston. He played with Fletcher Henderson and Roy Eldridge in the mid-40's, after which he took the Muslim name Sahib Shihab. From 1947 he worked with many prominent modern band leaders, such as Art Blakey, Thelonius Monk, Tadd Dameron, Dizzy Gillespie, and Oscar Pettiford. After a tour with Quincy Jones he remained in Europe, first settling in Sweden, but after 1962 in Copenhagen. 1973-76 he played in Los Angeles, after which he returned to Denmark. In Europe he played with the Kenny Clarke-Francy Boland Big Band (1961-72), the Danish Radio Jazz Group, The Ernie Wilkins' Almost Big Band, Thad Jones' Eclipse and others. In 1986 he returned to the USA where he died. Shihab was one of the first modern jazz musicians to take up the flute, but he is best known for his work on the baritone saxophone, on which he played with a beautiful, light tone and great imagination.

Buddy Tate

Among the Texas tenors George Holmes "Buddy" Tate (1913-) stands out as one of the finest, playing with a solid swing, a huge sound, and always with a stamp of high quality. He was born in Sherman, Texas and began his professional career already at the age of twelve. After several years in territory bands in the Southwest he joined Count Basie in early 1939, staying with him for ten years, after which he worked with Hot Lips Page, Lucky Millinder, Jimmy Rushing and Lucille Dixon. He then formed his own band which played for more than twenty years at the Celebrity Club in Harlem. Since then he has freelanced and toured regularly in Europe with his own band, Buck Clayton, Illinois Jacquet, the Saints and Sinners and others.

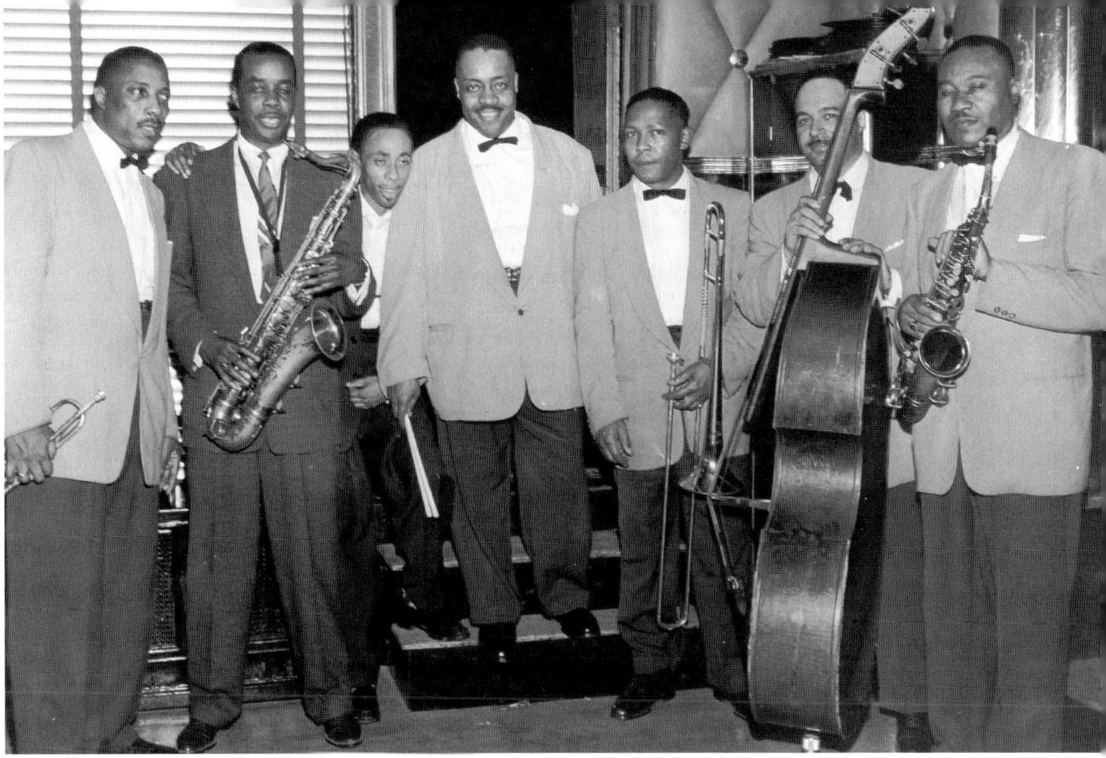

Buddy Tate and His Celebrity Club Orchestra ca.1953. From the left: Pat Jenkins (tp), Buddy Tate (ts), Skip Hall (p), Charles "Fats" Donaldson (dr), Eli Robinson (tb), Carl "Flat Top" Wilson (b), Ben Richardson (as).

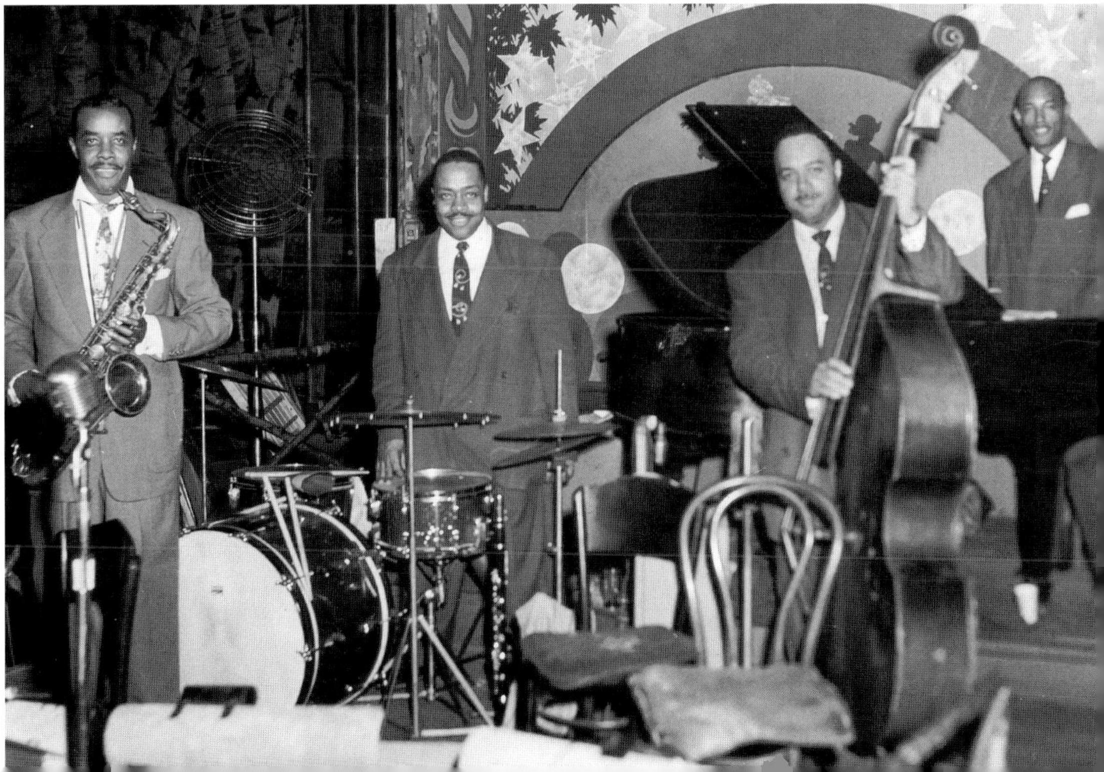

Buddy Tate and His Celebrity Club Orchestra around 1954 at the Celebrity Club on 125th Street in Harlem. Buddy Tate (ts), Charles "Fats" Donaldson (dr), Carl "Flat Top" Wilson (b), Sir Charles Thompson (p).

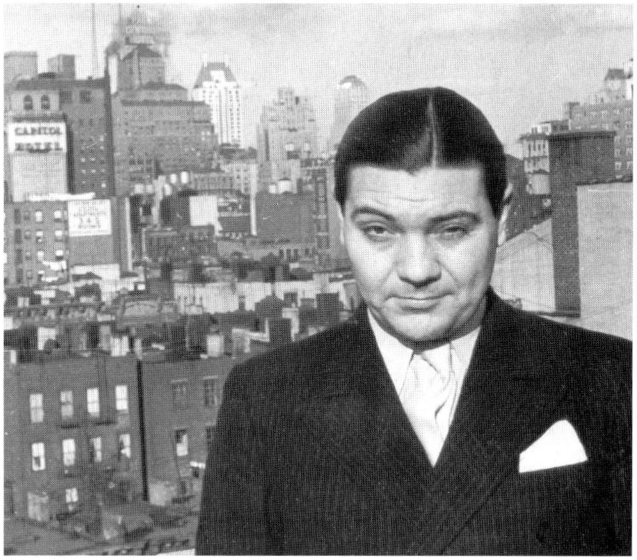

Jack Teagarden with a hangover captured by Rosenkrantz on top of the Plymouth Hotel in New York

JACK TEAGARDEN

Maybe the finest of all jazz trombonists was Weldon Leo "Jack" Teagarden (1905-1964). He was born into a musical family in Vernon, Texas, in which both parents and two brothers, Charlie and Cub, and a sister, Norma, also played instruments. In 1927 he came to New York where he joined Ben Pollack's band the following year. 1933-1938 he worked for Paul Whiteman, after which he formed his own big band with which he went bankrupt in 1946. After a spell with his own small group he joined Louis Armstrong in 1947. From 1951 until his death he led his own dixieland groups. Teagarden set new standards for playing the trombone with his astonishing, yet lightly-phrased technique which made everything he played sound natural. He was also a charming singer, with a lazy, Texan drawl.

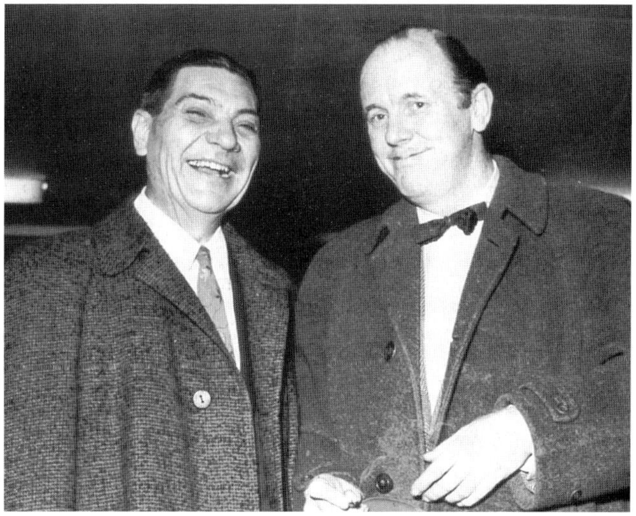

Jack Teagarden and Rosenkrantz at Copenhagen Airport, October 1957, when Teagarden toured Europe with his sextet.

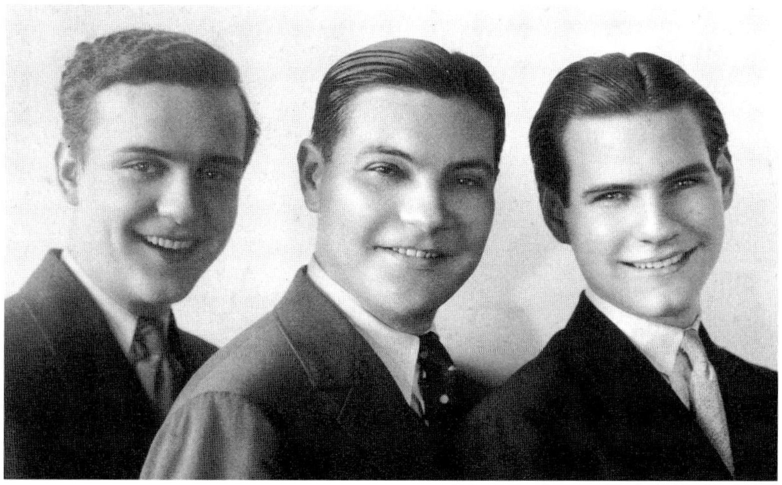

The Teagarden brothers. From the left, drummer Clois Lee "Cub" (1915-1969), Jack, and trumpeter Charles "Charlie" (1913-1984). The photo was taken in the early 30's, probably around 1933 when both Jack and Charlie joined Paul Whiteman's orchestra.

BILLY TAYLOR

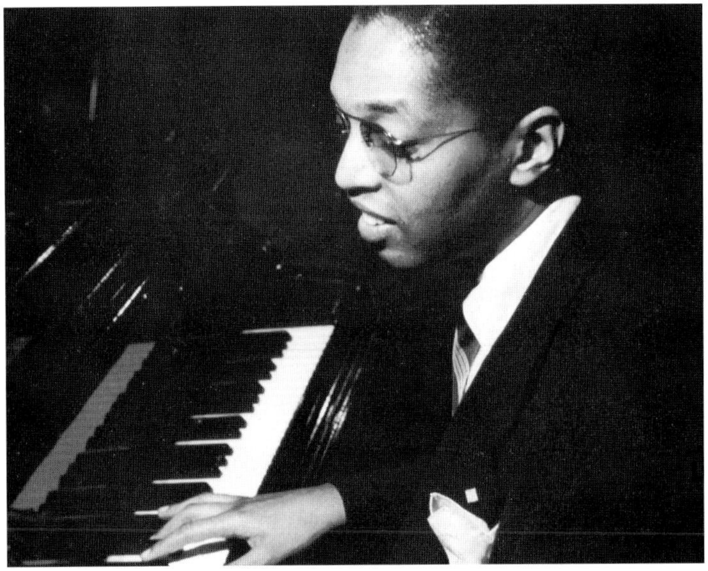

Born in Greenville, North Carolina, pianist William "Billy" Taylor (1921-) moved to New York in the early 40's with a degree in music from Virginia State College. During the following years he played with Ben Webster, Dizzy Gillespie, Eddie South, Stuff Smith, Slam Stewart, Don Redman, Charlie Parker and others. In 1951 he became the house pianist at Birdland, but from 1952 he has had his own trio, besides taking a great interest in jazz education, publishing books on jazz piano, running his own programs on radio and TV, arranging workshops and being the co-founder of the Jazzmobile organization. Taylor plays with technical finesse in a light and fluid bop style.

JOHN TCHICAI

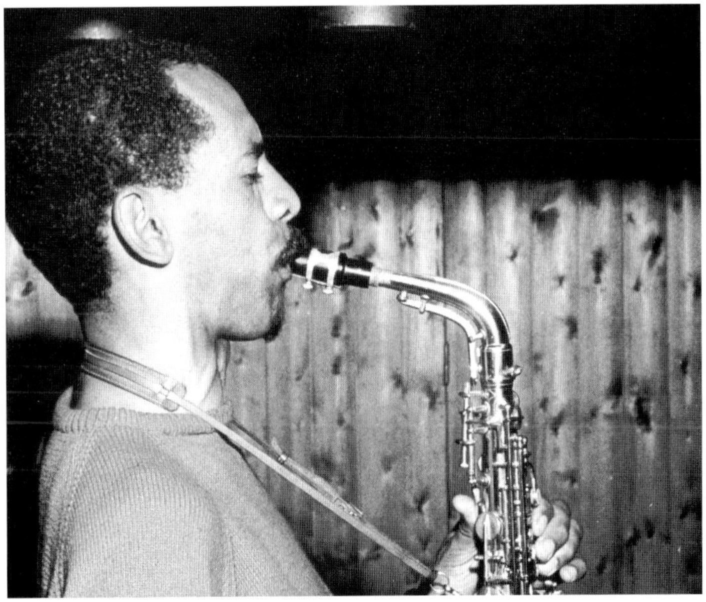

John Tchicai in the Jazzhus Montmartre, Copenhagen, September-Oktober 1963, as part of the New York Contemporary Five with Archie Shepp and Don Cherry.

The Danish saxophonist John Martin Tchicai (1936-) was born in Copenhagen but grew up in Aarhus where he attended the local Academy of Music for three years. In 1962 he played a festival in Helsinki when he met Archie Shepp, and in 1963 he moved to New York to play with Shepp, Don Cherry, Roswell Rudd, John Coltrane, and others. In 1966 he returned to Denmark but since the early 70's he has also played in other European countries with Han Bennink, Albert Mangelsdorf, George Gruntz, Johnny Dyani and the Dutch saxophone sextet De Zes Winden. Tchicai, who was a major force in the avant-garde jazz movement of the 60's, settled in California in 1991 where he founded his own group "The Archetypes".

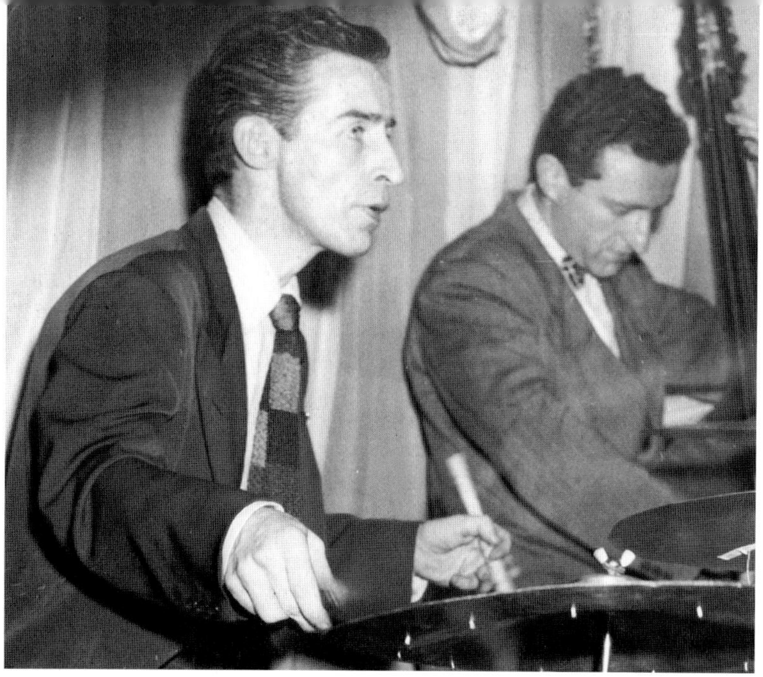

Dave Tough and Jack Lesberg at Eddie Condon's in New York, 1946.

Dave Tough

Though physically frail and tiny David Jarvis "Dave" Tough (1908-1948) was a powerful giant behind his drums, a swinger with a natural sense of musical quality, one of the finest drummers of the swing period and on a par with Sidney Catlett. He was born in Oak Park, Illinois, and played drums at an early age. In the mid-20's he became an influential member of the Austin High School Gang in Chicago, but due to illness he was inactive in 1932-35, after which he played with the best among the white bandleaders. After a short spell in the U.S. Navy during World War II he joined Woody Herman, after which he played with Eddie Condon, Joe Marsala and others. During his last years he was ill several times, and while on leave from New Jersey Veteran's Hospital he slipped on a street in Newark on a cold December day, receiving fatal skull injuries.

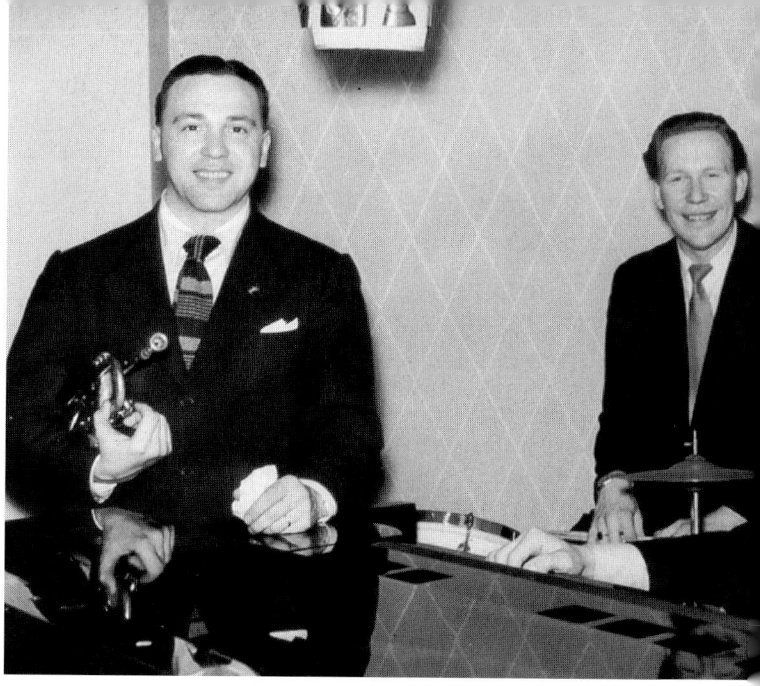

Gösta Törner at a recording session in 1947 with drummer Bertil Frylmark and Swedish-American pianist Bob Laine.

Gösta Törner

The Swedish trumpeter and bandleader Gösta Törner (1912-1982) was among the finest jazz musicians of his country, and one of its earliest and most consistent improvisers. He was born in Stockholm and played professionally from 1929 with a large number of Swedish bands, most notably those led by Sune Lundwall, Arne Hülphers and Thore Ehrling. He led his own group 1943-47, and played 1958-64 on the Swedish-American Line. He retired during the late 60's, but did occasional comeback appearances with a swing group during the 70's.

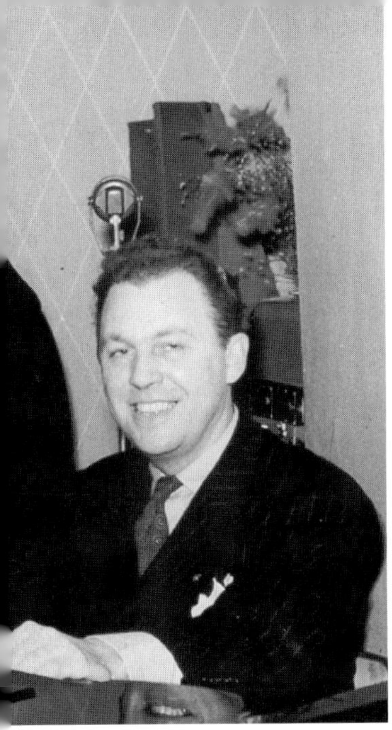

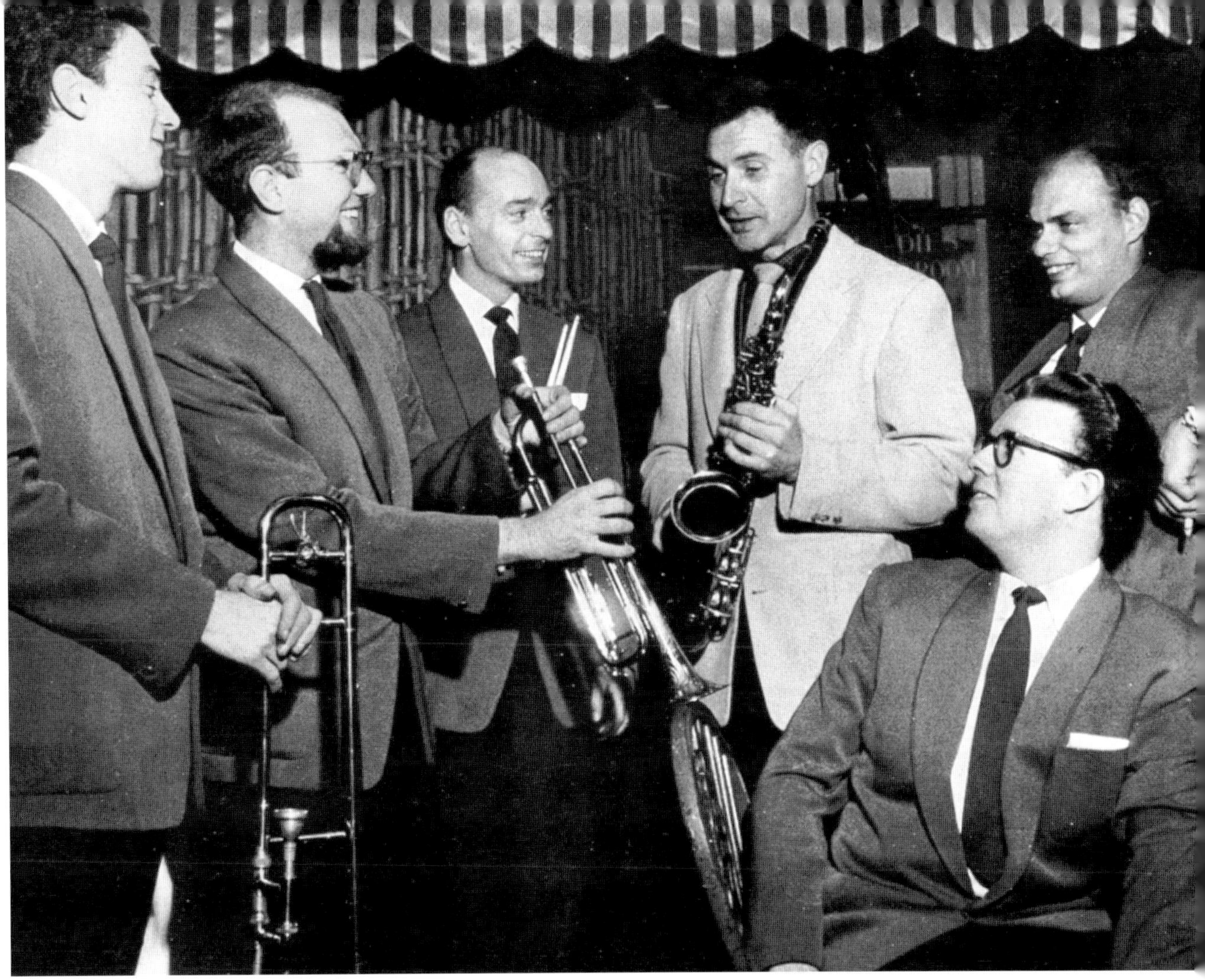

Bruce Turner's Jump Band in London, 1960. From left: John Mumford (tb), John Chilton (tp), John Armatage (dr), Bruce Turner (as), Collin Bates (p), and Jim Bray (b).

BRUCE TURNER

With his extraordinary eclecticism which enabled him to play everything from dixieland to avant-garde jazz, Malcolm Bruce Turner (1922-1993) was an outstanding musician on the British jazz scene. He was born in Saltburn, Yorkshire, but grew up in India where his father was a teacher. At fifteen he took up the clarinet, and began playing the alto saxophone during military service in World War II. After the war he played aboard the Atlantic liner Queen Mary, and in 1953 he joined Humphrey Lyttelton with whom he remained until he formed his own band in 1957. 1966-70 he was with Acker Bilk but in 1974 he rejoined Lyttelton, staying with him until 1988. He then led his own small bands until shortly before he died of a brain tumour.

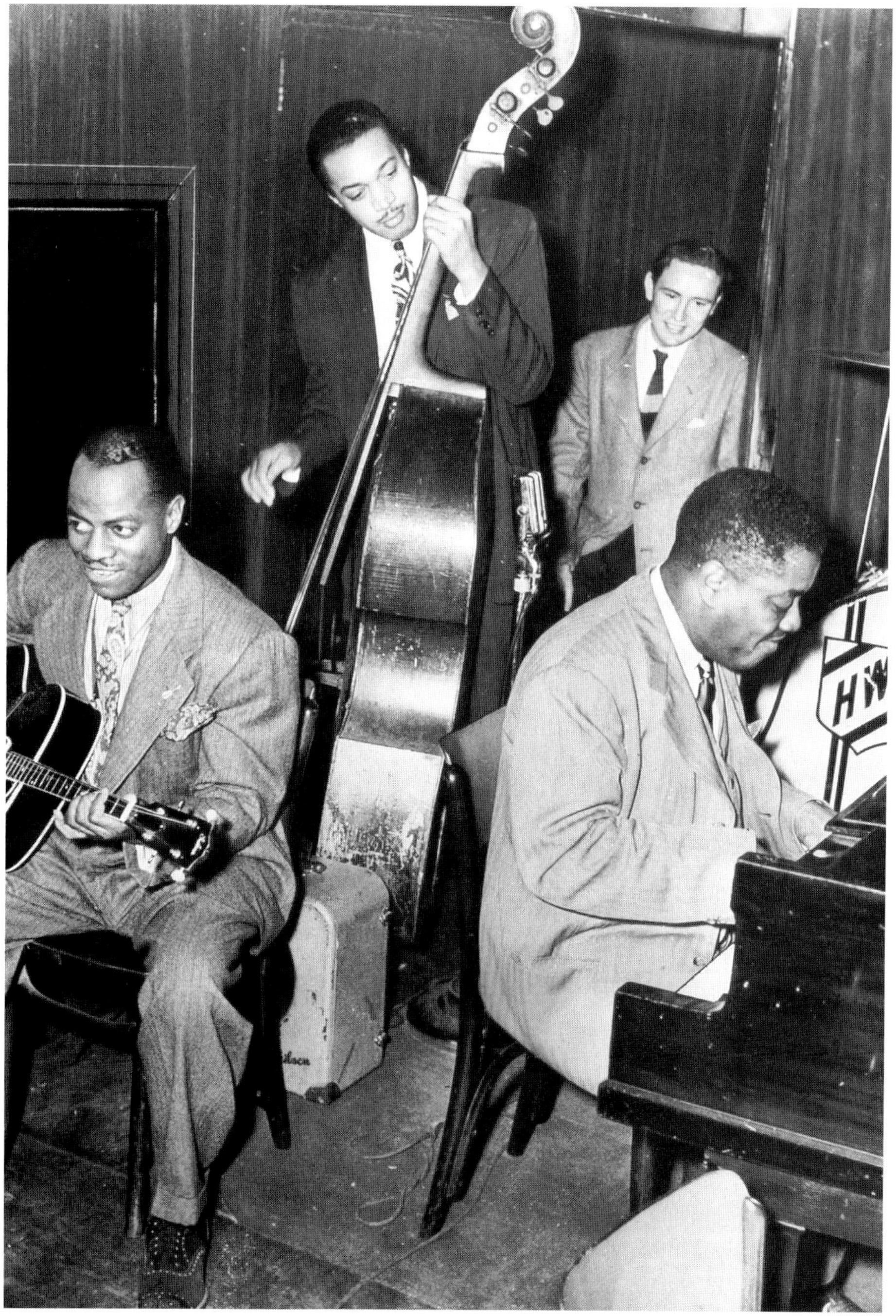

ART TATUM

Pianist Arthur "Art" Tatum (1909-1956) was one of the true geniuses in jazz. He was born in Toledo, Ohio, and was partially blind at birth. He was mostly self-taught and played professionally from 1926 with his own band in and around Toledo and Cleveland. He toured with Adelaide Hall 1932-33 after which he returned to Ohio. Following a couple of years in Hollywood, he moved to New York. After a tour of England in 1938 he worked mostly in California, until he settled in New York in 1940, working clubs and concerts, either as a soloist or with a trio. He settled in California in 1954 where he died of uremia. Tatum's influence on later pianists has been enormous. In his playing he summarized almost everything that had preceded him stylistically, integrating it with great technical virtuosity and adding to it his own unsurpassed inventiveness, rhythmic variations and harmonic subtlety.

The Art Tatum Trio at the Downbeat Club, New York, 1944, with Tiny Grimes (g) and Slam Stewart (b). Owner Morris Levy is enjoying the performance.

Pha Terrell

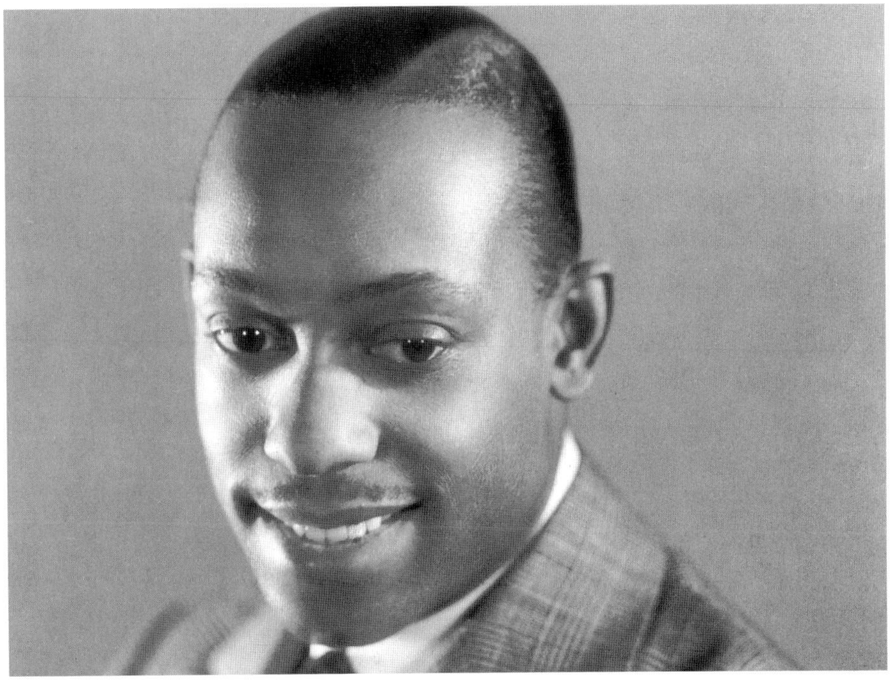

Singer Pha Elmer Terrell (1910-1945) was an outstanding vocalist with a smooth, mellow baritone, but was also capable of singing in falsetto, a popular feature among the singers of the time. He was born in Kansas City, Missouri and worked in local clubs, until he joined Andy Kirk's band in 1933. He stayed with Kirk until 1941 and worked afterwards with Clarence Love in Indianapolis for a while. He then worked as a solo act on the West Coast until he died of a kidney complaint.

The Three Sounds

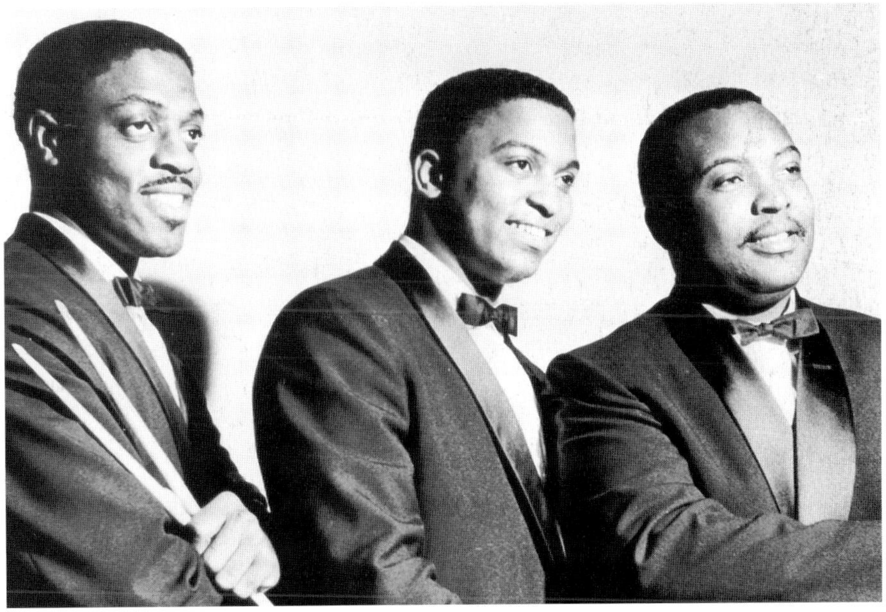

This instrumental trio was formed in 1957 by drummer Bill Dowdy. With pianist Gene Harris and bass player Andy Simpkins the trio remained unchanged until Dowdy left in 1966. The trio achieved considerable popularity in a mainstream style with hints of the blues, and recorded both alone and with guest musicians, such as Nat Adderley, Stanley Turrentine and Anita O'Day. From the left, on this publicity photo of the late 50's: Bill Dowdy, Gene Harris and Andy Simpkins.

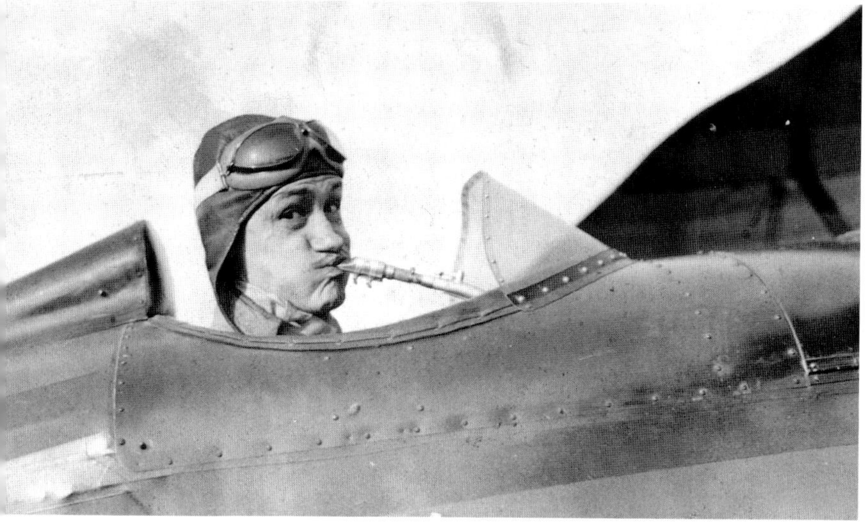

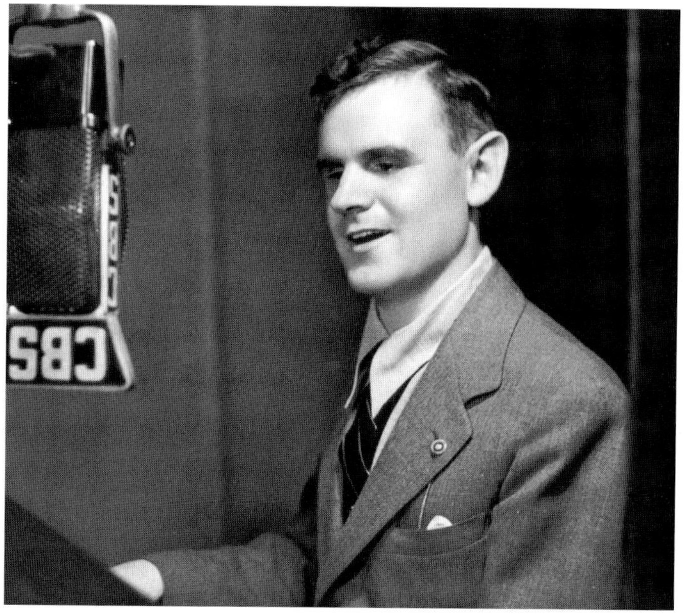

Alec Templeton broadcasting for CBS in June 1937.

FRANKIE TRUMBAUER

On this photo from around 1929 saxophonist Frank "Frankie" Trumbauer (1901-1956) combines two of his obsessions: music and aviation. He was born in Carbondale, Illinois and became a professional musician after Word War I. In the early 20's he moved to Chicago where he worked with Ray Miller and had his own band with Bix Beiderbecke before joining Paul Whiteman's orchestra in 1927. He remained with Whiteman to 1936, after which he organized his own bands. During World War II he worked as a test pilot, but after a couple of years as a sideman in New York he moved to California but retired from full-time music in 1947 to work in aeronautics. Trumbauer was a brilliant saxophonist, specializing on the C-melody saxophone. His improvisations were original, with a delicacy and a light phrasing which influenced many saxophonists, including Benny Carter and Lester Young.

ALEC TEMPLETON

English pianist and composer Alec Templeton (1910-1963) was born blind. He was born in Cardiff, Wales, and educated at Worcester College of Music, after which he also studied in London at the Royal Academy of Music and at the Royal College of Music. From seventeen he played in cinemas, and during the early 30's he also appeared with various symphony orchestras. In 1933 he joined Jack Hylton's orchestra and went with him to the USA in 1935. When Hylton returned, Templeton settled in New York, becoming an American citizen in 1941. Among his many compositions "Bach Goes to Town" is the most popular.

SARAH VAUGHAN

Singer Sarah Lois Vaughan (1924-1990) may be regarded as the most influential jazz vocalist after World War II. She was born in Newark, New Jersey, where she learned the piano and sang in church as a child. In 1942 she won an amateur contest at the Apollo Theatre in Harlem which led to her joining Earl Hines's big band. After stints with Billy Eckstine and John Kirby 1944-46 she worked only as a soloist until she died of lung cancer. Vaughan had perfect intonation, a wide range and a very flexible voice which she used brilliantly in her interpretations of songs. As she grew up with bop musicians she used her knowledge of this style to incorporate passing tones and other modern harmonic devices into her sung lines, thus setting new standards for jazz singing.

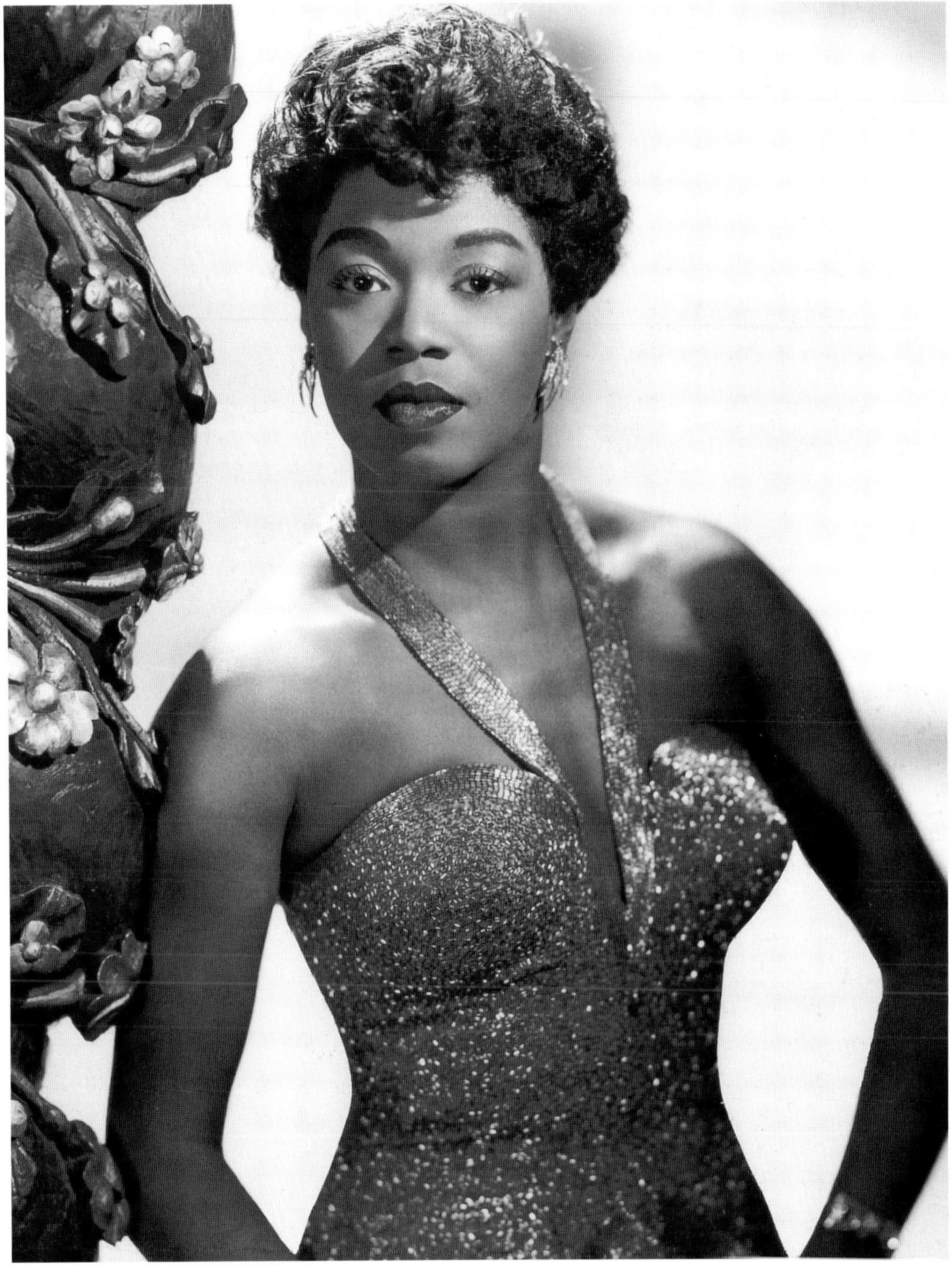

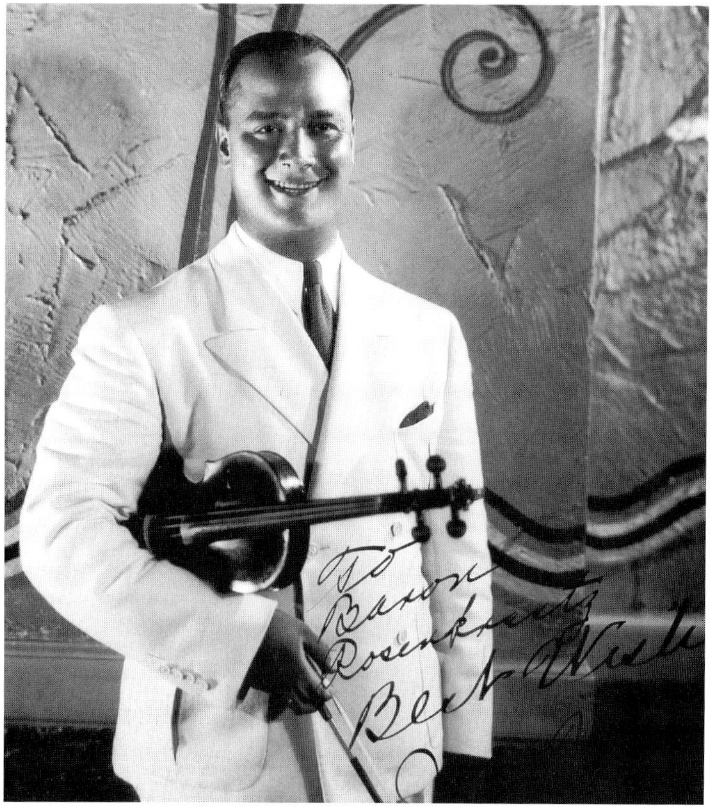

Publicity photo of Joe Venuti taken in the early 30's.
To Baron Rosenkrantz. Best Wishes Joe Venuti.

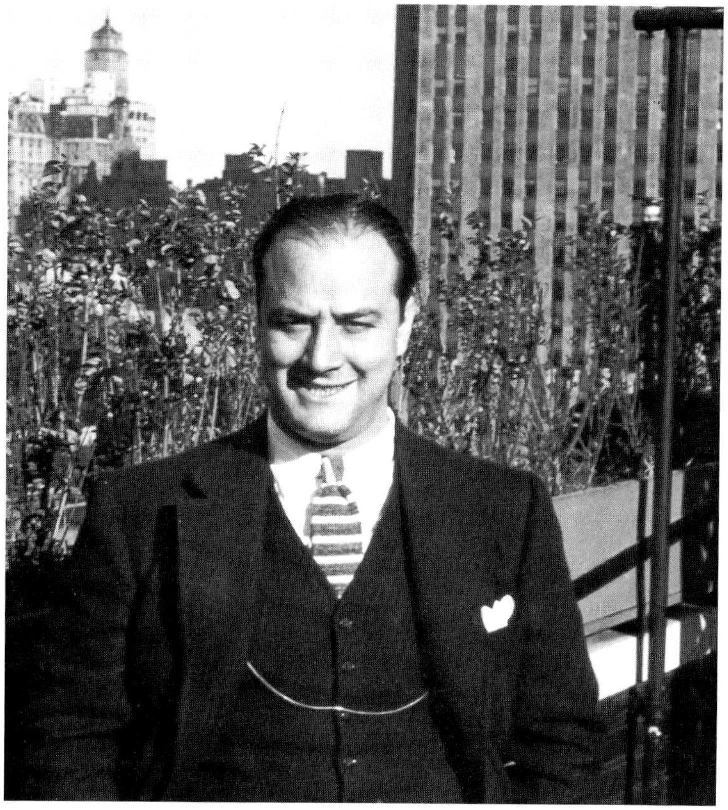

Joe Venuti photographed by Rosenkrantz in New York in 1934.

JOE VENUTI

A lover of practical jokes violinist Joe Venuti (1903-1978) was born in Philadelphia, and not onboard a ship when his parents emigrated from Italy, as one of his stories went. In Philadelphia he began a long partnership with guitarist Eddie Lang which lasted until Lang died in 1933. In 1925 they both moved to New York and began working with leading jazz musicians, such as Red Nichols, Benny Goodman and Jack Teagarden. From 1935-43 Venuti led a big band, after which he moved to California and worked in the studios. From the 60's he played regularly in public again, touring Europe several times. He died of cancer. Venuti played with sparkling energy, enormous swing and an inventiveness which made him a true giant of jazz.

FATS WALLER

A humorous entertainer and singer, a two-fisted giant at the piano, and a wonderful composer, these are some of the characteristics of Thomas Wright "Fats" Waller (1904-1943). He was born in New York and became a professional pianist at the age of fifteen after studies with private teachers. During the 20's he worked in cabarets and theatres and also wrote numerous popular songs for revues, such as "Keep Shuffling" and "Hot Chocolates". In 1934 he formed his six-piece group Fats Waller and His Rhythm, with whom he recorded hundreds of popular songs over the years. In 1941 he expanded his group to a big band and did national tours, but from 1942 he worked as a single. In late 1943 he toured military camps and worked in Los Angeles, but on his return to New York he died of pneumonia on the train.

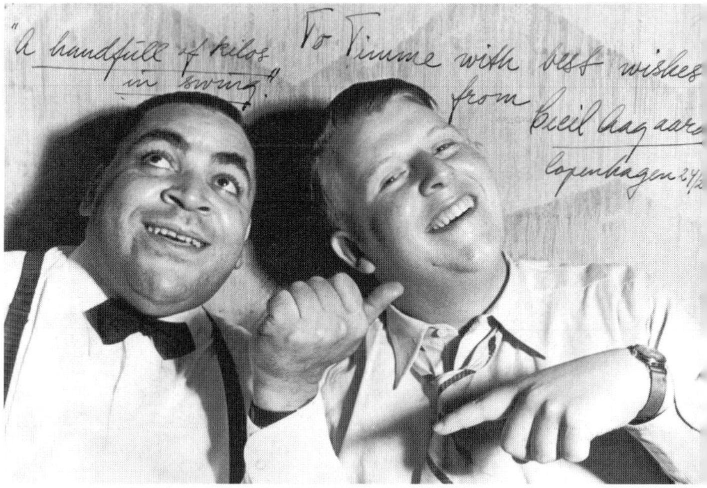

Fats Waller and Norwegian singer Cecil Aagaard. "A handfull of kilos in swing". *To Timme with best wishes from Cecil Aagaard. Copenhagen 24/2-38.*

On his way to an engagemet at the Apollo Theatre in Harlem in May 1937, Fats Waller buys a hot dog from a street vendor.

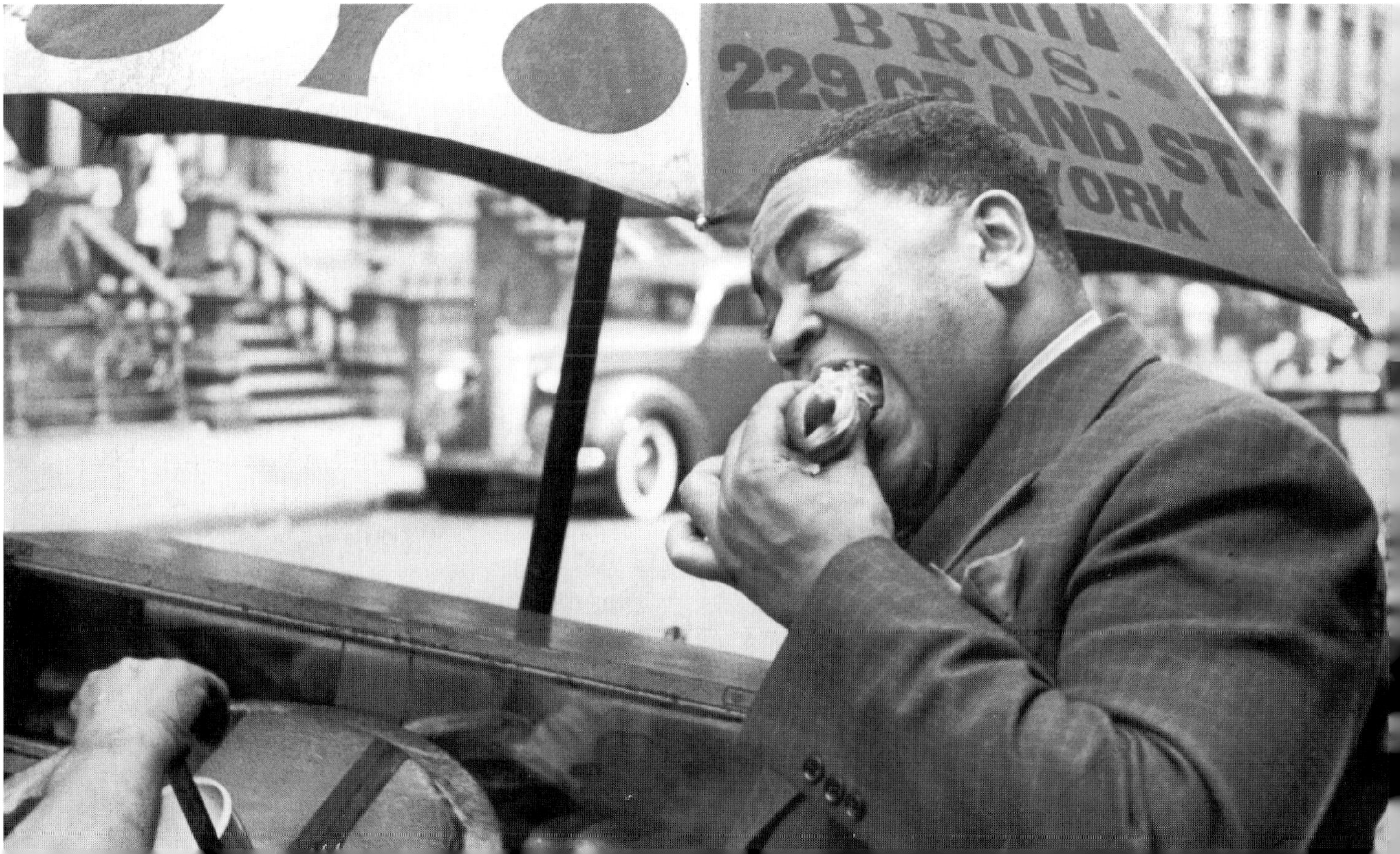

TEDDY WILSON

One of the most important and influential pianists of the swing era, Theodore Shaw "Teddy" Wilson (1912-1986), was born in Austin, Texas and grew up in Tuskegee, Alabama. After a visit to Chicago in 1928 he was determined to make jazz a living, and the following year he joined Speed Webb's band. In 1933 he came to New York to play with Benny Carter, and later on he was with Benny Goodman, and also recorded prolifically with small ad hoc groups with Billie Holiday and Mildred Bailey and others. 1939-40 he led his own musically successful, but economically disastrous, big band, after which he worked primarily with small groups or as a soloist. He worked also as a studio musician at CBS and as teacher at the Juilliard and Metropolitan music schools. Wilson was influenced by Earl Hines, but developed his own style characterized by elegant lines and a steady flow of ideas performed with a light swing.

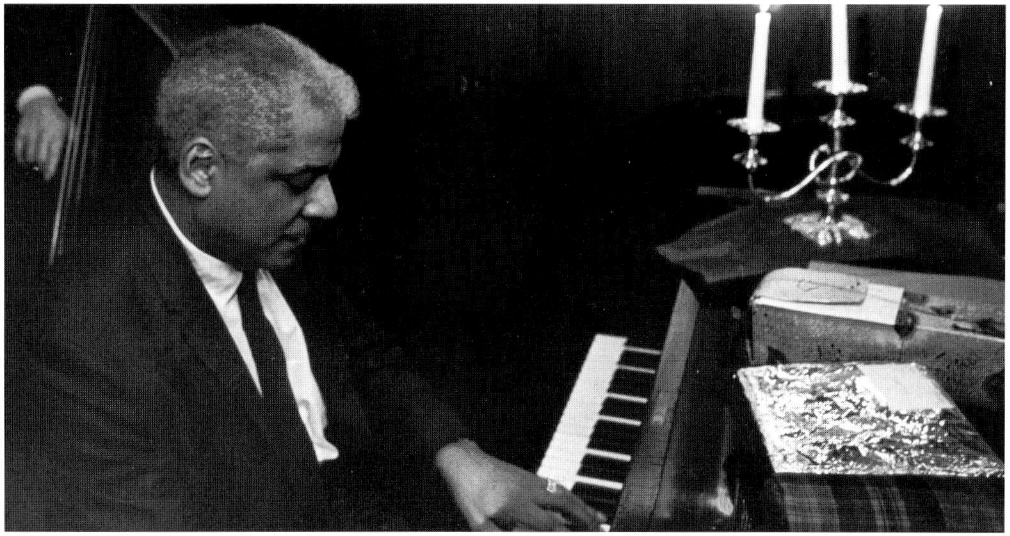

Teddy Wilson performing on his 56th birthday, November 24, 1968 at Timme's Club in Copenhagen accompanied by bassist Erik Mølbak. Still unopened birthday presents lie on top of the piano.

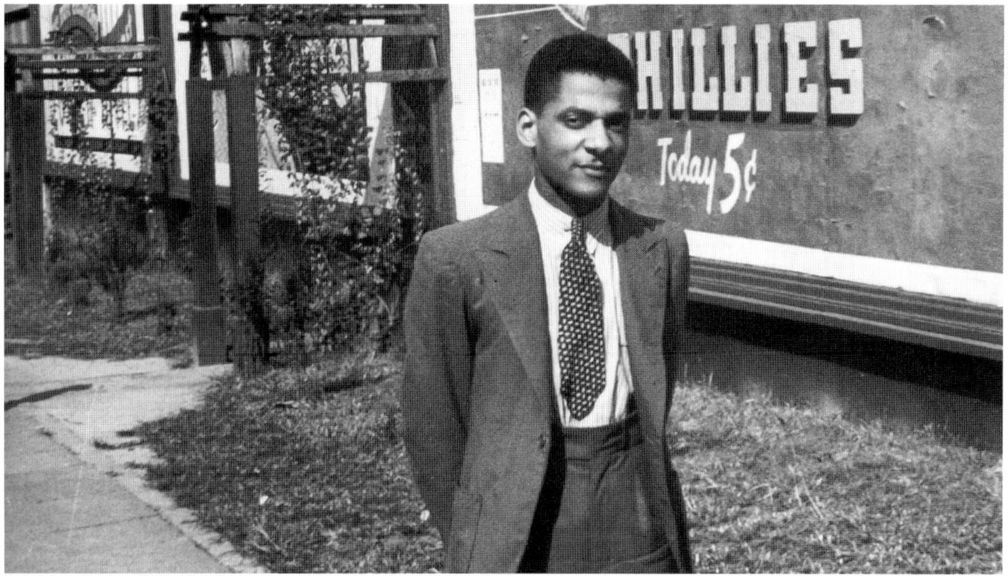

Teddy Wilson photographed by Rosenkrantz in New York, 1935.

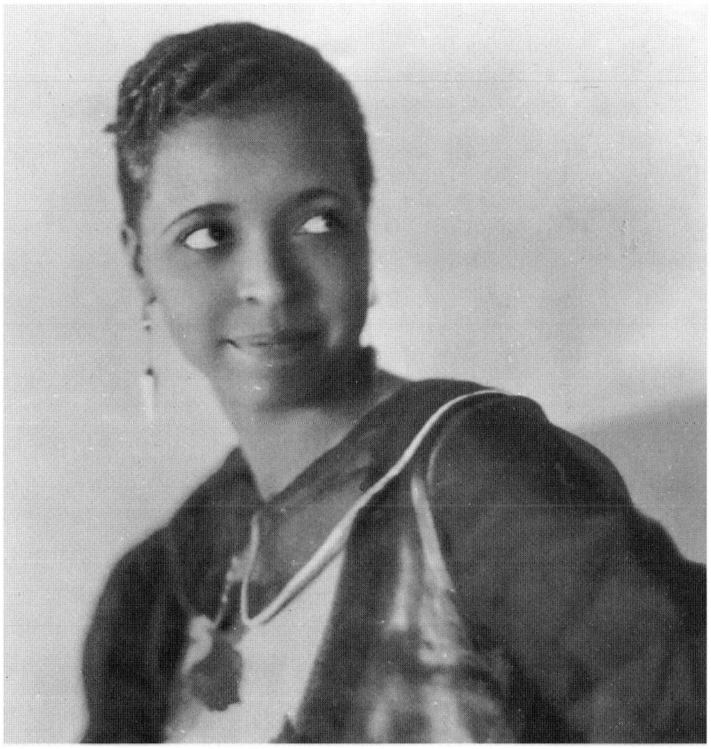

Ethel Waters in the late 20's. Tall and thin she was at that time known as "Sweet Mama Stringbean".

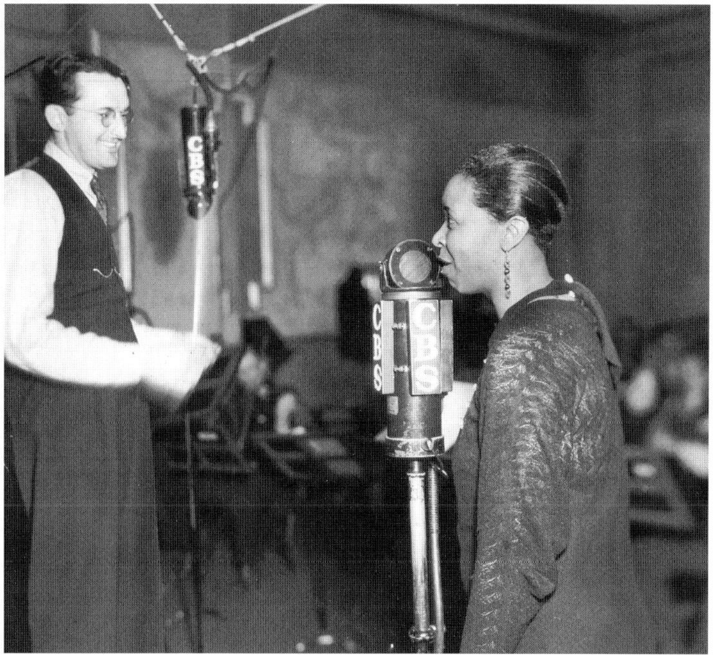

Ethel Waters and Tommy Dorsey broadcasting on either October 29, November 5, or November 12, 1933 at the CBS Studios in New York. On these dates the Dorsey Brothers' Orchestra went on the air featuring Waters on the "American Review" programme at 7:00-7:30 PM.

ETHEL WATERS

As a child Ethel Waters (1896-1977) sang in church choirs, but after she won a talent contest at a theatre in her hometown Philadelphia, she began performing in vaudeville. In 1917 she came to New York, and by the end of the 20's she had established herself as one of the most popular singers, performing at the best theatres and nightspots and being much in demand in revues and shows. From 1935 to 1939 she toured with her own show, and in the 40's she worked mostly in cabaret, but also appeared regularly as a movie actress. Being a deeply religious woman she joined evangelist Billy Graham in 1960 and toured with his organization until 1975. With her wonderful phrasing, a natural theatrical flair and a sophisticated style she became one of the most influential popular singers of the 20's and 30's.

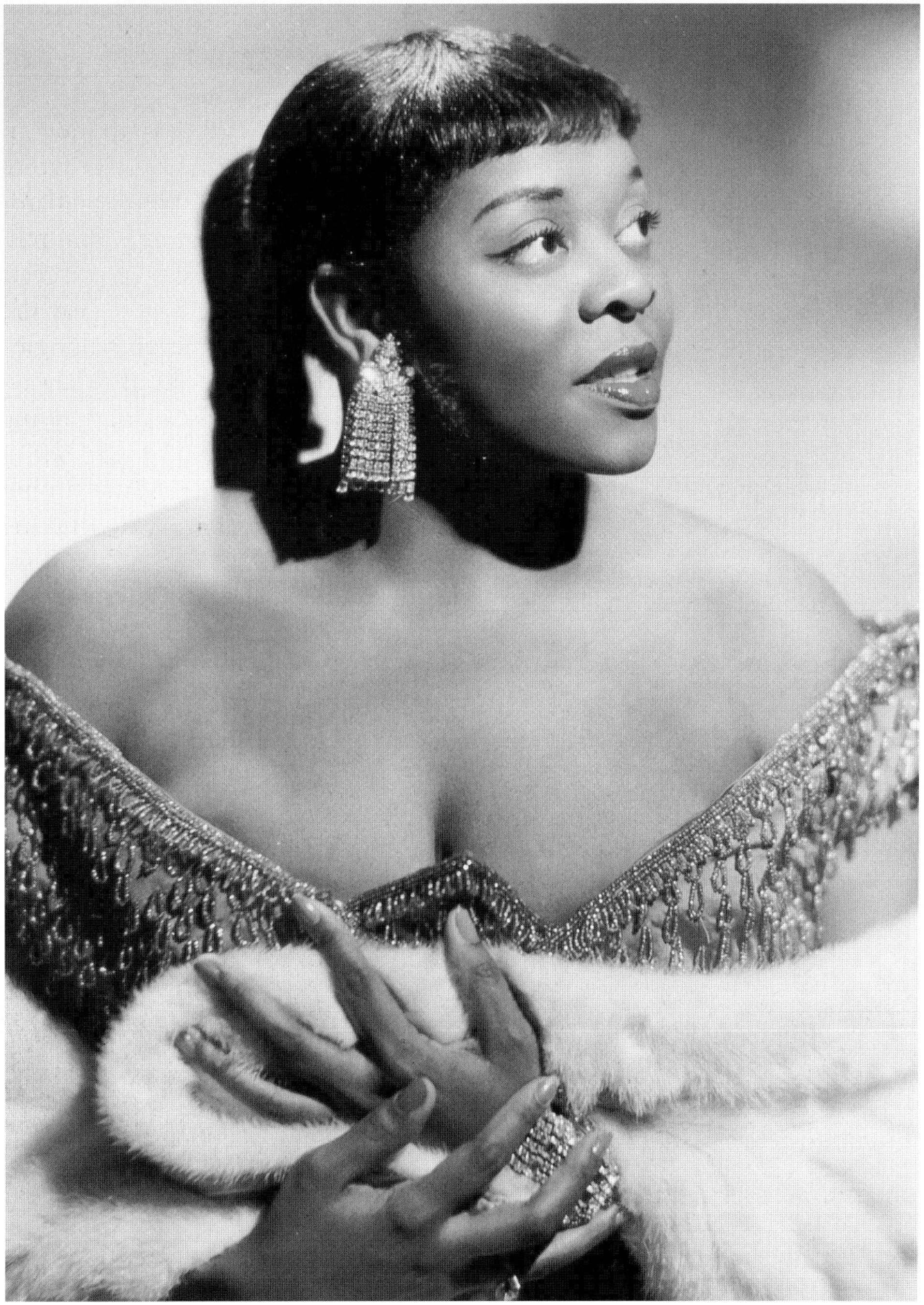

DINAH WASHINGTON

One of the most versatile of vocalists, Dinah Washington – née Ruth Lee Jones – was equally at home singing blues, standards, rhythm-and-blues, jazz, gospel, soul, and the popular songs of the day. She was born in Tuscaloosa, Alabama, but grew up in Chicago where she sang and directed a church choir. From the age of fifteen she also worked in clubs, and it was around this time she was given the name Dinah Washington by the manager of a bar. From 1943 she worked with Lionel Hampton, but from 1946 she enjoyed a successful solo career. She was a large-scale consumer of money, cars, furs, drinks, men, and drugs, and it was probably an accident that she took a fatal amount of sleeping, pills after an evening of heavy drinking. Washington put a lot of energy and emotion in her singing, had a rich voice, and like Billie Holiday was able to make much of trite material.

MARY LOU WILLIAMS

The most significant female musician in jazz is pianist, composer and arranger Mary Lou Williams (1910-1981). She was born Mary Elfrieda Scruggs in Durham, North Carolina, but grew up in Pittsburgh where she learned to play the piano at an early age. From 1929 to 1942 she was with Andy Kirk, after which she had her own small group in New York. In the mid-40's she was staff arranger for Duke Ellington, and in the same period she became involved in the bop movement, writing for Dizzy Gillespie's big band, but in the mid-50's she retired to devote herself to charity work. From 1957 she was active in music again, leading her own groups, playing and teaching until shortly before her death of cancer. Williams was unique in many ways. A deeply religious woman she wrote extended works which from the early 60's set standards for those musicians who began performing in church, including Duke Ellington. All the time she kept abreast of the development of jazz, and she was able to play the piano in any style, from ragtime, stride and boogie-woogie to swing, bop and avant-garde, but always inventively and interestingly, and with an underlying feeling of the blues. Though she received a number of honorary doctorates from American universities in her last years, she is still a very underrated musician, and her works deserve to be much better known.

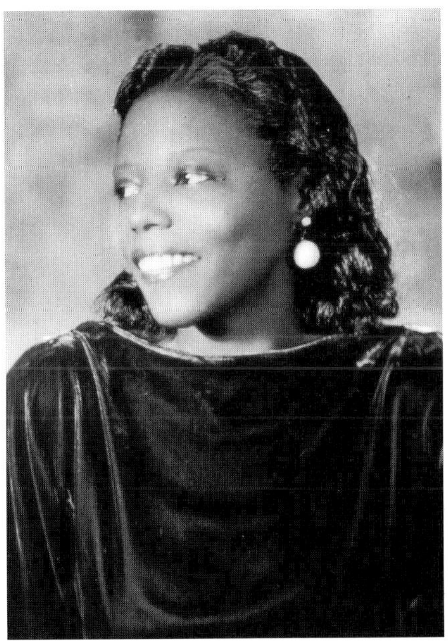

Mary Lou Williams in the mid-30's.

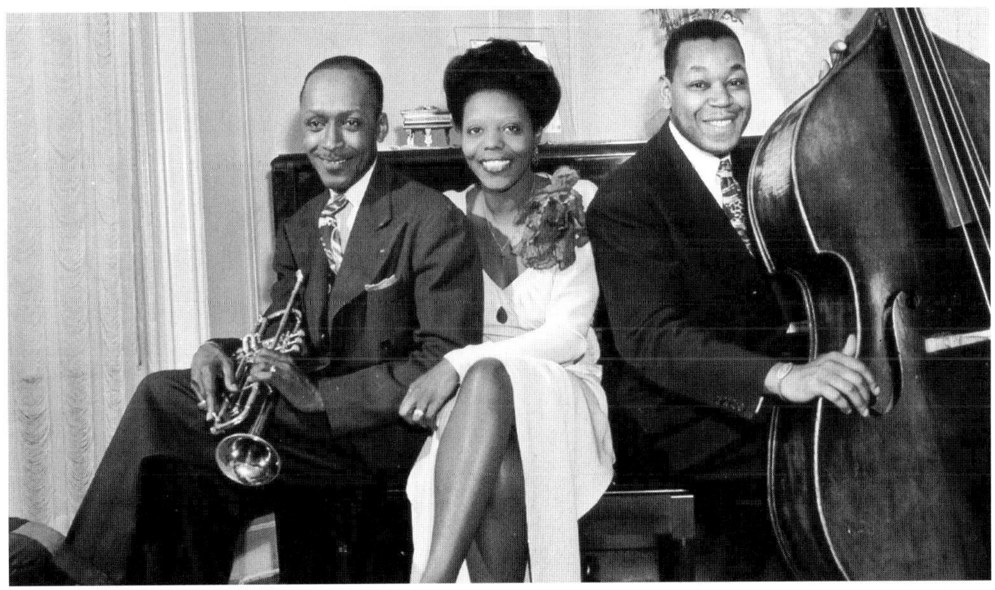

Mary Lou Williams and Her Trio in 1944. Bill Coleman is on trumpet, and Al Hall is holding the bass.

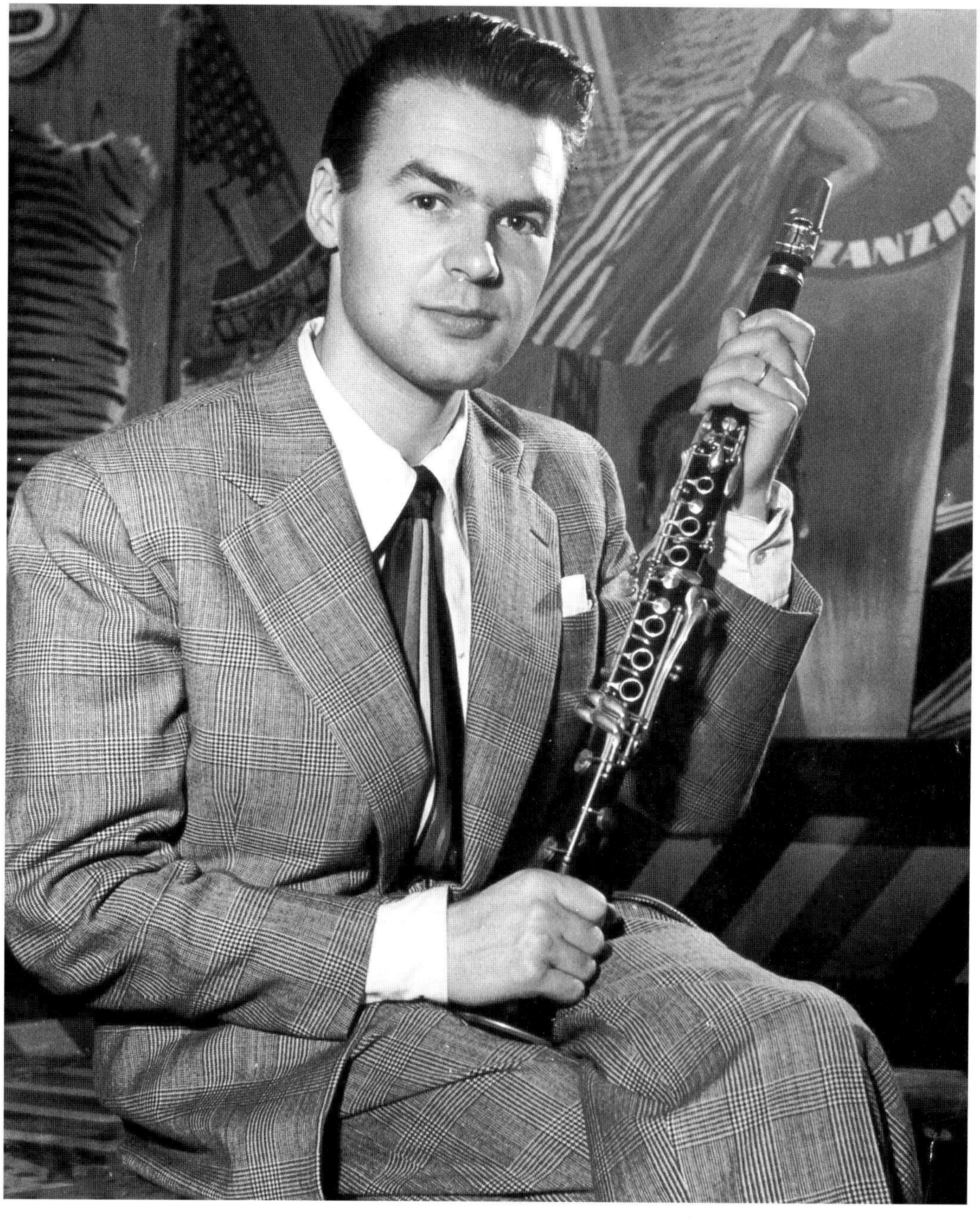

Putte Wickman in the late 40's.

PUTTE WICKMAN

The Swedish clarinetist Hans-Olof "Putte" Wickman (1924-) is an intense soloist, playing an ambitious repertoire in a modern, personal style. He was born in Borlänge and played the piano as a child, but at the age of sixteen he switched to the clarinet on which he is self-taught. Four years later he was playing professionally with Arthur Östervall after which he joined Simon Brehm, and 1948-61 he led his own small group. Then he formed a big band, but from 1967 he has been freelancing as a soloist, as well as doing classical concerts. He is held in high esteem by other musicians and is regarded as one of the outstanding soloists on his instrument.

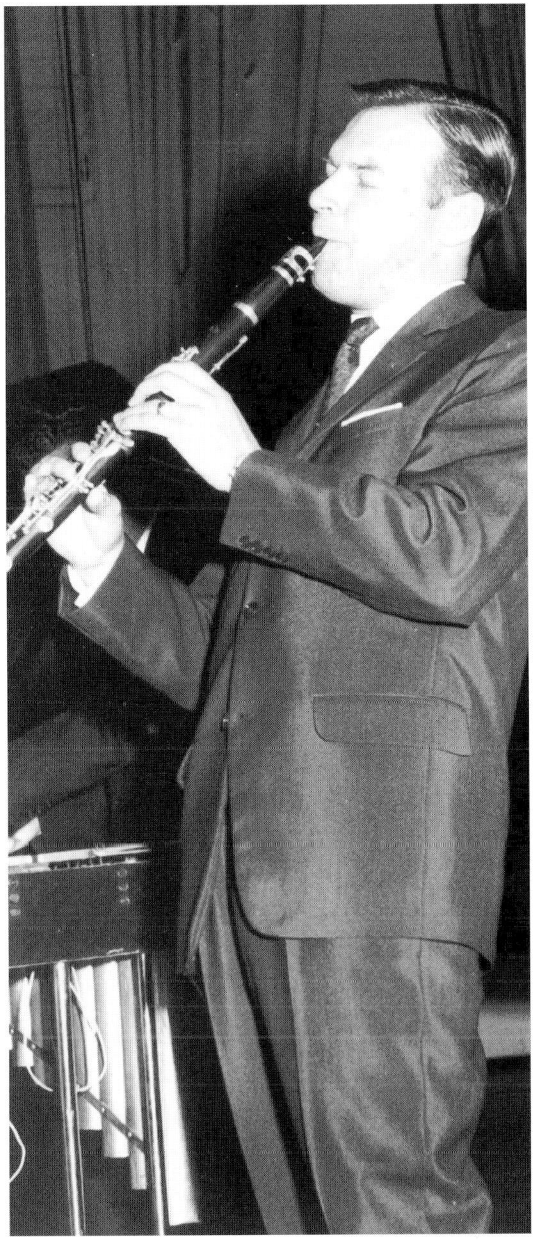

Putte Wickman on stage at Carnegie Hall during the Sidney Bechet Memorial Concert, June 14, 1959, with vibist Joe Roland.

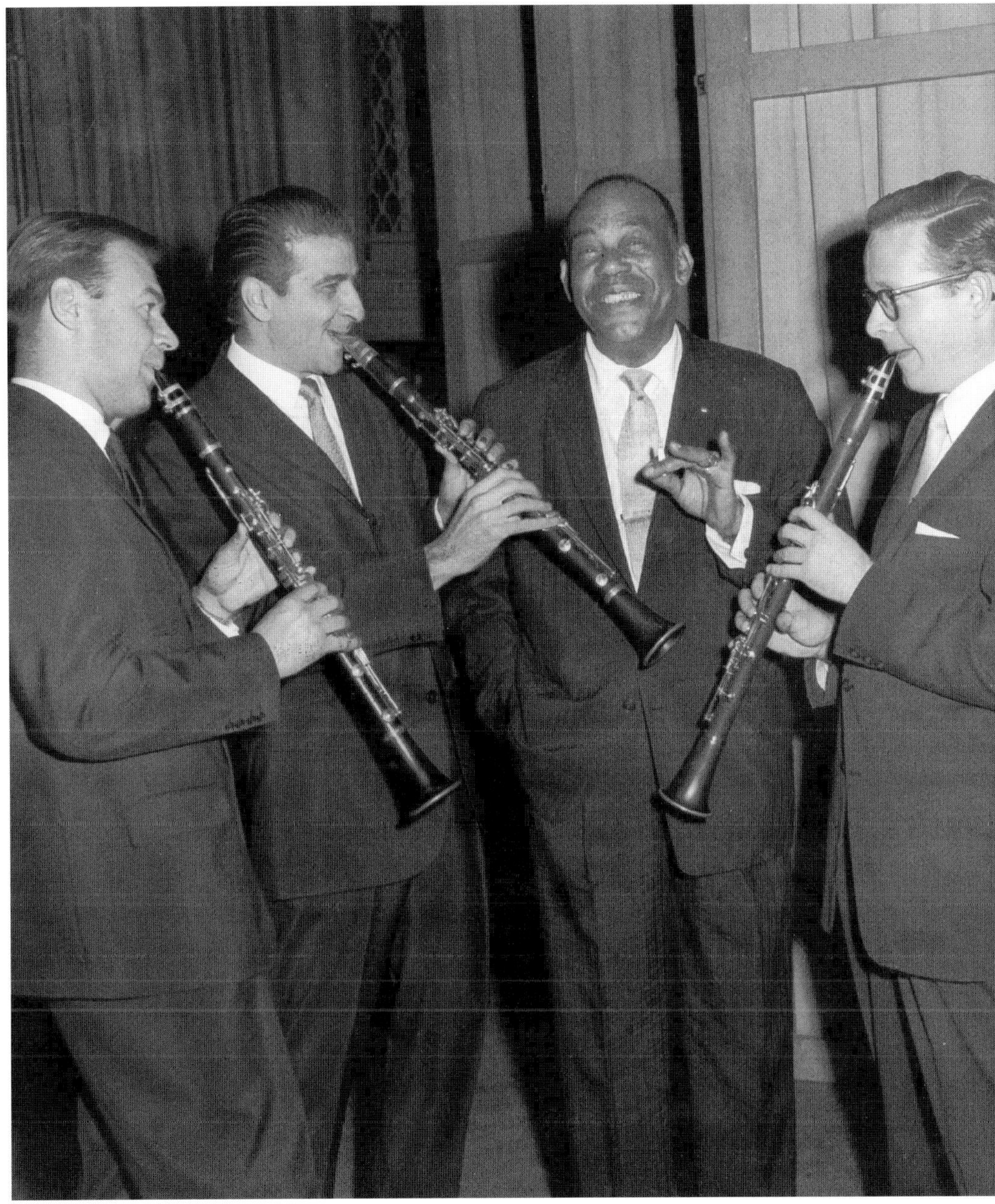

Backstage at Carnegie Hall, New York, during the Sidney Bechet Memorial Concert on June 14, 1959. Drummer Zutty Singleton is rehearsing the clarinet trio of, from left, Putte Wickman, Tony Scott, and Bob Wilber.

DICK WILSON

Jazz lost a bright tenor saxophonist when Richard "Dick" Wilson (1911-1941) died of tuberculosis only two weeks after his 30th birthday. He was born into a musical family in Mount Vernon, Illinois; both parents were musicians. He began playing piano at an early age, and after leaving high school took saxophone lessons with Joe Darensbourg. From around 1930 he played on the West Coast with Gene Coy's Band, after which he was with Zack Whyte 1934-35. In early 1936 he joined Andy Kirk in Kansas City and remained with him until shortly before his untimely death. Wilson played in a personal style influenced by Chu Berry, but with a brighter sound and a lighter attack.

ALEX WELSH

One of the most versatile British bands after World War II was led by cornetist and singer Alex Welsh (1929-1982). He was born in Edinburgh, Scotland, and after several years in local bands, he arived in London in 1954. Here he formed his own band which almost immediately gained a large following and well-earned reputation for its excellent dixieland style. The following years the band made several overseas tours and also accompanied many American soloists, such as Earl Hines, Wild Bill Davison, and Ruby Braff. From the 60's on the repertoire became more varied as more modern styles were introduced, but everything was played with enthusiasm and vitality. Unfortunately Welsh's health was poor, and he died shortly before he would have been 53.

HENRY WELLS

Trombonist and singer Henry James Wells (1906-) should not be confused with his instrument-colleague Dicky Wells (1907-1985). Henry Wells was born in Dallas and studied music at Fisk University and at the Cincinnnati Conservatory. From 1926 he played with the Boston Serenaders, and 1929-35 he worked for Jimmie Lunceford followed by three years with Andy Kirk. In 1939 he led his own short-lived big band, after which followed short stints with Gene Krupa and Teddy Hill before he rejoined Kirk. After service in the US Army during World War II he was with Sy Oliver until 1948, and during the 60's he performed in California.

LAUREL WATSON

Not much is known today about singer Laurel Watson. She came into prominence when she sang and recorded with Don Redman in 1938, and the following year she joined Roy Eldridge. During the early 40's she performed with other bands and also appeared as a solo act in nightclubs in New York but then she dropped out of sight. In this photo she is singing with Roy Eldridge's big band in the Arcadia Ballroom in New York, July 1939.

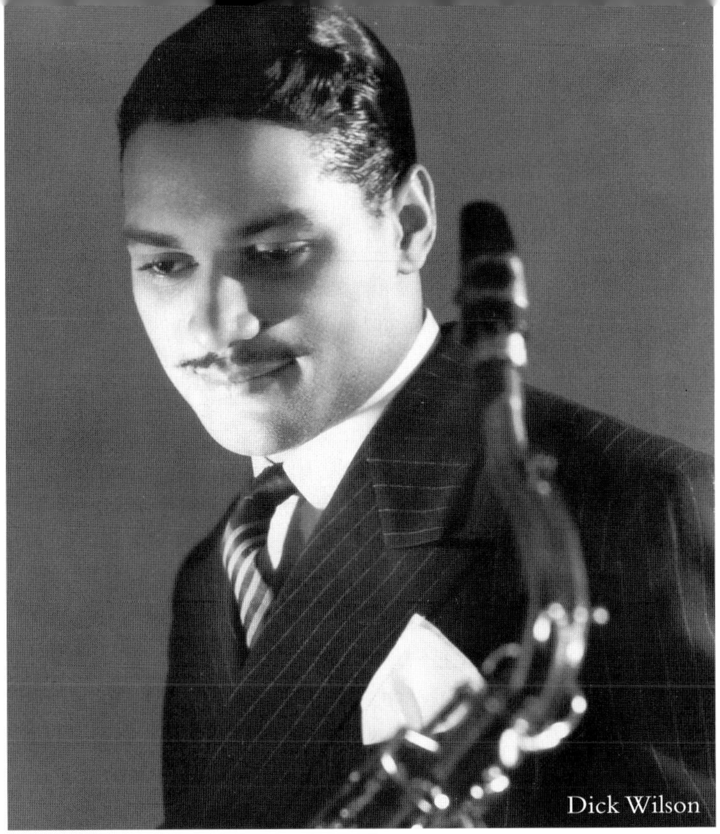
Dick Wilson

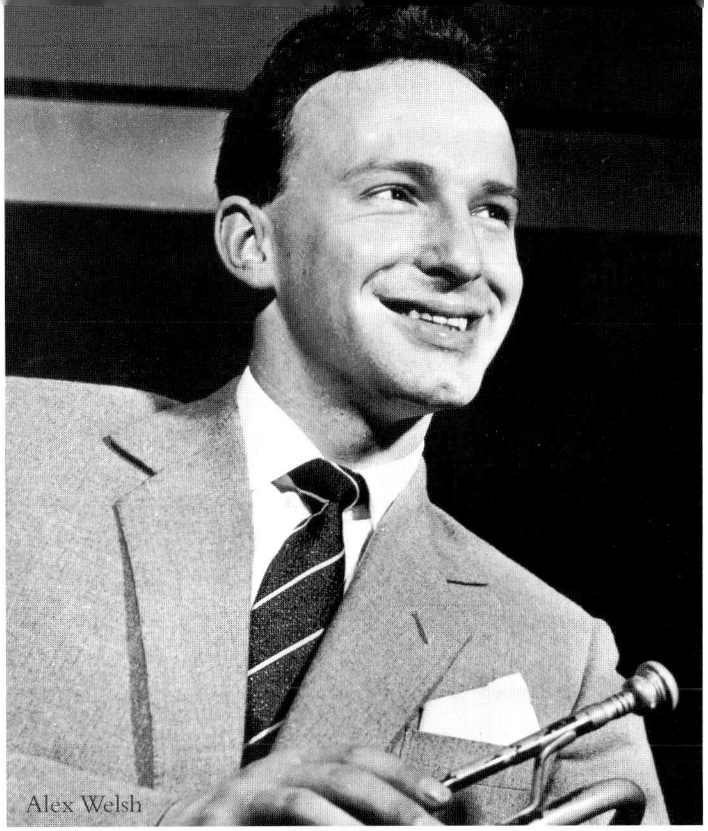
Alex Welsh

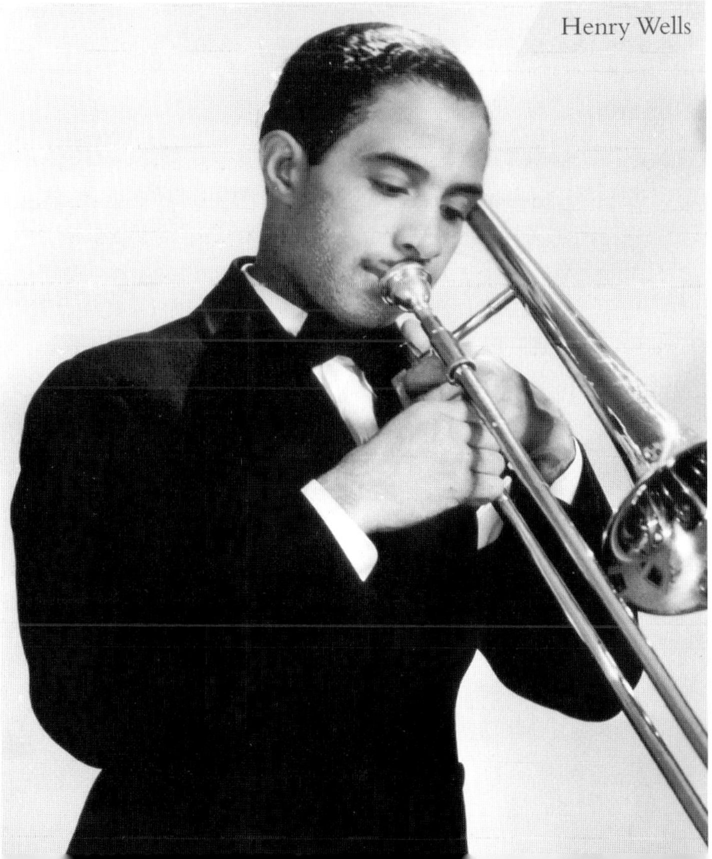
Henry Wells

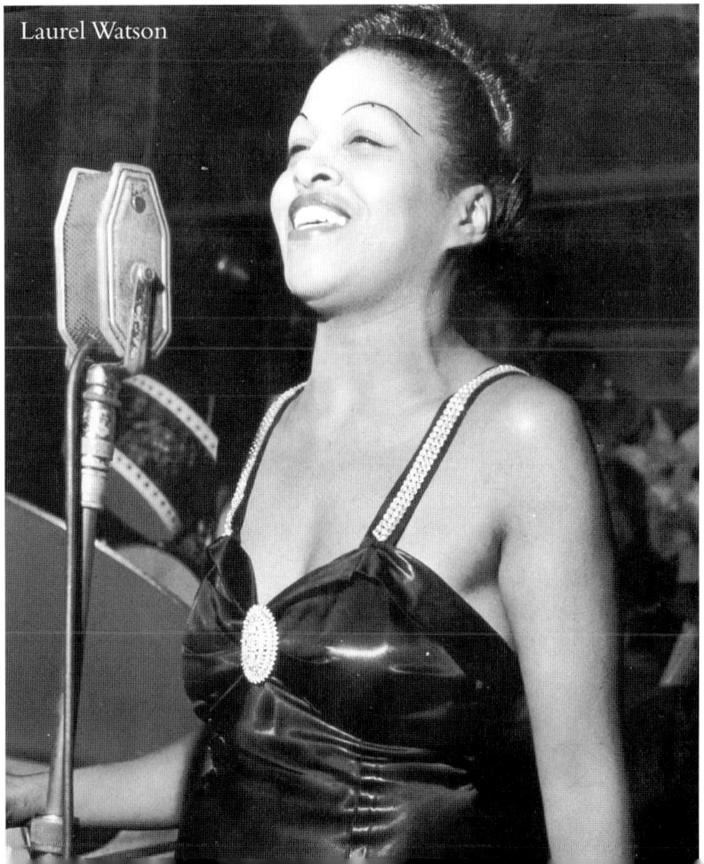
Laurel Watson

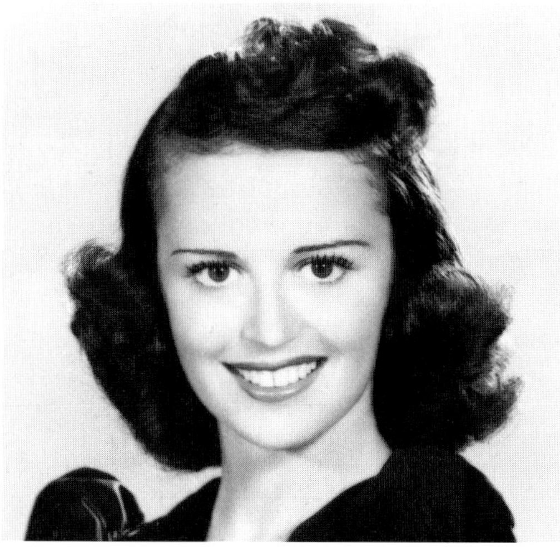

HELEN WARD

Singer Helen Ward (1916-1998) was born in New York and began singing in her teens. In 1933 she became a staff musician at NBC, where she performed with the Benny Goodman band in the "Let's Dance" radio show. Goodman hired her, and she was with his band 1934-36, after which she worked in studios the following six years. From 1943 until she went into retirement in 1959 she performed with Wild Bill Davison, Peanuts Hucko and others, and also toured with Goodman again, but in 1979 she made a comeback and performed up through the mid-90's. Ward was a lively singer, performing with a natural, easy swing.

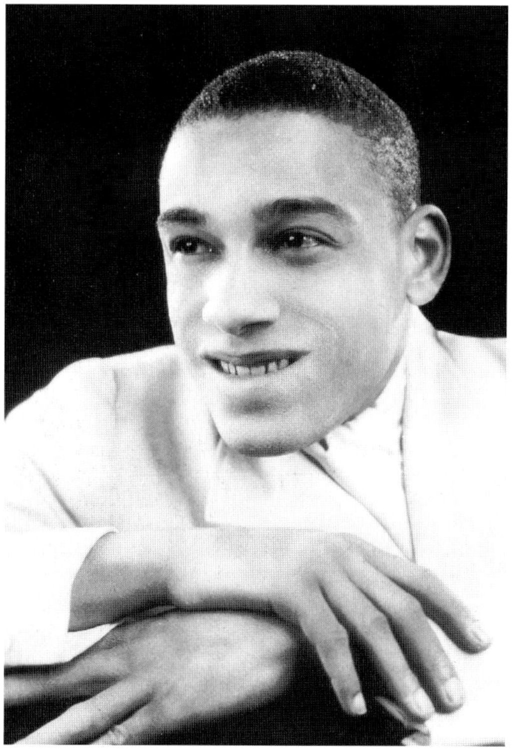

CHICK WEBB

Shortly after his birth in Baltimore, Maryland, William Henry "Chick" Webb (1909-1939) contracted tuberculosis of the spine, which crippled him for the rest of his life. But as he was determined about his future – he bought his first set of drums at the age of eleven – he overcame this deformity, and became an outstanding drummer with a wide influence, not least upon Gene Krupa who formed his own style after Webb's. In the early 20's Webb played on excursion boats, but in 1925 he came to New York and formed his own band. From 1927 to his death he played regularly at New York's Savoy Ballroom which became sort of a home for him and his band. Though his band never had a major soloist, it used excellent arrangers such as Edgar Sampson, and in 1935 he hired singer Ella Fitzgerald, which helped to establish his band as the most popular at the Savoy. During the late 30's his playing was affected by the tubercolosis, and from 1938 he had to be supported by another drummer. He died shortly after a major urological operation. Webb had great technical skill and played with drive and forceful swing. *Sincerely Chick Webb.*

BEN WEBSTER

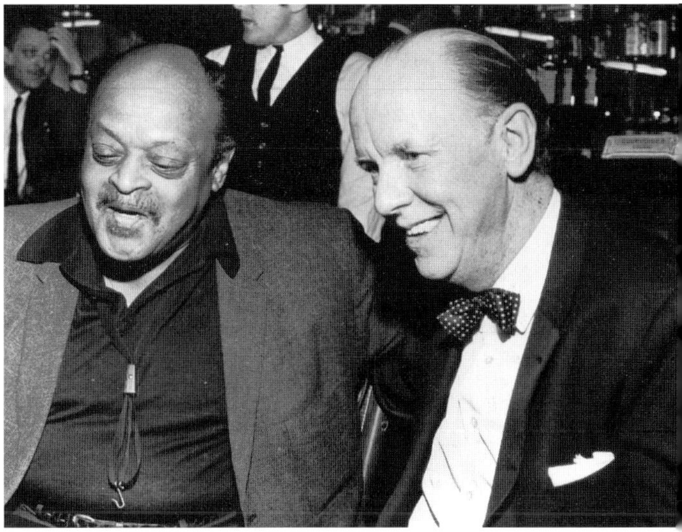

Ben Webster and Rosenkrantz in Timme's Club, Copenhagen around 1969. In September 1968 Rosenkrantz opened his Timme's Club with pianist Mary Lou Williams as its opening attraction.

Tenor saxophonist Benjamin Francis "Ben" Webster (1909-1973) was born in Kansas City, Missouri, and began as a pianist in movie houses and bars after studies at Wilberforce College. He then toured with territory bands, and in 1927, while playing with a family band led by Lester Young's father, he switched to the tenor saxophone. He then played with territory bands in the Midwest led by Gene Coy, Blanche Calloway, Bennie Moten and Andy Kirk, and in 1934 he joined Fletcher Henderson in New York. While with Duke Ellington (1940-43) he rose to international fame after which he led his own small bands in New York. Most of the 50's were spent in California but in late 1964 he moved to Europe, and in his last years he lived in Copenhagen. While in Holland he died in Amsterdam of a blood clot in the heart. With his wide vibrato and breathy sound, his powerful and extrovert playing in up-tempo numbers, and last but not least, his warm and heartfelt renditions of ballads, Webster was one of the giants of the tenor saxophone.

LEONARD WARE

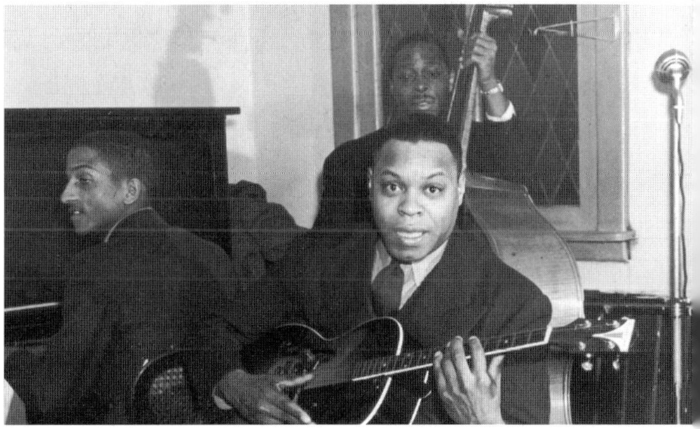

Leonard Ware Trio at the Village Vanguard around 1940. Pat Flowers is on piano and Eddie Robinson on bass.

Few know that Leonard Ware (1909-) was one of the pioneers of the amplified guitar. Eddie Durham is normally credited with having made the first amplified experiments in the mid-30's as well as the first recordings on an amplified guitar in March 1938 with the Kansas City Five. But the same year, in November, Ware used his amplified guitar on recordings with Sidney Bechet. Ware was born in Richmond, Virginia, and studied at the Tuskegee Institute where he played oboe in the college band. In 1934 he began playing guitar, and in the late 30's he formed a trio which was popular in New York clubs up through the 40's. He retired from full-time music in the late 40's to post office employment in New York.

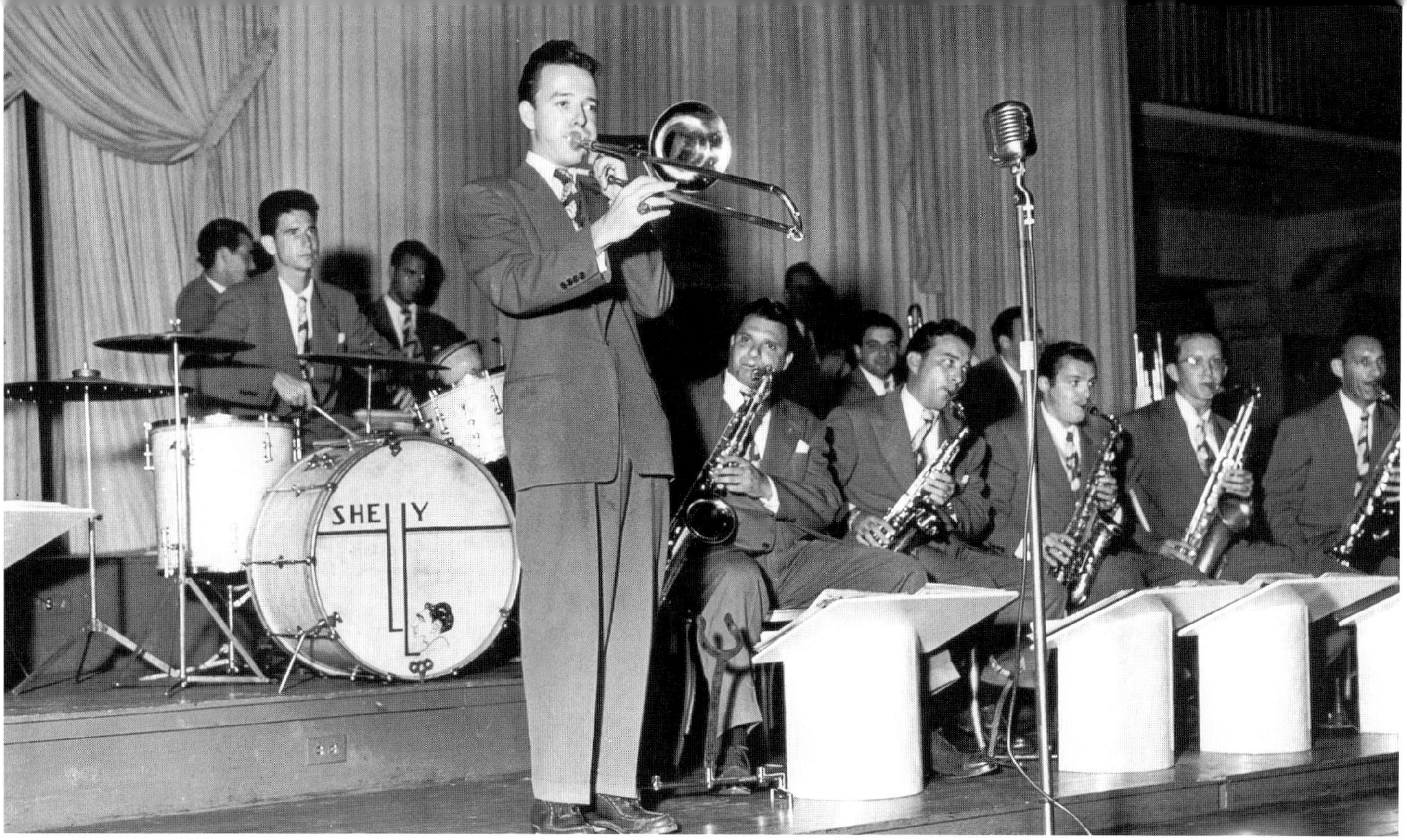

Kai Winding soloing with the Stan Kenton Orchestra 1947. In the rhythm section are José Mangual (bongos), Pedro Allendo (maracas) and Shelly Manne (dr). The visible trombonists are probably Milt Bernhardt and Harry Forbes, while the saxophone section consists of Vido Musso (ts), Boots Mussuli (as), Eddie Meyers (as), Bob Cooper (ts), and Bob Gioga (bars).

Kai Winding

Born in Århus, Denmark, Kai Chresten Winding (1922-1983) moved with his parents to USA at the age of twelve. While in his teens he took up the trombone and was soon playing with big bands led by Sonny Dunham and Alvino Rey. From 1946 to 1947 he was with Stan Kenton, but afterwards he played with small groups. 1954-56 he co-led a quintet with J.J. Johnson known as "Jay and Kai", and in the 60's he worked as musical director of the Playboy Clubs in New York. 1971-72 he toured with the Giants of Jazz, after which he semi-retired to Spain. 1979-80 he toured again, co-leading with Curtis Fuller the quintet Giant Bones, and playing with Lionel Hampton's big band. Winding was one of the earliest trombonists to be influenced by bop, but as an accomplished musician he was able to blend into many musical styles. He played with a coarser tone than his contemporaries, but developed a smoother sound while with "Jay and Kai".

LESTER YOUNG

The equal of Louis Armstrong and Charlie Parker, tenor saxophonist Lester Willis Young (1909-1959) was one of the most influential musicians in jazz. He was born in Woodville, Mississippi, but grew up in New Orleans. From the age of ten he played drums, touring with his father's carnival band, but switched to the alto saxophone in his early teens. In 1927 he left his family, joining Art Bronson's band now on tenor saxophone. He played in several other territory bands in Kansas City and Minneapolis during the early 30's before he joined Count Basie in 1936. With him he gained a wide national and international reputation. In 1940 he left Count Basie to form his own band, but in 1943 he was back with Basie again. In 1944 he was drafted into military service, but from 1946 he was back in the music business fronting his own groups, working as a soloist, and touring with Jazz at The Philharmonic. In 1959 he became ill while playing in Paris, and he died the day after his return to New York of liver complaints and oesophagial varicoses. Young's unique style, which was the only serious alternative to the rhapsodic style of the Coleman Hawkins school, was a primary force in the development of modern jazz. His articulate, relaxed, smoothly flowing lines was an inspiration to scores of younger musicians, regardless of instrument.

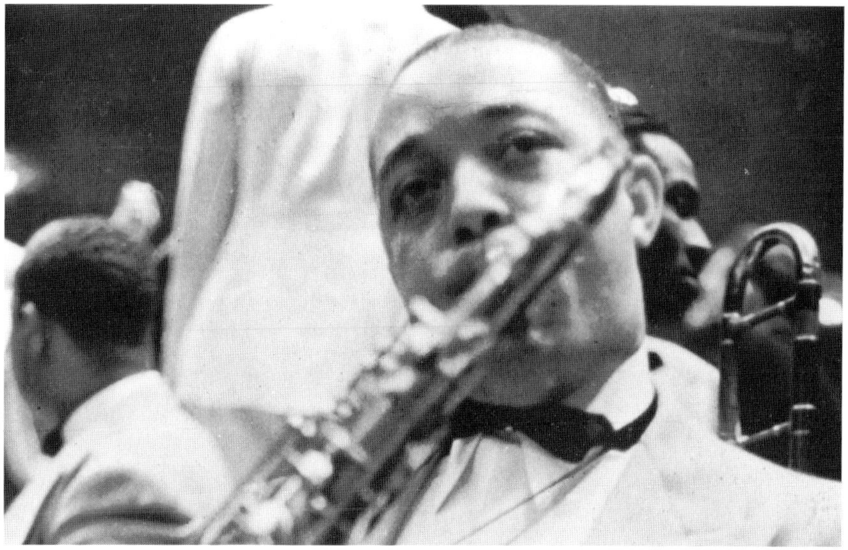

Lester Young immaculately dressed with Count Basie's orchestra in 1940.

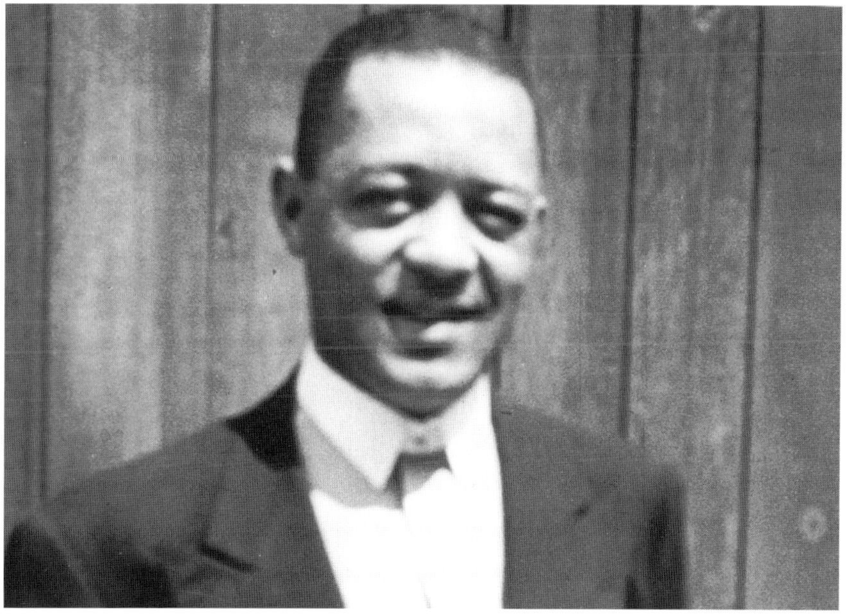

Lester Young photographed in New York by Rosenkrantz in 1938.

INDEX OF NAMES

Page numbers in bold-face refer to illustrations

PHOTO CREDITS

Please note that only photos with credit information are listed below.

Roland Anderson
182

Apeda Studios
48 (top, right), 80 (left), 115, 123 (bottom), 127 (top), 132 (top), 153

Art Foto Studios
130 (top)

Ava Studio
70 (right), 77 (bottom, left)

Bloom
69 (right), 87 (left), 87 (right), 88 (right), 89 (top), 139 (left), 160 (bottom)

Lamar Boren
188

J. Braae
120-121 (top)

Jack Bradley
11 (right), 28 (bottom) 29 (bottom), 81 (top)

John Brook
44 (top)

Bruno of Hollywood
68 (top), 75 (right), 159 (bottom, right)

Dunc Butler
29 (right), 102 (top), 102 (bottom), 145 (bottom)

CBS Photo
94 (top), 141 (bottom), 174 (right)

Alain Chevrier
106 (left)

Chilton-Butler
56, 77 (top, left), 77 (bottom, right), 79 (top), 83 (left), 103 (bottom), 104, 117 (right), 150 (top)

Gordon Conner
111 (top, right), 111 (bottom, right)

Daddio
17 (top)

DeBarron Studios
112 (right)

Devon-Studio
163

D'Orsay-Studio
46 (top), 145 (top, left)

George A. Douglas
161 (top)

Myron Ehrenberg
84 (bottom)

Empire Photographers
51

Franca Fiedler
187 (top)

Tom Fizdale
26 (left), 65

Flair Photography
12 (right), 13

Irvin Glazer
137, 143

Gottlieb Foto
149

Hascall
108 (bottom)

Herbert Hawkins
52 (left)

Otto F. Hess
32 (left), 96 (bottom), 135

Fritz Holm
148 (right)

Ray Lee Jackson
101

Tore Johnson
17 (bottom)

George Maillard Kesslere
159 (top, right)

James J. Kriegsmann
37, 42 (top), 60 (top), 69 (left), 96 (top), 97 (bottom), 107 (right), 124, 125 (right), 131, 142 (right), 159 (left), 175, 180

Peer Lauritzen
178 (top)

Jerry Lee
183 (left), 183 (right)

Loubé
127 (bottom)

Jean Mainbourg
117 (left)

Helge Mass
8, 120 (bottom, right), 168 (bottom, left)

Miners
119 (top), 133 (top)

Moss Photo
154 (left)

Charles B. Nadell
36 (right), 38, 58, 67 (right), 85 (left), 162 (bottom), 181 (right)

Nasib
141 (top)

NBC Photo, N.Y.
68 (bottom), 179 (left)

Nord Sørensen
71 (left)

Nordisk Pressefoto
71 (right)

N.T.B.s Billedavd.
33 (bottom)

Rockwell O'Keefe
14, 33 (top), 79 (bottom), 94 (bottom), 155, 173 (top), 185 (top, left)

Edward Ozern
64 (top, right), 148 (left)

Jan Persson
162 (top)

Charles Peterson
25 (middle), 27 (right), 59, 133 (bottom), 156, 165 (left), 177 (bottom), 185 (bottom, right))

Photo des Nations
169 (top)

K. Progress
11 (left), 43

Reprograph Studio
99 (top, left)

Ray Rising
48 (left)

Houston Rogers
70 (left)

Timme Rosenkrantz
30 (right), 57 (bottom), 132 (bottom), 164 (right), 168 (top), 176 (right), 178 (bottom), 189 (bottom)

Röster I Radio
18 (right)

Maurice Seymour
15 (left), 44 (bottom), 92 (top), 97 (top), 136, 139 (right), 151 (right)

Shaw-Boynton
164 (left)

Richard Stangerup
152 (top)

Harold Stein
40

Jimmy Sunshine
93 (top), 93 (bottom), 109 (top)

Richard M. Tucker
25 (right)

Vanderree
130 (bottom)

Vernon
108 (top)

Achille Volpé
119 (bottom)

Francis Wolff
55 (left), 82, 99 (top, right), 106 (right),
113 (left), 113 (right)

Ebbe Wraae
64 (bottom), 128, 129 (left), 142 (left),
166 (bottom), 169 (bottom)